The Renaissance of emotion

I0809674

MANCHESTER
1824

Manchester University Press

The Renaissance of emotion

Understanding affect in Shakespeare and his contemporaries

Edited by Richard Meek and Erin Sullivan

Manchester University Press

Copyright © Manchester University Press 2015

While copyright in the volume as a whole is vested in Manchester University Press, copyright in individual chapters belongs to their respective authors, and no chapter may be reproduced wholly or in part without the express permission in writing of both author and publisher.

Published by Manchester University Press
Altrincham Street, Manchester M1 7JA
www.manchesteruniversitypress.co.uk

British Library Cataloguing-in-Publication Data
A catalogue record for this book is available from the British Library

ISBN 978 1 5261 1691 8 paperback

First published by Manchester University Press in hardback 2015

This edition first published 2017

The publisher has no responsibility for the persistence or accuracy of URLs for any external or third-party internet websites referred to in this book, and does not guarantee that any content on such websites is, or will remain, accurate or appropriate.

Typeset by
Servis Filmsetting Ltd, Stockport, Cheshire
Printed in Great Britain by
TJ International Ltd, Padstow

Contents

Part III The politics and performance of emotion

Acknowledgements

We would like to extend our great thanks to the Leverhulme Trust, which supported this project in its early stages, as well as to our colleagues at the University of Hull and the Shakespeare Institute, University of Birmingham. We are deeply grateful to Matthew Frost and the team at Manchester University Press for their expert guidance in seeing this collection through to publication, and to our anonymous readers who helped shape and strengthen its focus with their perceptive advice. Finally, we would like to thank our wonderful team of contributors, whose talent, patience and affectionate collegiality has made this project a happy one – in all senses of the phrase – from beginning to end.

Notes on contributors

David Bagchi is Senior Lecturer in Ecclesiastical History at the University of Hull. He specialises in the history and thought of the Reformation, with a particular interest in the theology of Martin Luther, early modern religious polemic and the use of the printing press for disseminating theological ideas. His major publications include *Luther's Earliest Opponents: Catholic Controversialists, 1518–25* (Fortress, 2nd edn, 2009) and *The Cambridge Companion to Reformation Theology* (2004) (co-edited with David C. Steinmetz).

Frederika Bain works at the University of Hawai'i, where she recently completed her dissertation focusing on representations of bodily modification, primarily dismemberment, in medieval and early modern literature. She has also published a short edition of early modern fairy spells. Her other research interests include monstrosity and monstrous births, the animal–human boundary, and medieval and early modern midwifery.

Richard Chamberlain is Senior Lecturer in English at the University of Northampton. His main interests are in Renaissance literature, Shakespeare studies and critical theory, with particular focus on the politics of interpretation and the relationship between literature and society. His monograph *Radical Spenser: Pastoral, Politics and the New Aestheticism* (Edinburgh University Press, 2005) approaches these questions by tracing the ethical and political implications of an open-ended 'pastoral' logic at work in Spenser's writing. He is working on a new book, *Shakespeare's Refusers*, looking at figures who negate coercive social participation – that is, who 'just say no' to behaviour collectively enforced in the name of enjoyment.

Sara Coodin is Assistant Professor of Classics and Letters at the University of Oklahoma. Her research focuses on classical philosophy's importance to thought and action in Shakespeare's plays, as well as classicism and Christian Hebraism in Renaissance England. She has published on these topics in several Shakespeare journals and edited collections, and is currently completing a book-length study of Shylock's moral agency that focuses on his use of biblical citation in *The Merchant of Venice*.

Peter Holbrook is Professor of Shakespeare and English Renaissance Literature at the University of Queensland, and Director of the UQ Node of the ARC Centre of Excellence for the History of Emotions, Europe 1100–1800. He is the author of *Shakespeare's Individualism* (Cambridge University Press, 2010) and *Literature and Degree in Renaissance England: Nashe, Bourgeois Tragedy, Shakespeare* (University of Delaware Press, 1994), and co-editor, with David Bevington, of *The Politics of the Stuart Court Masque* (Cambridge University Press, 1998).

Ann Kaegi is Lecturer in English at the University of Hull, where she researches the historical dramas of Shakespeare and his contemporaries and 'unruly voices and unruly subjects' in early modern writing. She has a long-standing interest in early modern resistance theory, civic culture and the political languages of the sixteenth and seventeenth centuries. Her recent publications in these areas include articles in the *Journal of Early Modern Studies* and *Shakespeare*, and an introduction and revised set of notes for the Penguin Shakespeare edition of *Henry V*. She currently writing a monograph provisionally titled *England's Woeful History*.

Andy Kesson is Senior Lecturer in English Literature at Roehampton University and a guest lecturer at Shakespeare's Globe. His work focuses on performance theory, book history, representations of the body and sexuality on and off the stage, reception theory, pedagogy and the history of English as a scholarly discipline. He is the author of *John Lyly and Early Modern Authorship* (Manchester University Press, 2014) and with Emma Smith is the editor of *The Elizabethan Top Ten: Defining Print Popularity in Early Modern England* (Ashgate, 2013). He is currently working on a study of London's earliest playhouses.

Mary Ann Lund is Lecturer in English at the University of Leicester, where she works on prose writing, religion and medicine in the English Renaissance. She is the author of *Melancholy, Medicine and Religion in Early Modern England: Reading 'The Anatomy of Melancholy'* (Cambridge University Press, 2010), which was shortlisted for the CCUE Book Prize in 2011. She is currently editing volume 12 of *The Oxford Edition of the Sermons of John Donne* (gen. ed. Peter McCullough), and has a research interest in the experience of illness in early modern literature.

Richard Meek is Lecturer in English at the University of Hull. He has published articles in *SEL*, *English*, *Literature Compass*, *FMLS* and *Shakespeare Survey*, and his book *Narrating the Visual in Shakespeare* was published by Ashgate in 2009. He is interested in representations of sympathy and empathy in early modern literature, and his current research project is a monograph on this topic, provisionally entitled *The Relativity of Sorrows*. In 2012 he edited a special issue of *Shakespeare* entitled 'Shakespeare and the Culture of Emotion'.

Ciara Rawnsley is an early career researcher, currently working within the Australian Research Council Centre of Excellence for the History of Emotions at the University of Western Australia. Her role is to help develop and manage a new, web-based resource for researchers studying the history of premodern emotions. Her research interests are in Shakespeare, emotions and folk and fairy tales. She has published in *Journal for Early Modern Studies* and has contributed chapters to two volumes on Shakespeare and emotions. She is also currently co-editing a volume of essays on children's literature, childhood death and emotions 1500–1800.

Erin Sullivan is Lecturer and Fellow at the Shakespeare Institute, University of Birmingham, where she works on emotion, psychology and identity in the English Renaissance. She has published research in this area in *Cultural History*, *Studies in Philology*, *The Lancet* and *Emotions and Health, 1200–1700*, ed. Elena Carrera (Brill, 2013), and has also worked extensively on Shakespeare's role, emotional and otherwise, in the London 2012 Olympics. She is currently completing a monograph called *Beyond Melancholy: Sadness and Selfhood in Renaissance England*.

R. S. White is Winthrop Professor of English and Cultural Studies at the University of Western Australia and Chief Investigator for the Australian Research Council Centre of Excellence for the History of Emotion (1100–1700). From 2008 to 2013 he was an Australian Professorial Fellow. He has published widely on Shakespeare and the younger Romantics, including *John Keats: A Literary Life* (Palgrave Macmillan, 2010; paperback 2012). He is also the author of several monographs on English literature and the history of human rights, most recently *Pacifism and English Literature: Minstrels of Peace* (Palgrave Macmillan, 2008).

Nigel Wood is Professor of Literature at Loughborough University and a Senior Research Associate at the Shakespeare Institute, University of Birmingham. He has edited six volumes in the *Theory in Practice* series for Open University Press (1993–97), including those on *The Tempest*, *Antony and Cleopatra*, *Measure for Measure*, *Hamlet*, *Henry IV, Parts 1 and 2* and *The Merchant of Venice.* His most recent work on Shakespeare has been focused on the interface between his comedies and early modern notions of the public sphere, with specific reference to staging conditions, and he has recently edited *She Stoops to Conquer and Other Comedies* for the Oxford English Drama series (2007).

Introduction

Richard Meek and Erin Sullivan

IN THE PENULTIMATE SCENE of William Shakespeare's *Richard II*, Richard is alone in prison, reflecting upon his misfortunes – and his emotional state. In a typically comparative mode, Richard likens his empty cell to the world, and resolves to populate it with his own thoughts:

> My brain I'll prove the female to my soul,
> My soul the father, and these two beget
> A generation of still-breeding thoughts;
> And these same thoughts people this little world,
> In humours like the people of this world,
> For no thought is contented.[1]

In this complex passage, Richard's discontented thoughts are said to resemble the variety of 'humours' – that is, the unbalanced moods and temperaments – that can be found in the world at large. Echoing contemporary Aristotelian and Galenic thinking, Richard's material brain becomes the fecund matter into which his immaterial soul injects its potent form, producing a seething family of humorally inflected conceits. The passage illustrates Shakespeare's awareness of natural philosophy and medical humoralism as a means of explaining mental and emotional processes, both those of Richard and early modern individuals more generally. For some recent critics of Renaissance literature and culture (and Shakespearian drama in particular), Richard's comments might confirm the notion that humoral theory was the essential model for understanding the emotions in the period, rooting such phenomena in the materially bound 'ecology' of passion, sensation and embodied experience.

Yet what is striking in this passage is that Shakespeare explicitly uses humoralism metaphorically, as part of an extended simile that transforms Richard's thoughts into a self-generated audience that is at once real and imagined. In the lines that follow, Richard compounds his initial humoral account, layering on top of it biblical quotations, proverbial sayings and even more elaborate metaphorical conceits as he continues to explore his mental and emotional state. After quoting two passages from the Bible that emphasise the value of poverty and humility – suggesting his uncertainty, perhaps, about his chances of entering the kingdom of heaven – Richard likens his thoughts to 'silly beggars' sitting in the stocks, who take solace in the fact that 'many have and others must sit there; / And in this thought they find a kind of ease' (5.5.25–8). The sound of offstage music prompts Richard to consider his situation in more sonic terms: 'Music do I hear? / Ha, ha, keep time! How sour sweet music is / When time is broke and no proportion kept!' (41–3). Like 'a disordered string' (46), he imagines himself out of tune and out of time with the world around him, a proposition that leads him to figure himself next as a clock: 'My thoughts are minutes, and with sighs they jar / Their watches on unto mine eyes' (51–2). Alone in his cell, he imagines his finger, 'like a dial's point', wiping tears from his face, and his heart, like a clock's bell, counting out the hours with its 'clamorous groans' (53–6).

The elaborate and at times unwieldy conceits of this speech emphasise the difficulties in turning one's emotions into language, and suggest that all attempts to articulate inward feelings involve a certain degree of translation or metaphorical conceptualisation. As Emma Mason and Isobel Armstrong have written, '[a]rt can put the passions outside the self only by representing them through what they are not, through the substitutions of image, picture, or proxy enactment'.[2] Humoral theory is invoked in this speech, to be sure, but only as one of a series of metaphors that Richard employs to describe his fragmented self – a self too complex and disordered to be contained within any single paradigm or framework, or indeed any fixed form. His identity is figured as a continual performance, and an imperfect and unstable one at that, suspended between competing thoughts, quotations, metaphors and imagined roles: 'Thus play I in one person many people, / And none contented' (31–2). Taken as a whole, Richard's speech suggests something of the diversity and even mystery of early modern emotional experience, particularly as it related to the understanding of the self. While there are many ways to describe what such emotional experience might be like, there is no single or straightforward way of explaining what it actually is.

Recovering Renaissance emotion: humoralism and beyond

This book seeks to recover the plurality and creativity of Renaissance and early modern emotion, attending to the multiple intellectual frameworks and aesthetic strategies Shakespeare and his contemporaries used to probe the meaning of passion and its significance in human life. Such an ambition builds on a growing interest in emotion across Renaissance and early modern studies. Since the turn of the twenty-first century we might say that there has been a 'Renaissance of emotion' in the field, with scholars across various disciplines turning their attention to the centrality of emotion (or passion, or affect – more of which to follow) in all aspects of early modern literary, dramatic, cultural and political life. Indeed the expansion of emotion studies has been so striking and pervasive as to prompt several scholars to point to an 'emotional turn' across the humanities.[3] Whereas emotional experience may have once been seen as too ephemeral, unrecoverable or idiosyncratic for systematic scholarly analysis, critics are increasingly considering the ways in which the study of emotion connects with fundamental questions about the relationship between self and society, mind and body, biology and culture, and the representation of lived experience.

As has already been suggested, in Renaissance and especially Shakespeare studies, academic interest in emotion has largely been informed by the cultural history of medical thought, resulting in a picture of early modern emotion that stresses the centrality of the material, humoral body. Scholars in the field have tended to focus on the physiological determinism of emotion in early modern texts, arguing that feeling was something that happened *to* the body of the passive, receptive subject, who either gave way to these material impulses or attempted to resist them through stoical self-control. Perhaps the most influential study to adopt this approach has been Gail Kern Paster's *Humoring the Body: Emotions and the Shakespearean Stage* (2004), which emphasises the ways in which early modern passions were inseparable from physiological experiences. Paster suggests that, for early modern individuals, 'the passions actually *were* liquid forces of nature, because, in this cosmology, the stuff of the outside world and the stuff of the body were composed of the same elemental materials'.[4] She is keen to historicise early modern emotional experience, proposing that, no matter how 'natural' an emotion might feel, it always occurs 'within a dense cultural and social context' specific to time and place.[5] In the case of early modern emotional culture, Paster offers a vivid description of the psychophysiological holism she believes was produced by the context of Galenic humoralism:

> [T]he bodily humors and the emotion that they sustain and move the body to express in action can be lexically distinguished but not functionally separated. For the early moderns, emotions flood the body not metaphorically but literally, as the humors course through the bloodstream carrying choler, melancholy, blood, and phlegm to the parts and as the animal spirits move like lightning from brain to muscle, from muscle to brain. (p. 14)

For Paster, the individual is a fundamentally material entity, subject not only to humoral fluctuations in the body but also to elemental shifts in the wider natural world, or 'ecology', as she calls it. A similar approach is taken in *Reading the Early Modern Passions: Essays in the Cultural History of Emotion* (2004), which Paster co-edited with Katherine Rowe and Mary Floyd-Wilson. As the editors emphasise in their Introduction, several of the book's contributors explore how 'pre-Cartesian psychophysiology may have affected early modern self-experience', and the ways in which 'the very language of physiology … helps determine phenomenology'.[6] While *Reading the Early Modern Passions* includes work that explores methods and approaches beyond Galenic humoralism – for example, the chapters by Richard Strier and Douglas Trevor – the historiographical legacy of the book has been the emphasis on humoralism that is present in its framing introduction and several of its subsequent chapters. Along with Michael Schoenfeldt's *Bodies and Selves in Early Modern England* (1999) these studies have been highly influential, arguably setting the emotional agenda in Shakespeare and Renaissance studies.[7]

Such an approach reminds us of the extent to which emotions, as William Reddy puts it, 'have a kind of history', and suggests that some of the descriptions of emotion that we now think of as metaphorical – having a broken heart, or being infected with fear – had literal resonance in the period.[8] Moreover, the emphasis upon the bodily aspects of emotions can seem especially attractive, as it resonates with the concerns of late twentieth and early twenty-first century neuroscience, which increasingly questions dualistic assumptions about the disembodied mind.[9] Recent work in Shakespeare studies has continued to argue for the acceptance of this critical paradigm, extending it to the realm of early modern literary and theatrical reception. In *Shakespearean Sensations* (2013), Katharine Craik and Tanya Pollard argue that critics need to take seriously 'the complex and intimate reciprocity between books, bodies, and selves', and suggest that '[o]ur longstanding habit of separating bodily responses from intellectual reasoning has deterred critics from exploring their interdependence'.[10] For Craik and Pollard, early modern descriptions of somatic responses to literary texts are not merely rhetorical tropes, but instead offer accurate descriptions of readers' bodily sensations: 'Books and plays were among the external agents capable of profoundly altering humoral balance, implicating readers and theatregoers in complex processes of transaction or exchange.'[11] Their work highlights the profound impressionability of the humoral, emotional self, while also drawing attention to the ways in which readers and playgoers acted as agents in this process by seeking out the imaginative and sensory experiences offered in contemporary literature and drama.

Such scholarship has been extremely valuable in foregrounding the importance of humoralism in relation to historical phenomenology and embodiment, but it has to some extent obscured the way in which other intellectual and creative frameworks, such as religious and philosophical belief, political performance, or rhetorical and dramaturgical style also shaped cultural beliefs about emotional experience. Such frameworks complicate the humoral paradigm and point to more active and wilful experiences of emotion in the period, in which writers drew on multiple emotional discourses in order to construct their own particularised models of feeling. Indeed Richard Strier has questioned the ability of purely humoralist readings to recover the full variety of emotional experience on display in Renaissance writing, arguing that 'the early modern period is a period where all discourses are contested, and that to take a Galenic discourse as somehow a master-discourse is mistaken'. 'If we are trying to understand early modern persons', he continues, 'we need to take into account all the available resources the period offered, in all their abundance and contradiction, and see which ones are being mobilized in any particular instance.'[12] More recently, in *The Unrepentant Renaissance* (2011), Strier has suggested that 'the new humoralism' of the last decade is akin to new historicism in its questioning of individual agency, and that humoral theory is one of several tools used by scholars to characterise the period 'in dark and dour terms'. He writes that the focus of the new humoralists 'might be said to be on selves in the period as physiocultural rather than sociocultural formations', and suggests that more attention might be given to the ways in which such selves resisted 'systematizing' in favour of more 'bumptious, full-throated, and perhaps perverse' ways of feeling.[13] Bridget Escolme has voiced a similar 'desire to give pleasure equal weight with anxiety' in the study of Shakespeare and his contemporaries, while Brian Cummings and Freya Sierhuis have called for a 'realignment' of early modern emotion 'both with the ancient concerns of rhetoric and with contemporary reflections on intersubjectivity and self-reflection'.[14]

Even scholars largely interested in the medical nature of Renaissance and early modern emotion have begun to take issue with the totalising predominance of humoralism within the field. In her discussion of anger and health in late medieval and Renaissance Europe, Elena Carrera has challenged the assumption that a 'humoral inevitability' or 'determinism' single-handedly dictated medical interpretations of the passions. She argues instead that mind–body relations were not so 'unidirectional', and that mental and even rational phenomena such as *pneuma* – an entity she describes as 'approaching the substance of celestial beings' – played a larger role in the production of passion than has previously been recognised.[15] Likewise, in his work on melancholy and Galenic humoralism, Angus Gowland has posited that the kinds of emotional subjectivity found in Renaissance medical and philosophical discourse 'cannot be understood exclusively or even primarily in terms of the body and its humours, but rather in terms of the relationship between the body and the soul'. Through a careful examination of a range of European writings on the subject of melancholy, Gowland emphasises the complexity of the relationship between the material and immaterial self and notes that while 'occasionally these connections were suggestive of a radical materialism … the two domains [of body and soul] never collapsed into each other'.[16] Such work has drawn attention to the fact that early modern theories of mind, soul and will overlapped with those of the body in complex and often contested ways, destabilising any straightforward explanation of how emotional experience might be produced or what it might mean from a moral or social point of view. Understanding emotion in the Renaissance was part of the larger project of understanding the human, and accordingly it required insights from all of its philosophical, spiritual, physiological and creative engagements.

Emotional frameworks: religion, rhetoric, performance

If we do want to historicise the early modern passions, then, we need to give more attention to the other systems of knowledge and representation that people used to conceptualise and articulate emotional experience. While such frameworks are numerous, the contributors to the present book focus on what we believe to be three of the most important areas of influence: religious and philosophical belief, linguistic and literary form, and political and dramaturgical performance. In their investigation of these areas, the chapters below cover a range of texts by writers including Thomas Wright, Thomas Cranmer, Robert Burton, John Lyly, Thomas Preston and William

Shakespeare. Shakespeare emerges as a particular focus in several of the chapters, reflecting the fact that he exemplifies a wider early modern interest in the active, pluralistic and performative aspects of emotion. Some contributors go further, and make the case that Shakespeare was unusual among his contemporaries in the extent to which his characters' emotional states cannot be accommodated within the framework of medical-humoral theory. John Lee has made a similar argument about Shakespeare's distinctiveness in this regard, writing that, while Shakespeare was 'profoundly an Elizabethan in terms of style', he was 'also quite un-Elizabethan in the ways certain of his dramatic persons … conceive of their identity'. Lee suggests that Hamlet in particular seems to have 'found the materialist theories of his age unsatisfactory'.[17] We might extend such an observation to the soliloquy from *Richard II* quoted above, in which Richard's attempts to make sense of his plight appear to be as concerned with religious, proverbial, musical and dramatic frameworks as they are with physiological ones. This is not to deny, of course, that medical theory (including humoralism) played an important role in shaping contemporary approaches to emotion, very often at the same time as one or more of these other frameworks; yet the chapters below seek to complicate the medical-humoral approach by considering how engagements with religion, philosophy, rhetoric, politics and performance shaped the formulation of feeling in equally meaningful and culturally lasting ways.

Given the centrality of religion in Renaissance and Reformation culture, it should come as little surprise that theology and devotion played a central role in the experience of a wide variety of emotions. Andy Kesson and Emma Smith have recently estimated that, of the nearly eleven thousand books and papers published in the Elizabethan period, about 40 per cent were religious in nature.[18] If we take seriously the role that printed material plays in the shaping of cultural beliefs, practices and ways of feeling (and almost all major histories of emotion to date rely on such a precept), then we must acknowledge the deep influence that religious doctrine and guidance had on the understanding of emotion.[19] As Penelope Gouk and Helen Hills write in *Representing Emotions* (2005), '[a]s long as religious belief was central to society, with the Church assuming immense social and institutional power, arguments about emotions or *affetti* … ultimately revolved around the relationship between the individual and God'.[20] Several of the chapters in this volume show how this relationship as well as the relationships between different communities of believers fundamentally shaped the experience and valuation of emotion across a range of early modern texts. While Gouk and Hills's collection explores how such issues manifested themselves in music and art, literary critics such as Jan Frans van Dijkhuizen and Femke Molecamp have shown how devotional poetry and spiritual life writing in the period also reveal a deep emotionality concerned most centrally with the life of the soul.[21] Authors here extend such examination to Scripture itself, as well as to the contemporary theological treatises, stage plays and even medical texts that drew on this Scripture in their explanation and representation of the emotional life.

This fundamental connection between emotional identity and spirituality has recently come to prominence in two major historical studies of religious change in early modern Europe. Alec Ryrie devotes the first part of *Being Protestant in Reformation Britain* (2013) to a discussion of 'The Protestant Emotions', examining the intensive ways in which Protestants 'disciplined' their emotions before God, and in *The Reformation of Feeling* (2010) Susan Karant-Nunn shows how German reformers embedded particular emotional 'tenors' in their sermons in order to establish communities of Protestant feeling that were distinct from existing Catholic ones. In doing so, she emphasises the 'complexity and dynamism – as opposed to the purity and separateness – of emotions in practice', drawing attention once again to the active nature of affective experience.[22] These historical works underpin several of the literary and dramatic readings advanced in this book, while also heralding a wider shift in the field of early modern emotion studies.

In addition to religious beliefs, rhetorical practices and traditions dating to classical times also shaped the way in which early modern emotions were experienced and articulated. In *Ovid and the Politics of Emotion in Elizabethan England* (2009), Cora Fox acknowledges the importance of humoral theory, but proposes that we need to think more seriously about the influence of classical narratives and intertexts in studying the emotional culture of the period: 'in order to understand an individual or a society, and particularly such subtle but foundational aspects of everyday life as emotion, we need to turn to texts, and particularly to intertexts'.[23] Fox is especially interested in the influence of Ovid: 'In dialogue with humoral conceptions of the body, Ovidianism registers the interdependence of body and self, but it also reveals the way the self can outlive the body, even as it aestheticizes and attaches cultural value to the body as the site of metamorphosis' (p. 8). As Fox points out, many of the Ovidian narratives that are referred to by Renaissance writers involve female laments, such as the stories of Philomela, Daphne, Proserpina and Arachne. She argues that such early modern representations of emotion could be politically as well as rhetorically powerful, as female characters seek out classical exemplars as a way of articulating their passions in potent and oppositional ways.[24] Lynn Enterline's *Shakespeare's Schoolroom* (2012) also points to the importance of such classical figures, and emphasises the ways in which grammar-school training played a key role in providing pupils with 'influential emotion scripts'.[25] Like Fox, Enterline notes Shakespeare's awareness of Galenic medicine, but proposes that we need to investigate further why his reflections on the passions 'involve meta-theatrical or meta-rhetorical reflections on classical figures, texts, and traditions' (p. 27). Both of these critics, then, emphasise the extent to which emotions in the period were understood in relation to intertexual, narrative and literary models, as well as humoral ones.

One intriguing example of such emotional intertextuality occurs in Shakespeare's *The Two Gentlemen of Verona*.[26] Having been abandoned by Proteus, and disguised as a male page named Sebastian, Julia describes to Silvia how she (or rather 'he') once borrowed Julia's clothes in a pageant and performed the tragic role of Ariadne: 'And at that time I made her weep a-good, / For I did play a lamentable part. / Madam, 'twas Ariadne, passioning / For Theseus' perjury and unjust flight' (4.4.163–6). As the archetypal betrayed woman, Ariadne is an apt classical precedent for Julia to invoke, and provides a pattern for her grief.[27] Yet the passage is also noteworthy in terms of how it describes Sebastian's performance of Ariadne's grief, and its effect upon his mistress:

> Which I so lively acted with my tears
> That my poor mistress, moved therewithal,
> Wept bitterly; and would I might be dead
> If I in thought felt not her very sorrow.
>
> (4.4.167–70)

This description of a kind of emotional contagion between Sebastian and Julia might confirm the classical and early modern notion that an actor's performance of grief could provoke spontaneous tears in their audience.[28] At the same time, however, this moment suggests that early modern books and plays did not simply alter an audience's humoral balance but rather gave rise to a complex interaction of thinking and feeling: as 'Sebastian' states, he felt Julia's sorrow 'in thought'. This rich description of an entirely imaginary performance – which arguably points to Julia's agency and imaginative creativity – highlights the ways in which representing the passions challenged Shakespeare's creative resources, as he explored and extended his audience's emotional capacities as well.

The emphasis on performance and performativity in this passage – and the imaginative demands that it places on Shakespeare's audience – also draws attention to the significance of dramaturgical creativity and practice in representing and reshaping the passions. Steven Mullaney has emphasised the importance of the early modern stage as a place where emotions could be depicted and debated, suggesting that '[t]heater can provide a culture with a means of thinking about itself'. He argues that the playhouses of Elizabethan London constituted 'one of the more complex affective technologies of this or any other period'.[29] Mullaney thus offers a more optimistic view of the relationship between emotion, self and society than some critics have allowed, and argues that early modern playgoers were encouraged to experience innovative forms of emotional self-consciousness: 'The new playhouses demanded and produced new powers of identification, projection, and apprehension in their audiences, altering the threshold not only of dramatic representation but also of self-representation' (p. 81). Indira Ghose, in her study of Shakespeare and laughter, likewise stresses the ways in which the rhetorical and political performance of emotion – both on the stage and in highly charged social settings such as the court – allowed orators the 'capacity to refashion the world through art', often in very playful and unpredictable ways.[30] Together these critics recognise not only the early modern fascination with performing one's passions on both the theatrical and political stage but also the ways in which writers such as Shakespeare had the capacity to shape their culture, rather than simply being shaped by it. Of course Shakespeare was not the only early modern author to explore such concerns: as we shall see in the chapters that follow, his works borrowed from and influenced a range of writers including John Lyly, Samuel Daniel, Thomas Preston, Robert Baron and Richard Niccols. Nevertheless Shakespeare seems to have played a particularly important role in creating new words and vocabularies for expressing emotional states, which in turn enriched and complicated the emotional culture that he inhabited.

Reclaiming agency: language and meaning

Directly connected to such questions of authorial and emotional agency are the terms that were used to describe and debate emotion in this period. The most common of these – the *passions* – derived from the Greek word *pathe* and was part of the same etymological family as the Latin *patior*, which meant to suffer passively.[31] As Susan James has shown, this sense of passion as a passive experience related both to the physical and spiritual suffering endured by Christ in his Passion and to Aristotle's conception of passion and sensation as responsive states, arising not in and of themselves but in reaction to external stimuli. Summarising Aristotle's thinking on this point, James writes, 'our ability to feel passions is not an ability to transform one kind of thing into another; rather, as with sensory perceptions, it is a capacity to be affected by the world around us'.[32] But not all early modern writers were entirely at ease with this formulation. In his *The Use of the Passions* (published in English in 1649), Jean François Senault largely followed Aristotle in his definition and explication of his subject matter, but he nevertheless noted that these 'motions' produced in the soul and body were so 'violent ... that they do hardly deserve the name of passions'.[33] Implicit is the sense that there is a powerfully active force at work in the experience of the passions that is conceptually at odds with the idea of passivity. Though Senault still regarded the passions as detrimental, describing them subsequently as disorders, diseases and even monsters, he also pointed to the ways in which they were not simply autonomic responses to external stimuli, but were also the product of human imagination working in consort (or indeed contest) with the understanding, the appetite, the humours and in some cases even reason.[34]

The motive power of the passions, and its seeming incongruity with the word's etymological implications, is perhaps one of the reasons why a new term, *emotions*, emerged in late sixteenth-century England to signify these mental and physical states. Although the word did not become commonplace until much later in the nineteenth century, when it was widely adopted by the medical and psychological sciences, its limited emergence in the period in question is none the less significant.[35] As David Thorley has shown, *emotion* was 'a term whose meaning was in flux' in the seventeenth century, and could signify anatomical and political as well as mental and spiritual upheavals, depending on the context in which it was used.[36] Within this flux were a number of other sixteenth- and seventeenth-century emotion terms, most notably the *affections*, which could also indicate specific meanings according to the context in which they appeared, but were not so thoroughly particularised as to always mean something distinctive from one another.[37] As James puts it, among English writers in the sixteenth and seventeenth centuries, '[t]he view that these terms were all roughly synonymous quickly became fixed'.[38]

Nevertheless, the question of which term is most appropriate for historical, literary and dramatic investigations of emotion in the early modern period has become a vexed one, with scholars rightly reminding us that, just as the categories of feeling known in other times do not always match with our own, neither does the language used. Thomas Dixon in particular has highlighted the specific 'extensions' and 'intensions' at work in the words *passion*, *affection* and *emotion*, and he has argued convincingly for the historical specificity of each term and against naive elisions of present and past modes of experience. Dixon takes the word *emotion* as his central case in point, suggesting that its use in modern historical analyses too often brings with it a tradition of secular medicine and psychology that is anachronistic in the context of Renaissance and early modern thinking.[39] Along similar lines, current use of the word *affect* in cultural and critical studies generally implies a supremely embodied experience of emotion (to the extent that any rational or even cognitive component is sometimes denied), whereas in the Renaissance *affection* in its most technical sense signified quite the opposite, that is, an immaterial, disembodied and explicitly rational state.[40]

The contributors to the present book follow their Renaissance predecessors in taking a pluralistic and contextually specified approach to the language of emotion, drawing on the available terminology according to their methodological and theoretical approach. While some prefer a more historically or technically bounded idiom, many choose a language less intensively situated in a particular period. Such a decision may be particularly important as the study of emotion in early modern literature and drama begins to move beyond a strictly historicist approach, and starts to encompass presentist, performative and formalist analyses as well. In spite of such terminological differences, however, all of our contributors share an interest in the creative and dramatic work language performs when it is used to give shape to interior experience, both in terms of the specific vocabulary used and the wider social and aesthetic context in which it is deployed. Of particular interest is the fluidity of language and its constant development through different kinds of use. While Paster and others have emphasised the literal significance of emotive language in early modern writings, situating its meaning within the framework of Galenic humoralism, our contributors also attempt to reconsider the metaphorical, poetic and more generally unbounded potential of emotionally charged language in this period. As Strier has helpfully reminded us, 'the problem of what is literal and what is metaphoric in early modern humors discourse is extremely tricky', just as the meaning of particular emotion words is so.[41]

Rereading the passions

This book proposes, then, that we 'reread' the early modern passions, attending not only to their humoral engagements but also to the other historical belief systems and literary and dramaturgical styles that informed their conceptualisation and representation. While our contributors do not deny the important role the body might play in mediating early modern understandings and experiences of emotion, they do challenge the current scholarly hermeneutic by demonstrating how early modern interpretation and valuation of emotion were bound up in questions that could not be answered solely through humoral medical knowledge, including questions about the life of the soul, the creation of community, the cultivation of virtue, the power of language and the nature of literary and dramatic creativity. By bringing greater scholarly attention to the marked pluralism of early modern emotions theory, this volume shows how open, creative and agency-ridden the experience and interpretation of emotion could be, with writers in the period drawing on a variety of emotional ideas and tools to shape the representation and reception of feeling in their texts. Taken individually, the contributions in this volume offer much-needed investigations into previously overlooked areas of emotional experience and signification; taken together, they offer a significant re-evaluation of the cultural priorities and phenomenological principles that shaped the understanding of the emotive self in the early modern period.

The first part of the book examines how intellectual traditions beyond Galenic humoralism shaped Renaissance thinking about emotion. Focusing in particular on religious and philosophical approaches, this section explores how contemporary writers drew variously on teachings from Protestant, Catholic, Anglican, Judaic, Augustinian, Neoplatonic and neo-Stoic traditions to help frame their understanding of emotional experience and its consequent role in the earthly and spiritual life. In the opening chapter, Erin Sullivan examines the varieties of emotionality at work in Thomas Wright's *The Passions of the Minde in Generall* (1601), a book that she suggests 'has become something of a touchstone' for scholars interested in humoral materialism and early modern emotion. Her consideration situates the book instead within the context of its theological and 'immaterial' commitments, which she suggests arose from both Wright's life and work as a Jesuit priest and his engagement with natural philosophical questions about the possibility of passion in the intellective, and thus disembodied, soul. Through such an analysis she argues that Wright 'at once embraced the centrality of the integrated and embodied soul while nevertheless retaining scope for elements of dualism', exploring within *The Passions* a more intensively devotional and immaterial vision of emotion than has sometimes been acknowledged.

David Bagchi's chapter turns our attention from varieties of Catholic emotionality to those of Protestantism. Building on Karant-Nunn's study of emotion in German Protestant sermons, Bagchi considers how the English Church's standardised readings from the *Book of Common Prayer* and its associated *Homilies* acted as an 'officially imposed script' that framed, and at times tamed, biblical emotions for English congregants. Through close readings of the prayers and exegeses that the *Book of Common Prayer* and *Homilies* offered at potentially very emotive biblical moments – such as the spiritual highs and lows of the psalms, the supposed crimes of the Jews and the Passion of Christ – Bagchi demonstrates how these texts managed the 'confusing and even frightening emotions' to be found in 'the newly published vernacular' Bible, resulting in a view of devotional piety that above all emphasised spiritual quietness and tranquillity.

In the third chapter, Sara Coodin examines the relationship between 'thrift-as-thriving' and eudaimonia ('happiness' or 'the good life') across early moral philosophical, religious and literary writings. Her analysis reminds us once again of the pluralism inherent in contemporary approaches to emotion, which she shows 'made ready use of the discourse of humoral psychology, but did not begin and end with the body'. Moving us firmly into the realm of literature, Coodin examines Shakespeare's *The Merchant of Venice* within the context of contemporary moral-philosophical 'self-help' guides and Christian and Judaic exegetical literature, illustrating how Shylock's moral character as presented within the play is defined not so much by a humoral or financial materialism, but rather by a practised and agency-ridden awareness of thrift's powerful role in 'eudaimonistic flourishing, or … the life that is well-lived'.

Mary Ann Lund concludes the first part of the book by showing how Robert Burton's *The Anatomy of Melancholy* (1621), a work known principally for its exploration of sadness through the lens of humoral theory, includes within its pages a richly affective meditation on the happiness arising from the apprehension of God's beauty. In this 'prose hymn of heavenly beauty', Lund identifies an eclectic and at times surprising range of source material, demonstrating how Burton drew centrally on Augustine for his account – 'the central patristic authority of English Reformation theology' – while also incorporating ideas from contemporary Catholic and Neoplatonic writers. The result, Lund argues, is a treatment of divine beauty that is 'less squeamish' and more 'overtly sensuous' than its English counterparts, creating space for communion with the *visio dei* through moments of ecstatic rapture as well as more sustainable and wilful acts of loving charity.

The second part of the book explores three important emotion words – *spleen*, *sympathise* and *happiness* – and illustrates the ways in which linguistic and conceptual histories reflect the changing debates surrounding the meaning and valuation of emotional experience in the Renaissance. Nigel Wood explores the use of the word *spleen* in Shakespeare's comedies, and suggests that, while it was associated with the satyr, the term was capable of more positive associations, and summons up a 'range of contrasting significations'. A fit of the spleen was understood to involve a violent burst of passion, or a draining off of excess humours and passions; but the term evades straightforward definition, and thus becomes a figure for ungovernability in a wider, literary and rhetorical sense. Rather than being explicable via bodily or humoral models, Wood suggests that, in Shakespeare's hands, *spleen* 'indicated some aspect of the emotional that could not be adequately represented in verbal terms'. Wood thus uses the concept to open up larger questions of mimesis and representation, and argues that spleen does not allow for a 'speaking picture' that depicts affective experience, but is rather a term at the 'at the very boundaries of linguistic capture'. It also, he suggests, serves as a metaphor for the audience's mixed emotions.

Richard Meek is also concerned with the responses of audiences and readers, and the way in which such responses are shaped and manipulated by Shakespeare's *Richard II*. Various critics and editors have considered the emotionalism of the play, and debated whether or not audiences do or should feel sympathy for its central character. Meek's chapter adopts a different approach, and reads the play in relation to the development of the terms *sympathy* and *sympathise* in the period. He argues that Shakespeare's interest in pity and emotional comparability relates to the ways in which the play itself is embedded in a larger process of literary allusion and borrowing. The chapter culminates in a reading of Richard's description of a 'lamentable tale' that will be told about him in the future, which will 'send the hearers weeping to their beds' (5.1.44–5). In this speech Richard seemingly uses the term *sympathise* to mean 'to answer or correspond to'; yet the fact that this moment describes the compassion of a figured audience suggests that Shakespeare may have played an important role in reshaping and modifying the meaning of the term.

Richard Chamberlain's chapter explores *Hamlet*'s preoccupation with the relationship between event, chance and emotion. Through a close examination of Shakespeare's use of the terms *hap*, *perhaps* and *happy*, Chamberlain argues that *Hamlet* imagines happiness as serendipity, or the evasion of conventional moral goods and totalising social systems. He points out that, in the Renaissance, the primary meaning of *happy* was not a feeling of pleasure, but rather 'Having good "hap" or fortune; lucky, fortunate; favoured by lot, position, or other external circumstance' (*OED*, 2a). Chamberlain also shows that *happiness* could refer to felicity of expression, and that certain emotional states can lead to fortunate instances of verbal or literary creativity. By recovering these early modern meanings of emotion words, and drawing upon the writings of Marx and Adorno, Chamberlain reads *Hamlet*'s study of political repression as part of a broader thesis: that happiness lies in *hap* (suddenness, spontaneity, chance) rather than bureaucratic prescription.

The third part of the book moves from the linguistic and rhetorical dimensions of early modern emotion to the performative. Focusing on emotion as an element of both political and theatrical craft, the chapters in this section explore how Renaissance authors – including, but not limited to, Shakespeare – used emotion as a tool for dramatic representation and political expression. Andy Kesson explores how central 'discrepant and divergent emotional duress' proves to be in both the creation and reception of Lyly's work, which was frequently performed for a courtly audience. Challenging a received scholarly tradition that has tended to see Lyly as a static or schematic author, Kesson shows instead how continual movement, in both a kinaesthetic and an affective sense, characterises Lyly's drama and prose. Such movement directly implicates readers and audience members, inviting them to engage 'not [in] an act of removed, distanced spectatorship', but in a process of active, mutual and at times even violent participation. Likening the author–reader relationship in Lyly to a kind of dance, Kesson demonstrates how emotive agency and creativity in Lyly's works emerge through a performative and linguistic interplay between fictional and non-fictional worlds, a kind of imaginative 'maze' that cannot help but produce amazement.

Ann Kaegi's chapter on female lament in Shakespeare's *Richard III* considers how the performance of emotion could be a deeply political act. 'Pathos is a form of power, particularly in the theatre', she writes, and her chapter explores this idea in terms of both the religious politics of mourning in post-Reformation culture and the dramatic politics of tyranny and tyrannicide in Shakespeare's history play. Kaegi shows how Shakespeare reworked cultural expectations about the performance of grief as well as his historical source material in order to foreground the lamentations and curses of the play's female characters, including Lady Anne, Queen Elizabeth, Queen Margaret and the Duchess of York. But it is not until these characters give up cursing one another and focus their complaint solely on Richard that the 'potent political idiom' of their grief achieves its full effect. Through such affective consolidation, Kaegi argues, the grieving female voice becomes a form of 'treason by words' that establishes the basis for Richard's eventual overthrow.

Frederika Bain focuses on the performance of emotion in early modern accounts of execution and murder, including the plays *Cambyses, King of Persia* and *Richard III*, as well as broadside ballads, pamphlets and other forms of cheap print. In their representations of the passions of the key players, these texts illustrate not only how emotion might be communicated from one character to another but also how certain emotional effects can be achieved by manipulating linguistic and dramatic conventions. Through dramatic performances of passion these texts communicate larger – and at times subversive – political arguments about the nature of tyranny versus legitimate rule, and illustrate the potency of emotional performance on the early modern stage and page. Bain demonstrates that Shakespeare and his contemporaries were not constrained by such early modern 'emotion scripts', but rather exploited them in order to create a compelling illusion of emotional immediacy.

In the final chapter, R. S. White and Ciara Rawnsley explore how Shakespeare in particular constructed complex manifestations of mixed emotions in his plays, suggesting that 'this aspect of his drama is so characteristic as to be "the dyer's hand" in his work'. Through a close analysis of two sequences in *The Two Gentlemen of Verona* and *Cymbeline*, White and Rawnsley argue that discrepant emotional awarenesses between characters, as well as between characters and audiences, prove 'crucial to the dramatic effect and affect' of the plays as a whole. Shakespeare, they suggest, was often less concerned with 'narrative neatness' than with the dynamic interplay of 'structural and emotional' elements within a story, resulting in a layering of emotional experience through dramatic disclosure that resists straightforward explanation or historicisation.

Peter Holbrook concludes the book with an Afterword that meditates on the importance of emotional freedom in Shakespeare's works. His closing analysis calls for a freer, more agency-ridden approach to our understanding of emotional creativity in Shakespeare and his period, a process that might liberate not only our reading of Renaissance characters and texts but also the critical form itself. Together, then, the chapters in this collection demonstrate how unpredictable, dynamic and powerful emotion could be in the early modern period. Like Paster and her collaborators, we agree that 'the representation of affect resides at the very heart of artistic production', as well as daily cultural life, and we are indebted to these scholars for their pioneering work in what is, thanks to them, a burgeoning field.[42] At the same time, we welcome this further phase in early modern literary studies and emotion, in which researchers are building on work on Galenic humoralism and the passions while also taking it in new and more pluralistic directions. The contributors to our collection point to three major areas in which the understanding of early modern emotion still has considerable room to grow. While such an examination cannot offer a comprehensive exploration of the kinds of emotional experience and creativity on display in early modern literature, drama and culture, it seeks to demonstrate that emotion in this period did not follow a single template or social script, but rather was made up of multiple intellectual traditions and literary practices. The results, we suggest, are sometimes surprising and always exciting, offering ample material to take early modern emotions studies both through and beyond its current disciplinary turn.

Notes

1 *Richard II*, 5.5.6–11. Quotations are taken from Charles R. Forker's Arden 3 edn (London: Methuen, 2002). Further references will appear parenthetically in the text. For a more extended discussion of *Richard II* see Chapter 6, below.

2 Emma Mason and Isobel Armstrong, 'Introduction: "Feeling: An Indefinite Dull Region of the Spirit?"', *Textual Practice*, 22 (2008), Special Issue on 'Languages of Emotion', 1–19 (p. 2).

3 See Jan Plamper, 'The History of Emotions: An Interview with William Reddy, Barbara Rosenwein and Peter Stearns', *History and Theory*, 49 (2010), 237–65 (p. 237); Sharon Crozier-De Rosa, 'Popular Fiction and the "Emotional Turn": The Case of Women in Late Victorian Britain', *History Compass*, 8 (2010), 1340–51; Colin Jones, 'The Emotional Turn in the History of Medicine and the View from Queen Mary University of London', *Social History of Medicine*, Virtual Issue: Emotions, Health, and Well-being (2012), 1–2; Richard Meek, 'Introduction: Shakespeare and the Culture of Emotion', *Shakespeare*, 8 (2012), 279–85 (p. 279); and Erin Sullivan, 'The History of the Emotions: Past, Present, Future', *Cultural History*, 2 (2013), 93–102 (p. 94).

4 Gail Kern Paster, *Humoring the Body: Emotions and the Shakespearean Stage* (Chicago: University of Chicago Press, 2004), p. 4, her emphasis. See also Paster, 'The Tragic Subject and Its Passions', in Claire MacEachern (ed.), *The Cambridge Companion to Shakespearean Tragedy* (Cambridge: Cambridge University Press, 2013), pp. 152–70.

5 Paster, *Humoring the Body*, p. 8.

6 Gail Kern Paster, Katherine Rowe and Mary Floyd-Wilson, 'Introduction:

Reading the Early Modern Passions', in Paster, Rowe and Floyd-Wilson (eds), *Reading the Early Modern Passions: Essays in the Cultural History of Emotion* (Philadelphia: University of Pennsylvania Press, 2004), pp. 1–20 (p. 16).

7 Michael C. Schoenfeldt, *Bodies and Selves in Early Modern England: Physiology and Inwardness in Spenser, Shakespeare, Herbert and Milton* (Cambridge: Cambridge University Press, 1999). See also Mary Floyd-Wilson and Garrett A. Sullivan, Jr (eds), *Environment and Embodiment in Early Modern England* (Basingstoke: Palgrave Macmillan, 2007); Matthew Steggle, *Laughing and Weeping in Early Modern Theatres* (Aldershot: Ashgate, 2007); David Wood, *Time, Narrative and Emotion in Early Modern England* (Farnham: Ashgate, 2009); and Allison P. Hobgood, *Passionate Playgoing in Early Modern England* (Cambridge: Cambridge University Press, 2014).

8 William M. Reddy, *The Navigation of Feeling: A Framework for the History of Emotions* (Cambridge and New York: Cambridge University Press, 2001), p. x; Paster et al., 'Introduction', pp. 16–18. For dying of a broken heart see Erin Sullivan, 'A Disease unto Death: Sadness in the Time of Shakespeare', in Elena Carrera (ed.), *Emotions and Health, 1200–1700* (Leiden: Brill, 2013), pp. 159–83; for fear see Allison P. Hobgood, 'Feeling Fear in *Macbeth*', in Katharine A. Craik and Tanya Pollard (eds), *Shakespearean Sensations: Experiencing Literature in Early Modern England* (Cambridge: Cambridge University Press, 2013), pp. 29–46.

9 See, for example, Antonio Damasio, *Descartes' Error: Emotion, Reason and the Human Brain* (London: Picador, 1995), and *The Feeling of What Happens: Body, Emotion and the Making of Consciousness* (London: Heinemann, 1999); Joseph LeDoux, *The Emotional Brain: The Mysterious Underpinnings of Emotional Life* (London: Weidenfeld and Nicolson, 1998); John Sutton, *Philosophy and Memory Traces: Descartes to Connectionism* (Cambridge: Cambridge University Press, 1998); and Seth Duncan and Lisa Feldman Barrett, 'Affect Is a Form of Cognition: A Neurobiological Analysis', *Cognition and Emotion*, 21 (2007), 1184–211.

10 Katharine A. Craik and Tanya Pollard, 'Introduction: Imagining Audiences', in Craik and Pollard (eds), *Shakespearean Sensations: Experiencing Literature in Early Modern England* (Cambridge: Cambridge University Press, 2013), pp. 1–25 (pp. 4–5).

11 Ibid., p. 7.

12 Richard Strier and Carla Mazzio, 'Two Responses to "Shakespeare and Embodiment: An E-Conversation"', *Literature Compass*, 3 (2006), 15–31 (p. 16).

13 Richard Strier, *The Unrepentant Renaissance: From Petrarch to Shakespeare to Milton* (Chicago: University of Chicago Press, 2011), pp. 2, 17–18. It is important to note, however, that Michael Schoenfeldt (one of the 'new humoralists' that Strier identifies) specifically highlights the differences between his methodology and that of new historicism: 'Where New Historicism has tended to emphasize the individual as a victim of the power that circulates through culture, I stress the

empowerment that Galenic physiology and ethics bestowed upon the individual' (Schoenfeldt, *Bodies and Selves*, p. 11).

14 Bridget Escolme, *Emotional Excess on the Shakespearean Stage: Passion's Slaves* (London: Bloomsbury, 2014), p. xxv; Brian Cummings and Freya Sierhuis, 'Introduction', in Cummings and Sierhuis (eds), *Passions and Subjectivity in Early Modern Culture* (Farnham: Ashgate, 2013), pp. 1–9 (p. 7).

15 Elena Carrera, 'Anger and the Mind–Body Connection in Medieval and Early Modern Medicine', in Elena Carrera (ed.), *Emotions and Health, 1200–1700* (Leiden: Brill, 2013), pp. 95–146 (pp. 102–3, 107, 113).

16 Angus Gowland, 'Melancholy, Passions and Identity in the Renaissance', in Brian Cummings and Freya Sierhuis (eds), *Passions and Subjectivity in Early Modern Culture* (Farnham: Ashgate, 2013), pp. 75–84 (p. 83).

17 John Lee, 'Shakespeare, Human Nature, and English Literature', *Shakespeare*, 5 (2009), 177–90 (p. 184). Lee writes that 'Shakespeare's plays are not Jonsonian comedies of humours, but rather they set loose, in Western culture, optimistic narratives – often very optimistic narratives – about the degree to which we may remake ourselves and our societies' (p. 184).

18 Andy Kesson and Emma Smith, 'Introduction: Towards a Definition of Print Popularity', in Kesson and Smith (eds), *The Elizabethan Top Ten: Defining Print Popularity in Early Modern England* (Farnham: Ashgate, 2013), pp. 1–15 (p. 9).

19 The most influential theories and methodologies proposed for historical emotions research – including Peter and Carol Stearns's *emotionology*, William Reddy's *emotives* and Barbara Rosenwein's *emotional communities* – all fundamentally root their approaches in the power of the written word. See Stearns and Stearns, 'Emotionology: Clarifying the History of Emotions and Emotional Standards', *American Historical Review*, 90 (1985), 813–36; Reddy, *The Navigation of Feeling*; and Rosenwein, *Emotional Communities in the Early Middle Ages* (Ithaca: Cornell University Press, 2007).

20 Penelope Gouk and Helen Hills, 'Towards Histories of Emotion', in Gouk and Hills (eds), *Representing Emotions: New Connections in the Histories of Art, Music and Medicine* (Aldershot: Ashgate, 2005), pp. 15–34 (p. 19).

21 See Jan Frans van Dijkhuizen, *Pain and Compassion in Early Modern Literature and Culture* (Cambridge: D. S. Brewer, 2012); and Femke Molecamp, *Women and the Bible in Early Modern England: Religious Reading and Writing* (Oxford: Oxford University Press, 2013), esp. chs 4 and 6.

22 Alec Ryrie, *Being Protestant in Reformation Britain* (Oxford: Oxford University Press, 2013), p. 17; and Susan C. Karant-Nunn, *The Reformation of Feeling: Shaping the Religious Emotions in Early Modern Germany* (New York: Oxford University Press, 2010), p. 5.

23 Cora Fox, *Ovid and the Politics of Emotion in Elizabethan England* (New York and Basingstoke: Palgrave Macmillan, 2009), p. 3. Fox suggests that '[l]iterature … is often informed by conflicting epistemological systems and varying cultural

narratives', and notes that critics such as Jacqueline Miller have explored understandings of emotion 'based not on philosophical or protomedical discourse but on rhetorical theories of imitation' (p. 5). See Jacqueline T. Miller, 'The Passion Signified: Imitation and the Construction of Emotions in Sidney and Wroth', *Criticism*, 43 (2001), 407–21.

24 On the political aspects of female eloquence see Jennifer Richards and Alison Thorne (eds), *Rhetoric, Women and Politics in Early Modern England* (London and New York: Routledge, 2007).

25 Lynn Enterline, *Shakespeare's Schoolroom: Rhetoric, Discipline, Emotion* (Philadelphia: University of Pennsylvania Press, 2012), p. 26.

26 For further discussion of the play see Chapter 11, below.

27 See William C. Carroll's Arden 3 edn of *The Two Gentlemen of Verona* (London: Thomson, 2004), note to 4.4.165–6. Further references are included in the text. Carroll suggests that Shakespeare knew the tale from Ovid's *Heroides* and Chaucer's *The Legend of Good Women*. But see also T. W. Baldwin, who argues that Shakespeare was more likely to know the tale of Theseus and Ariadne from the grammar-school interpretation of Ovid than via Chaucer (*William Shakspere's Smalle Latine and Lesse Greeke*, 2 vols (Urbana: University of Illinois Press, 1944), vol. 2, p. 424).

28 See Joseph R. Roach, *The Player's Passion: Studies in the Science of Acting* (Newark: University of Delaware Press, 1985); and Robert Cockcroft, *Rhetorical Affect in Early Modern Writing* (Basingstoke: Palgrave Macmillan, 2003).

29 Steven Mullaney, 'Affective Technologies: Toward an Emotional Logic of the Elizabethan Stage', in Mary Floyd-Wilson and Garrett A. Sullivan, Jr (eds), *Environment and Embodiment in Early Modern England* (Basingstoke: Palgrave Macmillan, 2007), pp. 71–89 (pp. 73, 81).

30 Indira Ghose, *Shakespeare and Laughter: A Cultural History* (Manchester: Manchester University Press, 2008), p. 7. See also Kate Welch's analysis of theatrical publics and the performance of mourning in *Hamlet*, which draws attention to 'the performative nature of any public act' ('Making Mourning Show: *Hamlet* and Affective Public-Making', *Performance Research*, 16 (2011), 74–82 (p. 76)).

31 For a wide-ranging discussion of Shakespeare's creative use of the term *passion* see R. S. White, '"False Friends": Affective Semantics in Shakespeare', *Shakespeare*, 8 (2012), 286–99.

32 Susan James, *Passion and Action: The Emotions in Seventeenth-Century Philosophy* (Oxford: Oxford University Press, 1997), pp. 11, 41.

33 Jean François Senault, *The Use of the Passions*, trans. Henry Earl of Monmouth (London, 1649), p. 18.

34 Ibid., pp. 18–20.

35 See Graham Richards, 'Emotions into Words – Or Words into Emotions?', in Penelope Gouk and Helen Hills (eds), *Representing Emotions: New Connections in the Histories of Art, Music and Medicine* (Aldershot: Ashgate, 2005), pp. 49–65;

and Thomas Dixon, *From Passions to Emotions: The Creation of a Secular Psychological Category* (Cambridge: Cambridge University Press, 2003), pp. 1–25. See also Dixon's '"Emotion": The History of a Keyword in Crisis', *Emotion Review,* 4 (2012), 338–44.

36 David Thorley, 'Towards a History of Emotion, 1562–1660', *The Seventeenth Century*, 28 (2013), 3–19 (p. 3).

37 Carrera, 'Anger and the Mind–Body Connection', pp. 95–6; Gouk and Hills, 'Towards Histories of Emotion', pp. 17–18.

38 James, *Passion and Action*, p. 11.

39 Dixon, *From Passions to Emotions*, pp. 15–19.

40 For modern uses of *affect*, see Ruth Leys, 'The Turn to Affect: A Critique', *Critical Inquiry*, 37 (2011), 434–72 (p. 437). For historical analyses of *affection*, see Nicholas E. Lombardo, 'Emotions and Psychological Health in Aquinas', in Elena Carrera (ed.), *Emotions and Health, 1200–1700* (Leiden: Brill, 2013), pp. 19–46 (pp. 26–7); and Dixon, *From Passions to Emotions*, p. 40.

41 Strier and Mazzio, 'Two Responses to "Shakespeare and Embodiment"', p. 17.

42 Paster et al., 'Introduction', p. 19.

Part I

The theology and philosophy of emotion

1

The passions of Thomas Wright: Renaissance emotion across body and soul

Erin Sullivan

In the study of Renaissance emotion, especially in relation to Shakespeare and his contemporaries, it doesn't take long before coming across the work of Thomas Wright (*c.*1561–1623).[1] His *The Passions of the Minde in Generall*, first published in 1601, has become something of a touchstone for literary scholars, offering a detailed description of embodied passion that has often been used as a gloss on dramatic and poetic representations of affective experience. In 2004 Mary Floyd-Wilson described Wright's *The Passions* as 'a handbook on rhetoric and the management of one's emotions', and a decade later one could be forgiven for thinking it is *the* handbook, given the frequency with which it surfaces in studies of sixteenth- and seventeenth-century emotion and literature.[2] There are several reasons why Wright's book has proved so useful. First, the dates of its composition (late 1590s), publication (1601) and republication (1604) sit very well alongside Shakespeare's dramatic career, making it genuinely contemporary with the period's most-studied author. Second, Wright's writing is vivid, detailed and comprehensive, describing the workings of the passions at greater length and in richer language than many other writers on the subject. Third, Wright's philosophical approach to passionate experience is a permissive, humanistic and strikingly holistic one, prompting students and scholars of the period to read articulations of embodied feeling in exciting new ways – 'to literalize those locutions that we have long presumed to be figurative'.[3]

Bearing all this in mind, an argument could be, and has been, made querying the extent to which Wright's book is entirely representative of emotional understanding in the period. Several writers have pointed out that he was a Jesuit – adhering at least in part to a different worldview from that of most of his countrymen in late sixteenth- and early seventeenth-century England – and Christopher Tilmouth has suggested that too many scholars have treated Wright's work 'as if it were normative', arguing instead that his 'distinctly Thomist treatment of the affections is only one of several analytical frameworks with reference to which Shakespeare and his contemporaries could have conceptualized the emotions'.[4] Likewise, while critical responses to canonical works in the recent historiography of Renaissance emotion such as Gail Kern Paster's *Humoring the Body* and Paster, Katherine Rowe and Mary Floyd-Wilson's *Reading the Early Modern Passions* have deservedly praised these studies for their pioneering investigation of the embodied nature of Renaissance emotion, they have also suggested that Wright's role in such scholarship may be overemphasised at times. Fay Bound has described *Reading the Early Modern Passions* as 'critically-aware' and a 'welcome addition to the early modern history of emotion and subjectivity', but she has also critiqued its tendency to take 'medical writing – and a limited selection at that – as a measure of objective knowledge', suggesting in particular that '[t]his lack is illustrated by the uncontextualized (over)use of Wright's *Passions of the minde*'.[5] Likewise, Robert A. Erickson has noted that 'the influence of Scripture' receives minimal attention in Paster's *Humoring the Body*, adding that, while it 'refers usefully' to a selection of Renaissance writers, it relies 'above all (and perhaps too heavily) on Wright'.[6] Such responses rightly celebrate the significant findings of these important books, but they also suggest that, in their detailed examination of a particular approach to Renaissance passion, they may occlude other ways of feeling available in the period.

While this collection as a whole seeks to recover a more heterogeneous view of Renaissance emotion, situating Wright's psycho-physiological holism within a more pluralistic and less predictable network of affective strategies in Renaissance literature and culture, this chapter looks at the more specific question of Wright, his personal and political contexts, and the philosophy of the passions he ultimately puts forward in his treatise. It focuses in particular on the relationship between passions and the soul, both in Renaissance devotional practice (an area in which Wright was atypical of most of his English readers), and in Renaissance natural philosophy and its stance on the ontology of the passions (where he was less so). Placing Wright's *The Passions* within these contexts shows how his understanding of affective experience was part of a larger intellectual project addressing the complex relationship between the physical and the spiritual, the body and the soul, in both the private and public domains. In the first part of the chapter I trace Wright's training as a Jesuit priest and the subsequent religious and political controversies in England in which he became involved. In the second section I read *The Passions* alongside the other three publications he wrote in the late 1590s, highlighting their shared interest in a deeply affective, embodied and indeed Catholic form of devotion. And in the third and final part I show how he nevertheless retained scope for more dualistic and disembodied approaches to emotional experience, both in human life and in the wider celestial world. Such an analysis, this chapter argues, illustrates how Wright's understanding of the passions was both more particular and more complicated than has often been acknowledged, and it highlights the importance of accounting for both local contexts and the influence of multiple intellectual frameworks (medical, religious, political and philosophical) in the study of early modern emotion.

Thomas Wright: philosopher, theologian, controversialist

In order to appreciate Wright's *The Passions* in greater contextual detail, it is necessary to understand more about Wright himself, in particular his commitment to his Catholic faith. While some recent critics have characterised him as a 'physician', all of his formal and practical professional training was as a theologian and priest.[7] Born in York around 1561, Wright grew up as part of a strongly recusant family, a formative influence that shaped much of the rest of his life. His uncle, possibly also called Thomas, was known as 'a learned Marian priest', and both the younger Thomas and his brother William eventually followed in this uncle's footsteps, taking orders as Catholic priests later in their lives.[8] Around the age of sixteen Thomas's family sent him to northern France to live at the English College, Douai, a Catholic seminary where the poet Robert Southwell also studied. Wright's stay here was brief; in 1578 the College ran into opposition from its host institution, the University of Douai, forcing it to relocate to Rheims.[9] Rather than move with it, however, Wright went further south to the newly established English College, Rome, where he remained until at least 1580. Anthony Munday (1560–1633) visited the College at Rome during this time, famously describing daily life there in *The English Romayne Lyfe* (1582). The College, he writes, is 'a house bothe large and fayre', in which students study 'Divinitie', 'Phisique', 'Logique' and 'Rhetorique' and follow a strict spiritual regimen of prayer, meditation and penance. Munday was particularly interested in the latter, providing examples of atonement ranging from forgone meals to extra *Pater nosters* to public self-flagellation. In one instance he describes how a penitent student was required to enter the dining hall at mealtime, clothed anonymously 'in a Canvas vesture downe to the grounde, a hood of the same on his head', and then to go 'up and downe the Hall, whipping him selfe at that bare place, in somuch, that the blood dooth trickle on the ground after him'.[10] Alongside such graphic and arguably exoticised scenes, Munday includes more conspicuously English episodes such as antagonism between English and Welsh residents at the College and a great appetite among all students for news from 'home', especially as might relate to 'that proude usurping *Jezabell*', Queen Elizabeth.[11]

This strong interest in English current events and political news was part of the founding vision for the colleges, which the Oxford professor William Allen (1532–94) instituted in 1568 as a means of cultivating and maintaining an English Catholic clergy ready to return to England should Elizabeth die or the country reject her Protestantism: 'we thought it would be an excellent thing to have men of learning always ready outside the realm to restore religion when the proper moment should arrive', he writes in a letter to the fellow academic and theologian Jean de Vendeville, adding that 'it seemed hopeless to attempt anything while the heretics were masters there'.[12] Wright appears to have embraced this mandate fully, vowing to undertake an English mission and eventually returning to his home country in 1595. His return was not without controversy; having taken 'the unusual step' in 1580 of joining the Society of Jesus, which at the time had no English arm, he studied for several years in Milan, becoming a priest in 1586, and then taught at Jesuit colleges in Genoa, Milan, Rome and Valladolid.[13] Peter Milward has suggested that throughout this time, and 'against the judgement of his superiors', Wright remained dedicated to an English return, finally achieving his wish in his mid-thirties by forging an influential connection with Robert Devereux, Earl of Essex.[14] Although Wright never wavered in his commitment to the Catholic faith, he made himself palatable to Essex and others by supporting the current English government, including Queen Elizabeth, and writing against a Spanish invasion of England. Such 'extravagant propositions' led to his discharge from the Society of Jesus but also his entry back into England, where he reportedly provided Essex's secretary with information about a possible Spanish naval attack.[15]

Up until this point Wright's life had been marked by an immersion in humanist learning, Catholic theology and the Jesuit community, but his decision to write in support of Elizabeth's rule and in opposition to Spanish influence revealed an appetite for political controversy that would come to characterise the second half of his life, some of which was spent in England. During these years Wright found himself in and out of both prison and exile, reflecting the precarious positioning of Catholics in England during Elizabeth's and then James's reigns as well as the particularly polemical stances Wright repeatedly took in political and religious debates. Indeed, shortly after returning to England in 1595 he became involved in arguments with ecclesiastical authorities in his home town of York, resulting in his being put under house arrest and eventually imprisoned in Bridewell, the Clink and then Wisbeach Prison, from which he escaped in 1600. Ian Donaldson, among others, has suggested that Wright may have been the priest who visited Ben Jonson in 1598 and eventually converted him to Catholicism, prompting Jonson to write a 'tributary sonnet' as a preface to Wright's *The Passions* a few years later.[16] Even more certain is that during these years Wright wrote four of the five works that he published in print during his life-time, including two Catholic treatises on the Eucharist (published in 1596), one pamphlet attacking 'the palpable absurdities, and most notorious errours of the Protestants religion' (1600) and, finally, *The Passions of the Minde in Generall* (1601).

Of these four works, the latter stands out as the atypical one, avoiding the overtly religious debates present in the others and focusing throughout on an ostensibly secular topic. It was also the only one that Wright did not have to have covertly published and smuggled into distribution.[17] Reflecting on Wright's commitment to Catholic toleration in England, Thomas O. Sloan has suggested that he 'must have entertained hopes that this noncontroversial book would reflect favorably upon his own ethos, at least in the eyes of the government, and so assist him in advancing his greater cause'.[18] While we do not have any detailed evidence regarding how the book was received, it was at least a good seller: in spite of Wright's continued involvement in controversial matters, including acting as a witness in the 1600 trial of Essex and Southampton and being banished in 1603 and again in 1610 as a result of anti-Catholic legislation, *The Passions* was republished in England three times during Wright's life and once again after his death (1604, 1620, 1621, 1630). Although Wright spent much of the final portion of his life in exile on the Continent, publishing in 1614 one final set of theological disputations, he managed to return to his home country for a short time before his death. Called to England in 1623 to be a part of the newly established Chapter of Canons, a sign at last of growing Catholic toleration in the country, he spent the final year of his life much as he had lived the rest of it: working in the service of his Catholic faith and the country he called home.

Emotion and devotion in *The Passions*

Although Wright's *The Passions* stands out as the most secular of his literary engagements, it none the less reveals significant theological links with his other writings, particularly in its positive valuation of the productive work passionate sensitivity might accomplish in the devotional life. Such links reframe how we approach Wright's book and its relationship to other contemporary takes on the passions, illustrating the more specific intellectual and spiritual space it occupied within a wider cultural conversation about the nature and value of emotional experience. As both Tilmouth and Sloan have pointed out, Wright's book is a deeply Thomist work, relying heavily on Aquinas's *Summa Theologica* for its understanding of the nature of the passions, their journey through the body and soul, and their potential use or 'habituation' in the virtuous (or, indeed, the not-so-virtuous) life.[19] Wright objects to a strictly Stoical approach, highlighting places in the Bible in which Christ is said to feel passions or men are commanded to approach sin with anger or salvation with fear: 'And therefore it were blaspemous to say, that absolutely all passions were ill, for so the Scriptures should exhort us to ill.'[20] Wright adds support to this argument by emphasising how 'vertuous' passions, 'directed with the square of Gods law', help men carry out their Christian duties with 'much more ease, pleasure, and delight' than if they approached them impassively (p. 16).

While Wright was not unusual among his contemporaries in stating that he rejected Stoicism, it seems he *was* atypical in terms of the extent to which he actually did so. Tilmouth, in his survey of differing Aristotelian positions on the passions within late sixteenth- and early seventeenth-century thought, has shown how Wright's take on such matters differed considerably from those of some of his English contemporaries, in particular the Protestant clergyman Thomas Rogers (*c.*1553–1616), who in 1576 published his own treatise on the passions entitled *The Anatomie of the Minde* (reissued four years later as *The Paterne of a Passionate Minde*). Like Wright, Rogers challenges the Stoical desire to 'cut of, and as it were gelde men of those thinges which are grafted and planted in them by nature', but he does so not on the basis that passions are particularly virtuous in and of themselves, but rather that through their stern control man reveals his virtue: 'And therefore except there bee passions and perturbations in man, ther is no place for vertue. Even as there is no victorie, where as there is no adversary.'[21] Although Rogers notes elsewhere that the passions may contain some inherent benefit, this is an idea that receives little further consideration in his treatise, which Tilmouth has characterised as more Socratic, Stoic and Calvinistic than heavily Thomist works like Wright's.[22] Such an approach, Tilmouth argues, is particularly 'representative of later Tudor moral thought', and his conclusion points us to the possibility that works like Rogers's, which emphasise above all else the psychomachic struggle involved in battling the passions and mortifying the appetites they provoke, may be better reflective of Protestant England's overarching 'emotionology' – that is, the 'collective emotional standards' of the time – than Wright's more permissive treatise.[23] Along similar lines, Tilmouth suggests that emotional 'continence' and 'self-mastery' were the chief aims of major contemporary writers such as William Perkins and Edmund Spenser,[24] and Douglas Trevor identifies in Spenser's *The Faerie Queene* an aversion to reading human experience in overly Galenic, psycho-physiologal terms – a tendency that he ultimately concludes was somewhat atypical.[25] In light of the observations above, however, it seems very possible that Spenser's was in fact the more characteristic view, and his contemporaries' (such as Wright's) the more exceptional.

This is not to say that Wright was not also concerned with the potentially negative effects of passion and the consequent need for its regulation, but rather that the nature of his concern and his development of it over the course of his treatise ultimately takes a different shape. In the opening of *The Passions*, Wright, like Rogers, links unruly passion to both sin and disease (pp. 2–4), reiterating this connection between inordinate feeling and spiritual and physical corruption in a later chapter on passion and prudence: 'when we are moved with a vehement passion … our soules are then, as it were infected with a pestilent ague' (p. 89). In contrast to Rogers's treatise, however, this negative view of the passions does not dominate Wright's account; while he acknowledges the considerable psycho-physiological effects passions can have on the mind, body and soul, he does not conclude that their chief virtue is in their conquering. On the contrary, passions according to Wright can and should be used to propel people to good, if not through their own doing then through others' influence on them. 'Wright insists that the passions are not simply to be "mortified" but are rather to be *used*', Sloan argues, pointing in particular to the Catholic practice of devotional meditation Wright would have learned during his years on the Continent and very likely continued upon his return to England.[26]

Indeed, in his *A Treatise … of the Reall Presence of Our Saviour in the Blessed Sacrament*, a much more polemical work written as we know very close to the same time as *The Passions*, Wright emphasises the fundamental importance of passion and the stimulation of the senses in the cultivation of deep and lasting faith, precisely because purely intellectual devotion may not take hold in the entire, embodied person: 'True it is that wise and faithfull Christians conceave the presence of God in every place, but because it is so insensible, because it proceedeth from the intellectuall faculty, it causeth no great impression in the soule.'[27] For some of Wright's contemporaries, the fact that the intellective part of the soul was wholly incorporeal and thus not dependent on the body for its functioning was one of its chief virtues, but for Wright in this passage the intellective soul's separation from the materiality of the body proves problematic, making it more difficult for communion with God to move beyond mental abstraction and towards total enrapture and immersion. In an attempt to aid this process, Wright suggests that 'sensible' or physical objects may help focus prayer and thus deepen faith, making a stronger, more material impression in the sensitive, embodied part of the soul, and helping those who experience 'diffidence or doubting that they pray in vaine' to remain committed in their meditations. The 'corporall presence' of such objects, including images, emblems and crucifixes, helps believers 'stirre more deeply in their mindes a more lively conceite of the presence of God then they coulde imprint without it'.[28]

Wright's sentiments here show the influence of his Jesuit training and the ideas put forward in St Ignatius Loyola's *Spiritual Excercises* (first printed in 1548), in particular those emphasising the role sensation plays in the creation of deep spiritual experience through meditation: 'the soul's longing is satisfied not by abundant learning', we read in the annotations to Loyola's preface, 'but by inwardly sensing and tasting things'.[29] Although this directive relates most centrally to the five outward senses of sight, smell, taste, touch and hearing, each of these in turn provokes passionate responses that deepen and enrich the connection one makes with God during meditative prayer. Like Aristotle, Aquinas and most other Renaissance writers on the subject, Wright situates both sensation (including sight) and passion in the sensitive faculty of the soul, emphasising their mutuality in the creation of 'feeling', be it physical, mental, spiritual or all three at once. Likewise, in Book V of Wright's *The Passions*, which addresses 'the meanes to moove Passions', Wright begins by explaining how 'externall senses' and 'sensuall objects' facilitate passion, in particular sight and its apprehension of visual objects, a topic that verges dangerously on the very fraught question of devotional images and icons in Reformation England (p. 149).

Taken on its own, this section on the potency of images to move passions is at best as theologically ambivalent, and perhaps to divert any sectarian suspicion Wright goes on to provide several biblical examples emphasising the moral dangers of vision and the passions it inspires: 'no sense perverteth more perilous then this', he warns at one point, adding shortly thereafter that 'alluring sights' can lead to the creation of 'too much affection', as well as 'inordinate delights' in the human heart (pp. 151–2). But Wright also posits that under the right circumstances, 'no sense serveth the soule so much for knowledge, as this [i.e. sight]' (a sentiment we might compare with Mary Ann Lund's discussion of vision in the work of Burton and Sibbes, Chapter 4, below). If we read this section on the provocation of passion within the context of Wright's theological writing elsewhere on the Eucharist, in particular his celebration of the value of 'sensible objects' and their 'corporall presence', a more positive and indeed Catholic significance begins to emerge. '[T]he presence of any visible object, moveth much more vehemently the passion, than the imagination or conceit thereof in the absence', he concludes in *The Passions* (p. 158), echoing his earlier consideration in *A Treatise … of the Reall Presence* of the productive role images and other sensible objects can play in the facilitation of religious communion. The underlying argument is that both sensations and passions – and indeed the images that inspire them – perform positive work when marshalled in the direction of virtuous activity, be it worldly or divine.

This endorsement of passionate experience and its relationship to spirituality reaches its climax in Wright's later discussion of 'Motives to Love', also located in Book V of *The Passions*. Here his largely descriptive and secular authorial voice gives way to a much more sensuous, personal and religious use of language (again, not unlike Burton's change in style in his 'Beauty of God' section, as described by Lund). Acknowledging this shift in tone, Wright begins the section by appealing to God for a more passionate means of conveying his vivid subject matter:

> O My God, the soule of my soule, and the life of all true love: *these dry discourses of affections, without any cordiall affection, have long deteined, & not a little distasted me.* Now that I come towards the borders of Love, give me leave O loving God, to vent out and evaporat the affects of the heart, and see if I can incense my soule to love thee intirely and incessantly, and that all those motives which stir up mine affections to love thee, may be meanes to inflame all their hearts which read this treatise penned by me. (p. 193, my emphasis)

In the succeeding pages, Wright engages in a meditative conversation with God, admitting his own 'imperfection' and asking for God's 'fountaine of love' to 'endue [him] … with [the] grace' to praise him as best a human can (p. 194). In total this section on the cultivation of love runs to sixty-seven pages, making it considerably longer than the following sections on motives to 'Hatred, Detestation, Feare, and Ire' (twenty-six pages), 'Hope' (three pages), 'Joy and Delight' (five pages), and sorrow, which is conspicuously absent.[30] Notably, Wright characterises his holy love here as a kind of 'affection' rather than 'passion', a word that Thomas Dixon has shown signalled 'proper affect' in the writings of Augustine, Aquinas and their followers, as it was more specifically associated with divine, rather than worldly, affectivity.[31] The string of virtuous 'Motives to Love' that follows, however, blurs any hard and fast distinctions between earthly and godly feeling, mixing discussion of subjects as diverse as family, kindness, heroism, beauty and acts of generosity in its consideration of how soul-incensing 'affects of the heart' are produced. Love, Wright posits in a statement reminiscent of both Aquinas and Loyola, is the 'fountaine, root, and mother … [of] all other passions' (p. 146), and as such it offers believers the means to imbue their devotion to God with a vibrant affectivity that motivates as well as deepens religious practice.

Similarly, in both of his treatises on the Eucharist, Wright celebrates the value of a loving, passionate faith, describing how 'frendly affection' and 'amiable conversation' create a 'Union of affection' among congregants who come together to share their love of God, as well as a corresponding union between believers and God himself, who infuses them with his love through the material sacrament of the Eucharist: 'How doth not those veines swell with affection which are filled with the pretious bloud of their most affectious and zealous GOD?'[32] In private meditation, shared devotion and sacramental communion, loving affectivity emerges as a – even *the* – basis of spirituality and virtue, motivating a deeper form of religious experience than could be achieved without such feeling. Indeed, in his *The Disposition, or Garnishmente of the Soule*, Wright includes not only love and hope but also 'Feare' and 'Greefe' as essential steps in preparing oneself to receive the sacrament, describing how the experience of such feelings provokes a deeper knowledge of one's sins and a yearning for God's grace: 'Feare the beginninge of wisdom, is the first gate, by which we muste enter into the palace of wisdom, whose chamber of presence is this sacrament'.[33] This experience of fear – in particular 'filiall' fear of one's sins and 'angelical' fear of God's greatness – in turn facilitates greater spiritual awareness and humility in believers' souls, prompting them to ask themselves, '[h]ave I confessed them [my sins] with such diligence, with such greife as I ought?'[34] Thus love, fear and grief all maintain essential places in the spiritual life, offering a useful gloss on the role feeling may play in *The Passions*'s more secular pursuit of virtue.

Of course, in both arenas such passion (or affection) may also come with potential dangers, rendering people more vulnerable to unreasonable desires if allowed free and unruly rein. In *The Passions,* Wright frequently emphasises how these 'Passions, and Affections, or perturbations of the mind …

trouble wonderfully the soule, corrupting the judgement & seducing the will' (pp. 7–8), and likewise in his pamphlet on the *Palpable Absurdities … of the Protestants Religion* he warns that heretical teachings may 'inveagle the witt with errors … [and] also seduce the will with occasions of inordinate affections'.[35] Still, such warnings do not mean that Wright encourages his readers to shy away from the affective life. On the contrary, for those who subscribe to the central project he sets out in his *The Passions* – to 'come to a knowledge of himself' (p. 2) – conscientious engagement with and even cultivation of deeply felt passions and affections become an intrinsic part of the pursuit of virtue and, more covertly, of a truly saving, Catholic faith.[36] Particularly in his emphasis on the value of passionate meditation, Wright points his readers towards a Catholic form of devotion that he sees as intimately related to man's fulfilment both in heaven and on earth. Returning to this subject in the final pages of his book, Wright suggests that 'lack of prudent meditations' is one of the four chief reasons 'more men are wicked then vertuous' in the world. Such 'meditation & ponderation', he writes, produce a 'love & affection' that deepen both faith in God and a knowledge of oneself, allowing practitioners to 'live ever in peace and tranquility of mind, who dwelling in earth, converse in heaven' (pp. 345–7). Far from a destabilising force, such meditative affectivity facilitates even-mindedness and inner strength, allowing men to understand better the relationship between the worldly life and that which lies beyond.

The embodied soul and the ensouled body

In its emphasis on the value of both sensuality and affectivity, Wright's *The Passions* reveals a veiled connection with the Catholic devotional practices and beliefs that are at the centre of his more polemical and religious publications. Such engagements suggest a specificity at work in Wright's thinking that, while not negating his book's broader applicability to the prevailing 'emotionology' of sixteenth- and seventeenth-century England, does qualify and contextualise it, revealing how elements of his atypical religious agenda connected with and even shaped his medico-philosophical understanding of the passions. As we have already seen, such discussions focused intensively on the way in which the passions engaged both body and soul, straddling worldly, corporeal experience as well as more immaterial processes in the divine soul. Wright's thorough discussion of the physiology of passionate experience has proved especially interesting to scholars, with his emphasis in many sections of *The Passions* on integrated, holistic ways of feeling being taken as evidence more generally of 'the inseparability of body and soul, material and spiritual' in the period.[37] Such conclusions have led to the argument that dualism as a concept postdated the Renaissance, emerging only in the latter part of the seventeenth century as the mechanistic philosophy of Descartes and his followers took hold. As a result, Gail Kern Paster has argued that scholars must recognise 'that Shakespeare's dramatic narratives of passion take place in an imagined physical and psychological environment epistemically prior to post-Enlightenment dualism'. At the same time, however, she acknowledges that '[i]t is difficult for us to achieve such recognition, because we approach the plays, inevitably, with the mental and lexical habits that we have inherited from that dualism and are only now – thanks to the intellectual advent of cognitive science – beginning to discredit'.[38]

Paster's clear identification of the tendency to project modern conceptions of experience onto our understanding of the past has been extremely productive in pushing scholars to read Renaissance texts in new lights, making new space for the deeply material engagements present in contemporary descriptions and representations of passionate experience. What this emphasis on a thoroughly holistic 'historical phenomenology' has sometimes occluded, however, is the extent to which contemporary natural philosophy and theology accommodated different varieties of embodied and disembodied experience, reserving space for dualistic phenomena within a materially bounded 'ecology of the passions'.[39] 'To write off the discourse of immaterial selfhood as merely a figment of the Cartesian mind/body split is to miss the varying degrees of embodiment described in the soul–body discourse of Elizabethan and Stuart England', Sean McDowell has argued, with Paster herself suggesting that more work on the immaterial dimensions of Renaissance affect remains to be done: 'most of us as secular humanists no longer believe literally in the soul but have no choice but to believe literally in the body', she has written, adding that 'we need to think harder about the ensouled body as well as the embodied soul' if a comprehensive understanding of early modern phenomenology is ever to be achieved.[40]

Wright's treatise is no different in offering a mixed view of passion and its body–soul engagements, approaching the issue, we have seen, not only from the medico-philosophical perspective of gentlemanly self-comportment but also from the viewpoint of spiritual enrichment and devotional transformation. Given Wright's controversial religious commitments, it is unsurprising that this latter element always remains understated in *The Passions*, resulting in a correspondingly muted treatment of it in scholarly analyses of the book. More perplexing, however, is the fact that little to no attention has been paid to Wright's more explicit treatment of the immaterial dimensions of passion, a subject he explores in Book I, Chapter VIII, entitled, 'That there are passions in the reasonable Soule' (p. 30). In this chapter Wright unambiguously asserts that, under certain circumstances, passions can indeed occur independently from the body. Citing the fact that God acts with 'love, hate, ire, zeale' in the Bible, and that, having no body, God 'cannot be subject to any sensitive operations', Wright concludes that 'it cannot be doubted upon, but that there are some affections in the highest and chiefest part of the soule, not unlike unto the passion of the Minde' (p. 31).

As in Book V's discussion of love, Wright makes a subtle but important distinction here between 'passions' and 'affections', suggesting once again that the latter occupy a more holy and indeed disembodied space in the spectrum of human feeling. As previously discussed, natural philosophers regularly located the passions, alongside the senses, in the sensitive faculty of the soul, positing that, although passions were motivated by spiritual movements (made in response to the apprehension of external phenomena), they were realised through the physiological processes of the body. Thus Wright asserts at the start of his book that passions 'are drowned in corporall organs and instruments' and liable to 'alter the humours of our bodies', a system that he then contrasts to the workings of reason in the intellective faculty of the soul, which 'dependeth of no corporal subject, but as a Princesse in her throne, considereth the state of her kingdome' (pp. 8–9). Such sentiments help establish a hierarchical system of human experience in which disembodied reason presides over embodied passion and sense, and, while Wright frequently subscribes to this model in *The Passions*, he also qualifies and adds nuance to it throughout his discussion, particularly when dealing with matters theological. In his discussion of both godly affections and indeed *God's* affections, Wright follows medieval philosophers and theologians including William of Ockham, Augustine and Aquinas in suggesting that humans have a distinctively disembodied and intellectually circumscribed element to their soul that encompasses the faculties of reason and will and their related manifestations, including holy affections.[41] According to Wright, such affections in God 'are perfections, and [as] we are commanded, and may imitate him in them, there is no reason why they should be denied unto us in such sort as they be perfit, and that is principally in the Will' (p. 31). These sentiments, Tilmouth has shown, were 'typical of Thomist scholars of the time', who held that '"affections" of the will' were 'rather like a passion', except that they did not, as in the case of passions, 'induce a commotion [i.e. movement] within the soul'.[42]

For many moralists, this lack of motion was crucial, as it indicated that psycho-physiological instability was not always created as a result of affective experience. While experientially similar to passion, affection was nevertheless ontologically distinct, possessing the ability to manifest itself in the rational soul without the threat of physiological or moral corruption. Unsurprisingly, such affections were almost always linked with religious feeling and devotion, not least because the intellective, disembodied part of the soul was also understood to be its immortal, and therefore divine, part.[43] In this sense, religiously inspired feelings, such as the love, fear and grief for God previously described in Wright's treatise, could be positioned at the top of the hierarchical model of human functioning, taking a seat alongside reason in her royal throne. This differentiation between holy affections and 'naughty' passions, however, did not mean that the two were seen as categorically distinct in the realm of lived experience. As we have already seen, Wright in his discussion of affective devotion intermingles the experience of divine feeling with more worldly phenomena, and in Book I, Chapter II, entitled, 'What we understand by Passions and Affections', he likewise suggests that the words are roughly synonymous. 'The motions of the soule', he explains, have been known by various names, with the Greeks and Romans calling them 'perturbations, others affections, others affects, others more expresly name them Passions' (pp. 7–8). In his subsequent analysis he suggests these different terms each inflect the experience of feeling with a particular flavour ('perturbations' being particularly negative, 'affections' being particularly positive), but he does not insist on demarcating them ontologically with reference to the different faculties of the (dis)embodied soul. When he later comes to his section on 'Passions in the reasonable soule', his linguistic register does indeed shift towards a greater use of the word 'affection', but he nevertheless retains the word 'passion' in the title itself.

This blurring of the line between embodied and disembodied passion, and, by extension, unreasoning and reasoning passion, continues in Wright's subsequent discussion of the way in which the sensitive appetite and the will interact in the production of both understanding and feeling: 'as our wit understandeth whatsoever our senses perceive, even so our will may affect whatsoever our passions do follow' – or, in other words, just as sensual knowledge may become intellectual knowledge, sensitive passions may be taken up by the will and become rational feeling. The danger, Wright warns, is that most often this exchange is a negative one, with the passions having a corrupting influence on the will and reason. Embedded within this line of thought, however, and certainly condoned by Wright, is the possibility that embodied passion may apprehend something not only useful to, but also otherwise unattainable by, the disembodied will, promoting the creation of a kind of affection that is essentially a form of reason. In this sense, passion, affection and reason are part of the same virtuous project, bound by an integrated and holistic psycho-physiology that none the less retains scope for more dualistic and delimited forms of phenomenological experience.

This movement of passion and affection between sensitive and intellective realms is indicative, I would suggest, of a bigger question looming in the period about the relationship between the mind and the soul, and their respective levels of embodiment. Like 'passion' and 'affection', 'mind' and 'soul' could be both synonymous and distinctive, with sixteenth- and seventeenth-century writers (including Wright) often oscillating between the two terms in their discussions of passionate experience. On a technical level, the issue was largely one of translation, as both 'mind' and 'soul' were possible English renderings of the Latin *animus*, which generally referred to the rational portion of the *anima*. Gareth Matthews has shown how Augustine, so influential to the development of medieval and Renaissance thought on the passions, did not use Latin words for 'mind' and 'soul' in an entirely systematic way, helping establish a subsequent ambiguity in English. In Augustine's works the entire, animating soul is most generally known as the *anima* (as in Aristotle's *De Anima*), but when he discusses this force at work in a man (that is, a male) it is sometimes rendered as *animus*, a term that at other times he applies specifically, along with *mens*, to the intellective and incorporeal soul present in all humans.[44] In this linguistic schema, the disembodied portion of the soul – the *animus* – becomes most clearly aligned with *mens* – the 'mind' – producing a conception of mind as intellectively driven and disassociated (or at least capable of disassociation) from the body. Timothy Bright (1549/50–1615), an English physician-turned-divine contemporary to Wright, reinforces such a view in his *A Treatise of Melancholie* (1586), arguing that the 'mind' is the immortal, 'everlasting' and 'essentiall' part of a person, 'exempt from chaunge and corruption' and 'in action … next unto the supreme majestie of God'.[45]

And yet, in Wright's *The Passions of the Minde in Generall*, readers encounter a title that attributes the passions – largely if not uniformly mutable and embodied phenomena – to the province of this 'mind', complicating any easy or standardised definitions of the term. In this regard, Wright's book is in fact *more* representative than has often been acknowledged, illustrating how open and contextually determined key concepts like 'mind', 'soul', 'passion' and 'affection' could be in the period, producing an understanding of passionate experience that at once embraced the centrality of the integrated and embodied soul while nevertheless retaining scope for elements of dualism. Affectivity was a shared and extended experience, altering the body as it moved in and beyond the mind and soul, but it could still take the shape of a more abstracted, disembodied and wilful enterprise, particularly when linked to the divine yearnings of the intellective soul. Although brief in its treatment, Wright's *The Passions* explicitly acknowledges the possibility of 'reasonable' or at least disembodied affective experience, offering a subtle but important adjustment to our understanding of the historical phenomenology and concomitant emotionology of Renaissance England.

In its analysis of Wright's *The Passions*, this chapter has focused predominantly on the way in which matters of the soul fundamentally shaped Wright's approach to both his life and his literary works. In doing so it has sought at once to differentiate Wright's theories of the passions and to normalise them, highlighting how they were marked by his Catholic faith while also drawing attention to their more widely characteristic interest in the emotionality of the rational soul. In both instances these modifications to our understanding of Wright and his *The Passions* involve attending more seriously to the spiritual dimensions of Renaissance affect, which have sometimes been obscured by an emphasis on the body and humoral psychophysiology. This shift towards spirituality does not negate or undermine the undeniable medical humoralism to be found throughout Wright's treatise, but rather complements and complicates it. Further complications are no doubt possible – this chapter has said little, for instance, about the sustained interest in rhetoric and persuasion found running through Wright's book, a feature that suggests important links between Wright's understanding of how language and passion shape the process of decision-making, and how this in turn might be applied to his larger project of Catholic conversion, or at least toleration, in England. What underlines the mode of enquiry taken in this chapter and others yet to be pursued is an acknowledgement of the complex and at times unstable way in which passion was bound up in questions of mind, body and soul in the period, if not always holistically unifying their processes then certainly constellating them. Investigation into the nuances of such constellations reveals how pluralistic and at times idiosyncratic approaches to emotion in the Renaissance could be, freeing up writers like Wright, and those in turn who may have drawn on him, to avail themselves of established approaches to the passions while also combining and reworking them into something more particular and unpredictable than we may currently expect.

Notes

1 This chapter has benefited from the keen insights of Richard Parr, Andrew Wear and several members of the University of Birmingham's Centre for Reformation and Early Modern Studies. My great thanks to all of them for their help and support.

2 Mary Floyd-Wilson, 'English Mettle', in Gail Kern Paster, Katherine Rowe and Mary Floyd-Wilson (eds), *Reading the Early Modern Passions: Essays in the Cultural History of Emotion* (Philadelphia: University of Pennsylvania Press, 2004), pp. 130–46 (p. 132). Wright's influence is visible in several of the essays in *Reading the Early Modern Passions*, as well as in many of the books discussed in the Introduction to this volume.

3 Gail Kern Paster, Katherine Rowe and Mary Floyd-Wilson, 'Introduction: Reading the Early Modern Passions', in Paster, Rowe and Floyd-Wilson (eds), *Reading the Early Modern Passions: Essays in the Cultural History of Emotion* (Philadelphia: University of Pennsylvania Press, 2004), pp. 1–20 (p. 16).

4 Christopher Tilmouth, *Passion's Triumph over Reason: A History of the Moral Imagination from Spenser to Rochester* (Oxford: Oxford University Press: 2007), p. 7.

5 Fay Bound, 'Review: *Reading the Early Modern Passions*', *Medical History*, 50 (2006), 270–2.

6 Robert A. Erickson, 'Review: *Humoring the Body*', *Early Science and Medicine*, 11 (2006), 237–9 (p. 238).

7 Katharine A. Craik and Tanya Pollard, 'Introduction: Imagining Audiences', in Craik and Pollard (eds), *Shakespearean Sensations: Experiencing Literature in Early Modern England* (Cambridge: Cambridge University Press, 2013), pp. 1–25 (pp. 6–7).

8 Peter Milward, 'Wright, Thomas (*c.*1561–1623)', *Oxford Dictionary of National Biography* (*ODNB*) (Oxford University Press, 2004). For the biographical account that follows I am indebted to Milward's entry as well as to Katharine A. Craik, 'Wright, Thomas', in Garrett A. Sullivan, Jr, and Alan Stewart (eds), *The Encyclopedia of English Renaissance Literature* (Oxford: Blackwell, 2012), pp. 1075–6; and Thomas O. Sloan, 'Introduction', in *The Passions of the Minde in Generall: A Reprint Based on the 1604 Edition* (Urbana: University of Illinois Press, 1971), pp. xv–xxv. For an older but influential account, see Theodore A. Stroud, 'Father Thomas Wright: A Test Case for Toleration', *Biographical Studies*, 1 (1951), 189–219.

9 Eamon Duffy, 'Allen, William (1532–1594)', *ODNB*; John Bossy, 'Communications: 1. Rome and the Elizabethan Catholics: A Question of Geography', *The Historical Journal*, 7 (1964), 135–42 (p. 136).

10 Anthony Munday, *The English Romayne Lyfe* (London, 1582), pp. 21–3.

11 Ibid., pp. 56–67, 12–14.

12 Quoted in Scott R. Pilarz, *Robert Southwell and the Mission of Literature, 1561–1595: Writing Reconciliation* (Aldershot: Ashgate, 2004), p. 81.

13 Craik, 'Wright, Thomas', p. 1075.

14 Milward, 'Wright, Thomas'. For an extended consideration of Essex's attitudes towards religious tolerance and the significance of Wright's return, see Alexandra Gajda, *The Earl of Essex and Late Elizabethan Political Culture* (Oxford: Oxford University Press, 2012), ch. 3.

15 Milward, 'Wright, Thomas'.

16 Ian Donaldson, *Ben Jonson: A Life* (Oxford: Oxford University Press, 2011), pp. 138–41; and Theodore A. Stroud, 'Ben Jonson and Father Thomas Wright', *English Literary History*, 14 (1947), 274–82. Gajda also shows how Wright's unpublished letters evidence hope that Essex and even Queen Elizabeth herself might be tempted to convert (*The Earl of Essex*, p. 129).

17 The title pages of his other three books indicate that they were published in Antwerp, but Sloan and others have argued that they were in fact published on 'secret Catholic presses in London'. See Sloan, 'Introduction', p. xix n. 11; D. M. Rogers, 'A Bibliography of the Published Works of Thomas Wright', *Biographical Studies*, 1 (1952), 262–80 (pp. 266–8); Gajda, *The Earl of Essex*, pp. 129–30 n. 99.

18 Sloan, 'Introduction', p. xx.

19 For more on habituation see Tilmouth, *Passion's Triumph*, pp. 23–6.

20 Thomas Wright, *The Passions of the Minde in Generall: A Reprint Based on the 1604 Edition*, ed. Thomas O. Sloan (Urbana: University of Illinois Press, 1971), pp. 16, 22–6. Further references are to this edition and will appear in the text. The 1604 version greatly expanded on the text of the original 1601 imprint, organising it into six books and elaborating on it in many places. The text of 1604 became the basis for the 1620, 1621 and 1630 publications, which, in substantive terms, are identical (see Sloan, 'Introduction', p. xlvi).

21 Thomas Rogers, *The Anatomie of the Minde* (London, 1576), sigs B1v–B2r.

22 Interestingly, a large part of Rogers's literary legacy is bound up in his translation and adaptation of Latin Catholic texts into English, a process that reflected his simultaneous interest in Catholic exegesis and his disapproval of certain devotional practices. See John Craig, 'Rogers, Thomas (*c.*1553–1616)', *ODNB*.

23 Tilmouth, *Passion's Triumph*, p. 33; Peter N. Stearns and Carol Z. Stearns, 'Emotionology: Clarifying the History of Emotions and Emotional Standards', *The American Historical Review*, 90 (1985), 813–36 (p. 813).

24 Tilmouth, *Passion's Triumph*, pp. 20–36 (pp. 33, 38). Such aims are similar to those emphasised in Michael C. Schoenfeldt's *Bodies and Selves in Early Modern England: Physiology and Inwardness in Spenser, Shakespeare, Herbert and Milton* (Cambridge: Cambridge University Press, 1999), although Tilmouth

highlights their deeply religious and spiritual, rather than humoral, imperatives. For further discussion of different forms of Stoic 'mastery' see David Bagchi, Chapter 2, below.

25 Douglas Trevor, 'Sadness in *The Faerie Queene*', in Gail Kern Paster, Katherine Rowe and Mary Floyd-Wilson (eds), *Reading the Early Modern Passions: Essays in the Cultural History of Emotion* (Philadelphia: University of Pennsylvania Press, 2004), pp. 240–52 (p. 250).

26 Sloan, 'Introduction', p. xxxii.

27 Thomas Wright, *A Treatise, Shewing the Possibilie, and Conveniencie of the Reall Presence of Our Saviour in the Blessed Sacrament* (Antwerp, 1596), sig. 33r.

28 Ibid.

29 Quoted in Sloan, 'Introduction', p. xl. See also Bradley Rubidge, 'Descartes's Meditations and Devotional Meditations', *Journal of the History of Ideas*, 51 (1990), 27–49 (pp. 31–3).

30 For a consideration of reasons for sorrow's absence, see Erin Sullivan, 'A Disease unto Death: Sadness in the Time of Shakespeare', in Elena Carrera (ed.), *Emotions and Health, 1200-1700* (Leiden: Brill, 2013), pp. 159–83.

31 Thomas Dixon, *From Passions to Emotions: The Creation of a Secular Psychological Category* (Cambridge: Cambridge University Press, 2003), pp. 41, 46.

32 Thomas Wright, *The Disposition, or Garnishmente of the Soule to Receive Worthily the Blessed Sacrament* (Antwerp, 1596), pp. 54–5, and *A Treatise ... of the Reall Presence*, sigs 21v–22r.

33 Wright, *Disposition, or Garnishmente of the Soule*, pp. 32–7 (p. 32), 69–73.

34 Ibid., p. 35.

35 Thomas Wright, *Certaine Articles or Forcible Reasons Discovering the Palpable Absurdities, and Most Notorious and Intricate Errors of the Protestants Religion* (Antwerp, 1600 [1604]), sig. 3Ar.

36 In Chapter 3, below, Sara Coodin highlights how important knowledge of self, or *nosce te ipsum*, was to any early modern writer interested in the proactive cultivation of virtue – a project that she shows was linked to humoral physiology, but not solely predicated upon it.

37 Mary Floyd-Wilson, Matthew Greenfield, Gail Kern Paster, Tanya Pollard, Katherine Rowe and Julian Yates, 'Shakespeare and Embodiment: An E-Conversation', *Literature Compass*, 2 (2005), 1–13 (p. 2).

38 Gail Kern Paster, *Humoring the Body: Emotions and the Shakespearean Stage* (Chicago: University of Chicago Press, 2004), p. 244.

39 Paster, Rowe and Floyd-Wilson, 'Introduction', p. 18. For an exploration of this material ecology in the works of Thomas Middleton, see Paster, 'The Ecology of the Passions in *A Chaste Maid in Cheapside* and *The Changeling*', in Gary Taylor and Trish Thomas Henley (eds), *The Oxford Handbook of Thomas Middleton* (Oxford: Oxford University Press, 2012), pp. 148–63.

40 Sean McDowell, 'The View from the Interior: The New Body Scholarship

in Renaissance/Early Modern Studies', *Literature Compass*, 3 (2006), 778–91 (p. 787); Floyd-Wilson et al., 'Shakespeare and Embodiment', p. 3.

41 Paul S. MacDonald, *History of the Concept of the Mind: Speculations about Soul, Mind and Spirit from Homer to Hume* (Aldershot: Ashgate, 2003), pp. 1–2, 245–64; Emily Michael, 'Renaissance Theories of Body, Soul and Mind', in John P. Wright and Paul Potter (eds), *Psyche and Soma: Physicians and Metaphysicians on the Mind–Body Problem from Antiquity to Enlightenment* (Oxford: Oxford University Press, 2002), pp. 147–72 (pp. 158–62, 170). For further discussion of the emotionality of God in the Bible, and the problems it raised for some theological commentators, see David Bagchi, Chapter 2, below.

42 Tilmouth, *Passion's Triumph*, p. 27 (including n. 55). See also Dixon, *From Passions to Emotions*, pp. 39–48.

43 R. W. Serjeantson, 'The Soul', in Desmond M. Clarke and Catherine Wilson (eds), *The Oxford Handbook of Philosophy in Early Modern Europe* (Oxford: Oxford University Press, 2011), pp. 119–41 (p. 124); Eckhardt Kessler, 'The Intellective Soul', in Charles B. Schmitt and Quentin Skinner (eds), *The Cambridge History of Renaissance Philosophy* (Cambridge: Cambridge University Press: 1988), pp. 485–534.

44 Gareth Matthews, 'Internalist Reasoning in Augustine for Mind–Body Dualism', in John P. Wright and Paul Potter (eds), *Psyche and Soma: Physicians and Metaphysicians on the Mind–Body Problem from Antiquity to Enlightenment* (Oxford: Oxford University Press, 2002), pp. 133–45 (pp. 137–8). See also Gerard J. P. O'Daly, *Augustine's Philosophy of Mind* (Berkeley: University of California Press, 1987), pp. 7–8.

45 Timothy Bright, *A Treatise of Melancholie* (London, 1586), pp. 60–1, 70.

2

'The Scripture moveth us in sundry places': framing biblical emotions in the *Book of Common Prayer* and the *Homilies*

David Bagchi

IN 1549, WHEN THE *Book of Common Prayer* was first published, the people of the West Country rose up against it. 'We will not receive the new service', they protested to the young Edward VI, 'because it is but like a Christmas game'.[1] Seven thousand Cornish rebels were prepared to fight and to die for this conviction. But less than a century later, on the eve of the Civil War, the people of Cornwall issued another set of demands to another king. This time, they petitioned Charles I in near bibliolatrous terms 'to eternize (as far as in you lies) the divine and excellent form of Common Prayer'.[2] Cornwall was not alone in expressing such warm support for the Prayer Book: we know of twenty-nine similar petitions, from counties and other localities, from the years 1641–42. For example, the people of Cheshire (which in Tudor times had been as staunchly conservative as Cornwall) claimed that, among them, 'scarce any Family or Person can read, but are furnished with the Books of Common Prayer; in the conscionable Use whereof, many Christian Hearts have found unspeakable joy and comfort'.[3]

It is perhaps surprising to find such affective language applied in defence of the Prayer Book. After all, the Prayer Book, in its successive editions, was famously criticised by the hotter sort of Protestant for its cold, formulaic rigidity and its inability either to respond to the affections or to evoke them. The first *Admonition to the Parliament* in 1572 declared that liturgical freedom was a chief characteristic of the early Church. Then 'ministers were not so tied to any one form of prayers, but as the Spirit moved them, and as necessity of time required, so they might pour forth hearty supplications to the Lord. Now they are bound of necessity to a prescript order of service.'[4] After the execution of Charles I, John Milton, in an extended essay on how to kick a man when he is not only down but beheaded, made the definitive case for the emotional stuntedness of the Prayer Book and its users: 'This is evident, that those who use no set forms of prayer, have words from their affections; while others are to look for affections fit and proportionable to a certain dose of prepared words.'[5]

It is also surprising to come across phrases such as 'Christian Hearts' and 'unspeakable joy and comfort' in the context of a parliamentary petition. It suggests that the petitioners had invested in the Prayer Book not only financially (they claimed to be furnishing themselves with books of *common* prayer, intended for public worship, for private use at home) but also emotionally.[6] Indeed, the very phrase 'unspeakable comfort' is a direct quotation from the Thirty-nine Articles, which since 1571 had been bound with the Prayer Book, and so physically part of it.[7] The people of Cheshire had over the years evidently internalised a Protestant culture and a Protestant sensibility; more particularly, they had borrowed the emotional vocabulary associated with the *Book of Common Prayer* and adopted it as their own.

There are of course different ways of explaining this process of internalisation and borrowing. One is to see it as part of the 'the civilising process', which Norbert Elias defined as the attempt by the early modern state to control the emotional volatility of its subjects and make them more governable.[8] Another is to explain the process as not so much 'top-down' and hegemonic as collaborative and reciprocal. For this view one might appeal to the thesis of Anna Wierzbicka that 'every culture offers … a set of "scripts" suggesting to people how to feel, how to express their feelings, how to think about their own and other people's feelings, and so on'.[9] The two most recent studies of the *Book of Common Prayer* from a literary perspective represent this choice of approaches, with Ramie Targoff's 2001 study depicting the Prayer Book, in new historicist colours, as a deliberate attempt to manipulate the populace, and Timothy Rosendale's 2007 study tending more towards the reciprocal model.[10]

In order to adjudicate between the hegemonic and the reciprocal approach, more data are required. Data of a comparative nature are particularly valuable, for what do they know of the Church of England who only the Church of England know? Fortunately, the results of a recent ground-breaking study on religious emotions in early modern Germany, which can be applied *mutatis mutandis* to late sixteenth-century England, are now available to us. This gives us a context for asking whether, and to what extent, we can say that the *Book of Common Prayer* (*BCP*), together with the books of *Homilies*, provided a 'script' (to borrow Wierzbicka's term) by which English men and women could express their religious emotions, and by which those religious emotions could be mediated, moderated and controlled. Because the

Protestantisation of England is normally attributed to the reign of the first Elizabeth, I shall be referring to the 1559 edition of the *BCP* and the 1563 edition of the *Homilies*.[11]

The 'reformation of feeling': from Germany to England

In 2010, Susan Karant-Nunn published her study of religious emotions in early modern Germany, *The Reformation of Feeling*.[12] Taking as her starting-point both Wierzbicka's theory of the 'emotional script' and Barbara Rosenwein's concept of 'emotional communities', Karant-Nunn showed how sermons on the Passion, or about dying and death, given by Catholic, Lutheran and Reformed preachers helped to create or at least to reinforce three markedly different 'communities of emotion'.[13] Pre-Reformation Catholic sermons on the Passion were, she argued, characterised by intense emotionality. Preachers represented Christ's undeserved suffering and death at the hands of wicked men in order to move their hearers to tears, and thence to a sincere resolve to amend their lives. Even in the seventeenth century, when Catholic preaching attained a 'homiletic maturity', Catholic sermons showed 'a striking degree of similarity' to fifteenth-century examples in this regard.[14] Lutheran sermons delivered at Passiontide, on the other hand, deliberately avoided such affectivity. The contrast was presented starkly by the Lutheran preacher Johannes Kymaeus (d. 1552), who critiqued late medieval approaches to the Passion:

> And thus it was the final purpose, when someone preached the Passion to us, how one could move the people to weeping, to howling, and to lamenting over the unkind Jews and mean-spirited peoples who killed Christ, God's Son. But the recognition of sins, and faith, which one was above all supposed to bring about by means of the Passion – these remained behind.[15]

While Lutheran preachers also meant to move their hearers to repentance, they sought to move them quickly beyond sorrow over sin to the assurance (*Trost*) of their forgiveness in and by Christ. Overmuch dwelling upon every stripe and blow Christ received shifted the salvific focus away from God's merciful agency towards the quality and quantity of the congregation's tears, a species of justification by works.[16] Reformed preaching, according to Karant-Nunn's analysis, departed even more drastically than Lutheran preaching from Catholic tendencies. It depicted Christ's suffering as psychological rather than physical – the torment of abandonment represented by the great cry of dereliction from the cross. But it also differed from Lutheran sermons on the subject. In Calvin's own preaching, Karant-Nunn found, the theme of assurance was wholly lacking: his purpose was neither to move his hearers to tears by reciting the lachrymose events of the Passion nor to fill their hearts with the assurance of sins forgiven, but to affirm the wisdom of divine Providence.[17]

This is certainly a pioneering work, which asks fresh questions of an extensive and hitherto underused corpus of evidence. It is also highly nuanced (more so than this summary might suggest) and is as sensitive to the commonalities between the traditions, especially as these developed over time, as to the differences. By describing the different confessions equally as 'communities of emotion', Karant-Nunn affirms the obvious point that none of the traditions regarded Christianity as lacking in affectivity. All three, indeed, had preachers and writers who strove to stir their hearers' and readers' emotions. But her overall impression was that, in the Protestant communities, inner emotions were expected to be contained within an 'outward tranquillity'.[18] And she concludes that '[t]here is a direct correlation between the curtailment of emotional display in religiosity and the definition of upright Christianity as quiescent'.[19] This conclusion accords well with the findings of such historians of the emotions as Michael Schoenfeldt and others who have identified a Christianised Stoicism at the heart of early modern reformed and humanist understandings of the self. It accords less well with the view of Richard Strier, who has warned against such a one-sided emphasis on Stoic restraint at the expense of other voices of the Renaissance which celebrated emotional exuberance.[20]

Karant-Nunn has therefore given us a helpful template for looking at the role of emotions, and the ways in which they were shaped by the theological elite, which can arguably be applied to England. Fortunately, the English evidence is far more manageable than the German for two reasons. First, the 1559 Prayer Book itself, and the Act of Uniformity which enforced its use, ensured a degree of liturgical homogeneity which was perhaps unmatched in Europe at this time, given the size and geographical extent of the English population.[21] Secondly, the Anglican *Homilies* (consisting of twelve sermons dating from Edward's reign, and a further twenty-one authorised under Elizabeth) ensured that the message from the pulpit was almost as uniform as the liturgy.[22] Every minister without a licence to preach was bound to read one of the homilies every Sunday. Bishops who were especially conscientious – or especially distrustful of their clergy – sometimes required even licensed ministers to use the *Homilies* as a matter of course.[23] Deviation from the script was strictly prohibited, and the consequent length and tedium of the process seems to have been on occasion as painful to the homilist as to the hearer, at least to judge from a line that William Shakespeare gave to Rosalind in *As You Like It*: 'O most gentle pulpiter, what tedious homily of love have you wearied your parishioners withal, and never cried: "Have patience, good people!"' (3.2.152–4).[24] We can therefore be certain that we know almost exactly what was preached week by week.[25]

Between them, the *Book of Common Prayer* and the *Homilies* constituted an unchanging form of words that was drummed into the hearts and minds of churchgoers week by week. Attendance at at least one Sunday service was enforced by law, on pain of a twelvepenny fine. Attention to the sermon was enforced for schoolboys, at least, who would be tested individually each Monday on the content of the previous day's homily.[26] The effect was deep and lasting. As indirect testimony to the persistence of the Prayer Book in the memories of even the humblest sort from a later century, we have the poet John Clare's assertion that chapbooks and sixpenny romances 'have memorys as common as Prayer Books and Psalters with the peasantry'.[27] So let us turn to the texts themselves, to see what sort of emotional discourse this officially imposed script presented.

The Prayer Book, the *Homilies* and the Bible

The authors of the Prayer Book and the *Homilies* clearly did set out to impose a 'script' upon their audience and readership. The script they intended to be so inscribed was not, however, a liturgy or even a sermon, but Holy Scripture itself. And, to describe this process, they chose an image more technologically up to date than one drawn from a scribal age, as is apparent from the very first homily.

> This worde [of Christ], whosoever is dylygent to reade, and in hys heart to print that he readeth, the great affection to the transitorye thynges of thys worlde, shalbe minished in hym, & the great desyre of heavenly thynges (that be therein promysed of God) shall increase in hym.
>
> For that thing, which (by continuall use of reading of holy scripture …) is depely prynted and graven in the hart, at length turneth almost into nature … And in reading of Gods word, he most profiteth not alwayes, that is most ready in turninge of the boke, or in saying of it withoute the booke, but he that is most turned into it, that is moste inspyred wyth the holy ghost, most in his hearte & lyfe altred and changed into that thing, which he readeth.[28]

It was no accident that the first homily of the first book of *Homilies* was an exhortation to the reading of Scripture. The extent to which the homilies were consciously based on Scripture would have been evident to even the most fitful of listeners, for each sermon bristled with numerous claims to scriptural fidelity: 'Therefore saieth Saint Paul', 'Saint John writeth in this wise', 'Read the book of Judges, and therein you shall find', and suchlike formulae. Similarly, the most striking feature of the regular Prayer Book services – that is, Morning Prayer (daily), Evening Prayer (daily) and to a lesser extent Holy Communion (ideally monthly) – was that they consisted chiefly of listening to large chunks of the Bible. The assiduous churchgoer would hear a chapter from the Old Testament and one from the New every morning, and a further chapter from each testament in the evening. At Holy Communion, two chapters from the New Testament would be read, one from an epistle and one from a gospel. In addition, there would be read perhaps two or three psalms at each service. And in addition to that were the canticles, all of which, with the exception of the *Te Deum*, were taken from the Bible or the Apocrypha. The rest of the service consisted of prayers, said either by the minister alone or in conjunction with the congregation: those prayers which were not taken verbatim from Scripture would be larded with scriptural themes. In this way the regular churchgoer would hear the entire Scripture read through in the course of a year, and the Psalter recited once a month. The framer of the Prayer Book, Thomas Cranmer, gave his rationale for this approach in the Preface.

> For they [the ancient fathers] so ordred the matter, that all the whole Bible (or the greatest part thereof) should be read over once in the year, intendyng thereby, that the Cleargie, and specially suche as were Ministers of the congregacion, should (by often readyng and meditacion of Gods worde) be stirred up to godlines themselfes, and be more able also to exhorte other by wholsome doctrine, and to confute them that were adversaries to the trueth. And further, that the people (by daily hearyng of holy scripture read in the Churche) should continuallye profite more and more in the knowledge of God, and bee the more inflamed with the love of his true religion.[29]

It is clear that, for Cranmer, it was Scripture which was affective, 'stirring up' and 'inflaming with love' its hearers. The liturgy was not merely designed as a vehicle for conveying daily deliveries of Scripture but intended to conform with Scripture, for 'here … is ordeyned nothyng to be read, but the very pure worde of God, the holy scriptures, or that whiche is evidently grounded upon the same' (p. 5). This programmatic focus on the Bible was signalled by the fact that Morning Prayer (and in due course Evening Prayer as well) invariably opened with sentences from Scripture, followed by an invitation to repent which began '[d]erely beloved Brethren, the Scripture moveth us in sondry places, to acknowledge and confesse our manifolde sinnes and wickednes ...' (p. 103).

While Cranmer was no doubt sincere in his conviction that the Prayer Book was as transparent of the Word of God as 'any thing by the wit of man ... devised' could be, we can more easily see it as providing a necessary interpretative framework for the public's consumption of Scripture.[30] Such a framework was necessary for two principal reasons. First, the Bible did not align as conveniently with the requirements of English Protestantism as most English Protestants might wish: the Epistle of James, for instance, with its assertion that one is justified by works and not by faith alone (2:24) was always a thorn in the flesh for a strictly Pauline doctrine of justification;[31] and the prophet Samuel's warning (in 1 Sam. 8) about the incompatibility of national monarchy with fidelity to God was difficult to square with the notion of a supreme royal governor of both Church and state.[32] By setting the Bible within the interpretative framework of the *BCP* and the *Homilies*, such inconvenient passages, while they could not be suppressed, could at least be managed and harmonised with other, more favourable passages. The idea that the Bible needed to be set in some sort of domesticating framework was far from unusual – in fact it was the norm. The late medieval Church in England had, after 1407, reserved the Bible from the laity by keeping it in Latin. The Evangelical and the Reformed vernacularised it, but framed it with Luther's prefaces or with Calvin's *Institutes* or with Bullinger's *Decades*. The authorised English translations – the Great Bible and the Bishops' Bible – carried no prefaces or marginal notes, and so another sort of framework was required, which the *BCP* and the *Homilies* would provide.

It was however not just the doctrinal but also the emotional world of the Bible that needed to be managed. This emotional world was varied and confusing and not always obviously edifying. The God of the Old Testament is portrayed as highly susceptible to his passions. In the Torah, the 'experiencing subject' of strong emotion in almost a quarter of all instances is God himself.[33] Even more tellingly, it has been calculated that, of the 714 occurrences of verbs denoting anger in the entire Hebrew Bible, three-quarters of them have God as their subject.[34] Sometimes these divine emotions have some foundation – humanity's wickedness leads to God's sorrow for having made Adam and Eve and his resolve to destroy their descendants in the Flood. But often God's passions seem to be driven by mere caprice – 'Jacob I loved but Esau I hated' (Romans 9:13; see also Malachi 1:2, 3). Human agents in the Bible seem no less emotionally unstable. The worshipper who reads the Psalms rebounds from one deep emotion to another, so that the plaintive weeping by the rivers of Babylon in Psalm 137 turns within nine verses to undisguised glee at the thought of dashing one's enemy's children against the rocks. In the remainder of this chapter, we shall look more closely at the ways in which the *BCP* and the *Homilies* might be seen as providing an affective, as well as an interpretative, framework for the Bible.

Framing biblical emotions I: 'in rest and quietness'

Karant-Nunn's study of the German evidence revealed a strong tendency in sixteenth-century Protestant communities towards the 'curtailment of emotional display' and the promotion of 'outward tranquillity', of 'quietude' and 'quiescence'. Karant-Nunn attributed this both to a particularly Lutheran suspicion of overt emotionality as an ostentatious good work and to the neo-Stoicism of the age. There is certainly much evidence from the Prayer Book to suggest that this tendency was no less characteristic of mainstream English Protestantism. 'Quietness' and its cognates occur fairly frequently in the *BCP*. Worshippers weekly, if not daily, at Evening Prayer petitioned for peace '[that we] may passe our time in rest and quietnes' (p. 114, second collect). At the Communion service they would have prayed 'that under [Elysabeth our Quene] we may be godly and quietly governed' (p. 129, the prayer for the Church militant), and have heard this invitation to auricular confession:

> [T]herfore yf there be any of you, which … can not quiet his owne conscience, but requireth further comforte or counsail, then let him come to me, or some other discrete and learned minister of gods word, and open his griefe, that he may receive such ghostly counseil, advise, and comfort, as his conscience may be releved, and that by the ministery of Gods word, he may receyve comfort, and the benefyte of absolution, to the quieting of his conscience, and advoiding of all scruple and doubtfulnes. (p. 132, the second exhortation)

Less regularly, they would have heard the minister ask on their behalf that 'thy congregacion may joyfully serve the in al godly quietnes' (the collect for Trinity 5), and 'that they may … serve the with a quyet mynde' (the collect for Trinity 21).[35]

The attribute of quietness in the *BCP* seems at first sight to be patient both of a new historicist and of a 'new humoralist' reading. As a virtue to be cultivated by every English worshipper, it accorded with the specific priorities of the Tudor state, which set such store by obedience to royal authority and the avoidance of civil unrest. And as a signifier of the absence of violent emotion, it corresponds to the neo-Stoicism that one associates with the Renaissance. But we should perhaps be wary of jumping to conclusions. 'Quietness' translates the Greek word *hesychia*, which appears in the New Testament in precisely this sense of civil and domestic peace.[36] It was a desideratum of first-century Christianity and therefore of Christianity in all ages (including the Sarum Rite and other sources from which the Prayer Book was adapted), not one exclusively valued by the practitioners of Tudor statecraft. Nor are we necessarily correct in assuming that the Prayer Book's 'quietness' denoted the absence of high emotion. In his experience of Prayer Book services, John Donne – no stranger to fervid passions – found the two to be intimately connected.

> And, O the power of Church-musick! that harmony added to this Hymn has raised the Affections of my heart, and quickned my graces of zeal and gratitude; *and I observe*, that I always return from praying this publick duty of *Prayer* and *Praise* to God, with an inexpressible tranquillity of mind, and a *willingness* to leave this world.[37]

Finally, we should be careful to avoid any suggestion that neo-Stoicism was simply a repristination of the original. Christian Stoicism was a different beast, which did not regard unfeeling, autonomous detachment as a virtue to be emulated. In his classic study of Julius Lipsius, Gerhard Oestereich reminded us that the neo-Stoic understanding of reason (*ratio*) also included piety (*pietas*).[38]

A word that recurs throughout Cranmer's liturgy is 'joy' and its cognates. This is again largely because the words appear frequently in the Bible, both in the Psalms and in the New Testament – and of course because that emotion is the very basis of the worship being choreographed by the Prayer Book. The order for Morning Prayer illustrates this choreography well. It demonstrates the framing of biblical emotions by acting as a sort of *vade mecum* through the confusing emotional world of the Bible, progressing from divine anger to divine love, and from human fear to human joy. Indeed, Morning Prayer can be seen as the liturgising of the characteristically Lutheran progression from Law to Gospel. The first emotion-words to be encountered in the order of service occur in the introductory sentences from Scripture. The faithful are told rather familiarly by Joel that God is 'such a one that is sory for your afflictions', and in the words of Jeremiah they ask God to '[c]orrecte us, O Lorde, and yet in thy judgement, not in thy furie' (pp. 102–3). These are among the Scriptures 'in sondry places' which in turn 'moveth us' to confess our manifold sins and wickedness. In the prayers of confession and absolution which follow, divine and human emotions are contrasted. Selfish human desire ('we have folowed to much the devises and desires of our owne hartes') is counteracted by God's gracious desire to save ('which desireth not the deathe of a sinner, but rather that he maye turne from his wickednesse and lyve'). The result of forgiveness is the first mention in the service of joy ('that at the last we may come to his eternall joye'), though it is perhaps significant that the joy referred to is God's. The Lord's Prayer which follows both echoes ('forgeve us our trespasses') and brings to an end the first, penitential part of the service (pp. 103–4).

The second part consists of the two lessons from Scripture, framed by psalms. Now for the first time the emotion of joy is appropriated by worshippers ('let us hartely rejoyce in the strength of our salvacion'; 'let us … shewe ourselfe gladde in hym wyth Psalmes'; 'O be joyfull in the Lorde (al ye lands): serve the Lorde wyth gladnes, and come before hys presence with a song' (p. 105)). The final part of the service consists of prayers which repeat the key emotion of joy ('make thy chosen people joyful'). Much of the credit for the emotional vocabulary is due of course to the source material which Cranmer used. But inasmuch as Cranmer simplified and reduced three medieval services into one, the essential shape of this liturgy is his.

The order for Morning Prayer illustrates how the emotional world of the Bible was framed and to some extent tamed by the *BCP*. The psalms appointed for the day, with their effusions of conflicting emotions, are bracketed by other psalms and canticles which are more univocal in their expression of joyfulness in and thankfulness for God's mercies and which are relatively stable and unchanging in their message. The psalmist's expressions of bottomless grief and abject despair are heard, and heard frequently; but they occur within a daily and weekly framework of comfort and assurance.

Framing biblical emotions II: 'only the ministers of our wickedness'

In her study of contemporary German evidence, Karant-Nunn reported that, in sermons on the suffering and death of Christ given during Holy Week and especially on Good Friday, Catholic preachers tended to elaborate on the sufferings of Christ and the cruelties he endured, far beyond the detail provided by the gospel accounts, and in particular to expatiate on the malice and spite of his tormentors. An invariable element of this elaboration was reflection on Jewish culpability for Christ's death. This was embedded in the gospel account of the crucifixion by Matthew, who in a fateful verse has the Jewish crowd exclaim, '[h]is blood be upon us and upon our children' (Matthew 27:25). In Continental Europe, violence against the persons and property of Jews was a not infrequent concomitant of Good Friday devotions, and Jews were often banned from leaving their homes on that day, partly so as not to offend pious Christians, partly for their own safety. It was one of the most palpable effects of affective piety. Lutherans and Reformed preachers, on the other hand, tended to play down the culpability of the Jews, according to Karant-Nunn. Even Luther himself, who is no one's idea of a philosemite, insisted, '[o]ne should not do as those do who rebuke the Jews'.[39] For both sets of Protestant preachers, it was important that their Christian hearers recognised their own responsibility for the crucifixion. The Jews were merely the instruments appointed to carry out God's work. As one might imagine, Protestant sermons still contained anti-Jewish sentiments, but they were far less marked than in Catholic sermons.[40]

The *Homilies* fit very well into the Lutheran and Reformed pattern. In the Homily for Good Friday, Jews are cleared of culpability of Christ's death, and even the role which Matthew's gospel accords them is played down:

> If we (my friends) consider this, that for our synnes, this most innocent lambe was driven to death, we shall have muche more cause to bewayle oureselves, that we wer the cause of hys death, than to crye oute of the malyce and crueltye of the Jewes, whych pursued hym to hys death. We dyd the dedes wherfore he was thus stryken & wounded, they were onely the ministers of our wickednesse.[41]

Where Jews are criticised in the *Homilies*, and where the traditional epithets of 'stubborn' and 'stiff-necked' are trundled out, it is because of their refusal to acknowledge Jesus as the Messiah, not because of any accusation of deicide. But even these old insults are mitigated to some extent by those homilies (especially those written by John Jewel, Bishop of Salisbury (1522–71)) in which Jews are held up as model worshippers and servants of God, whose piety puts Christians to shame – the homilies on prayer, on keeping the Lord's house clean, on obedience to the sovereign and on idolatry.[42] The evidence is historical, taken from the Old Testament, but this is hardly surprising as there were no examples of Jewish piety in Elizabethan England that Jewel could have known about – at least not officially.[43] But, as Vincenette d'Uzer has pointed out, the *Homilies* represent an interesting development, caused at least in part by the exposure of their composers to the Old Testament. Jewel spells out the new paradigm for Christian attitudes towards Jews – 'we abhorre the very name of the Jewes, when we heare it, as of a moste wicked and ungodlye people', yet it is they whose diligence in worship condemns our negligence. The reason for this is that they 'have the true sense and meanyng of Gods lawe so peculierly geven unto them'.[44] Interestingly, Jewel always refers to the Jews in the *present* tense, so he can say not that they *were*, but that they *are*, the people of God. The words of the Old Testament, he seems to be saying, are as alive and present to the Christian as are the words of the New. It was this typically Reformed attitude, which saw the Old Testament not merely as a historical document of antiquarian interest but as a blueprint for a godly society, that kept alive in the minds of the hearers of the homilies the idea that the promises of God to the Jews were still valid. This message, repeated so regularly to the people of England through the *Homilies*, might arguably have prepared the ground for the re-admission of the Jews to England.[45]

The same moderation of anti-Jewish sentiment that we find in the *Homilies* is reflected also in the Prayer Book. In Cranmer's liturgy for Good Friday, for instance, the traditional 'Reproaches' – words put into Christ's mouth in which he reproaches 'his people' (the Jews) for their harsh treatment of him – were immediately dropped. And although the third collect for Good Friday, a prayer for the conversion of 'all Jews, Turks, infidels, and heretics', can cause offence nowadays for its proselytising spirit, it should be noted that in adapting the various prayers from the Missal to create this collect, Cranmer silently dropped the reference to the 'perfidy' of the Jews, with its sinister double-meaning of both 'infidelity' and 'treachery'.

> Merciful God, who haste made all men, and hatest nothinge that thou haste made, nor wouldest the deathe of a synner, but rather that hee should be converted, and live; have mercy upon all Jewes, turks, infidels, and heritikes, and take from them all ignoraunce, hardnes of herte, and contempte of thy worde: and so fetche them home blessed Lorde, to thy flocke, that they may be saved emonge the remnaunte of the true Israelites, and be made one folde under one shepherde, Jesus Christ our Lord; who lyveth and reigneth with thee and the Holy Ghost, now and ever. Amen.[46]

This was an example of liturgy and sermon working together to frame the emotions, and more specifically to restrain anti-Jewish emotionality. Although the practical impact of such a strategy was much less in England than in those lands (few as they were in the sixteenth century) in which Christians and Jews co-existed, it was none the less a revealing one. Those who heard the Homily for Good Friday and who said 'amen' to the collects were provided with a framework for interpreting the Bible. This framework mitigated the otherwise incendiary impact of such biblical verses as 'His blood be upon us', at the most emotionally charged point in the Church's calendar.

Framing biblical emotions III: 'which of you in such a case would not be moved?'

A similar process can be found in the Prayer Book's Order for Holy Communion, to which we now turn. The affective piety of the Middle Ages was to a large extent focused on the saving Passion of Christ, which was commemorated not only annually at Eastertide but also in the Mass. In the late Middle Ages, it was rare for lay people to communicate rather than simply hear Mass, and it was part of the Protestant programme that communion should become much more frequent. But while neglecting communion was sinful, receiving the sacrament unworthily was an equal and opposite sin, and indeed a far worse one if compounded by being out of charity with a neighbour. And so the Elizabethan Prayer Book, like its 1552 predecessor, was furnished with no fewer than three different exhortations, to be used as occasion warranted. The first was to be used 'at certayne tymes when the Curate shal see the people negligent to come to the holy communyon', and it contained a pathetic appeal, with a strong echo of a gospel parable:

> Ye know howe grevous and unkynde a thing it is, when a manne hath prepared a riche feaste: decked his table with al kynde of provisyon, so that there lacketh nothinge but the gestes to site downe; and yet they whych be called wythout anye cause mooste unthankfully refuse to come. Whyche of you in suche a case woulde not be moved? Who woulde not thyncke a greate injurie and wrong done unto hym? (p. 130)

The second exhortation was to be used in cases where the congregation was all too ready to receive communion. And the third, which was always to be used, followed a middle way by containing *both* a blood curdling warning of the danger of eating and drinking 'our owne dampnation' (thereby risking 'divers diseases, and sundrye kyndes of death') *and* a heart-warming invitation:

> Therfore if any of you be a blasphemer of god, an hinderer or slaunderer of his worde, an adulterer, or be in malyce, or envye, or in anye other grevous crime, bewaile your Sinnes, and come not to this holy table, lest after the taking of that holy sacrament, the devil enter into you, as he entred into Judas,

> and fil you full of al iniquities, and bring you to destruction both of bodye and soule. And to the ende that we should alwaie remembre the exceadinge greate love of our master and onelie saviour Jesu Christ, thus diyng for us, and the innumerable benefites (which by his precious bloud sheading) he hath obteined to us, he hath instituted and ordeined holy misteries, as pledges of his love, and continuall remembraunce of his death, to our great and endles comfort. (p. 133)

The optional nature of the first and second exhortations arguably not simply makes the *BCP* a framing device for biblical emotions but takes it to the level of a mechanism of control. For a congregation whose devotion might be cooling, the first exhortation gave the minister an opportunity to remind them of Christ's work in warm and emotive words: 'exceeding great love', 'his precious bloodshedding', 'our great and endless comfort'. But for a congregation already too emotional or frenetic in their piety, judicious use of the second exhortation provided the liturgical equivalent of a bucket of cold water. No doubt many ministers used or abused the scope this gave them for discretion. But the realities of the Elizabethan parish meant that one's minister might be under-qualified, or even Papist, and in such circumstances the obligatory nature of the third exhortation insured a fixed framework quite independent of the incumbent's skill.

Conclusion: framing and taming the Bible

A comparison of the 'emotional scripts' provided by religious authorities in sixteenth-century Germany and England shows, naturally enough, that emotions were acknowledged as a necessary concomitant of Christian life and worship. The role of a renewed Stoicism in inhibiting the expression of emotions has arguably been overstated: neo-Stoicism was still *Christian* Stoicism.[47] None the less, there was in Lutheran Germany a distrust of outward emotionality based on theological rather than philosophical grounds, namely the danger of tears as good works. Across the North Sea, a different priority emerged. Here it was recognised that the newly published vernacular Bible provided its own emotional script, but one that had to be read carefully if the unstable, confusing and even frightening emotions (both human and divine) to which it bore witness were to be understood correctly. The *BCP* and the *Homilies* combined to provide a device for framing and taming the emotional world of the Bible, one which emphasised God's loving-kindness over his sometimes capricious wrath and which emphasised Christian joy over fear. The up-and-down emotional world of the Bible was not suppressed. Indeed, the English reformers took pains to insure that the entire Bible (including the Old Testament apocrypha) was read out during the course of the year. But it was set firmly within a proleptic 'salvation history' which elevated Gospel over Law, and the order of Morning Prayer exemplifies this 'emotional framing'.

The Scriptures, and in particular the psalms, read within these services testify that other, more negative emotions, such as grief and despair, are part of the Christian condition. But these are framed within orders of service which emphasise a realistically positive emotion: joy. It is positive, because the Prayer Book's notion of joy is based on a firm assurance of God's love. It is realistic, because any triumphalistic tendency is tempered by the acknowledgement that in this vale of tears we remain 'miserable offenders' even when redeemed. Such a middling message was neither as blood-curdling on the one hand, nor as heart-warming on the other, as some of the Prayer Book's sixteenth- and seventeenth-century critics would have liked. It certainly did not provide the emotional freedom that the Admonitioners and John Milton desired. But that was the point. Few people in the first Elizabeth's England could read the Bible except as mediated by the *Book of Common Prayer*. It has been credibly suggested that 'perhaps the Book of Common Prayer, not the English Bible, is the foundational and paradigmatic text of Anglicanism'.[48] By the same token, one might suggest that it was the Prayer Book, rather than the Bible, which helped to form the emotional culture of the English.

Notes

1 As quoted by Cranmer in his refutation of the rebels' demands. See J. E. Cox (ed.), *Miscellaneous Writings of Thomas Cranmer* (Cambridge: Cambridge University Press, 1846), p. 179.

2 Judith Maltby, 'Petitions for Episcopacy and the Book of Common Prayer on the Eve of the Civil War, 1641–1642', in Stephen Taylor (ed.), *From Cranmer to Davidson: A Church of England Miscellany*, Church of England Record Society, vol. 7 (Woodbridge: Boydell Press, 1999), pp. 105–67 (p. 147).

3 Judith Maltby, *Prayer Book and People in Elizabethan and Early Stuart England* (Cambridge: Cambridge University Press, 1998), p. 27.

4 John Field, *An Admonition to the Parliament* (Hemel Hempstead, 1572), sig. Aiijv.

5 John Milton, *Eikonoklastes*, in *Complete Prose*, ed. Merrit Y. Hughes, 6 vols (New Haven: Yale University Press, 1962), vol. 3, p. 505.

6 These petitions were not a clerically organised response to similar petitions by the hotter sort of Protestant against episcopacy and fixed liturgy, but according to Maltby represented 'an authentic lay voice in the provinces' ('Petitions', p. 107).

7 '[T]he godly consideration of Predestination, and our Election in Christ, is full of sweet, pleasant, and unspeakable comfort', Article XVII. The *Articles of Religion* were designed as terse statements of doctrinal orthodoxy capable of commanding the broadest range of pan-Protestant support. Affective language occurs only twice, in this article on predestination and in Article XI on justification. (The latter hails the teaching 'that we are justified by Faith only' as 'a most wholesome Doctrine, and very full of comfort, as more largely is expressed in the Homily of Justification'.) Its use in Article XVII serves to emphasise that article's contention that the purpose of the doctrine is to provide believers with assurance of salvation, not to furnish material for pointless and dangerous speculation. But it may not be without significance for later controversies in the English Church that the language of the *Articles* takes an affective turn when dealing with the most 'Protestant' of the Protestant articles of faith.

8 Norbert Elias, *Power and Civility* (*The Civilizing Process*, vol. 2) (New York: Pantheon, 1982), p. 291.

9 Anna Wierzbicka, *Emotions across Languages and Cultures: Diversity and Universals* (Cambridge: Cambridge University Press, 1999), p. 240.

10 Ramie Targoff, *Common Prayer: The Language of Public Devotion in Early Modern England* (Chicago: University of Chicago Press, 2001); and Timothy Rosendale, *Liturgy and Literature in the Making of Protestant England* (Cambridge: Cambridge University Press, 2007).

11 Earlier accounts tended to regard Protestantisation as a process which began in the reign of Edward or even that of his father, and (allowing for the ecclesiastical hiccup represented by Mary's short reign) was effectively over by the beginning of Elizabeth's reign. Current historiography tends to regard Elizabeth's accession as marking the actual beginning of the process. See, for example, Peter Marshall, *Reformation England, 1480–1642* (London: Hodder Arnold, 2003), p. 113.

12 *The Reformation of Feeling: Shaping the Religious Emotions in Early Modern Germany* (New York: Oxford University Press, 2010).

13 The phrase itself comes from Barbara Rosenwein, *Emotional Communities in the Early Middle Ages* (Ithaca: Cornell University Press, 2006).

14 Karant-Nunn, *Reformation of Feeling*, ch. 1.

15 Ibid., p. 84.

16 Ibid., ch. 2.

17 Ibid., ch. 3.

18 Ibid., p. 68. For examples of similar 'containment' among English Protestant writers such as Richard Sibbes and Thomas Rogers, see Mary Ann Lund, Chapter 4, below, and Erin Sullivan, Chapter 1, above.

19 Ibid., p. 242. Karant-Nunn relates this quiescence to an early modern revival of Stoicism: 'Within the arena of quietude, we may see the gentleman's affinity for that stoic revival that characterized some educated men's interests' (p. 243).

20 See Michael C. Schoenfeldt, *Bodies and Selves in Early Modern England: Physiology and Inwardness in Spenser, Shakespeare, Herbert and Milton* (Cambridge: Cambridge University Press, 1999). Often associated with the 'Stoic' position are those studies which interpret early modern understandings of the emotions in terms of the balance of Galenic humours, as discussed in the Introduction to this volume; but early modern neo-Stoicism also involved theology and spiritual ways of being. For Strier's response to what he characterises as 'the new humoralism', see his *The Unrepentant Renaissance: From Petrarch to Shakespeare to Milton* (Chicago and London: University of Chicago Press, 2011). This contains much material of direct relevance to the current discussion, not least his helpful analyses of Luther. On this see also his earlier *Love Known: Theology and Experience in George Herbert's Poetry* (Chicago: University of Chicago Press, 1983), and 'Against the Rule of Reason: Praise of Passion from Petrarch to Luther to Shakespeare to Herbert', in Gail Kern Paster, Katherine Rowe and Mary Floyd-Wilson (eds), *Reading the Early Modern Passions: Essays in the Cultural History of Emotion* (Philadelphia: University of Pennsylvania Press, 2004), pp. 23–42.

21 The even wider dissemination of the Elizabethan Prayer Book was ensured by translations into Latin in 1560, for use in both the universities, and into Welsh in 1567. On the *Book of Common Prayer*'s status as an Elizabethan 'bestseller', see Brian Cummings, 'Print, Popularity, and the *Book of Common Prayer*', in Andy Kesson and Emma Smith (eds), *The Elizabethan Top Ten: Defining Print Popularity in Early Modern England* (Farnham: Ashgate, 2013), pp. 135–44.

22 The Elizabethan edition of the Edwardian homilies was entitled *Certaine Sermons Appoynted by the Quenes Maiesty, to be Declared and Read, by Al Parsons, Vicars, & Curates Everi Sunday and Holi Day, in Their Churches: and by Her Graces Advise Perused & Oversene, for the Better Understanding of the Simple People* (London, 1563). The second book, first published in 1563, consisted of twenty homilies under the title *The Second Tome of Homelyes of Such Matters as Were Promised and Intituled in the Former Part of Homelyes, Set Out by the Aucthoritie of the Quenes Maiestie: and to Be Read in Every Paryshe Churche Agreablye* (London, 1563). A further homily, 'Against Disobedience and Wilful Rebellion', was added in 1571. Although the two books were sometimes printed in uniform editions from 1582, to facilitate their being bound together by the owner, they were not printed in a single volume until 1623. This was also the last volume to be printed under royal authority. For convenience sake, I shall refer in the text to the first and second books of *Homilies*, even though such a generic title is not strictly accurate for this period.

23 See the entry 'Homilies, the Books of', in Frank Leslie Cross and Elizabeth A. Livingstone (eds), *The Oxford Dictionary of the Christian Church*, 3rd edn (Oxford: Oxford University Press, 1997), p. 786.

24 Quoted from Juliet Dusinberre's Arden 3 edition of *As You Like It* (London: Thomson Learning, 2006). The reading 'Jupiter' is preferred by some editors to 'pulpiter', though the reference to a lengthy homily is still clear. See Michael

Hattaway's New Cambridge edition (Cambridge: Cambridge University Press, 2009), esp. the note at 3.3.130. I am grateful to Erin Sullivan for alerting me to this point.

25 Karant-Nunn's German evidence consisted of printed editions containing tens of thousands of sermons, and for that reason she limited her study to sermons dealing with the Passion and with dying and death. She admitted that it was impossible to discover how faithful the printed versions were to the sermons as originally delivered. In many cases, vernacular sermons would be turned into Latin for publication. See Karant-Nunn, *Reformation of Feeling*, pp. 5, 13. The English Homilies, by their nature, present no difficulties in terms either of the sheer variety of source material or of the fidelity of the surviving records to the original spoken word. Of course, neither the 'godly' nor the secretly practising Catholics would have restricted themselves to this official diet of sermons. For the 'godly', the alternative to the restrictive homilies were 'prophesyings' and (when these were suppressed by Queen Elizabeth in 1576–77) 'combination lectures'. On these unofficial sermons, see the valuable introduction in Patrick Collinson, John Craig and Brett Usher (eds), *Conferences and Combination Lectures in the Elizabethan Church: Dedham and Bury St Edmunds, 1582–1590*, Church of England Record Society, vol. 10 (Woodbridge: Boydell Press, 2003), pp. xxvi–xxxii. It is arguable that the affective style of later, and hotter, Protestants like Richard Sibbes and Robert Bolton derives from this unofficial homiletic tradition rather than from the official one.

26 The statutes of some schools required pupils to render the substance of the sermon into Latin or Greek verse, Latin or Greek prose, or English, according to their seniority. See Norman Wood, *The Reformation and English Education* (London: Routledge, 1931), p. 167. Even where such elaborate exercises were not required by school statutes, the Church, following Archbishop Grindal's canons of 1571, would insist on some degree of interrogation. See, among many examples, the visitation articles of Bishop William Chaderton for his Lincoln diocese in 1607, who asked his incumbents 'Doth your schoolemaster … bring his schollers to church, and … doth he examine them after their returne, what they have learned of the sermon?' See Kenneth Fincham (ed.), *Visitation Articles and Injunctions of the Early Stuart Church*, Church of England Record Society, vol. 1 (Woodbridge: Boydell Press, 1994), p. 76.

27 *John Clare's Autobiographical Writings*, ed. Eric Robinson (Oxford: Oxford University Press, 1983), pp. 56–7.

28 Extracts from the conclusion of the opening homily, 'The fruitful exhortation to the reading and knowledge of Holy Scripture', in *Certaine Sermons*, sigs Bir–v.

29 *The Book of Common Prayer: The Texts of 1549, 1559, and 1662*, ed. Brian Cummings (Oxford: Oxford University Press, 2011), p. 4. Cranmer's preface to the 1549 *BCP*, from which this extract is taken, was reprinted unchanged in the second

Edwardian Prayer Book of 1552 and the Elizabeth Prayer Book of 1559. In 1662 its spelling and punctuation were modernised, and some other minor changes were made (none affecting this quotation). Further references to the *BCP* are to Cummings's edition and will appear in text unless otherwise noted.

30 Cranmer had begun his preface to the *BCP* by declaring of previous liturgies that '[t]here was never any thing by the wit of man so well devised, or so surely established, which (in continuance of time) hath not been corrupted' (p. 4).

31 It was left to the *Homilies* to provide puzzled parishioners with the official solution to this conundrum. The third homily, 'Of the salvation of mankind, by onely Chryst', states the orthodox Protestant doctrine of justification by faith alone. This is immediately followed by a shorter homily, 'Of the true, lyvely and Chrystian fayth', which explains that 'the holy Apostle Saint James' meant merely that true faith always brings forth good works. The third homily in this set, 'Of good workes annexed unto fayth', immediately corrects any misunderstanding of James by reminding its hearers in Paul's words that a good work done without faith is sin. See *Certaine Sermons*, sigs Diiv–Kiiiv.

32 Here the strategy seems to have been to hide the offending chapter, as far as possible, from the congregation's earshot. It is not referred to in either of the two homilies on obedience, and 1 Samuel 8 was not scheduled to be read at a Sunday service (the proper lessons go from 1 Samuel 3, read at evensong on the Third Sunday after Trinity, to 1 Samuel 12, read at matins on Trinity 4). One would need to attend evening prayer on 2 April (but only if a weekday) to hear this chapter read aloud. Even so, it is balanced by the second lesson, Hebrews 8 – which happens to contain a dire warning against disobedience. See *BCP*, pp. 219, 225.

33 As reported in an intriguing, though methodologically questionable, study of the text of the standard eighteenth-century Italian translation of the Vulgate. See Dario Galati, Renato Miceli and Marco Tamietto, 'Emotions and Feelings in the Bible: Analysis of the Pentateuch's Affective Lexicon', *Social Science Information*, 46 (2007), 355–76 (p. 366).

34 Ellen van Wolde, 'Sentiments as Culturally Constructed Emotions: Anger and Love in the Hebrew Bible', *Biblical Interpretation*, 16 (2008), 1–24 (p. 8). On the significance of God's passions for the English Jesuit Thomas Wright, see Erin Sullivan, Chapter 1, above.

35 *The Prayer-Book of Queen Elizabeth 1559*, ed. Edward Benham (Edinburgh: John Grant, 1909), pp. 78, 83.

36 In 1 Timothy 2:2, prayer is enjoined 'for kings and all who are in high positions, that we may lead a peaceful and quiet (*hesychion*) life'. In 1 Peter 3:4, wives are besought to let their adorning be 'the imperishable beauty of a gentle and quiet (*hesychiou*) spirit'. See Kurt Aland, Matthew Black, Carlo M. Martini, Bruce M. Metzger and Allen Wikgren (eds), *The Greek New Testament*, 3rd edn (New York: United Bible Societies, 1975), pp. 722, 796.

37 Cited in *The Book of Common Prayer*, ed. Cummings, p. xxxvi (emphasis original). Cummings points out that the 'hymn' to which Donne refers would have been a psalm.

38 Gerhard Oestreich, *Neostoicism and the Early Modern State* (Cambridge: Cambridge University Press, 1982), p. 7.

39 Karant-Nunn, *Reformation of Feeling*, p. 142.

40 Ibid., pp. 153–7.

41 *The Second Tome of Homelyes*, sig. 191r.

42 On this rich subject, see for example David Katz, *Philosemitism and the Readmission of the Jews to England, 1603–1655* (Oxford: Oxford University Press, 1982); Eliane Glaser, *Judaism without Jews: Philosemitism and Christian Controversy in Early Modern England* (Basingstoke: Palgrave Macmillan, 2007); Achsah Guibbory, *Christian Identity, Jews and Israel in Seventeenth-Century England* (Oxford: Oxford University Press, 2010); and Charles W. A. Prior, 'Hebraism and the Problem of Church and State in England, 1642–1660', *The Seventeenth Century*, 28 (2013), 37–61.

43 There is evidence of a substantial Jewish presence at the Tudor court from the 1540s onwards. See Roger Prior, 'A Second Jewish Community in Tudor London', *Transactions of the Jewish Historical Society of England*, 31 (1990), 137–52.

44 *The Second Tome of Homelyes*, sigs 5r–47v.

45 See Vincenette d'Uzer, 'The Jews in the Sixteenth-century Homilies', in Diana Wood (ed.), *Christianity and Judaism*, Studies in Church History, vol. 29 (Oxford: Blackwell, 1992), pp. 265–77, esp. pp. 276–7. For the view – fully consonant with Jewel's approach in the *Homilies* – that Shakespeare's Shylock had a more privileged access to the interpretation of Genesis than a Christian, see Sara Coodin, Chapter 3, below.

46 *Prayer-Book of Queen Elizabeth*, ed. Benham, p. 71.

47 '[T]he Judaeo-Christian tradition, insofar as it is biblical, is a tradition that allows for strong, even uncontrolled emotion' (Strier, 'Against the Rule of Reason', p. 23). In a recent essay, Joe Moshenska goes so far as to argue that Cranmer's Eucharistic theology reflects not simply an affective but a 'bodily and sensual devotion', though in such a way as to be deniable ('"A Sensible Touching, Feeling and Groping": Metaphor and Sensory Experience in the English Reformation', in Brian Cummings and Freya Sierhuis (eds), *Passions and Subjectivity in Early Modern Culture* (Farnham: Ashgate, 2013), pp. 183–200).

48 Rosendale, *Liturgy and Literature*, p. 6.

3

'This was a way to thrive': Christian and Jewish eudaimonism in *The Merchant of Venice*

Sara Coodin

In the opening lines of Shakespeare's *The Merchant of Venice*, Antonio insists upon the profound effects of his sadness – and upon his utter ignorance of its causes.

> In sooth, I know not why I am so sad,
> It wearies me, you say it wearies you;
> But how I caught it, found it, or came by it,
> What stuff 'tis made of, whereof it is born,
> I am to learn;
> And such a want-wit sadness makes of me
> That I have much ado to know myself.[1]

Antonio's strong externalist description of emotion as something that happens to him – 'I caught it, found it, or came by it' – and insistence that it has in some fundamental way remade him, turning him into a 'want-wit', echo some of the critical mainstays of recent scholarship surrounding the early modern passions, particularly Gail Kern Paster's and Mary Floyd-Wilson's post-structuralist work discussing the embodied nature of early modern emotion. Both Paster's and Floyd-Wilson's scholarship has focused heavily on emotion's material dimension, targeting the early modern body's susceptibility to the destabilising physiological upheavals generated by strong passions.[2] In their accounts, the bodies that experienced passions like anger and sadness were labile entities continually being reshaped in response to shifting environmental cues. When Antonio pronounces that sadness is something that he 'caught', 'found' or 'came by', and that it has changed him into someone he no longer recognises, he would therefore appear to confirm their conclusions about the material nature of early modern inwardness and its fundamental imbrication with environmental forces. Salerio's and Solanio's responses to Antonio appear to further develop this set of ideas;

they suggest that Antonio's bad mood is caused by merchandise, pirates and perilous storms, remarks that rehearse the Renaissance trope of the self as an only tentatively stable body easily rocked by external material forces, which Paster also foregrounds in her introduction to *Humoring the Body*.[3]

In addressing complex emotional states such as happiness and sadness that straddle a range of discursive fields and signal multiple cultural scripts, the recent scholarly preoccupation with the material body has remained stubbornly singular in its focus. As much as the self to which Antonio refers at the outset of the play signals a tentative balance of early modern humoral fluids, his comment that 'I have much ado to know myself' suggests even more straightforwardly at a philosophically conceived self capable of making decisions that impact the material body, its moods, complexions and dispositions. Antonio makes clear that he does not see his passion sourced in material goods – 'my merchandise makes me not sad' – and scholars of early modern emotion might, like Antonio, usefully question the utility of reducing passions, moods and emotions so deterministically to material forms, including the physical body.

It is significant that Antonio professes not to know the sources of his own sadness; sources of emotion in *The Merchant of Venice* and in Shakespeare's plays generally are often bound up with not-knowing and with characters' incomplete views into their own emotional motivations. In early modern England, the drive to shed light on those sources of motivation formed a crucial part of the discourse of self-management. Well into the seventeenth century, those discussions continued to bear the marks of a classical eudaimonism concerned with actualising the good life in practical terms. Vernacular moral-philosophical texts, including handbooks on the passions and guides to happiness and the management and care of the body, made ready use of the discourse of humoral psychology, but did not begin and end with the body. Rather, it was through the discourse of humoral psychology that these texts initiated practical discussions about the well-lived life.

The discourse of self-help in Shakespeare's era was deeply immersed in questions of what it was possible to control and how to effect a reshaping of the self in accordance with objective ideals. Accordingly, self-cultivation, as it was outlined in many vernacular English Renaissance guides to health and happiness, was profoundly concerned with the exercise of moral agency. Human subjects were understood not as passive vessels but, rather, as entities positioned within a field of small-scale choices imagined to carry enormous consequence for the cultivation of human happiness. Early modern emotion may have become nearly synonymous in recent years with decentred material selves subject to the overarching swell of environmental forces; however, the early modern discourse of eudaimonism, which emphasised individuals' capacity – and responsibility – for moral self-cultivation, poses serious challenges to that paradigm. I begin this chapter with a discussion of the philosophical context for early modern writings on emotion, one that stems from self-help texts' own emphasis on lifelong self-cultivation that was understood in eudaimonistic terms, that is to say, concerned with moral flourishing. I argue that, in dwelling so persistently on the material languages through which eudaimonistic ideas were being expressed, the current materialist preoccupation with emotion effectively mistakes the forest for the trees, and fails to address the larger issues of agency and self-management that underwrote those discussions. I then turn to Shakespeare's *The Merchant of Venice* and the question of moral flourishing in that play. Typically, questions of moral thriving in *Merchant* have been tied to Christian allegory. Within the terms of that allegory, Shylock has been figured as a greedy, crude materialist; he is the vice that counterpoints Antonio's Christian virtue, and he must be overcome in order for Christian virtues – mercy, forgiveness, etc. – to flourish. I propose a very different reading of *Merchant*, one that foregrounds the ethnographic identity of Shakespeare's characters, but reads the language of ethnography and the scriptural exegesis that is its primary vehicle as part of a larger discussion of eudaimonistic flourishing and 'way[s] to thrive', as Shylock refers to it (1.3.80). Shakespeare takes up that conversation about thrift, I argue, in complex ways by giving voice to two distinct models of moral flourishing in *The Merchant of Venice*: Christian and Jewish.

Eudaimonia and the early modern moral life

One of the dominant ideas that Shakespeare's contemporaries relied on to figure a comprehensive notion of happiness was eudaimonia, a classical concept that has been variously interpreted as the well-lived, well-realised or beautiful life, as moral thriving or flourishing and more commonly simply as 'happiness'. In both the *Nicomachean* and *Eudemian Ethics*, Aristotle takes up the question of happiness by deliberating about the kinds of character-traits and virtues worth cultivating, focusing in the *Nicomachean Ethics* on practical virtues. More modestly but no less earnestly, sixteenth- and seventeenth-century guides to the passions, complexions and humours pick up on elements of Aristotelian eudaimonism, particularly Aristotle's emphasis on the practical virtues of prudence and temperance. In *A Touchstone of Complexions*, a popular sixteenth-century Dutch guide to health first translated into

English in 1576, Levinus Lemnius (1505–68) advocates caring for the body, but also regards the care of the body as an important adjunct to care of the soul. In his introduction, Lemnius states the importance of self-awareness as the foundation for health and happiness, likening the body dominated by unruly passions and vices to a ship dashed upon the rocks by fierce winds. 'By the ignorance or not knowing of our own selves, and by negligence looking to the state of our own bodies and minds, we are thrown into sundry diseases and innumerable affections, and (like a ship full freight with wares in tempestuous and boisterous weather) carried and dashed upon the rocks of perturbation'.[4]

The metaphor of the body as a sea-swept vessel appears often in Renaissance writings on emotion. Shakespeare makes ready use of it in the opening scene of *Merchant* when Salerio and Solanio hypothesise about the causes of Antonio's melancholy. Salerio comments that Antonio's 'mind is tossing on the ocean' where his ships' fortunes are being determined (1.1.8). He dwells on the interconnectedness of the body and its environment. 'My wind cooling my broth / Would blow me to an ague when I thought / What harm a wind too great might do at sea' (1.1.22–4). In Salerio's view, the human body, Antonio's body, is exquisitely vulnerable to meteorological shifts, so vulnerable that the mere reminder of harsh weather prompts anxiety. What Salerio actually describes here, however, are his own anxieties about the kinds of risks that attend the merchant's life. Salerio figures those risks as overwhelming, threatening at every moment to capsize the literal and figurative vessel, and he imagines that this accounts for Antonio's bad mood. But Antonio rejects this account, and reveals no such anxiety about the risks of commercial venturing, even when he is faced much later with certain news about his ships' failure to come in. The ship-tossed-at-sea metaphor that Salerio uses to figure the moods of the unstable self is more accurately figured in Antonio's case as a willingness to venture risk in order to profit tidily. In other words, Antonio's venturing reflects his deliberate choices about what he is willing to risk; it does not suggest at a self that is fundamentally subject to destabilising external forces.

Lemnius's appeal to the passion-wracked body as a vessel tossed on turbulent seas expresses a similar concern with the effects of deliberation and choice. His discussion of the impassioned body not only describes the body's proneness to perturbations; it also proffers a set of instructions for positively impacting one's physiology and, ultimately, attaining a measure of equilibrium. And although *A Touchstone of Complexions* relies heavily on the language of humoral psychology and the microcosm–macrocosm analogy, it is through this discourse that Lemnius manages to articulate a vision of moral self-cultivation that is remarkably focused on human agency and practical choice.

Lemnius begins with an incentive to self-awareness. Throughout *Touchstone*, he is emphatic that self-awareness represents the basic starting-point that facilitates prudent decision-making and self-regulation. He insists that 'every man must search out his own inclination and nature'; such self-discovery leads to a form of knowledge that he regards as crucial to effective lifelong decision-making. Self-knowledge determines whether 'dancing, singing, womens flatteryes, allurements, and embracings' constitute dangerous incentives to vice or harmless diversions.[5] Conversely, lack of insight into the state of one's body and mind leads to the kinds of poor decisions that exacerbate humoral imbalances. *Touchstone* cites a roster of entertainments – a Renaissance version of 'sex, drugs and rock and roll', including dancing, singing and women's flatteries – posited as diversions that can potentially unbalance or rebalance a person's humoral equilibrium. Lemnius describes how this list of enticements operates very differently on different personality types:

> If a man throughe abundance of humours, and stoate of bloude and spirites, feel hymselfe prone to carnalitye and fleshiye luste, let him, by altering his order and diet, enjoyne to himselfe a most strict ordinary and frame his dealings to a more stayed moderation. But if hee feele himself to bee of a nature somewhat sulleyne and sterne, and given somewhat to a wayward, whining testye, churlish, and intractable spirit … it shall not be ill for such a one to frequent dancing, singing, womens flatteryes, allurements, and embracings, provided always, that all the same be not otherwise done nor meant, but in honestye and comeliness, within a reasonable measure.[6]

Each personality type – sanguine, melancholic, phlegmatic, choleric – corresponds to a particular set of fortifying actions in the face of sensual delights. Lusty hedonists enflame their underlying excesses by engaging in certain merry-making pursuits. Conversely, for withdrawn, depressive individuals, these same entertainments can be beneficial in moderation. Happiness and balance, in other words, are a function of knowing which choices suit an individual constitution. Also worth noting is that Lemnius's anecdote focuses on a highly charged moment of temptation: there is dancing, music, sensual pleasure – elements imagined then, as now, to evoke powerful responses more than capable of overriding practical judgement. Self-knowledge is essential to the exercise of practical judgement for Lemmius and essential for moderation, which, in true Aristotelian fashion, requires careful assessment of context in relation to individual subjects.

Self-awareness and self-knowledge for Lemnius and other Renaissance self-help writers entails a diligent care of the body in all of its subjective nuances. Many self-help discussions in the sixteenth and seventeenth centuries are explicitly framed in terms of human health, physiology and diet and exercise intended to rebalance the body's humours. As Michael Schoenfeldt has argued, the care of the body formed an important part of self-fashioning in the period, and the self at the centre of such practices was undoubtedly conceived, at least in part, as a physiologically constituted one.[7] But the self at the centre of these kinds of self-help practices was also a moral self, one whose complexional and humoral identity was importantly tied to moral identity, and subject to refashioning through human agency. Melancholia and sanguinity do not only refer to physiological humours in this period; they also correspond to a set of behaviours and dispositions inseparable from their moral aspects. In an important sense, physiological self-fashioning not only leads to a better, more balanced body; those kinds of adjustments are also strongly linked to the cultivation of a more virtuous disposition and philosophically refined character.

Like Lemnius's *A Touchstone of Complexions*, other writings on happiness, health and the moral life that circulated in early modern England went to great lengths to spell out how best to retain moral integrity in the face of contingent practical circumstances. In some of these works, readers are encouraged to find ways to adaptively translate moral ideals into the practical domain. Many accounts emphasise the need to remain self-present in moments that require practical decision-making. In Lemnius's example, self-presence constitutes a basic precondition for keeping moral ideals in play, even within circumstances where it no longer feels pleasurable or immediately desirable to be 'good'. His recipe for moderating humoral imbalances crucially relies upon an accurate self-assessment of whether an individual is lusty or melancholy and, even more crucially, relies on subjects' continued awareness of their own strengths and weaknesses during moments when they most tend to forget themselves – in other words, very practical, situated moments when individuals may not be able or willing to engage in lengthy deliberation about what is good for them. In *The First Part of Consideration of Humane Condition* (1600), James Perrott also emphasises self-knowledge, advocating self-awareness as the primary means of managing the body, mind and soul. Perrott (1571/2–1637) was a career politician who pursued a classical education at Oxford's Jesus College that was far richer in Aristotelian moral philosophy than Galenic physiology.[8] And yet despite his lack of medical training, Perrott adopts many of the same strategies of emotional self-management that scholars typically cite in discussions of Galenic materialism, directing them towards more explicitly philosophical ends. In his treatise, Perrott focuses on self-understanding and describes it as a basic precondition for the successful grasp of reality. 'The knowledge of thy selfe being the beginning of all true knowledge', he writes, 'and without this no knowledge or consideration can profit thee, be it of matters never so exquisite, or of mysteries never so high'. Perrott then goes on to describe self-knowledge as the epistemic foundation that conditions the human experience of the world.

> For as it doth concerne every man to learne what is done at home, before hee goe abroad: for doth it behove him to knowe himselfe, before he looke into others. It is true that many men seeme to knowe many things, and yet, not knowing themselves, they knowe nothing at all; or at least, they knowe nothing in that, which doth most availe them.[9]

Perrott's recommendations to embrace the domestic and eschew the foreign resonate with political implications; in earlier writings, he discourages scholars and soldiers from settling abroad lest they be ensnared in plots to invade England.[10] But these same comments also resonate philosophically. When Perrott makes reference to the human capacity for self-knowledge, he appeals to the Socratic *nosce te ipsum*, that most sententious of Renaissance moral-philosophical imperatives. Although sententious, the kind of knowledge that Perrott signals was, however, anything but schematic; the kind of self-knowledge that is useful requires practical deliberation about what course of action to pursue within particular, contingent circumstances. In this sense, the Renaissance *nosce te ipsum* is like many of the detailed, voluminous catalogues of circumstantial and complexional particulars from the sixteenth and seventeenth centuries that appear wholly schematic in focus, and yet still insist upon an important degree of self-reflection and selective application on the part of the reader. The kind of self-cultivation encouraged by self-help writings like Perrott's requires vigilant self-transparency, transparency that is imagined to be under continual threat by episodes of wilful self-deception in which individuals 'forget' just how harmful certain actions, in fact, are. The kind of awareness Perrott describes as self-knowing, the very kind 'which doth most availe' us, calls for a recognition of the detailed variations that characterise subjective human experience. Rather than a one-size-fits-all solution, these guides advocate a much more subject-centred approach to attaining health, happiness and fulfilment. They argue for a form of vision that is attuned to the nuances of the particular, the detailed and the subjective, which in turn forms part of the more comprehensive process through which the well-lived life is actualised and human agency is expressed.

Jacob's success and Shylock's way to thrive

Philosophical approaches to human happiness have important implications for the study of emotion in early modern culture. They can also help us better understand Shakespeare's fictional characters and those intentional and emotional states that fortify their words and actions. To be sure, paying attention to fictional characters' motivational states requires looking beyond humoral materialism to the broader philosophical questions that underwrite it, questions such as why and to what ends individuals sought to regiment themselves, and what moral ideals those interventions reflect. By considering emotional responses philosophically, as components of how individuals like Shylock behave as moral agents, their thoughts and actions begin to reflect something more than subjugation to environmentally determined bodies; they express deliberate, often flawed attempts to actualise moral flourishing in response to contingent practical circumstances.

Of course, considering Shakespeare's characters as moral agents requires that we admit that they are in some important sense decision-making agents and not just flat allegories, manifestations of symbolic abstractions, or empty ciphers through which social energies or authorial designs are expressed. Despite recent efforts to banish subjectivity from the critical vocabulary of early modern studies, many scholars still turn to questions of motivation when they discuss characters such as Hamlet and Iago, even scholars who have openly disavowed character criticism.[11] But what about for *The Merchant of Venice*'s Shylock? Within *Merchant* scholarship, Shylock is routinely treated as something other than a decision-making moral agent. Well before the current vogue for cultural materialism took root in Shakespeare studies, criticism dating back to the nineteenth century focused on *Merchant*'s theological implications, and reduced Shylock's character to an allegory for another kind of materialism: economic acquisitiveness and greed, which were thought to signal Shylock's profound spiritual depravity. Shakespeare's Jewish moneylender was often read via patristic theology, which cast Jews as depraved 'Letters' relative to Christian 'Spirit'. Antonio's passive acceptance of his fate and Portia's homily on mercy were assumed to correspond to the Christian 'Spirit' that transcended Shylock's spiritually depraved materialism. Shylock thereby became a symbol for moral-theological viciousness, a figure who prioritised his ducats over his daughter within the Christian allegory of the play.[12]

This view of Shylock's character and of the play did not fall as deeply out of fashion as we might imagine; in fact, it has enjoyed a lasting influence on *Merchant* criticism well into the late twentieth and early twenty-first century. Barbara Lewalski's seminal 1962 interpretation in 'Biblical Allusion and Allegory in *The Merchant of Venice*' picks up on many of its central tenets, arguing that Shylock and his Jewishness function as allegories for 'thrift' and 'niggardly prudence'.[13] It has informed discussions of Shylock as a stock comic character, sometimes imagined in his original performance with a hooknose and red wig; it has also influenced the widespread critical designation of Shylock as a usurer, another stock Elizabethan Jew. John Drakakis appeals to this view of Shylock to introduce and explain the play in the Arden 3 edition.[14]

But the Letter-versus-Spirit dichotomy has limited utility as an explanatory principle for the text of Shakespeare's play and the words uttered by its characters; in fact, its convenient schema reads past many of those utterances in favour of a reductive typology. Shylock is no mere foil for Christian ethics; he is a character whom *Merchant* emphatically designates as Jewish. Where Shylock's Jewishness has frequently been read through Antonio's anti-Semitic mindset, Shylock in fact does speak on his own behalf. He does so by citing Scripture, appealing to a set of stories that even Elizabethans recognised as foundational to both Christians and Jews, each of which interpreted them differently. In Act 1, scene 3 Shylock makes explicit and detailed reference to a story from the Hebrew Bible as he negotiates the loan with Antonio, discussing a biblical parable that features Jacob's unlikely successes breeding his uncle Laban's parti-coloured cattle. This scene is typically read and discussed – and glossed by the play's editors – as Shylock's attempt to justify usury.[15] It is important to point out that there is no specific mention of usury in this scene, or indeed anywhere in the play; in fact, the word 'usury' occurs only four times in Shakespeare's entire canon. The term 'usurer' is used once, and Shylock makes it clear that this is Antonio's word for describing Shylock's business practices: 'he [Antonio] was wont to call me usurer' (3.1.35–6). There is no suggestion that he agrees with Antonio's designation. More commonly, *The Merchant of Venice* makes reference to 'usance' – a term mentioned by Shylock for the rate of interest at 1.3.35, and on another occasion in relation to the act of borrowing at 1.3.132. The question of usury in the play only accounts for Shylock's motivations and behaviour in this scene if we accept at face value Antonio's ugly designation of him as a 'devil' who 'can cite Scripture for his purpose' (1.3.89).

The longstanding attribution of usurious motives to Shylock in this scene, even by exemplary recent critical editions of the play, is itself an odd move. 'Just usury' is an oxymoronic concept; either a lending practice is usurious or it isn't, and if it is usury then there is no justifying it morally. Shylock makes clear in Act 3, scene 1 that *he* does not accept Antonio's designation of him as a 'usurer'. What Shylock also makes clear is that he cites the biblical parable in order to explicate his intentions in relation to the loan as well as his approach to generating material wealth. He aligns his vision with Jacob's success at breeding cattle, success that, in his words, constitutes a 'way to thrive'. 'Mark what Jacob did', Shylock proclaims:

When Laban and himself were compromised
That all the eanlings which were streaked and pied
Should fall as Jacob's hire, the ewes, being rank
In the end of autumn turnéd to the rams,
And when the work of generation was
Between these woolly breeders in the act,
The skillful shepherd peeled me certain wands,
And in the doing of the deed of kind
He stuck them up before the fulsome ewes,
Who then conceiving did in eaning time
Fall parti-coloured lambs, and those were Jacob's.
This was a way to thrive, and he was blest;
And thrift is blessing, if men steal it not.

(1.3.69–81)

In citing scriptural precedent, Shylock articulates more than just a series of economic practices; he offers an account of his moral agency as a character, agency that is importantly sourced – and prefigured – in the biblical Jacob. Much like Lemnius's self-help manual on the passions and complexions that functions as a kind of do-it-yourself guide to happiness, requiring the intelligent, discriminating and judicious selection of appropriate complexional types and behaviours from an authoritative register, the Genesis Jacob cycle of stories functions as a digest of authoritative narratives, characters and moral scenarios from which Shylock selects what he imagines is the most relevant model for his present circumstances. For Shylock, Jacob represents an ethical model to be emulated. Moreover, his citation of biblical example appeals to a profoundly eudaimonistic aim: in no uncertain terms for Shylock, 'This was a way to thrive' (1.3.80).

Biblical narratives such as the one cited by Shylock have long represented sites of ethical deliberation, spiritual guidance and normative standards for a range of daily practices, including commercial ones relating to moneylending for both Christians and Jews.[16] The biblical passage that Shylock references, centred on the tale of Laban and Jacob breeding and dividing their respective flocks of cattle, offers important clues into the ethical considerations that inform his choices. Shylock's interpretative gloss on Jacob's story helps delineate the space of moral questions he confronts as he progresses through the play, because he interprets those questions through Jacob's experiences in Genesis 30.[17] It is through the language of scriptural citation that Shylock offers an account of his moral decision-making, including the ethos that underwrites his practice of lending at interest.

Antonio's response to Shylock's citation is equally revealing of his own moral landscape. In Act 1, scene 3 of *The Merchant of Venice*, which features the only scene of exegetical debate in Shakespeare's entire dramatic canon, Shakespeare foregrounds the distinctive ways that Antonio and Shylock – a Christian and a Jew – view a singular authoritative story. As Shylock lapses into his account of Jacob breeding cattle for his uncle Laban in 1.3, Antonio initially appears nonplussed by Shylock's digression and fails to see its relevance to the matter of whether Shylock will, in fact, agree to loan him three thousand ducats. 'And what of him [i.e. Jacob]? Did he take interest?' he asks (1.3.66). This mild curiosity is followed by their exegetical dispute about the meaning of these verses. Antonio claims that, 'This [i.e. Jacob's success at breeding cattle] was a venture, sir, that Jacob served for, / A thing not in his power to bring to pass, / But swayed and fashioned by the hand of heaven' (1.3.82–4). In Antonio's mind, the biblical passage suggests that Jacob's success at multiplying cattle owes everything to divine intercession.

In fact, Antonio's comments share important parallels with early modern Christian exegesis of Genesis 30, which worries over the question of Jacob's moral agency in this story. Although not all of the commentaries are as explicit as Antonio that 'this was a venture Jacob served for, a thing not in his power to bring to pass', the debate about who exactly was responsible for the multiplication of speckled cattle remains a consistent point of discussion for Renaissance Christian commentators. For these exegetes, the moral status of Jacob's actions in the cycle as a whole is problematic, and stands in need of substantial and often lengthy justification. The Christian commentaries are full of what Arnold Williams refers to as 'hair-splitting distinctions' that attempt to excuse Jacob of the various sins he commits: lying, dishonouring his father, tricking his brother.[18] 'The means which Jacob used, was not artificial or fraudulent, but natural, not depending on man's skill, but God's blessing', writes Andrew Willett (1561/2–1621) in his 1608 *Hexapla in*

Genesin. 'Although then that nature had her work, we cannot say that nature wholly did it', he adds.[19]

Commentators place a great deal of emphasis on divine intercession as the most and perhaps only satisfying way of absolving Jacob of these moral offences. Willett's 1633 edition of *Hexapla in Genesin Exodum* devotes a whole subheading in *The Explanation and Solution of Doubtful Questions and Places* to the question of '[w]hether Jacobs device were by miracle or by the workes of nature'.[20] In the same spirit, Henry Ainsworth (1569–1622), in his 1616 edition of *Annotations upon the First Book of Moses*, writes that 'naturally the cattel would bring forth others like themselves, and so Jacobs part should be few. But by Gods extraordinary providence, it fell out otherwise.'[21] Christian commentators worry tremendously over the problem of moral responsibility in these verses. Did God make Jacob commit these actions, or did he perform them of his own volition? And if he performed them of his own volition, how can we regard him as a moral exemplar? Throughout the commentaries, divine agency is emphasised far more than Jacob's own role in making the speckled and spotted cattle breed successfully. Jacob's success is a morally virtuous one only in so far as it is orchestrated by divine will; where it appears to reflect Jacob's natural abilities, the story instead inspires anxiety.

That same anxiety is reflected in a number of cultural scripts that accompany this story in Renaissance England, which align it with the imagination and its power to reshape material forms. In *The Secret Miracles of Nature* (1559 in Latin, 1658 in English), Levinus Lemnius cites this parable as an example of the mind's ability to affect matter in mysteriously powerful, sometimes unwitting ways.

> [W]hilest the Man and Woman Embrace, if the woman think of the mans countenance, and look upon him, or thinks of any one else, that likenesse will the child represent ... *Jacob* used that stratagem, who was afterwards called *Israel*, laying rods he had pilled off the rinds from, before them every where, and so he made the greatest part of the flock spotted and party-coloured.[22]

This same formulation is repeated in Thomas Wright's (*c.*1561–1623) *The Passions of the Minde* (1604) when he discusses the power of women's imaginations to alter the appearance of unborn offspring.

> Galen also reporteth, that a woman beholding a most beautiful picture, conceived and brought forth a beautiful child by a most deformed father, we have also in the Scriptures the like experience in Jacob, who to cause his ewes conceive speckled lambs, put sundry white rods in the channels where the beasts were watered, and thereby the lambs were yeaned party-colored.[23]

Although anxiety about women's unique ability to influence material forms through everyday actions aligns these uses of the parable with many Christian theologians' concern over what Jacob does, these uses of the Jacob story also reflect a concern with human agency. Both Wright's and Lemnius's discussion of the parable focus on how ordinary, natural human capacities – looking and imagining – can affect the appearance of material forms.

Several rabbinical commentaries on Genesis 30 rehearse this same Galenic theory of reproductive mutation; however, among rabbinical writers there is a far more positive evaluation of the lambs' natural workings. The medieval Torah commentator Shlomo Yitzchaki (Rashi) (1040–1105) remarks,

> many are amazed at what is reported in our verse, and say that it can only be described as an out of the ordinary phenomenon. Really, what Scripture describes is indeed one of the wonders of nature. However, it is a natural law. Even a woman who is created in the image of the angels affects her fetus by what she looks at while she is pregnant.[24]

The manipulation of a fetus may be a 'wonder of nature' to many, but to Rashi it actually looks more like a 'natural law'. His comment reflects the broader tendency within rabbinical commentary to emphasise the natural aspects of seemingly 'wonderful' occurrences. This is particularly the case for the episodes surrounding Jacob's multiplication of speckled cattle, where there is a concerted focus on the skill involved both in the production of the cattle and in Jacob's ability to broker the initial arrangement with his uncle. To this same end, the thirteenth-century Catalonian commentator Nahmanides (1194–1270) writes of Jacob's use of the peeled rods:

> As soon as they [Laban and Jacob] agreed that his hire would be these colors it was permissible for Jacob to do whatever he could to cause them to give birth in this manner. Perhaps Jacob had made a condition that he may do with them whatever he wants since Laban did not know of the ramifications of this measure, nor did Laban's shepherds sense anything when they saw the sticks in the gutters once a year during the days of Nisan.[25]

Nahmanides concludes that Jacob's stratagem was permissible because it abided by the rules governing their arrangement, rules to which both parties had agreed in advance. But the real reason Jacob succeeds in Nahmanides's view is that he was smarter than Laban and his sons. He found a way around the obvious constraints, and saw options that neither Laban nor his sons were able to anticipate, despite Laban's mystical divinations. The real substance of Jacob's success consists of his intelligent resolution of a practical problem, just as the moral substance of the episode consists of a skill-based resolution to a complex problem, rather than a passive submission to supernatural force.

Many rabbinical commentaries on these verses display a marked interest in the dynamics of what Jacob manages to accomplish by virtue of his own ingenuity. Going into great detail, they elaborate on the skilful interventions that make Laban's sheep breed more slowly and less abundantly than his own; they discuss the correct work ethic for situations in which an employee must tend to his employer's as well as his own flocks; and they venture opinions about the precise terms of Jacob and Laban's initial agreement. One commentator explains, '[w]e may learn from Jacob that an employee who works faithfully receives his reward in this world in addition to the portion stored up for him in the World to Come'.[26] Indeed, the emphasis in many of the Hebrew commentaries that discuss Jacob's feat is on effort, work and worldly progress. Conversely, Antonio insists that Jacob's success is praiseworthy solely because it reflects divine providence; the success is God's, not Jacob's. By implication, since Shylock has misread the meaning of the Scriptural passage, he claims undue credit for what amounts to a miraculous feat. Shylock's success at breeding money is like Jacob's stripped of any vestiges of virtue.

Many scholars have tacitly accepted Antonio's designation of Shylock as an illegitimate appropriator of Scripture and a usurer. But Shylock's view of Genesis 30 differs significantly from Antonio's appeal, and his account of it outlines a much more complex response than Antonio gives him credit for. Shylock emphasises lineage and generational entitlements – 'This Jacob from our holy Abram was, / As his wise mother wrought in his behalf, / The third possessor; ay, he was the third'(1.3.63–5). He emphasises human intervention in the form of hard work. The word 'wrought' is especially significant as the present tense of 'work' – a term that implies the application of human ingenuity and endeavour as is the case with metalworking, where metal is moulded into a desired form such as wrought iron.[27] In Jacob's case, his fate is carefully and masterfully worked into shape thanks to the ingenuity and substantial efforts of his mother Rebecca, who succeeds in positioning her youngest-born son in line for the firstborn's blessing. Throughout the Genesis cycle of stories, Jacob manages to succeed in his endeavours largely thanks to his clever innovations upon what look like firmly established rules and conventions. He manages to get around the natural fact of his own late-born status and claim the rights of his elder brother, Esau. In the case of the blessing, Isaac's affective preference for Esau is the non-negotiable principle, and yet Jacob manages to circumvent that, too.

Jacob functions as more than just a casual reference for Shylock or a means to justify what looks like moneylending for interest. In an important sense, Jacob's story represents a site for moral-philosophical deliberation that is both practical and eudaimonistic for Shylock. In that regard, Shylock's strategy is not all that unlike the strategies outlined in Renaissance self-help manuals, in which mimetic repetition is married with the creative and intelligent selection of appropriate models to follow. Shylock's is, ultimately, a self-servicing use of biblical examples; he uses biblical models judiciously by selecting a role model appropriate to his own circumstances and characterological strengths. It is that process of responding to practical, present-day circumstances in view of a comprehensive vision of success that makes Shylock's use of biblical citation in the play both philosophical and characteristically eudaimonistic, even where it prefers the language of theology over that of moral philosophy, or the humoral discourse deployed by Lemnius. The debate over the significance of these biblical stories in *Merchant* in no uncertain terms features competing ideas of the good life, ideas that Shakespeare encodes in the language of Scripture, but which remain deeply philosophical in their attention to 'thrift'. Underwriting Shylock's appeal to the biblical Jacob is a comprehensive notion of what it means to thrive.

Shylock appeals to 'thrift' on two separate occasions over the course of his loan negotiations in 1.3. In the first instance, he describes an unpleasant past encounter with Antonio. 'He [Antonio] hates our sacred nation, and he rails, / Even there where merchants most do congregate, / On me, my bargains, and my well-won thrift' (1.3.38–40). The second usage occurs in his conclusive summary of Jacob's success: 'This was a way to thrive, and he was blest; / And thrift is blessing, if men steal it not' (1.3.80–1). Although both usages can and often are read in the distinctly unflattering modern sense as penny-pinching, in both cases Shylock appeals more directly to the older sense of thrift as thriving. In the second instance, 'thrift' follows immediately after 'thrive'. The sense of thrift-as-thriving here is especially appropriate to Shylock's understanding of the biblical passage's meaning, which has nothing whatsoever to do with being frugal. For Shylock, the 'way to thrive' is importantly bound up with the strategies of Jacob, whom he views as a moral exemplar.

In the Genesis Jacob cycle, Jacob's divine entitlement and his wealth are made possible because of his labour; the two elements are, in an important sense, coterminous, and form part of his essential disposition, reinforced and reaffirmed by a habitual practice. His behaviour in a number of key instances in the Jacob cycle, such as the procurement of his brother's birthright and the stealing of his father's blessing, speaks to his ability not only to survive but also achieve enviable levels of prosperity through cunning, perseverance and the ability to anticipate future consequences. These very abilities also appear to play a role in Shylock's business practices in *The Merchant of Venice*. Shylock certainly aspires to Jacob's cunning, success and thrift. These assets, and thrift in particular, have been regarded somewhat unkindly within the critical tradition, bound up with the suspicion of Shylock's usurious business practices and his supposed ill intentions toward Antonio in this and other pivotal scenes of the play. The story Shylock references deals much more explicitly with questions of thrift in the older, classical sense – that is to say, questions of human flourishing rather than penny-pinching. The kind of thrift Shylock admires in Jacob, which he picks up on in the story of Laban and the cattle, considers the material basis for thrift as an adjunct to a much more comprehensive notion: eudaimonistic flourishing, or concern for the life that is well-lived.

Reading Shylock's passion

Act 1, scene 3 is one of several scenes from *The Merchant of Venice* to dramatise how cultural scripts from the past can inform interpretative choices in the here-and-now. There is also Portia's predicament with her suitors, where her choice of partner is constrained by a love-test decreed by her dead father, and Jessica's frustration about her identity which has been determined by her Jewish 'blood' rather than her more Christian-seeming 'manners'. This network of plots hardly illustrates the ideal that Aristotle likely had in mind when he wrote of philosophical self-determination, but neither does it necessarily imply the kind of hardened determinism that denies these characters any agency at all. Rather, it illustrates the moral realism that characterises Shakespeare's dramatic universe, in which individuals are always situated within contingent practical circumstances that imply certain limitations. The challenge for so many of Shakespeare's characters consists of acting with a more concerted awareness of those boundaries, while attempting to actualise subjectively held desires and plans.

Self-awareness in Shylock's case appears to entail an awareness of those events that precede his individual lifespan, reaching back to a national history that predates his personal lived experience. His is, ultimately, a genealogical claim to certain privileges and strategies for success that he aligns with Jacob. It is a claim heavily determined by the kind of religious identity that the play foregrounds, one that outlines a virtue ethics that reads as distinctively

Judaic. Shylock's systematic application of details from the Genesis story on to his present circumstances is very much in keeping with Jewish-midrashic hermeneutics, which seek to 'coordinate the narrative and the prescriptive dimensions of Torah' by applying those stories to the exigencies of daily life, as Julia Reinhard Lupton has argued.[28] For Shylock, the Genesis episode establishes a set of fixed parameters for his present-day negotiations with Antonio. In so far as they are biblical, those fixed parameters importantly predate him.

If Shylock's wealth functions like Jacob's, as an adjunct to both his determined efforts to thrive and his preordained status as a member of God's elect, then the loss of that wealth represents a moment of extreme characterological disorientation and crisis. In fact, this is what happens when Jessica absconds with his money and jewels. Shylock, for whom money signals Jacob-like prosperity and dynastic success, hears of Jessica trading his turquoise ring for a monkey. She treats that same wealth as an expendable resource and a diversion. When Shylock finally speaks of her betrayal, his explanation suggests that the ring's value was complex and profound, material and sentimental. 'It was my turquoise; I had it of Leah when I was a bachelor. I would not have given it for a wilderness of monkeys' (3.1.90–2). The mention of a ring belonging to 'Leah' reinforces that this is not only Shylock's personal story but Jacob's too, bound up with the ethical and emotional rhythms of that narrative. Although Leah is the older, less desirable of Laban's daughters – Jacob is tricked into marrying her, and works an additional seven years for the chance to marry Rachel – Leah is the one who offers Jacob the occasion for an extended stay in Haran, resulting in a materially and dynastically fruitful sojourn. By the time we encounter him at Genesis 30, Jacob is equipped with all the glittering signs of that success, including a retinue of camels, goats and sheep, manservants and maidservants, wives and children, and God's blessing. It is the kind of wealth that does not go unnoticed; Laban even considers that he has gained advantage through his proximity to Jacob. 'I have learned by experience that the Lord hath blessed me for thy sake' are Laban's words at verse 27. Antonio has no such words for Shylock or anything resembling praise for the financial and social opportunities that his loan promises to generate.

Jacob's story provides a window into the severity of Shylock's losses in the play, losses that may well represent an important tipping point for him. Soon after, he becomes consumed with vengeful passion, turning his sights on the murder of Antonio and declaring, 'I will have the heart of him if he forfeit' (3.1.95). Shylock's rage is admittedly not a sympathetic turn for his character. But it is a motivated turn. The biblical intertext offers a way to understand it as a feature of Shylock's moral vision, as part of how he sees and responds to the world and his place within it. But it is a small, easily overlooked window, and Shakespeare's play poses important challenges to an audience's ability to consider Shylock as a character endowed with complex emotions. One of a series of such challenges occurs in Act 2, when Solanio recounts Shylock's response to the loss of his daughter and money.

> I never heard a passion so confused,
> So strange, outrageous, and so variable
> As the dog Jew did utter in the streets:
> 'My daughter! O, my ducats! O, my daughter!
> Fled with a Christian! O, my Christian ducats!
> Justice! The law! My ducats and my daughter!'
>
> (2.8.12–17)

Solanio's report dwells on the interchangeability of ducats and daughters, implying that for Shylock the real loss is financial, not familial. His is a deliberately slanderous send-up of Shylock that reads as comedic because, in his version, the greedy man has got his comeuppance. The Jew's 'passion' here is treated as part of a broader cultural stereotyping of Jews; Shylock's emotion is not an expression of a sensitive, complex man's moral architecture, but rather merely a stock comic script that the Jew acts out in public, and which Solanio rehearses here for a laugh. This description of Shylock's demeanour as 'strange', 'outrageous' and 'variable' is deliberately dehumanising. His passion is not presented as a measured response to grief, nor is it tragic or noble; it is the experience of a man turned into passion's slave and driven to extremes, a mere caricature of a man. In that sense, it is not unlike Salerio's and Solanio's initial characterisation of the melancholy individual as a ship tossed about on rough seas – a creature wholly subject to the whims of forces beyond his control. Perhaps these two cannot help but conceive of the nuances of their friend's suffering, or any human suffering at all, except through such crude formulations. But Antonio refuses to characterise himself thusly at the beginning of the play, and we should refuse to typecast Shylock in these terms, too. After all, he has not always been such a man; he has been reduced to one over the course of the play, at the hands of particular characters. At the play's end, he is reduced even more, stripped of what remains of his wealth and compelled to live out his days as a New Christian. By attending to the subjective forces that shape and direct Shylock's responses and those intentional and emotional cues that condition his behaviour, we as audiences and critics have the power to refuse to reduce him further.

Notes

1 William Shakespeare, *The Merchant of Venice: Texts and Contexts*, ed. M. Lindsay Kaplan (Boston: Bedford/St Martin's, 2002), 1.1.1–7. Further citations to the play will appear in text.

2 Gail Kern Paster, *The Body Embarrassed: Drama and the Disciplines of Shame in Early Modern England* (Ithaca: Cornell University Press, 1993); Gail Kern Paster, Katharine Rowe and Mary Floyd-Wilson (eds), *Reading the Early Modern Passions: Essays in the Cultural History of Emotion* (Philadelphia: University of Pennsylvania Press, 2004); Mary Floyd-Wilson and Garrett A. Sullivan, Jr (eds), *Environment and Embodiment in Early Modern England* (New York: Palgrave Macmillan, 2007).

3 Gail Kern Paster, *Humoring the Body: Emotions and the Shakespearean Stage* (Chicago: University of Chicago Press, 2004), pp. 1–24.

4 Levinus Lemnius, *A Touchstone of Complexions*, trans. Thomas Newton (London, 1576), p. 3.

5 Ibid., p. 6.

6 Ibid.

7 Michael C. Schoenfeldt, *Bodies and Selves in Early Modern England: Physiology and Inwardness in Spenser, Shakespeare, Herbert, and Milton* (Cambridge: Cambridge University Press, 1999).

8 Andrew Thrush, 'Perrot, Sir James', *Oxford Dictionary of National Biography* (Oxford University Press, 2004).

9 James Perrott, *The First Part of Consideration of Humane Condition* (Oxford, 1600), p. 9.

10 James Perrott, *Discovery of Discontented Minds* (Oxford, 1596).

11 Margreta de Grazia's *'Hamlet' without Hamlet* (Cambridge: Cambridge University Press, 2007) is an excellent example of a work that has continued to press the issue of characterological motivation, despite being formally opposed to the notion of character and its centrality within Shakespeare criticism.

12 For this perspective on the play and Shylock's character, see Karl Elze, *Essays on Shakespeare* (London: Macmillan, 1874), p. 73; William W. Lloyd, *Critical Essays on Plays of Shakespeare* (London: George Bell, 1875), p. 103; Richmond Noble, *Shakespeare's Biblical Knowledge and Use of the Book of Common Prayer* (New York: Octagon Books, 1970), p. 270; Elmer Edgar Stoll, *Shakespeare Studies: Historical and Comparative in Method* (New York: Macmillan, 1927), p. 323, and *From Shakespeare to Joyce: Authors and Critics; Literature and Life* (Garden City: Doubleday, 1946), p. 123; Harold R. Walley, *Essays in Dramatic Literature: The Parrott Presentation Volume* (Princeton: Princeton University Press, 1935), p. 237; Cary B. Graham, 'Standards of Value in *The Merchant of Venice*',

Shakespeare Quarterly, 4 (1953), 145–51; and Leah Woods Wilkins, 'Shylock's Pound of Flesh and Laban's Sheep', *Modern Language Notes*, 62 (1947), 28–30.

13 Barbara K. Lewalski, 'Biblical Allusion and Allegory in *The Merchant of Venice*', *Shakespeare Quarterly*, 13 (1962), 327–43 (p. 330). I cite her essay here because it is still so frequently cited as recommended reading in modern editions of the play, including Kaplan's *Texts and Contexts* edition.

14 Drakakis discusses usury as the play's major theme in his introduction to the Arden 3 edition. In his view, Shylock's characteristic speech patterns and tendency towards repetition 'require to be read symptomatically as evidence of the propensity to a devilish duplicity that owes its scriptural origin to St Matthew's gospel'. John Drakakis (ed.), *The Merchant of Venice* (London: Bloomsbury, 2010), p. 45.

15 See John Russell Brown's Arden 2 edition of the play as a good example of a reputable scholarly edition that glosses the episode this way, as well as Lindsey Kaplan's *Texts and Contexts* edition and Drakakis's more recent Arden 3 edition.

16 See Aaron Kitch, 'Shylock's Sacred Nation', *Shakespeare Quarterly*, 59 (2008), 131–55, for an extensive discussion of this point in a Renaissance context. Arnold Williams also discusses this issue with reference to the Renaissance understanding and use of the Book of Genesis, which was widely regarded as a sourcebook for practical guidance about agriculture, farming and other practical trades. Arnold Williams, *The Common Expositor: An Account of the Commentaries on Genesis, 1527-1633* (Chapel Hill: University of North Carolina Press, 1948), esp. the introduction.

17 I rely here on Charles Taylor's very useful discussion of identity as an orientation in a space of moral questions in *Sources of the Self: The Making of the Modern Identity* (Cambridge, MA: Harvard University Press, 1992).

18 Williams, *Common Expositor*, p. 169.

19 Andrew Willet, *Hexapla in Genesin* (London, 1608), pp. 320–1.

20 Andrew Willet, *Hexapla in Genesin and Exodum* (London, 1633), p. 275.

21 Henry Ainsworth, *Annotations upon the First Book of Moses, Called Genesis* ([Amsterdam], 1616), Genesis 30:32.

22 Levinas Lemnius, *The Secret Miracles of Nature* (London, 1658), p. 11.

23 Thomas Wright, *The Passions of the Minde in General*, in William Webster Newbold (ed.), *Renaissance Imagination*, vol. 15 (New York: Garland Publishing, 1986), p. 140.

24 *Rashi: Commentaries on the Pentateuch*, trans. Chaim Pearl (New York: W. W. Norton, 1970), p. 295.

25 *Ramban (Nachmanides) Commentary on the Torah: Genesis*, trans. Charles Chavel (New York: Shilo Publishing, 1971), pp. 376–7.

26 Cited in Menahem Kasher, *Encyclopedia of Biblical Interpretation: A Millennial Anthology*, trans. and ed. Harry Freedman, 9 vols (New York: American Biblical Encyclopedia Society, 1953), vol. 4, p. 112.

27 Michael Bristol first made this point during our collaborative presentation for the Shakespeare and Performance Research Team at McGill University in March of 2009 entitled 'Is Shylock Jewish?'

28 Julia Reinhard Lupton, 'Exegesis, Mimesis, and the Future of Humanism in *The Merchant of Venice*', *Religion and Literature*, 42 (2002), 123–39 (p. 125). On this point, Lupton also cites Jacob Neusner, *A Midrash Reader* (Minneapolis: Fortress, 1990), p. 76.

4

Robert Burton, perfect happiness and the *visio dei*

Mary Ann Lund

> A pound of sorrow is familiarly mixt with a dram of content, little or no joy, little comfort, but every where danger, contention, anxiety, in all places; goe where thou wilt, and thou shalt finde discontents, cares, woes, complaints, sicknesse, diseases, encumbrances, exclamations ...
>
> (*The Anatomy of Melancholy* (1621), vol. 1, p. 272)[1]

Happiness is in short supply in *The Anatomy of Melancholy*. At the beginning of the main body of his book, Robert Burton (1577–1640) reminds us that, before the Fall, humankind was 'pure, divine, perfect, happy' (vol. 1, p. 121). All this was lost with the advent of sin. A state of permanent discontent took its place, which, in the broadest sense of the word, is what constitutes melancholy:

> from these Melancholy Dispositions, no man living is free, no *Stoicke*, none so wise, none so happy, none so generous, so godly, so divine, that can vindicate himselfe, so well composed, but more or lesse some time or other, he feeles the smart of it. Melancholy in this sence is the Character of Mortalitie. (vol. 1, p. 136)

Although Burton claims to restrict himself to writing about melancholy in 'habit' ('a Chronicke or continuate disease') rather than 'disposition' ('that transitory *Melancholy*, which goes & comes upon every small occasion of sorrow', vol. 1, p. 136), the universal latter condition is as much his preoccupation as the former. The *Anatomy* is structured as a long satirical preface followed by three 'Partitions', and for much of the first Partition (on causes, symptoms and prognostics of melancholy) we hear the same emphatic lament: 'for an inch of mirth an ell of mone, as Ivy doth an oke these miseries encompasse our life. And 'tis most absurd and ridiculous, for any mortall man to looke for a perpetuall tenor of happinesse in this life' (vol. 1, p. 137).

In the second Partition (on cures), however, there is a new note of hope. Although permanent happiness might be out of reach on earth, a degree of contentment may be possible. Classical moral philosophy, particularly Stoicism, underlies a consolation against melancholy which looks to the mind, not to external circumstances, for emotional tranquillity. Whether a person is rich or poor, healthy or ill, young or old, he or she may be able to escape worldly troubles, since 'all things then being rightly examined and duly considered as they ought, there is no such cause of so generall discontent, 'tis not in the matter it selfe, but in our minde, as we moderate our passions and esteeme of things' (vol. 2, p. 170). Despite this, the ability of the mind to exercise control over the passions through reason is often questioned by Burton, for whom melancholy as 'the Character of Mortalitie' is a disease which corrupts the imagination and affects one's rational powers. The distinction between 'matter' and 'minde' is not as clear-cut as the quotation implies, a complexity that the chapters in this volume seek to address.[2] In the 'Consolatory Digression', Burton aims to persuade the reader towards an ideal state of mental balance. In doing so, he is less in line with the Stoic belief in *apatheia* or the complete riddance of passions than with Aristotle's ideal of *metriopatheia* or moderate passions.[3] While Burton's approach to earthly happiness bears a strong debt to classical ethics, it also draws on the tradition of medieval medical regimens, which promote the health-giving properties of moderate *laetitia*, or cheerfulness. Yet the *Anatomy* is caught in a tension between scepticism and hopefulness about how far real peace of mind is sustainable: 'if there bee true happinesse amongst us, 'tis but for a time' (vol. 1, p. 275).[4]

Alongside this imperfect, unstable, flawed happiness, the *Anatomy* also provides an alternative vision of happiness, the opposite of troubled earthly contentment since it is unmoderated, complete, perfect: the *summum bonum* of human wishes. It is this happiness which forms the subject of this chapter.[5] In a brief and dazzling interlude at the beginning of his section on 'Religious Melancholy' (in the third Partition), Burton considers the joy of divine fruition as experienced through the contemplation of God's beauty. The sight of God (*visio dei*), experienced fully in heaven but available in glimpses to a rare few on earth, is the state of true happiness. In reaching this conclusion, Burton stands in the long shadow of St Augustine, but he also marshals in support Neoplatonic and contemporary Catholic authorities. As I will argue, Burton's meditation on *visio dei*, and particularly on divine beauty, adds a dimension to his text, tonally distinct and contemplative in its outlook, which has largely been overlooked by critics. Appearing at the beginning of 'Religious Melancholy', it performs an important rhetorical function in balancing the satirical material later in this section. His treatment of his subject matter points to a preoccupation which is concerned not solely with an intellectual understanding of God but with emotional activity, as he stresses a principally affective route towards union with God. The contemplation of God can be experienced within the embodied self, and Burton's treatment follows an Augustinian path from creature to creator, but, in its highest sense, it involves a taking leave of the body. The 'Beauty of God' subsection thus presents a different approach to emotion from the physiologically based models which have been privileged in recent studies of early modern emotion.[6] Much of Burton's exploration of the emotions elsewhere in the *Anatomy* is linked to the humoral disruption of melancholic disease; indeed, he cautions that both anxieties about abandonment by God and claims to divine inspiration may be the result of bodily disorder (vol. 1, p. 418; vol. 3, pp. 360–1). The satirical thrust of 'Religious Melancholy' – that superstition and zealotry are a form of illness – finds particular pointedness in the link between the humours and the authenticity, or otherwise, of emotional experiences. In the later decades of the seventeenth century, this connection would lead to the critique of non-conformist religious experience as enthusiasm.[7] None the less, Burton's solidly Galenic framework is not an all-encompassing one, as his treatment of Platonic and Augustinian ideas in this section reveals. Here, his approach moves beyond humoralist explanations of emotion, drawing instead on philosophical and theological theories about a happiness achieved, as St Paul said, 'whether in the body, I cannot tell, or whether out of the body, I cannot tell' (2 Corinthians 12:2).[8]

'This lustre of his divine majesty'

In order to understand Burton's interest in the beauty of God more fully, one must first observe how the subsection fits into the *Anatomy* as a whole, and how its argument develops. He opens his long final section on 'Religious Melancholy' by noting that he has 'no patterne to followe as in some of the rest, no man to imitate' (vol. 3, p. 330), since most other writers treat it as a symptom or cause, but few as a separate species of melancholy. It stands in parallel to the preceding sections on love (or 'heroic') melancholy, following the twofold division of earthly and heavenly loves, in Neoplatonic terms the two Venuses.[9] The division is found in Renaissance Neoplatonic authors such as Leone Ebreo (*c.*1465–1535) and Marsilio Ficino (1433–99) (cited vol. 3, pp. 11–12), but also further back in the Platonic-infused theology of Augustine, in whose *City of God* Jerusalem and Babylon represent love of God and love of the world (vol. 3, p. 12). Augustinian and Neoplatonic thinking will become important for Burton's treatment of divine beauty.

Burton states at the beginning of 'Religious Melancholy' that he will examine how it arises, causing superstition, heresy, enthusiasm and error, but first 'I must say something necessarily of the object of this love, God himselfe, what this love is, how it allureth, whence it proceeds, and (which is the cause of all our miseries) how we mistake, wander and swarve from it' (vol. 3, p. 332). If this rhetorical *divisio* suggests a rather drily analytical approach, what follows is anything but that. God's beauty is identified as one of his essential attributes (with Plato as authority for this view), and Burton weaves together Bible verses, patristic and modern commentaries, and his own words to create a prose hymn of heavenly beauty. He begins with Psalm 27:4 – '*One thing, saith* David, *have I desired of the Lord, and that will I still desire, to behold the beauty of the Lord*' – which acts as his text for the occasion. God's creation is beautiful:

> If ordinary beauty have such a prerogative and power, and what is amiable and faire, to draw the eyes and eares, hearts and affections of all spectators unto it, to move, win, intice, allure, how shall this divine forme ravish our soules, which is the fountaine and quintescence of all beauty? (vol. 3, p. 332)

As this example shows, Burton's typically copious language becomes increasingly impassioned: the balanced pairs of nouns and adjectives ('prerogative and power', 'amiable and faire') which begin this sentence yield to breathless asyndeton with his synonymous verbs ('move, win, intice, allure'), each more sensual than the last, leading towards the climax of 'ravish'.[10] The verbs emphasise that the contemplation of God's beauty is not an activity to be mediated through the intellective faculty alone but a profoundly emotional one, rooted in the affections.[11] His words on the 'prerogative and power' of ordinary beauty remind us of the countless tales of lovers falling under the spell of beautiful women and men earlier in the Partition; Burton argues there that 'the most familiar and usuall cause of Love, is that which comes by sight, which convayes those admirable rayes of Beauty and pleasing graces to the heart' (vol. 3, p. 66). The parallels between earthly and heavenly loves are extended as Burton cites Augustine's description of the Bible as a '*love letter*' (vol. 3, p. 333), and quotes extensively from that key scriptural text of erotic and holy desire, the Song of Songs. God's beauty, he continues, is beyond the powers of human description, stronger than the sun (an image used of human beauty in vol. 3, p. 88). 'In this life we have but a glimpse of this beauty and happinesse' (vol. 3, p. 334), but in the life to come we shall have 'a full fruition of it'.

The barrier to loving God, and by extension to this fruition, is the corrupt will: 'the world, & that infinite variety of pleasing objects in it, doe so allure & enamor us that we cannot so much as looke towards God' (vol. 3, p. 334), he warns, gathering several Augustinian references in support. Burton's discourse then takes a more mystical turn. '*It is the eye of contemplation by which we must behold it, the wing of meditation which lifts us up*' (vol. 3, p. 335), he says, quoting Gregory the Great via Bonaventura, and he proceeds to cite Philo Judaeus, Ficino and Plotinus: 'If we desire to see him, we must lay aside all vaine objects, which detaine us and dazell our eyes, and as *Ficino* adviseth us, get us solar *eyes … to see this divine beauty*' (vol. 3, pp. 335–6). Another important authority here and throughout the passage is Leone Ebreo (Leo Hebraeus or Judah Abravanel), the Portuguese Jewish Neoplatonic philosopher and physician whose dialogues on love inform both the division of erotic and divine loves, and the notion that happiness consists in both knowing and loving God, not one or the other alone:

> Because God is the true and only object of our happiness, we love Him through both knowledge and love. The sages held divergent opinions regarding these two activities, that is, whether happiness really consists in knowing God or in loving Him. But you must be content to know that both activities are necessary to beatitude.[12]

Ebreo provides an important authority for Burton in his overlapping of emotional and rational responses to God. Indeed he tends to stress the affective side of Ebreo's formulation more strongly, and his discussion of contemplation moves into an exploration of the link between loving God and charity to others. It might be considered surprising to find Burton taking this stance, especially since the affections and passions are elsewhere seen as a source of humoral melancholic disorder.[13] Yet it is a mistake to see Burton, cloistered scholar though he claimed himself to be, as opposed to emotional forms of experience, and when he turns his thoughts to the emotional experience of devotion, the whole complexion of his writing changes. The meditation on the beatific vision which I have outlined holds a unique place in the *Anatomy*, as over a few pages Burton circles back to the same ideas, even the same words and phrases – 'amiable and faire', 'quintescence of all beauty' (both p. 332), 'lustre of his divine majesty' (p. 333) – in an attempt to express the inexpressible.

Augustine and Burton

'For now we see through a glasse, darkely: but then face to face: now I know in part, but then shall I know even as also I am knowen' (1 Corinthians 13:12). St Paul's words to the Corinthians promise a direct, unmediated vision of the divine. Seeing God is the heavenly fulfilment of earthly existence. The beatitudes hold out this supreme joy as the reward of the holy: 'Blessed are the pure in heart: for they shall see God' (Matthew 5:8). The question of whether or not it is possible to see God in this life (*in via*) or only in heaven (*in patria*), and indeed how that seeing might take place – corporeally, spiritually through interior images, or intellectually through the understanding – formed the subject of debate from Augustine onwards, with much attention devoted to the questions throughout the Middle Ages, particularly in response to the growth of visionary mysticism.[14] The Bible itself suggested different answers. As Burton paraphrases it, '*Moses* himselfe, *Exod. 33. 18.* when he desired to see God in his glory, was answered that hee might not endure it, no man could see his face and live' (vol. 3, p. 334). Yet St Paul's veiled autobiographical account of being 'caught up to the third heaven' (2 Corinthians 12:2) suggests a direct encounter with God which gave a foretaste of heavenly bliss.

St Augustine returned to the topic of the divine vision numerous times throughout his writings, and it is to him that Burton bears his greatest debt in linking perfect happiness with seeing God. Although Burton does not refer to Augustine's *City of God* at the beginning of 'Religious Melancholy', he cites it extensively elsewhere, and would probably have assumed that his readers were well acquainted with that work's final chapters, where the nature of the beatific vision and of eternal felicity are explored: 'there we shall rest and see, see and love, love and praise', Augustine concludes.[15] Burton mines major quotations on the beauty of God from Augustine's *Enarrations on the Psalms*, specifically on Psalms 41, 64 and 85. As a minister himself, Burton would have consulted the *Enarrations* when composing sermons on the Psalms, and the many references to that work in the *Anatomy* suggest that it was a favourite text.[16] Yet he also uses less well-known works:

> The Sunne it selfe and all that we can imagine are but shadowes of it, 'tis *visio praecellens*, as *Austin* calls it, the quintescence of beauty this, *which farre exceeds the beauty of heavens, Sun and Moone, Starres, Angells, gold and Silver, woods, faire fields, and whatsoever is pleasant to behold.* (vol. 3, p. 334)

This quotation is wrongly identified in Burton's footnote (where the Latin is also given) as coming from the *Enarration on Psalm 85*, whereas in fact it derives from the fourth of the *Ten Homilies on the First Epistle of John*.[17] Possibly Burton misread his notes (since a previous reference is to the Psalm 85 *Enarration*), or misconstrued a quotation found in a mediating source, whether a patristic anthology or another theological work. Whatever the case, the conspicuous references to 'Austin' in this part of the text, and their pivotal role in developing the argument of this subsection, flag up to the reader Burton's solid alignment with the central patristic authority of English Reformation theology.

That said, Burton's words on the experience of seeing God have a distinctive flavour. Early on in his account of God's beauty, he quotes Augustine on the relationship between the experience of earthly beauty and the divine:

> *I am amazed, saith Austin, when I looke up to heaven and behold the beauty of the starres, the beauty of Angels, principalities, powers, who can expresse it? who can sufficiently commend, or set out this beauty which appeares in us? so faire a body, so faire a face, eyes, nose, cheekes, chin, browes, all faire and lovely to behold, besides the beauty of the soule which cannot be discerned. If we so labour and be so much affected with the comelinesse of creatures, how should we bee ravished with that admirable lustre of God himselfe?* (vol. 3, p. 332)

Burton does not give a source for this passage, although the presentation of it here and in the Latin text in the footnote suggests a single text. In fact, he is splicing passages from two Augustinian works, the *Enarrations* on Psalms 42 and 26, with some intriguing alterations.[18] Both concern the beauty of God's creation, compared to God himself the creator. In the *Enarration* on Psalm 26 Augustine lists the faculties of human bodies and minds which are worthy of admiration – the body, limbs, senses, memory, intellect – but Burton alters this to name instead specific body parts, 'a face, eyes, nose, cheekes, chin, browes', as if he is turning patristic prose into a Petrarchan blazon. Burton's rewriting of Augustine encourages the reader to think of beauty in immediate, bodily terms. These do not transfer directly to God, however: Augustine ridiculed the Manichees for wondering, since God made man in his own image, whether he had a nose, teeth and a beard, and Burton nowhere raises the question of what God might look like.[19] Yet his alteration does fully embrace the visual experience of beauty. I have already remarked on the correspondences between this subsection and his earlier writing on the power of beauty in secular love. Like Augustine's movement from creature to creator, Burton's work gestures from the earthly to the eternal in its understanding of how we might see God face to face. We shall later see how his contemporary the Calvinist preacher Richard Sibbes takes a very different approach in order to avoid the potentially idolatrous overtones of regarding divine beauty.

Continental sources

Augustine's reading of the '*visio praecellens*' is layered over by a more surprising set of sources. Burton quotes from two Continental Catholic writers, the German Jesuit Jeremias Drexel (1581–1638) and the Portuguese churchman Jerónimo Osório (1545–1611), nephew to the theologian (1514–80) of the same name. The first quotation is from Drexel's *Nicetas, sive triumphata incontinens* (1624), a treatise on moral incontinence and how to avoid it (it was translated into English in Rouen as *Nicetas or the Triumph over Incontinencie* (1633)). Drexel extends the Augustinian idea that we can begin to imagine God's beauty only by looking at the beauty of his creation. As Burton quotes him,

> *Omnis pulchritudo florum, hominum, angelorum & rerum omnium pulcherrimarum ad dei pulchritudinem collata, nox est & tenebrae*, all other beauties are night it selfe, meere darknesse, to this our inexplicable, incomprehensible, unspeakable, eternall, infinite, admirable and divine beauty. (vol. 3, p. 332)

Burton omits to translate the examples of earthly beauty that Drexel gives ('*pulchritudo florum, hominum, angelorum*': the beauty of flowers, men, angels), but then adds a list of adjectives describing the 'incomprehensible' and 'infinite' nature of God's beauty, for which there is no equivalent in the Latin source. Drexel's words just before the quoted passage bear a strong resemblance to Augustine's *Enarration on Psalm 26*, and Burton must have noticed this link in bringing the two together. However, his adjustment of the Jesuit's text subtly redirects a passage which is conventionally Augustinian towards the apophatic theology of Pseudo-Dionysius, which taught that divine mystery could be approached only through the negative description of what God is not. It formed a counter-current to Augustine's teaching on the beatific vision by suggesting that God's essence could never be seen or understood by humans, whether on earth or in heaven.[20] There are signs elsewhere that Burton was drawn to this tradition (a little later he quotes Clement of Alexandria on charitable actions, vol. 3, p. 337), and, while I do not think that this note significantly disrupts the fundamental Augustinianism of the passage, it does add a new inflection to his argument.

Along with Drexel, the other Continental Catholic authority used in this section is Jerónimo Osório. Burton quotes from the younger Osório's annotations on the elder's Psalm commentary, at the rhetorical climax of his own paean to divine beauty,

> with sight of which wee shall never be tired, nor wearied, but still the more wee see the more we shall covet him. *For as one saith, where this vision is, there is absolute beauty, from the same fountaine comes all pleasure and happinesse, neither can beauty, pleasure, happinesse, be separated from his vision or sight, or his vision from beauty, pleasure, happinesse.* In this life we have but a glimpse of this beauty and happinesse, wee shall hereafter, as *John* saith, see him as hee is, thine eyes, as *Isay* promiseth, 33. 17. *Shall behold the King in his glory*, then shall we be perfectly inamored, have a full fruition of it, desire, behold and love him alone, as the most amiable and fairest object, our *summum bonum*, or chiefest good. (vol. 3, p. 334)

The italicised passage '*For as one saith* …' is part paraphrase, part direct translation from Osório, who is commenting on the fourth verse of Psalm 26 (i.e. 27), the same verse with which Burton begins his discourse on divine beauty.[21] Osório notes the difference between the Septuagint and Hebrew versions of the Psalm verse in the Vulgate, preferring the Hebrew 'ut videam pulchritudinem Domini' ('to behold the beauty of the Lord' in the King James Version) over the Septuagint 'voluntatem Domini' (the will or favour of the Lord). The elder Osório has paraphrased the verse as 'ut videam voluptatem tuam' (to see your pleasure or delight), and his nephew remarks that this pleasure and the vision of God are inseparable. In Burton's handling, Osório's point becomes further intensified as 'voluptas' translates into the triplet of 'beauty, pleasure, happinesse'. The terms become near synonyms as he repeats them, underscoring the way in which, according to Osório and Burton, the experience of *visio dei* in heaven will blur the act of seeing God with the experience of happiness which it produces. This is comparable to the sequence of verbs at the end of *The City of God* – 'there we shall rest and see, see and love, love and praise' – where the anadiplosis implies that all these activities are inextricably bound to one another.

What does the presence of a German Jesuit and a Portuguese counter-Reformation theologian suggest about Burton's own approach to the *visio dei*? It does not, I think, provide compelling evidence of crypto-Catholicism, or even of Catholic sympathies. Although neither writer today commands the instant recognition of a Bellarmine, both Drexel and Osório found a fairly wide circle of readers in Burton's England. Drexel was renowned for his devotional works in particular: Latin copies appeared in seventeenth-century booksellers' catalogues and private libraries, while English translations of his works were 'both popular and respectable'.[22] Jerónimo Osório the Elder, the most well-known Portuguese author in England during the sixteenth century, was known chiefly as a controversialist (among his writings is a letter to Queen Elizabeth urging her to return to the Catholic faith) and a Latin stylist. He was widely read in Oxford and Cambridge, where T. F. Earle has found over a hundred copies of books by him of early provenance.[23] Throughout the *Anatomy* Burton often has recourse to Catholic material, and like many of his age he sees no inconsistency in using it as a supporting authority at one point ('I can excuse my studies with [Leonhard] *Lessius* the *Jesuite* in like case', vol. 1, p. 22) and making it the target of polemic at another ('a *Capuchine*, a *Franciscan*, a *Pharesiacall Jesuite*, a Man-Serpente', p. 39). It is worth noting that Burton's uncle, Arthur Faunt (1553/4–91), was a Jesuit priest, but left England before Robert was born and never returned; it is unlikely his nephew had any contact with him.[24] Certainly, later in 'Religious Melancholy' Burton does not restrain himself in his polemic against a 'new sceane of superstitious imposters and heretickes, a new company of Actors, of *Antichrists*, that great *Anti-christ* himselfe: A rope of Popes' (vol. 3, p. 383). At a time when not everyone in the English Church identified the Pope as Antichrist, Burton's Reformed credentials seem robust.

None the less, Drexel and Osório receive more than a passing reference. In both cases they are quoted and translated, and Osório's words are given a place of special prominence at the climax of Burton's discussion of divine beauty. They act as the cement binding together Burton's thoughts on the vision of God, 'absolute beauty' and perfect happiness. Both Drexel's and Osório's words chime in with Augustine's theology of the *visio beatifica*, and so from a Reformed perspective their arguments as represented here are hardly objectionable. However, I think that their presence highlights the distinctive nature of Burton's approach to his subject matter, by the standards of English Protestantism. Drexel and Osório provide support for an unflinchingly visual approach to God. There is no trace of anxiety about the dangers of idolatry here, although later he will launch a searing attack upon 'superstitious Idolaters' (vol. 3, p. 338) old and new. It is significant that in 'Love Melancholy' Burton repeatedly cites the idea that Christ was beautiful (see vol. 3, pp. 26, 77, 88, 91–2). Although he cites patristic support for this view (including Augustine and Origen), his major sources are two Iberian Jesuits: the Spanish Pedro de Morales (1538–1614), who claims that the Virgin Mary was beautiful too, and the Portuguese Sebastião Barradas (1542–1615). Burton merely reports their opinions, neither endorsing nor contesting them, but the fact that the idea receives three separate outings suggests sustained interest in the notion of divine beauty which, although sanctioned by numerous patristic sources, receives little attention from Protestant theologians contemporary to him.[25] Continental Catholic authorities contribute a form of spirituality which Burton does not find elsewhere. In the 'Beauty of God' subsection, the quotations from Drexel and Osório are reproduced neither for academic interest alone, nor for controversial purposes, but for their devotional power.

To gauge the extent to which Burton's perspective on divine beauty is distinctive, it is instructive to compare him with one of his contemporaries, Richard Sibbes (1577?–1635), the stoutly Calvinist author of numerous godly sermons and popular devotional works. Sibbes's posthumously published treatise *A Breathing after God* (1639) takes as its text Psalm 27:4, the same verse Burton quotes at the beginning of his discussion of God's beauty. Sibbes is noticeably reluctant to interpret the words 'behold the beauty of the Lord' in the literal, visual sense that Burton embraces. The thrust of his argument is evident when he states that 'concerning the beauty of God, I will not speake of it at large, or singly of the excellencies of God. The Text aymes especially at the beauty of God, as discovered in his Ordinances, in his Church'.[26] Sermons, public prayer, the *ordo salutis*, orderliness among the faithful: these are the ways in which divine beauty is made manifest. In this he follows Calvin, whose commentary on the verse has nothing to say about *visio dei* but stresses that, when David speaks of 'the beawtifulnes of the Temple … he placeth that beawtifulnesse, not in the godlynesse that was too bee seene with the eye' but in a spiritual sense; beauty is found instead in 'the woord, the Sacraments, the Comon prayers, and other helpes of the same sorte'.[27] Sibbes likewise avoids the bodily interpretation of vision, claiming (in a veiled reference to Augustine) that 'sight is put for the more full enjoying, one sense put for another, as indeed sight is taken for all the senses, inward and outward', and he tends towards the 'inward' or 'spiritual' interpretation throughout his text.[28] Burton steers a similar course in his conventional exposition of the Song of Songs as an '*Epithalamium*' between Christ and the Church, '[t]hat by these figures, that glasse, these spirituall eyes of contemplation, we might perceave some resemblance of his beauty, the love betwixt his Church and him' (vol. 3, p. 333). Yet, unlike Sibbes, his discussion of the Church is subordinate to his primary interpretation of Psalm 27:4 as concerned with the experience of seeing God in heaven: 'this vision of his, this lustre of his divine majesty', which '*no tongue can tell, no heart can conceave it*, as *Paule* saith' (vol. 3, pp. 333–4), he writes, alluding to the classic text on the *visio beatifica*, 1 Corinthians 2:9.

Burton's approach is far more overtly sensuous in nature than Sibbes's, less squeamish about attempting to explore the nature of God's beauty, even though it is 'incomprehensible, unspeakable' (vol. 3, p. 332). He even displays a sympathetic attitude (albeit temporarily) towards 'those Heathens, Pagans, Philosophers, [who] out of those reliques they have yet left of Gods Image, are so farre forth incensed, as not only to acknowledge a God; but, though after their owne inventions … to love him, seeke him, feare him, though a wrong way, to adore him' (vol. 3, p. 333). It is the emotional experience of seeing beauty that provokes this reaction, by drawing people towards love. If absolute happiness is the end point of vision, emotion is also the means towards it. Even Sibbes, in his more indirect vision of God through his Church, is interested in the emotional mechanics of sight:

> Of all senses, sight hath this propertie above the rest, (as it is more spirituall, more refined, and more capable: a man may see many things at once, it is a quick sense: so) it hath this priviledge it stirs affections more than any sense, more then hearing, that is a more dull sense: things stirre affections more that are seene, then by that we heare, hee desired therefore to see the beautie of Gods house that he might be enamoured. Of sight comes love.[29]

It is unusual, particularly in a godly preacher, to find sight elevated above hearing for its emotional effects. Given the primacy of preaching, it is normal for hearing to be attributed the prerogative in stirring emotions, while sight is seen as more refined and connected with reason.[30] Burton is likewise interested in the power of sight, devoting a lengthy subsection of 'Love Melancholy' (vol. 3, pp. 65–90) to the ways in which beauty allures: 'Sight of all other, is the first step of this unruly love' (vol. 3, p. 65).

In via and *in media*

In the 'Beauty of God' subsection, sight does not receive any theoretical discussion, but Burton does pay attention to the ways in which it might take place, including its mystical possibilities. Quoting Gregory:

> *It is the eye of contemplation by which we must behold it, the wing of meditation which lifts us up and reares our soules* … And as *Philo Judeus* seconds him, *hee that loves God will soare aloft and take him wings, and leaving the earth fly up to heaven* … as *Ficinus* adviseth us, [we must] get us solar *eyes, spectacles as they that looke on the Sunne, to see this divine beauty*. (vol. 3, pp. 335–6)

The cluster of citations from Philo Judaeus, Ficino and later Plotinus raises an important question: what relationship does Burton envisage between the experience of seeing divine beauty and the activities of this life? For Neoplatonists, the rejection of worldly affairs is the only route to communion with the divine. Plotinus urges us to '*forsake the kingdomes and empires of the whole earth ... if we desire to be engrafted into him*' (vol. 3, p. 336). Yet while Burton's interest in Neoplatonic theory is evident (its influence is also felt strongly in 'Love Melancholy'), this forsaking of the whole earth is at odds with his prevailing advice to melancholics to '*be not solitary, be not idle*' (vol. 3, p. 445). The contemplative life might be an attractive one but it holds dangers for the melancholic, who (as Burton urges throughout the second Partition) needs company, exercise and occupation.

The possibility of experiencing *visio dei* on earth is given a conventional, and brief, treatment by Burton earlier in the subsection. 'In this life we have but a glimpse of this beauty and happinesse, wee shall hereafter, as *John* saith, see him as hee is' (vol. 3, p. 334). This 'glimpse' is often identified as divine rapture or ecstasy, as experienced by St Paul in his ascent to the third heaven. While Burton's prominent references to Philo and Ficino suggest a degree of interest in this topic, he does not explore it explicitly at this stage. Later in 'Religious Melancholy' he does address the subject, sounding a caution about ascribing all sorts of melancholic symptoms to authentic rapture: '*Extasis is a taste of future happinesse, by which we are united unto God, a divine melancholy, a spirituall wing,* Bonaventure *tearmes it*, to lift us up to heaven: But as it is abused, a meere dotage, madnesse, a cause and symptome of *Religious Melancholy*' (vol. 3, p. 361). The initial quotation (up to 'God') is taken from Erasmus's May 1515 letter to Martin Dorp, in which he responds to Dorp's attack on the *Praise of Folly*, a work which famously concludes with what M. A. Screech calls 'a powerful exposition of Christian ecstasy'.[31] The phrase '*divine melancholy*' seems to be Burton's interpolation, and surely has a positive sense here, bearing in mind that Erasmus twists the senses of folly and madness in the final paragraphs of the *Praise of Folly* to denote a state towards which the Christian should aspire. That Burton appeals to one of the classic humanist texts on ecstasy, and one which already provides a significant precedent for the *Anatomy* since it prompted Burton's pseudonym Democritus Junior, suggests a serious investment in the topic.[32] Yet even as Bonaventure's imagery of the '*spirituall wing*' brings us back to Philo's wings of divine contemplation, Burton sounds a warning note. Whereas earlier the rejection of worldly affairs in favour of spiritual vision is presented as an ideal, here the process by which it occurs is cast in doubt: the 'meere dotage' of religious enthusiasm can easily be mistaken for the true '*taste of future happinesse*'. This approach to ecstasy was widely held in the period; John Donne

(1572–1631), for instance, another churchman who displayed a sustained interest in the *visio dei*, warned his London congregation that 'you are not to looke for Revelations, nor Extasies, nor Visions, nor Transportations, but to rest in Gods ordinary meanes'.[33] Yet it is noteworthy that Burton does give some positive attention to ecstasy, a sign that he is not ready to dismiss all earthly 'glimpses' of heaven, as many clerics were.

The experience of ecstatic revelation or contemplative flight is not the only possible means of tasting future happiness *in via*, however. Directly after quoting Plotinus, Burton moves on to the safer territory of charity, a subject to which he has already devoted a memorably powerful subsection (vol. 3, pp. 29–38). The transition is a significant one. 'Wee must pray to God that hee will open our eyes, make cleare our hearts, that we may be capable of his glorious rayes, and performe those duties that he requires of us' (vol. 3, p. 336). Contemplation and charity are by no means opposed (and indeed Burton cites Leone Ebreo on the importance of charity) but, while Neoplatonic ascent may be available only to a few, the latter is a duty that all must follow, and as Burton describes it he does so firmly in the first person plural. He elucidates the meaning of loving one's neighbour in terms of positive, embodied actions: 'cloath the naked, visit the sicke, and performe … workes of mercy' (vol. 3, p. 337). These might seem to have little relation to his main topic, the beauty of God, but the underlying connection is a strong one, for charity was seen to be a major part of the *visio beatifica*.[34] In his *Summa Theologica*, Thomas Aquinas makes this clear as he argues that some will see God more perfectly than others in heaven:

> the intellect which has more of the light of glory will see God the more perfectly; and he will have a fuller participation of the light of glory who has more charity; because where there is the greater charity, there is the more desire; and desire in a certain degree makes the one desiring apt and prepared to receive the object desired. Hence he who possesses the more charity, will see God the more perfectly, and will be the more beatified [Latin: 'beatior' (happier, more blessed)].[35]

Burton does not refer to this passage explicitly but he does begin the paragraph with a quotation from Thomas's major discussion of charity in the *Summa* (II^{a}–IIae q. 23). Burton's relatively few references to the *Summa* (eleven in the whole of the *Anatomy*) conceal a greater debt to Aquinas than is immediately evident; like other clerics of his age, Burton may have wished to conceal his scholastic borrowings to present a 'purer' line of descent from the Church Fathers, in particular Augustine.[36] Yet Aquinas's link between charity, seeing God and ultimate happiness – the beatitude of heaven – underlies the structure of Burton's argument.

This issue of structure is an important one, for Burton's ordering of his argument is unusual, and this is reflective of a wider rhetorical pattern in his text. In the final sentence from Aquinas quoted above, the logical order is charity – seeing God – beatitude; this order mirrors the movement from earth to heaven, from what takes place *in via* to its reward *in patria*. Burton reverses this order, first considering the beauty of God, alongside the happiness that is part of it, and then turning to charity. Despite his interest in Neoplatonic writings, he does not imitate the trajectory of heavenly ascent in his writing. Instead, he considers the beauty of God and the bliss of seeing it at the beginning of 'Religious Melancholy', before following his cause-to-cure structure once more. As Ruth Fox has perceptively noticed, the *Anatomy* 'does not end with angel voices welcoming elect souls' but with 'a human scene', advising readers how to stave off their melancholic condition.[37] The movement from divine beauty to charity has a similarly practical aspect: whereas commentators treat *ecstasis* as something possible only for a very few, Burton treats charity as a series of performable activities, which make manifest the love which 'unites us to God himselfe' (vol. 3, p. 336). This positive picture of wilful action as a route to divine union is disrupted, however, in the second of two rhetorical 'falls'.[38] Having looked first to the moment in heaven when 'we shall be perfectly inamored, have a full fruition of it [God's beauty], desire, behold and love him alone, as the most amiable and fairest object, our *summum bonum*, or chiefest good' (vol. 3, p. 334), in the next paragraph he reminds us that '[t]his likewise should we now have done, had not our will beene corrupted'. Likewise, when he asserts the importance of charitable acts as 'the extent and complement of love' (vol. 3, p. 337, translating Clement of Alexandria), he continues, '[t]his we shall doe if we be truely enamored, but we come short in both, we neither love God, nor our neighbour as we should'. These moments conform to what I have elsewhere described as Burton's 'unhappiness motif', in which he 'begins by presenting an image of true human happiness, then topples it by showing the utter insufficiency of humans to reach such a standard, through their own fault'.[39]

Burton, then, does the opposite of what we might expect. In general, other writers of the period who display a similar interest in the *visio dei* fittingly leave their discussion for the end. John Donne devotes only the last part of his Candlemas 1627 sermon on the beatitude 'Blessed are the pure in heart, for they shall see God' (Matt. 5:8) to 'that *Visio beatifica*, to see God so, as that that very seeing makes the seer Blessed'.[40] Likewise, his Easter 1628 sermon on the key text 1 Corinthians 13:12 leaves the consideration of God 'face to face' until its closing stages.[41] Burton's upturning of the usual (and more logical) rhetorical pattern may strike us as more negative in its outlook, and certainly his 'unhappiness motif' works to draw attention to the gulf between what humans should be like, and the failures of sinful, earthly existence. At the same time though, his paean to the beauty of God stands out all the more because its placement at the beginning of 'Religious Melancholy' is unusual, and contrasts so greatly with what surrounds it (in particular the polemic against error and superstition). Despite being only a short subsection, the 'Beauty of God' offsets (although does not blunt) the sharpness of his satirical attack. He sets before his readers 'a stupend, vast, infinite Ocean of incredible madnesse and folly' (vol. 3, p. 331), but in order to do so he must first 'say something *necessarily* of the object of this love, God himselfe' (p. 332, my emphasis); in view of the impassioned language which follows, 'necessarily' denotes not a duty but a compulsion. The 'errors and obliquities' must be seen in relation to one absolute value.

The beauty of God – the source of perfect happiness – of which Burton gives his own 'glimpse' in the *Anatomy*, takes his text beyond the humoralist framework of the medical textbook. While Burton is thoroughly conversant with Galenic discourse, his wide and eclectic reading in theology and philosophy is equally important for his treatment of emotion, as this short section shows. It provides the emotional counterweight to the earthly melancholy which fills the rest of his book. He is a writer little given to emotional transports, and it is the rareness of such a moment that makes it worthy of special attention. In studying Burton's treatment of his source material, I have attempted to trace how the distinctive qualities of his writing come out of his notably varied reading matter. His writing is at once solidly Augustinian and inflected with a Continental Catholic spirituality, which addresses divine beauty with a directness little encountered in Protestant commentators. He draws substantially on Neoplatonic writers such as Ficino too, but tempers this with his Augustinian and Thomist emphasis on charity as a route to the vision of God. Throughout, he is little interested in entering the scholastic disputes which surround the topic, such as whether God can ever be seen in his essence, or what kind of seeing takes place, although he does seem to lay greater weight on love rather than knowledge as the route to union with God. As this affective approach suggests, his primary interest in the topic seems to be in its emotional dimension. Melancholy may be the character of mortality and the subject of the *Anatomy*, but for a brief moment, Burton banishes it from his text to give instead a vision of the immortal happiness of heaven.

Notes

1 All further references are to Robert Burton, *The Anatomy of Melancholy*, ed. Thomas C. Faulkner, Nicolas K. Kiessling and Rhonda L. Blair, commentary by J. B. Bamborough with Martin Dodsworth, 6 vols (Oxford: Oxford University Press, 1989–2000), by volume and page number, incorporated in the text.

2 On definitions of the mind in this period, see Erin Sullivan, Chapter 1, above.

3 For a full account of ancient attitudes to emotion, particularly Stoic, and their Christian heritage, see Richard Sorabji, *Emotion and Peace of Mind: From Stoic Agitation to Christian Temptation* (Oxford: Oxford University Press, 2000).

4 See further Mary Ann Lund, *Melancholy, Medicine and Religion in Early Modern England: Reading 'The Anatomy of Melancholy'* (Cambridge: Cambridge University Press, 2010), pp. 189–95. On moral philosophy in the *Anatomy* see Angus Gowland, *The Worlds of Renaissance Melancholy: Robert Burton in Context* (Cambridge: Cambridge University Press, 2006), esp. pp. 271–5.

5 For other approaches to happiness, see Sara Coodin, Chapter 3, above, and Richard Chamberlain, Chapter 7, below.

6 See, for example, Gail Kern Paster, *Humoring the Body: Emotions and the Shakespearean Stage* (Chicago: University of Chicago Press, 2004), and the discussion in the Introduction to this volume.

7 See John F. Sena, 'Melancholic Madness and the Puritans', *Harvard Theological Review*, 66 (1973), 293–309; and Michael Heyd, *'Be Sober and Reasonable': The Critique of Enthusiasm in the Seventeenth and Early Eighteenth Centuries* (Leiden: Brill, 1995).

8 All quotations from the Bible are taken from the King James Version, in *The Bible in English* database, http://collections.chadwyck.com/ [accessed 24 July 2012].

9 For further discussion of Burton's consideration of love melancholy, see Gowland, *Worlds of Renaissance Melancholy*, pp. 65–70, 158–61.

10 On this stylistic feature elsewhere in the *Anatomy*, see Lund, *Melancholy, Medicine and Religion*, p. 174.

11 Although, as we will later see, there are signs in Burton's text of an interest in Dionysian approaches to *visio dei*, Burton seems to be more aligned with the 'affective Dionysianism' of Bonaventura (whom Burton quotes) and the Franciscans than the 'intellective Dionysianism' of Albert the Great and the Dominicans; see Bernard McGinn, 'Visions and Visualizations in the Here and Hereafter', *Harvard Theological Review*, 98 (2005), 227–46 (pp. 232–3). On the rational soul, subjectivity and divine contemplation, see Angus Gowland, 'Medicine, Psychology, and the Melancholic Subject in the Renaissance', in

Elena Carrera (ed.), *Emotions and Health, 1200–1700* (Leiden: Brill, 2013), pp. 185–220 (pp. 198–201).

12 Leone Ebreo, *Dialogues of Love*, ed. Rosella Pescatori, trans. Damian Bacich and Rosella Pescatori (Toronto: University of Toronto Press, 2009), p. 59.

13 For the theoretical underpinnings of this see Gowland, *Worlds of Renaissance Melancholy*, pp. 47–9, 79–80.

14 A full account of this subject is given in McGinn, 'Visions and Visualizations'. See also McGinn, '*Visio Dei*: Seeing God in Medieval Theology and Mysticism', in Carolyn Muessig and Ad Putter (eds), *Envisaging Heaven in the Middle Ages* (Abingdon: Routledge, 2007), pp. 15–33; Christian Trottmann, *La Vision Béatifique: Des Disputes Scolastiques à sa Définition par Benoît XII* (Rome: Ecole Française de Rome, 1995); and Carolyn Walker Bynum, *The Resurrection of the Body in Western Christianity, 200–1336* (New York: Columbia University Press, 1995), pp. 279–317.

15 'Ibi vacabimus, et videbimus; videbimus, et amabimus; amabimus, et laudabimus', Augustine, *De Civitate Dei*, 22.30 (*Patrologia Latina*, 41.804). All references to patristic authors are taken from *Patrologia Cursus Completus. … Series Latina*, ed. J. P. Migne et al., 221 vols (Paris, 1844–1903), hereafter abbreviated as '*PL*'. The relevant chapters are Book 22, Chapters 29 and 30. Other important texts include the *Retractationes*, 1.2 (*PL*, 32.588) and various places in the *Confessions* (*PL*, 32.657–868). For further texts see McGinn, 'Visions and Visualizations', p. 229 n. 6; and Katrin Ettenhuber, *Donne's Augustine: Renaissance Cultures of Interpretation* (Oxford: Oxford University Press, 2011), p. 207.

16 The Oxford commentators identify references to thirty-three Augustinian works (four of them spurious); see vol. 6, pp. 309–10.

17 Augustine, *In Epistolam Joannis ad Parthos Tractatus Decem*, 4.5 (*PL*, 35.2008). The source given in the commentary to the Oxford edition of the *Anatomy*, vol. 6, p. 211, is incorrect.

18 The Oxford editors concluded that it was 'apparently based on a passage' in *Enarr. in Ps. 41*, 'but much expanded and altered' (vol. 6, p. 210). Burton's Latin footnote reads '*Miror & stupeo cum cœlum aspicio, & pulchritudinem syderum, angelorum &c. & cuis dignè quod in nobis viget, corpus tam pulchrum, frontem pulchram, nares, genas, oculos, intellectum, omnia pulchra, si sic in creaturis laboramus, quid in ipso deo?*' (vol. 3, p. 332). The relevant passages from Augustine are 'Ostendo magnitudinem circumfusi maris, stupeo, miror; artificem quaero: coelum suspicio et pulchritudinem siderum', *Enarr. in Ps. 41* (*PL*, 36.468); 'Quis digne laudet Angelos, Sedes, Dominationes, Principatus, et Potestates? Quis digne laudet hoc ipsum quod in nobis viget, vegetans corpus, movens membra, sensus exserens, et memoria tam multa complectens, intellectu tam multa discernens, quis digne laudet? At si in istis creaturis Dei sic laborat humanus sermo, in creatore quid agit, nisi sola restet sermone deficiente jubilatio?', *Enarr. in Ps. 26*, 2 (*PL*, 36.206).

19 *De Genesi contra Manichaeos*, 1.17.27 (*PL*, 34.186).

20 McGinn, 'Visions and Visualizations', pp. 231–2.

21 A Latin version of this appears in Burton's footnote: '*Ubicunque visio & pulchritudo divini aspectus, ibi voluptas ex eodem fonte omnisque beatitudo, nec ab ejus aspectu voluptas, nec ab illa voluptate aspectus separari potest*'. From '*nec ab ejus*' onwards is a near-direct quotation, while the rest is a paraphrase; see *Hieronymi Osorii … Opera Omnia*, 4 vols (Rome, 1592), vol. 3, p. 564.

22 J. M. Blom, 'A German Jesuit and His Anglican Readers: The Case of Jeremias Drexel (1581–1638)', in G. A. M. Janssens and F. G. A. M. Aarts (eds), *Studies in Seventeenth-Century English Literature, History and Bibliography* (Amsterdam: Rodopi, 1984), pp. 41–51.

23 T. F. Earle, *Portuguese Writers and English Readers: Books by Portuguese Writers Printed Before 1630 in the Libraries of Oxford and Cambridge* (Oxford: Oxford Bibliographical Society, 2009), pp. xx, xxx, 122; see also his 'Portuguese Scholarship in Oxford in the Early Modern Period: The Case of Jerónimo Osório (Hieronymus Osorius)', *Bulletin of Spanish Studies*, 81 (2004), 1039–49.

24 Burton cites his uncle, '*Laur. Arcturus Fanteus de Invoc. Sanct.*', in a list of Catholic writers who claim miraculous cures of the sick through holy water, relics and the like. Yet he makes clear that 'we on the other side, seeke to God alone' (vol. 2, p. 9). See G. Martin Murphy, 'Faunt, Arthur (1553/4–1591)', *Oxford Dictionary of National Biography* (Oxford University Press, 2004); Gowland, *Worlds of Renaissance Melancholy*, p. 5; and Kathryn Murphy, 'Jesuits and Philosophasters: Robert Burton's Response to the Gunpowder Plot', *Journal of the Northern Renaissance*, 1 (2009), 109–28.

25 As Erin Sullivan shows in Chapter 1, above, Thomas Wright inherits and further articulates the Jesuit emphasis on sensory and specifically visual experience in meditative practice.

26 Richard Sibbes, *A Breathing after God* (London, 1639), p. 117.

27 Jean Calvin, *The Psalmes of David and Others. With M. Iohn Calvins Commentaries* (London, 1571), sig. 101v; compare with Sibbes, *A Breathing*, pp. 125–60.

28 Sibbes, *A Breathing*, pp. 116–17, 170–1. Augustine distinguished between three types of seeing – *corporalis*, *spiritualis* and *intellectualis* – and it seems likely that both Sibbes and Burton are drawing on this division. See McGinn, 'Visions and Visualizations', p. 230.

29 Sibbes, *A Breathing*, p. 169.

30 Arnold Hunt, *The Art of Hearing: English Preachers and their Audiences, 1590–1640* (Cambridge: Cambridge University Press, 2010), pp. 81–94; and Mary Ann Lund, 'Early Modern Sermon Paratexts and the Religious Politics of Reading', in James Daybell and Peter Hinds (eds), *Material Readings of Early Modern Culture, 1580-1700* (Basingstoke: Palgrave Macmillan, 2010), pp. 143–62.

31 M. A. Screech, *Ecstasy and the Praise of Folly* (London: Duckworth, 1980), p. 8.

32 Erasmus's speaker, Folly, says that there are so many new types of folly that 'a thousand Democrituses wouldn't be enough to laugh at them, and we'd always have to call in one Democritus more', *The Praise of Folly*, in *Collected Works of Erasmus*, trans. Betty Radice, 89 vols (Toronto: University of Toronto Press, 1975–), vol. 27, pp. 120–1.

33 John Donne, *The Sermons of John Donne*, ed. George R. Potter and Evelyn M. Simpson, 10 vols (Berkeley: University of California Press, 1953–62), vol. 8, p. 46. See also Ettenhuber, *Donne's Augustine*, pp. 205–24.

34 See 'vision spéculaire', in *Dictionnaire de Spiritualité: Ascétique et Mystique: Doctrine et Histoire*, 17 vols (Paris: Beauchesne, 1937–95), vol. 3, p. 886.

35 Thomas Aquinas, *Summa Theologica*, Ia q. 12 a. 6 co. ('intellectus plus participans de lumine gloriae, perfectius Deum videbit. Plus autem participabit de lumine gloriae, qui plus habet de caritate, quia ubi est maior caritas, ibi est maius desiderium; et desiderium quodammodo facit desiderantem aptum et paratum ad susceptionem desiderati. Unde qui plus habebit de caritate, perfectius Deum videbit, et beatior erit', in *Corpus Thomisticum* (Fundación Tomás de Aquino), www.corpusthomisticum.org/sth1003.html [accessed 30 July 2012]). Translation by Fathers of the English Dominican Province, *The Summa Theologica of St. Thomas Aquinas* (1920), available online at *New Advent*, www.newadvent.org/summa/1012.htm [accessed 30 July 2012].

36 This point is powerfully made by Katrin Ettenhuber in connection to John Donne (*Donne's Augustine*, pp. 5–6, 83–6). Burton's debt to Aquinas has received little attention and is worthy of further study.

37 Ruth A. Fox, *The Tangled Chain: The Structure of Disorder in 'The Anatomy of Melancholy'* (Berkeley: University of California Press, 1976), p. 198.

38 For a discussion of emotions as agency see the Introduction to this volume.

39 Lund, *Melancholy, Medicine and Religion*, p. 171.

40 Donne, *Sermons*, vol. 7, p. 341.

41 Ibid., vol. 8, pp. 219–36. Another writer who discusses a similar topic is Sir Thomas Browne, who at the end of *Hydriotaphia* (1658), p. 83, remarks that 'if any have been so happy as truly to understand Christian annihilation, extasis, exolution, liquefaction, transformation, the kisse of the Spouse, gustation of God, and ingression into the divine shadow, they have already had an anticipation of heaven'. This seemingly technical perspective on Christian ecstasy in Browne's penultimate paragraph is one of the strangest moments in his writing.

Part II

Shakespeare and the language of emotion

5

Spleen in Shakespeare's comedies

Nigel Wood

In *A Midsummer Night's Dream*, Lysander realises early in the action that lovers resemble poets and the mad in that they have access to perceptions that confound common sensibilities. Any 'sympathy in choice' is prey to 'war, death, or sickness', rendering it 'momentany as a sound',

> Swift as a shadow, short as any dream,
> Brief as the lightning in the collied night,
> That, in a spleen, unfolds both heaven and earth,
> And, ere a man hath power to say 'Behold!',
> The jaws of darkness do devour it up:
> So quick bright things come to confusion.
>
> (1.1.144–9)[1]

But we know we are watching a comedy, so such scepticism is presumably diluted by the inexorability of the fortunate ending; Puck provides an apology for any offending 'shadows' – or unskilful actors – and the 'visions' they have offered that can now safely appear but a 'weak and idle theme' true only of dreams (5.1.417–21). Seasoned theatregoers know, however, that no final effort at comic closure actually terminates or exorcises the potential discomfort or doubt experienced earlier, and that the generic distinctions between comedy and tragedy are often nominal.

The precision with which the word *spleen* is used in the above passage can be part of an investigation into how so much of the play gestures towards the very limits of human comprehension. 'Spleen' is here associated not only with the 'jaws of darkness' but also with a revelation of 'heaven and earth', a vision that proves untenable and even unbearable. It disorders one's 'sympathy' and produces – ultimately – 'confusion'. The strength of the emotion is registered; the cause is not. For Theseus, what the lovers recount of their midsummer night is 'more strange than true', part of the 'shaping fantasies' that occur in the minds of the madman as well as the lover. Whilst 'cool reason' might comprehend its ratio of experience, the imagination is apt to 'apprehend' (emotionally, sensorily) much more: 'the forms of things unknown' that, in the hands of the poet, can be named and expressed – so that 'airy nothing' is manifest (5.1.2–15). At the back of Theseus's consternation is a common impasse: the imagination defies categorisation and so it also evades analysis. The 'fine frenzy' of Plato's *furor poeticus* is philosophically akin to an Ovidian grasp of nature's perverse mutability. As Golding's Ovid notes, nature can provide many instances of 'shapes transformde ... to bodies straunge'.[2] Yet Theseus's poet, in his glance 'from heaven to earth, from earth to heaven' (5.1.13), also accomplishes something more: a link between the transitory and the eternal, between the tangible and the ineffable.[3] Theseus's attempt to comprehend the night's events seems to echo Lysander's earlier concern at the fragility of the affections, and to a large extent it does, but in one significant particular it does not; whereas the 'shaping fantasies' of the poet challenge reason, they are neither as threatening nor as instantaneous as the perspective offered by the spleen. One may be poetical by constitution or persuasion, yet one shapes one's fantasies by design, irrational, yet still possessing some pattern or purpose. Lysander's 'spleen' is 'swift' and 'short' and its illumination is similarly elemental yet the reverse of illuminating in the accepted sense.

The association of spleen with lightning is a particularly self-conscious one. In *Romeo and Juliet* it is thematic. When Benvolio considers the chain of events that leads to Mercutio's death he attributes it to Tybalt's 'unruly spleen' in the face of which parley proves impossible; the breakdown of normal association leads to a scene wherein 'to't they go like lightning' (3.1.151, 173). This metaphorical thread is introduced by Juliet in 2.2, where she fears the suddenness of Romeo's affection for her, an emotion

> too rash, too unadvis'd, too sudden,
> Too like the lightning, which doth cease to be
> Ere one can say 'It lightens' ...
>
> (2.2.18–20)

This coupling of the meteorological with the perceptive faculties, the too-piercing illumination that the flash of lightning brings to the night sky, provokes the dramatic action; one would not wish Romeo's affections to keep within bounds if one has any dramatic sense at all. Similarly, the pity at Mercutio's slaying provokes the main tragedy, and arrested and sudden thoughtlessness is its catalyst. We return – with Romeo – to this motif when he surveys Paris's corpse at the Capulet monument, and he muses upon the paradox that, at the point of death, men may be merry, sometimes called a 'lightning before death', and yet he cannot conclude that it is indeed 'a lightning' (5.3.90–1) in the sense that it actually provides definite insight.[4] This rush of emotion before action is an ingredient of the spleen, and is part of the significantly punning *adnominatio* on light and vision true of both *A Midsummer Night's Dream* and *Romeo and Juliet*.

And yet enlightenment – in its primary sense – is not promised by Shakespeare's use of the term. A fit of the spleen exceeds exact description; in that it, anatomically, might aid a balanced constitution by draining off diseased impulses and humours, it is a corporeal safety valve, yet it also, figuratively, signifies a concentration of the excessive emotions (the atypical yet also impulsively natural), a threat to such a balance. For Lysander, the lightning of a dream is merely an intensification of what he acknowledges well before Puck's intervention. Rhetorically, it is akin to a Longinian sublime, where the rush of perception cannot be calibrated or controlled.[5] The language may be simple, yet its full significance is not. It is out of this clash between denotation and association that the word has such a complex function in many of his works.

Defining (and undefining) spleen

In this chapter I want to trace the appearances of the word *spleen* in some of Shakespeare's comedies, and to dwell on its valency. The simple observation is that Shakespeare does not use it in any streamlined or predictable way, and that it often captures some of the liminal meanings of tragicomedy at significant moments. In Lysander's speech, the perspective on transience derives from the being in a 'spleen', a point difficult to square with the later understanding of it as bad temper or vapours, that underworld of suppressed emotions that Alexander Pope explores in his Cave of Spleen in *The Rape of the Lock*, canto IV. Spleen in the *Dream* is here equated with sympathy and the transient illumination of lightning – not the morbid transformations and settled nervous melancholy of Pope's imagination. Inevitably, this goes some way to supplementing a modern critical concern with accounting for emotional states when reading literature now – and then. As the editors of *Reading the Early Modern Passions* (2004) have explored, we enter a foreign country when we try to conceptualise how past feelings and impulses are captured textually; so many of the essays in the collection find early modern abstractions of impulse and instinct beyond a modern compass.[6] For example, '[w]e are accustomed to viewing … the metereological analogy that likens sighs and tears to winds and storms as one-sided: human emotional expressions are analogous to the weather. But the correspondences ran both ways: the weather is correspondent with human emotions.'[7] One's emotional capacities are therefore involved in levels of projection and assumption that take a creative hold of the Real and wilfully fashion it. This is not, however, quite how Lysander views the 'collied night', its coruscating aspects defying a frame or consistent definition.

Defining the word for the *Dream*'s editors has demonstrated some similarities, but also some crucial differences. R. A. Foakes's New Cambridge edition glosses Lysander's 'spleen' as 'fit of temper'; Gail Kern Paster and Skiles Howard for Bedford/St Martin's term it as 'swift impulse' or 'violent flash'; Harold F. Brooks's Arden 2 edition calls it a 'fit of anger, or passion'; while Peter Holland for Oxford glosses it as 'fit of passion'.[8] If there is any common line here it might reside in the violence of the moment producing some level of bright and explosive revelation, and a depth of emotion that is ungovernable, a world away from the decrees of a Theseus or the 'ancient privilege' that Egeus invokes (1.1.41). On the other hand, the strength of the passion may or may not be identified just as anger. The *OED* claims Lysander's speech for its meaning 7a for *spleen*: 'A fit of temper; a passion', and includes examples from Shakespeare's comedies for meaning 3, 'Merriment, gaiety, sport' from *Love's Labour's Lost* and *The Taming of the Shrew*; 4b, 'Caprice, changeable temper' (*Taming*); and 8a, 'Amusement, delight' (*Twelfth Night*). The more we try to pin the word down, to get it to denote consistently, the less we succeed, as its connotations exceed the frame.

Without enumerating the compounds that comprise the word, *spleen* has, according to the *OED*, eight main meanings current in the sixteenth into the seventeenth centuries, with a further seventeen semantic sub-sets, ranging from the anatomical to the freakishly illuminating to the figurative seat of either melancholy or merriment. Crucially, ten of these sub-sets do not survive as accepted usage far beyond the Restoration, and the *OED*'s editors identify several shades of signification that either originate with Shakespeare or that he seems to have exclusively used. Thus, meaning 3, 'Merriment, gaiety, sport' stems only from *Love's Labour's Lost* and *Taming*; 4a, 'A sudden impulse; a whim, or caprice' from *Venus and Adonis* and *1 Henry IV*, where the 'hair-brained' Hotspur is regarded as 'governed by a spleene'; 4b, 'Caprice, changeable temper' again from *1 Henry IV*, and *Taming*; 5b, 'Impetuosity, eagerness' only from two instances in *King John*, and its use with the definite article (8a) only from *Twelfth Night*. It is first used in specific *OED* records to illustrate 5a, 'Hot or proud temper; high spirit, courage, resolute mind' (as quoted above, to help define Tybalt from *Romeo and Juliet*) and 6a, 'Violent ill-nature or ill-humour; irritable or peevish temper – with a possessive pronoun' from *Richard III*. Shakespeare is not noted in the *OED* to use it to indicate melancholia or dejection, a current option for him (theoretically) from meaning 1b.

Dictionaries are functional in mapping and marking distinctions; artistic aims are, by comparison, vagrant and opportunistic, seizing on the possibility of valency to express by initial lexicographic confusion. The evidence from the *OED* leads to two main hypotheses: (*a*) the word was exploited in Shakespeare's time because of its fertile slipperiness, and (*b*) that Shakespeare himself favoured it as comprising a remarkably broad spectrum of meaning, frequently returning to the ungovernable qualities of emotional excess, a state equally amenable to tragic as comic narratives. The major conundrum about the word *spleen* derives from a doubt about the anatomical value of the organ itself; now understood to offer some protection against serious disease and as a regulator of the blood, it is associated with moments of physical crisis when blood-flow needs extra regulation, such as in childbirth or other strenuous physical exertions. In the *Timaeus*, Plato identified the spleen as a cleanser of the liver and other neighbouring organs; it collected a surfeit of substances that might be toxic in great quantities, and somehow removed or transformed them.[9] Aristotle even regarded it as a second or bastard liver in his *De Partibus Animalium*, where 'the spleen attracts the residual humours from the stomach, and owing to its bloodlike character is enabled to assist in their concoction. Should, however, this residual fluid be too abundant, or that the heat of the spleen be too scanty, the body becomes sickly with over-repletion with nutriment'.[10] In other words, it ensures a balance of humours or fluids, and adds to the theory that the result of extremes, such as laughter or overbearing temper, is met with in the organ. In the Hippocratic corpus, its main function was to regulate water, yet, far more influential was Galen's assertion, when accounting for humoral imbalance, that the spleen's main task was to rid the body of too much black bile, the main constituent of melancholy. Far from appearing as the reservoir of elements that promoted melancholia, Galen – as both Plato and Aristotle had before him – regarded it as a means by which they may be dissipated or diluted.[11] As Isadorus had noted, this opened the way for an image quite the opposite from the Enlightenment one: as a manic antidote to a depression of spirits, a function briefly noted also by Aristotle. As Andrew Wear has made clear, even attempts at detailed anatomy – by Vesalius in his *De Humani Corporis*

Fabrica (1543) and Piccolomini in his *Anatomicae Praelectiones* (1586) – left this classical observation largely unchallenged.[12]

In lexicographical, or, indeed, aesthetic, investigations, this agreement as to the purgative function of the spleen could be appropriated to assumptions about irascibility and immoderate mirth: that they were safety-valves that ensured the balance of the body's constitution. What both Theseus and Lysander realise on the other hand is that the excessive and extreme can be revelatory; one would not wish to damn the poet or lover as lunatic *tout court*, and the 'jaws of darkness' that would eventually obscure all distinction may only be combated by the lightning of a splenetic perspective that opens to our view both 'heaven and earth'. *Spleen* is not a word that is casually chosen; its connotations derive from a process whereby changes of meaning are promoted not by a word's mimetic aptness but rather by its capacity to combine potentially alternative senses metaphorically. Polysemy seems often 'vague' in Paul Ricoeur's technical sense, to be understood 'not exactly as that abstraction which is itself a phenomenon of order, a taxonomic feature, but in the "generic" sense, that of not ordered, indefinite and imprecise, which always demands that a further discrimination be made on the basis of actual context'.[13] Its semantic consistency is less one consisting in a 'name–sense' relationship than what Wittgenstein terms a 'family resemblance', where the auditor or reader cannot enter the process of meaning creation at any consistent point;[14] we conjecture and read on or hear incrementally, where a primary meaning might finally establish itself but not at the expense of others that are lexically related. That initial struggle to decide between equally available, though apparently contending, senses is essential, just as the most complex narratives express meaning through time not in a moment of sublime revelation or *renversement*. One might argue that this is the more likely if the available lexicon is destabilised by a lack of established linguistic hierarchy, such as that derived from an authoritative dictionary or settled syntax, where sense units are arranged through a clear distribution of elements. Where 'spleen' is regularly concerned in Shakespeare's usage, 'further discrimination' is demanded if any clarity is to be achieved.

This is what Robert Burton discovered about melancholy in his *Anatomy of Melancholy* of 1621. Spleen's contribution to a melancholic outlook is to extract melancholy from the system in order to regulate the whole: 'For our body is like a clock; if one wheel be amiss, all the rest are disordered, the whole fabric suffers: with such admirable art and harmony is a man composed'.[15] The affections are apt to disturb the smooth operation of the body, yet melancholy is of three kinds and is affected in alternative ways. The first strain 'is the sole fault of the brain', whereas 'whole body' melancholy is a disorder more the result of behaviour; spleen, on a par with the bowels and liver, contributes to 'hypchondriacal or windy melancholy' a result of bad diet or grief and, crucially, 'some sudden commotion or perturbation of the mind'.[16] Burton's train of reasoning appears to proceed from conjectures about physiological anatomy to its more figurative consequences, yet his more pervasive preoccupation is not with the means by which the body determines mood or ethical choice, but rather with the overlaying of what we would now claim to be psychosomatic symptoms. Cure is the aim, and undue revelation a disorder.

For Shakespeare, the spleen challenges this positive aim: if any stable entity, it undoes the foundations of figurative 'art and harmony' upon which Burton depends in his ideal of the ordered human individual. In the *Dream*, in any case, the lovers do not fully escape their dreams – indeed, it is a moot point whether Lysander embraces his future with Helena quite in his right mind, and Hermia's dream in 2.2 achieves a figurative accuracy that she cannot fathom at the time when she 'sees' a serpent eating 'her heart away' (2.2.147). Bottom cannot fathom his own experiences at 4.1.202–17, in a parody of both 2 Corinthians 12:4 and 1 Corinthians 2:9–10. The celebratory ballad that he will commission of Peter Quince will explore the 'rare vision' (4.1.203) that has no bottom and that is beyond easy summary. As Paul concluded at 2 Corinthians 12:4: 'How that he was caught up into paradise, and heard unspeakable words, which it is not lawful for a man to utter'.[17] At 1 Corinthians 2:10, this reaching beyond sense is a heart's language: 'for the spirit searcheth all things, yea, the deep things of God'. As with the most provocative allusions, the source, though parodied, survives vestigially; Bottom cannot capture such traces in normative language (indeed, he has problems with normative language in any case), but then most of the Athenian court fare no better.

Witty spleen

In the sense that there are depths to which normative language cannot bring us, the ambiguity surrounding 'spleen' is potentially strategic and artful; in comic vein, this is derived from verbal wit, where exact sense disappears or a single orthographic existence belies semantic riches. In a tragic context, there is an irony where humans ultimately lack the control that language promises. Equivocation for Macbeth or Julius Caesar or Mark Antony, for example, can be tragic only if denotation were expected. In *The Merchant of Venice* Lorenzo voices a profound exasperation at Gobbo's torrent of wordplay:

> How every fool can play upon the word! I think the best grace of wit will shortly turn into silence, and discourse grow commendable in none only but parrots ... I pray thee understand a plain man in his plain meaning ...
>
> (3.5.42–56)

The quest for 'unwitty' plainness does indeed come near to the rejection of all certain sense whatsoever. Feste in *Twelfth Night* is also well aware of the relativity that attends all steadfastness of purpose or character; he has the temerity (and licence) to invoke the 'melancholy god' to protect Orsino and to wish that his tailor might 'make [his] doublet of changeable taffeta' as he possesses a mind that 'is a very opal' (2.4.73–5). Even considering the ironic possibilities of that statement, he does advance a proposition that has a general application: 'I would have men of such constancy put to sea, that their business might be everything and their intent everywhere, for that's it that always makes a good voyage of nothing' (2.4.75–8). The iridescence of an opal and the silkiness of taffeta are, one could claim, the acceptable face of wit – glossy and variegated – providing a mixture perhaps too rich for plainness of meaning or, perhaps, of intent.[18] Feste's closing reflection is less reassuring: at the same time as good might come of nothing, all is on the hazard as, following the proverb, 'he is not any where, who is everie where', true also of the speaker himself.[19] An interest in fits of the spleen is, thus, part of a wider preoccupation with what lies beyond language.

Spleen is then only 'vague' in a technical sense. It is used twice in *The Taming of the Shrew* and, on each occasion, there is a fear of its excesses. In the first scene of the Induction, the Lord expects that his presence at the Players' pretence or 'flatt'ring dream' practised upon Christopher Sly might 'well abate the over-merry spleen' that 'otherwise would grow into extremes' when his men see the duping of the beggar (Induction, 1.43, 136–7). Katherina is similarly wary of an apparently mad Petruchio, a 'mad-brain rudesby, full of spleen' and a 'frantic fool' (3.2.10, 12). Here, the word is used to capture the ungovernable rush of emotion both of immoderate laughter and also of whimsy and caprice. In *The Taming of the Shrew*, Sly is finally wakened from a dream that he seems to remember in that he thinks that it has instructed him the way to tame a wife, yet it is unlikely that it will be more than a 'rare vision' for him; we know that he has been a figure of fun, material for the spleen of those watching him. Katherina, too, cannot fathom her 'mad-brain' suitor's behaviour. It is only as an act, as a means to the end of taming, that it can be rationalised by the play's end, yet the doubt that such extremes of behaviour were in fact true of the man lingers, too, and Katherina's abject speech of capitulation at 5.2.137–80 is a willing entry not quite to a patriarchal way of the world but rather as a reinforcement of such unfathomable *mores*, this time to disconcert Bianca, her favoured younger sister, as well as win a bet for her husband. Indeed, the point of the encounter with Hortensio at 4.5, where Petruchio's taming is less a physical set of rebukes than an invitation to break out of the constraining norms of resentment and duty (as the elder daughter), and discover the faults of her 'mistaking eyes' that regarded the world as 'green' (an immature perspective rather than a fresh or natural one) (4.5.44–6), might be to illustrate a strategy not an authentic character. In other contemporary tamings, such as *Tom Tayler and His Wife* (*c*.1560) or *The Ballad of the Curst Wife Wrapt in Morell's Skin* (*c*.1550), the subduing of the strong woman is accompanied by beatings; here it is more insidious, one could claim, but thematically distinct and makes greater sense of the hints at a splenetic perspective – an escape from, even a challenge to, an easy acceptance of normative values.

It is a consistent value of 'spleen' in Shakespeare's comedies that it occurs at moments where the darker purpose of the form is suggested; just as a fit of the spleen can reveal hidden desires and aspirations, it also tussles with the more conservative paradigms of comic form, where eventually successful romantic love incorporates a younger generation into tradition. The perceptions unlocked by the unprompted energies of spleen exceed this and might render any conventional closure as merely formally pleasing. In *As You Like It*, Rosalind regards her love for Orlando as an emotion that 'cannot be sounded. [Her] affection hath an unknown bottom like the Bay of Portugal' (4.1.199–200). She is thus tyrannised by 'that same wicked bastard of Venus, that was begot of thought, conceived of spleen, and born of madness' (4.1.203–5). Cupid, begot out of wedlock by Mercury with Venus – not her husband, Vulcan – is not an example of a Hymeneal barring of confusion, the abrupt convergence of the play's closing marriages. Indeed, as Celia notices, its effect on her erstwhile friend is to introduce a sieve-like fickleness that puts their relationship at some risk, for 'as fast as you pour affection in, it runs out' (4.1.201–2). Although there is a pragmatic reason for the next scene where Jaques celebrates the killing of the deer with the 'Lords dressed as foresters' (an elapse of time to allow the return of Orlando to Rosalind), its expressions of licentiousness and recent violence surely spill over into Celia's sleep, perhaps as dream, and illustrate a cupidity where the affections are concerned, in stark contrast to the talk of marriage and fidelity in the previous scene. Rosalind's triad of causes for the illicit coupling of Venus and Mercury may now seem strange – madness and the splenetic might cohere, yet Cupid is also 'begot of thought'. Steevens, in 1773, had suggested 'melancholy' as a primary meaning of 'thought', yet Alan Brissenden in his Oxford edition is disarmingly honest in his note: 'several meanings are possible; "imagination" is as good as any and better than some'.[20] One wonders at the possible consequences of seeing 'thought' here as 'melancholy'. Is it a perhaps regrettable tendency in human nature that a fear of consequences is null and void when the 'spleen' strikes? Juliet Dusinberre, in her Arden 3 edition, conjectures a parody at work here of the Apostles' Creed, 'conceived of the holy ghost, borne of the virgin Mary'.[21] If so, then, like Bottom's allusions to Corinthians, it offers a diabolic counterpoint to 'holy' creativity on the one hand with a divine mystery on the other.

If we have the courage of our convictions thus far, then the valency of the word might summon up a range of contrasting significations even when the dramatic context seems to encourage just one main emphasis or sub-set of meanings. Take three other occurrences; two from *Love's Labour's Lost* and one from *Twelfth Night*. Don Armado is so taken by Costard's unlettered attempt at plainness that it provokes immoderate laughter – to the point where his 'silly thought' provokes the Don's spleen. This is, however, stilled by the pedantic analysis of the figures that both have used; the 'ridiculous smiling' (3.1.74–6) at the start is dissipated in the next forty or so lines, in attempting to decipher a moral in the epilogue or *envoi* that Armado supposes had been expressed by Moth and Costard. Well might he break in at lines 103–4 with the desire for some originating signified: 'How did this argument begin?' and also then dismiss the 'wit' of the exchange with 'we will talk no more of this matter' (3.1.117).[22] The Princess of France reports the arrival of her entourage's suitors dressed as Muscovites in what seems to be mere reportage. It is the prelude to the broadest comic moment of the play, the discomforting of Berowne and the courtiers:

> With that they all did tumble on the ground,
> With such a zealous laughter, so profound,
> That in this spleen ridiculous appears,
> To check their folly, passion's solemn tears.
>
> (5.2.115–18)

The maskers, the courtiers in disguise, aim to press their suits, yet the description that the Princess provides is Janus-faced; the precise species of laughter indicated here is the very reverse of thoughtless escape, 'zealous' and 'profound' mirth leads to ridicule and the solemnity of 'passion', a corrective to 'folly'. The syntax could yoke 'ridiculous' with 'spleen', or qualify 'passion's solemn tears'; in both cases (and I have not discounted it qualifying both nouns), the mocking intent of the maskers' reception is not calculated to be merely innocent merriment. Forty lines later the Princess anticipates the unmasked maskers departing 'away with shame' (5.2.156), an effect of the auditors being determined to 'render … no grace' (5.2.147), and an eventuality noted by Boyet: 'Why, that contempt will kill the speaker's heart / And quite divorce his memory from his part' (5.2.149–50) – which it does.

Maria, in *Twelfth Night*, anticipates a scene of Malvolio in yellow stockings and cross-gartered that 'will laugh' spectators 'into stitches', suitable for those who might 'desire the spleen' (3.2.66–7). She is to lead us to a scene of most unchristian and 'impossible … grossness' (3.2.69–70). Well may Olivia claim that this is 'midsummer madness' (3.4.56), and the imprisoned Malvolio cannot prove his sanity under these conditions, 'in hideous darkness' (4.2.30), claiming (in vain) that he is 'as well in [his] wits' as 'any man in Illyria' (4.2.107–8) – a dangerous yardstick of reason. His consternation is all the more marked by his confinement in a confused obscurity. As John H. Astington has noted, he is also likely to have been out of sight of the audience, perhaps in the tiring-house, depending on how we are to take the Folio's stage direction, 'MALVOLIO *within*' (s.d. 4.2.19).[23] Indeed, it is a relatively recent tendency in staging to reveal Malvolio, even if through a grate, and it makes sense of Maria's advice to Feste that he might have run through his antics as Sir Topas 'without thy beard and gown, [for] he sees thee not' (4.2.63–4). Malvolio's disembodied voice is heard and his possible madness registered, yet the spleen is with his spectators, Feste, Maria and Sir Toby, and, unless the perspectives on the scene, that it is 'madness', impossibly gross and unchristian, are just smoky stage rhetoric, then the absence of the victim – partial or complete – accentuates both Feste's comic versatility and his cruelty. The discomfort it causes even Sir Toby is confirmed with his desire to be 'well rid of this knavery'; his motives might be those of self-preservation, to remain in good standing with Olivia, yet he regards it so much as a probable 'offence' that he cannot 'cannot pursue with any safety this sport to the upshot' (4.2.66–70). Perhaps this would be to peer too closely at the text, and, for example, Lothian and Craik's reminder that Feste is the presiding genius of the scene and even the whole play might lead us to treat such scruples as token gestures to accepted good – and uncomic – behaviour.[24] Yet we might also conclude that Shakespeare's conclusion to the play is clearly provisional in plotting and verbal texture. How celebratory might any play be that concludes with Feste's song that reminds us that the 'rain it raineth every day', and that poor players will 'strive', therefore, to please us as recompense (5.1.384–400)? Or that it will be a requirement of the happy marriages that Malvolio be entreated to a peace (5.1.372)? Barnabe Riche's *Riche His Farewell to Militarie Profession* (1581), the most direct source for the play, concludes with no such loose ends: 'they passed the residue of their daies with suche delight, as those that have accomplished the perfection of their felicities'.[25]

If we were to take seriously Maria's sense that Malvolio's incarceration would attract the immoderate – and perhaps uncomfortable – mirth of the spleen, then his 'enlightenment' in 5.1 – as Lothian and Craik have it – is not simply an effect of the plot (he comes to know the degree of his deception), but rather a perception that is of much wider and unpalatable application: that he will never cross the class divide and the representatives of the class he has so devotedly wished to join are in effect antagonists.[26]

Unmimetic spleen

Taken seriously, 'spleen' challenges the bases of imitative art, for its swift and erratic power unsettles the usual relationship between tenor and vehicle, or between *res* and *verba*. For Sidney, Aristotelian *mimesis* resembled a 'speaking picture', yet before we conclude that this gestures towards a securely framed *topos* or grounded expressiveness, he takes the peculiar talent of the poet to lie in a supplementing of a philosopher's exhortations:

> he giveth a perfect picture of it [what a philosopher 'saith should be done'] in some one by whom he presupposeth it was done, so as he coupleth the general notion with the particular example. A perfect picture I say, for he yieldeth to the powers of the mind an image of that whereof the philosopher bestoweth but a wordish description, which doth neither strike, pierce, nor possess the sight of the soul so much as that other doth.[27]

Horace's famous formula, *ut pictura poesis*, has frequently been interpreted more in line with *ut pictura poesis erit* – that poetry should aspire to the condition of painting[28] – yet his original sense was more to plead for an expressive power in poetry itself, less that it should offer just a graphic quality, linked perhaps to *ekphrasis*.[29] As such, it is more a gloss upon the needs of Aristotelian *energeia,* a goal of stylistic vigour.[30] Indeed, in Quintilian's hands, the related term *enargeia* provides an immediacy that exceeds the graphic, 'a quality which makes us seem not so much to be talking about something as exhibiting it. Emotions will ensue just as if we were present at the event itself.'[31] In Shakespeare's hands, the special attraction of the splenetic was that it indicated some aspects of the emotional that could not be adequately represented in verbal terms. It also indicated some aspects of the full textual representation that could only be completed imaginatively.

This is also clearly demonstrated in his narrative poetry. In both *Venus and Adonis* and *The Rape of Lucrece*, the denial of passion in the former and its indulgence in the latter both provide Shakespeare with an opportunity to explore emotional affects rather more than their direct causes. Venus, when approaching what she fears is the fearful sight of Adonis harmed, is afflicted by 'a thousand spleens' that 'bear her a thousand ways', and that cause her to tread and yet also untread her way forward. Haste and delay are commingled 'like the proceedings of a drunken brain', a predicament wherein she is (actively) at a stand, 'full of respects, yet naught at all respecting, / In hand with all things, naught at all effecting' (907, 911–12). The link between intention and its effects is severed, a prelude to the desperation that 'beauty dead, black chaos comes again' (1020). It is the chaos that Othello fears when his love for Desdemona leads his soul to 'perdition', a loss of direction and even identity (3.3.90–2), and also the primeval condition before light renders illumination and so distinction in the Genesis myth.[32] In *Lucrece*, the enormity of the despoliation is beyond words. Lucretia has no confidence in 'idle words', and is clear in her own mind that 'this helpless smoke of words [of pleading] doth [her] no right' in the face of Tarquin's might (1016, 1027). Consequently, her grief – as with Philomel or Procne – 'hath no words' (1105). This progress towards some zero degree of feeling seems to have recourse to the Horatian equation of painting with words when Shakespeare describes at length her feelings of dishonour:

> To see sad sights moves more than hear them told,
> For then the eye interprets to the ear
> The heavy motion that it doth behold,
> When every part a part of woe doth bear.
>
> (1324–7)

For Sidney, it was specifically the example of Lucretia that best encapsulated the poetic possibilities of a speaking picture, an improvement on the 'meaner sort of painters' who represent merely the outward lineaments of their subject; on the contrary, we should expect not a facsimile of a person we had never met, but rather a painting of the 'outward beauty of such a virtue'.[33]

Shakespeare's Lucrece, however, in viewing the picture of the fall of Troy, is in no position to derive just an ethical lesson from its images. When spying Hecuba's plight, she receives the impression of 'time's ruin, beauty's rack, and grim care's reign' (1451), a sight that 'shapes her sorrow to the beldam's woes' (1458).[34] When viewing paintings of Troy ablaze, she lends the images words, but she in turn 'their looks doth borrow' (1498), and, in dwelling on the image of 'perjured Sinon', the response is emotive and ultimately not iconographical: '[his] words like wildfire burnt the shining glory / Of rich-built Ilion, that the skies were sorry' (1523–4). This is privileging the condition of poetic appropriation where the graphic images are mere foundation stones, and this is not an instance of the poet aligning himself to the skilled artist, but rather a demonstration of interpretative 'poetry', granting, pre-eminently, the silent images an imaginative life that exceeds the scope of a figurative canvas or tapestry – and even regular colours of rhetoric.

Dramatic spleen

One could approach the use of the word *spleen* in terms that are not strictly philological; there are several words or phrases in Shakespeare's dramatic language that are densely packed with alternative or contending senses, where deciphering the primary linguistic meaning is a complex business but where registering the dramatic impact is not. An excess of humoral effect is one of these. I stress 'an excess', for we do not understand Shakespeare's 'spleen' by recourse to humoral explanations.[35] It is as if the audience is also invited at certain moments to share the disorientation of certain of the *dramatis personae*. An opposite perspective on verbal power was expressed by Samuel Daniel, whose *Cleopatra* (1594) seems to have been a source for Shakespeare's *Antony and Cleopatra*. Daniel noted how it was a poet's higher duty to clear his works of 'oppressing humors' so that the 'words thou scornest now / May live, the speaking picture of the mind'. This was the method by which the soul might be commemorated and the 'just proportion of the spirits' regained. This is humanism at its most aspirational, for it is 'blessed letters' that can help us converse across the ages, 'and make one live with all'.[36] Apt choice is the key, for there may be a 'streame of words' that 'now doth rise so hie / Above the usuall banks', and these are liable to be 'ever amplified / With th'abounding humours that do multiplie'. If these are not to mar the clarity of antique wisdom, then we must call to our aid

heavenly *Eloquence*,
That with the strong reine of commanding words,
Dost manage, guide, and master th'eminence
Of mens affections, more than all their swords.[37]

The pen may indeed be mightier than the sword, but, in Daniel's hands, it is by no means an effortless victory; the emphasis is rather more on the tidal wave of rhetorical possibilities that could conspire to flood the senses and grant too much display to raw emotion. This was a common preoccupation of Daniel's, and in Sonnet 20 of *Delia* (1592) it is the peculiar power of deep love that threatens most this calculated art:

What it is to breathe and live without life;
How to be pale with anguish, red with feare,
T'have peace abroad, and nought within but strife:
Wish to be present, and yet shun t'appeare;
How to be bold far off, and bashful neare;
How to think much, and have no words to speake.[38]

This wall between utterance and feeling is a trope by which we gauge depth of emotion; we do, however, in Shakespeare's work trace a fascination with a loss of linguistic control – the very opposite of Daniel's at times desperate grasp at the structuring word. In Sonnet 85, his 'tongue-tied Muse' produces (of course) a quieter eloquence, disdaining others' rhetorical flights, their 'polished form of well-refined pen'. As Katherine Duncan-Jones puts it, he is here 'playing the Cordelia role', preferring the zero degree of language to express emotion too deep for words.[39] The sonnet claims that all this poet can do is assent to others' verbal dexterity, where his own 'words come hindmost', because the emotion is 'in my thought'. His emotional life produces 'dumb thoughts', where the only available speech must be 'in effect' – in action, in gesture. Indeed, the cycle permits several associated sonnets – from 82 to 86 – that play with this perception. From the search for 'true plain words' in sonnet 82 to the need to remain 'dumb' to avoid impairing beauty by inevitably inappropriate rhetoric in 83 to the determination to copy merely what is 'in you is writ' and what 'nature made so clear' in 84 to the distrust of polished praise in 85 Shakespeare reaches beyond the verbal.[40] To return to *Lucrece*, it is precisely Collatine's false step that he broadcasts his wife's beauty to Tarquin, where 'Beauty itself doth of itself persuade / The eyes of men without an orator' (29–30).

Perhaps at first reading an unlikely example of splenetic transformation, *Love's Labour's Lost* frequently pits rhetorical accomplishment, the craft of expression, with a more mature, yet less definable emotion. On hearing of the King of France's death and also observing the depth of grief experienced by the Princess and her entourage, Berowne understands that 'honest plain words best pierce the ear of grief' (5.2.747). The 'spleen ridiculous' that has led the maskers to exhibit themselves so foolishly is now forgot, 'fashioning our humours / Even to the opposed end of our intents' (5.2.751–2). It is especially the eye that forms the 'unbefitting strains' that love introduces:

> All wanton as a child, skipping and vain,
> Formed by the eye, and therefore, like the eye,
> Full of strange shapes, of habits and of forms,
> Varying in subjects as the eye doth roll
> To every varied object in his glance;
> Which parti-coated presence of loose love
> Put on by us, if, in your heavenly eyes,
> Have misbecomed our oaths and gravities,
> Those heavenly eyes that look into these faults,
> Suggested us to make.
>
> (5.2.755–64)

The rolling eye of 5.2.758 takes us back to Theseus who has his poet in a 'fine frenzy rolling' in the imaginative glance 'from heaven to earth, from earth to heaven', and where 'the forms of things unknown' are given 'shapes' and a 'local habitation and a name' (*A Midsummer Night's Dream*, 5.1.12–17). Love's suggestions (5.2.764) are also temptations, and the inexorable variety of perspective that this frenzy promotes can only provide a 'parti-coated presence' (5.2.760), no settled proportion or focus.

The spleen, therefore, does not quite allow a 'speaking picture', because it lacks fixed 'habitation' in being incessantly nomadic and transient. This misalignment of *res* and *verba* Berowne attributes to love, but it is also part of the *grotesquerie* of spleen; it is fitting that it is here associated with an effect at the very boundaries of linguistic capture. The play concludes with a claim that the 'words of Mercury' seem 'harsh after the songs of Apollo'.[41] Thus, the sobering (and brief) embassage of Mercade (5.2.705–9) ends the time of song and energy, and/or Winter's grasp succeeds Summer's heat. On closer inspection, though, Mercade, although a messenger, does not quite fit the role of Mercury, associated with eloquence and sometimes sophistry, and Summer's apparent consolation is attendant – at least for 'married men' – with the mockery of the cuckoo (5.2.896). Equilibrium is suggested yet not quite delivered; indeed, the Folio ends with a disjunction of some kind: 'You that way, we this way' (5.2.912).[42]

Berowne's understanding of where rhetoric might end is prefigured by earlier concerns about its permanence and even relevance. It is Armado who hails the 'sweet smoke of rhetoric' (3.1.60), a trope taken up – but with significant difference – by Lucrece.[43] It is only when noting the pain that can inhere in excessive emotion that Shakespeare lays particular emphasis on spleen. In caricaturing Achilles's love of paradox in *Troilus and Cressida*, Ulysses imagines his banter with Patroclus as misplaced; 'all our abilities, gifts, natures, shapes' as well as military achievements become fuel for their idle flyting, wherein they risk splitting their sides 'in pleasure of [their] spleen' (1.3.178–9). Distinction, military prowess, heroism and even 'what is or is not' (1.3.183) sinks into the one rhetorical void, but Ulysses is not the privileged voice of the play. Indeed, the play may not have one, so intent is it in disrobing monuments from Homer.[44] Despite Ulysses's confidence at this point, spleen might be the tutelary god of the piece. For Plato, in his *Philebus*, comedy involved a blending of pain with pleasure, where ignorance of self led to self-delusion.[45]

Comedic characterisation often involves the invitation for an audience to sense a superiority over them, but, accompanying that, also a discomfort when we witness their disorientation. We may laugh at Sly or Bottom, yet, at the same time, register the inexorability of their plight. In this, their own anagnorisis is shared with that audience – akin to the tragic variety. Without the verbal skills to express their perceptions, they *and we* are presented with perceptions that elude precise definition, largely because these notions are themselves ineffable. The spleen is invoked to suggest the mingle of associations and rush of emotion that an audience is also forced to contemplate even if in a cooler spirit. Far from framed and 'placed' by its context – a linear narrative or any consistency of character – attacks of the spleen display their own irrational power, a challenge to norms of linguistic range and unitary meaning – and also a strictly humoral explanation of human behaviour. Portia may, indeed, wish that her 'ecstasy' be allayed and that her joy may be reined 'in measure' as she watches Bassanio prepare himself for the fateful choice of caskets (*The Merchant of Venice*, 3.2.111–14). Her fear of 'excess' and 'surfeit' is true, perhaps, to her character at this moment, yet not so of her author.

Notes

1 All Shakespeare quotations are taken from Richard Proudfoot, Ann Thompson and David Scott Kastan (eds), *The Arden Shakespeare Complete Works*, revd edn (London: Thomson, 2001).

2 Arthur Golding, 'The first booke of Ouids Metamorphosis, translated into Englyshe Meter', l.1, in *The. XV. Bookes of P. Ouidius Naso, Entytuled Metamorphosis, Translated oute of Latin into English Meeter, by Arthur Golding Gentleman, a Worke Very Pleasaunt and Delectable* (London, 1567), p. 1.

3 For more on this 'circuit' of reference see Bruce Clarke, 'Paradox and the Form of Metamorphosis: Systems Theory in *A Midsummer Night's Dream*', *Intertexts*, 8 (2004), 173–89.

4 Cf. 5.1.1–5, and Juliet's beauty, which 'makes / This vault a feasting presence full of light' (5.3.85–6).

5 'The Sublime leads the listeners not to persuasion, but to ecstasy: for what is wonderful always goes together with a sense of dismay, and prevails over what is only convincing or delightful, since persuasion, as a rule, is within everyone's grasp: whereas, the Sublime, giving to speech an invincible power and [an invincible] strength, rises above every listener' (*Longinus on the Sublime*, trans. William Rhys Roberts (Oxford: Oxford University Press, 1899), p. 34).

6 Gail Kern Paster, Katherine Rowe and Mary Floyd-Wilson (eds), *Reading the Early Modern Passions: Essays in the Cultural History of Emotion* (Philadelphia: University of Pennsylvania Press, 2004). See especially Richard Strier's 'Against the Rule of Reason: Praise of Passion from Petrarch to Luther to Shakespeare to Herbert' (pp. 23–42), and John Staines's 'Compassion in the Public Sphere of Milton and King Charles' (pp. 89–110), where the intersection of public display and private intensity is unlike a modern division between inner and outer or between the individual psyche and rhetorical projection.

7 Gail Kern Paster, Katherine Rowe and Mary Floyd-Wilson, 'Introduction: Reading the Early Modern Passions', in Paster, Rowe and Floyd-Wilson (eds), *Reading the Early Modern Passions: Essays in the Cultural History of Emotion* (Philadelphia: University of Pennsylvania Press, 2004), pp. 1–20 (pp. 17–18). This perception also allows for an improvement to strictly Galenic definitions of bodily health; see also the discussions by Sara Coodin, Chapter 3 above, and R.S. White and Ciara Rawnsley, Chapter 11, below.

8 R. A. Foakes (ed.), *A Midsummer Night's Dream* (Cambridge: Cambridge University Press, 1984), note to 1.1.146; Gail Kern Paster and Skiles Howard (eds), *A Midsummer Night's Dream: Texts and Contexts* (Basingstoke: Palgrave Macmillan, 1999), note to 1.1.146; Harold F. Brooks (ed.), *A Midsummer Night's Dream* (London: Methuen, 1979); note to 1.1.146; Peter Holland (ed.), *A Midsummer Night's Dream* (Oxford: Oxford University Press, 1994), note to 1.1.146.

9 'Timaeus', 72c, 72d, in *The Dialogues of Plato*, trans. Benjamin Jowett, 6 vols (London: Sphere Books, 1970), vol. 3, p. 278.

10 'De partibus animalium', Book III, ch. 7 (669b, 670a), in *The Works of Aristotle*, ed. J. A. Smith and W. D. Ross, 12 vols (London: Oxford University Press, 1912).

11 *Galen: On the Usefulness of the Parts of the Body*, 2 vols, trans. M. T. May (Ithaca: Cornell University Press, 1968), vol. 2, pp. 221–3.

12 Andrew Wear, 'The Spleen in Renaissance Anatomy', *Medical History*, 21 (1977), 43–60.

13 Paul Ricoeur, *The Rule of Metaphor: Multi-disciplinary Studies of the Creation of Meaning in Language*, trans. Robert Czerny with Kathleen McLaughlin and John Costello (London: Routledge, 1978), p. 113. Ricoeur is here engaging with Stephen Ullmann's *The Principles of Semantics* (Oxford: Blackwell, 1951), pp. 159–75.

14 Ludwig Wittgenstein, *Philosophical Investigations*, trans. G. E. M. Anscombe (Oxford: Blackwell, 1953), par. 67.

15 Robert Burton, *The Anatomy of Melancholy*, ed. Holbrook Jackson, 3 vols (London: J. M. Dent, 1932), vol. 1, p. 171. Yet this equilibrium is constantly threatened by melancholic states of mind; see Mary Ann Lund, Chapter 4, above.

16 Ibid., vol. 1, p. 380.

17 All biblical references are to the King James Version, in *The Bible in English* database, http://collections.chadwyck.com/ [accessed 24 July 2012].

18 In like vein, Berowne in *Love's Labour's Lost* distrusts his own 'taffeta phrases, silken terms precise' that inevitably convey 'ostentation' (5.2.406, 409).

19 M. P. Tilley, *A Dictionary of the Proverbs in England in the Sixteenth and Seventeenth Centuries* (Ann Arbor: University of Michigan Press, 1950), E194.

20 Alan Brissenden (ed.), *As You Like It* (Oxford: Clarendon Press, 1994), note to 4.1.195.

21 Juliet Dusinberre (ed.), *As You Like It*, The Arden Shakespeare (London: Thomson, 2006), note to 4.1.200.

22 The clearest tracing of some punning sense in the exchange (mainly sexual) is summarised by H. R. Woudhuysen in his Arden 3 edn of *Love's Labour's Lost* (Walton-on-Thames: Thomas Nelson, 1998), note to 3.1.118-19. Its accuracy is not in doubt when we also note the complexities of the implications, where words pile up obscuring clear sense.

23 John H. Astington, 'Malvolio and the Dark House', *Shakespeare Survey*, 41 (1988), 55–62. See also Mariko Ichikawa, '"Maluolio within": Acting on the Threshold between Onstage and Offstage Spaces', *Medieval and Renaissance Drama in England*, 18 (2005), 123–41; and David Carnegie, '"Maluolio within": Performance Perspectives on the Dark House', *Shakespeare Quarterly*, 52 (2001), 393–416.

24 J. M. Lothian and T. W. Craik (eds), *Twelfth Night* (London: Methuen, 1975), pp. lxxv–lxxviii.

25 Geoffrey Bullough (ed.), *Narrative and Dramatic Sources of Shakespeare*, 8 vols (London: Routledge, 1958–75), vol. 2, p. 363.

26 Lothian and Craik, 'Introduction' to *Twelfth Night*, p. lxxviii.

27 Philip Sidney, *An Apology for Poetry, or The Defence of Poetry*, ed. R. W. Maslen, 3rd edn (Manchester: Manchester University Press, 1989), pp. 86, 90.

28 See Horace, *The Art of Poetry*, in D. A. Russell and M. Winterbottom (eds), *Classical Literary Criticism* (Oxford: Oxford University Press, 1989), p. 107; for further discussion see Henryk Mankiewicz, '"*Ut Pictura Poesis*: A History of the Topos and the Problem', *New Literary History*, 18 (1987), 535–58.

29 See Wesley Trimpi, 'The Meaning of Horace's *Ut Pictura Poesis*', *Journal of the Warburg and Courtauld Institutes*, 36 (1973), 1–34.

30 Aristotle's *Rhetoric*, III: 1411b22ff. See also Quintillian, *Instituto Oratoria*, trans. Donald A. Russell, 5 vols (Cambridge, MA: Harvard University Press, 2001), 8.3.88–9; and George Puttenham, *The Arte of English Poesie* (1589), ed. Gladys Doidge Willcock and Alice Walker (Cambridge: Cambridge University Press, 1936), 3.3.

31 *Instituto Oratoria*, 6.2.32.

32 It is also a pervasive motif of the poem that human and natural workmanship are often set at odds; see especially ll. 289–94 (when trying to capture the 'life' of Adonis's horse), and the 'statue contenting but the eye alone' (213).

33 Sidney, *Apology*, p. 87.

34 See also Collatine's inability to frame his own distress, where 'Weak words, so thick come in his poor heart's aid / That no man could distinguish what he said' (1784–5). Richard Meek's consideration of Collatine's plight (*Narrating the Visual in Shakespeare* (Farnham: Ashgate, 2009), pp. 60–3), sheds light on how the poem constructs its own perspective on visual metaphors; see also Stephen Cheeke, *Writing for Art: The Aesthetics of Ekphrasis* (Manchester: Manchester University Press, 2008), pp. 124–41.

35 This is not to claim that he did not exploit such explanations at certain junctures; see Robert L. Reid, 'Humoral Psychology in Shakespeare's *Henriad*', *Comparative Drama*, 30 (1996–97), 471–503.

36 Samuel Daniel, 'Musophilis', in *The Poeticall Essayes of Samuel Daniel* (London, 1599), p. 116.

37 Ibid., p. 131.

38 Samuel Daniel, *The Complete Works*, ed. Alexander B. Grosart (Aylesbury, 1885), pp. 49–50. See also Richard Meek, Chapter 6, below, where Daniel's goal of 'sympathy' is analysed in relation to *Richard II*.

39 Katherine Duncan-Jones (ed.), *Shakespeare's Sonnets*, The Arden Shakespeare, revd edn (London: Thomson Learning, 2010), p. 280.

40 A similar point is offered in Alison Scott, 'Tainted Exchanges: Giving Truth in Shakespeare's Sonnets', *Journal of the Australiasian Universities Modern Language Association*, 101 (2004), 1–25: 'Speech ruins friendship; it corrupts by speaking, degrades, belittles, undoes the speech of friendship; but this evil is done to it on account of truth. If silence must be kept among friends, concerning friends, this is just as much so as not to tell the truth, a murderous truth' (p. 17).

41 Unattributed in the quarto text; in the Folio given to Armado.

42 Either signalling the departure to France of the Princess and her attendants, or, if metatheatrically, the end of the play and its communion between actors and audience.

43 See above.

44 This satiric project and its bodily associations is detailed in David Hilman, 'The Gastric Epic: *Troilus and Cressida*', *Shakespeare Quarterly*, 48 (1997), 295–314.

45 *Philebus*, trans. A. E. Taylor (London: Nelson, 1956), pp. 167–9.

6

'Rue e'en for ruth': *Richard II* and the imitation of sympathy

Richard Meek

In Act 1 Scene 3 of *Richard II*, Mowbray describes his sorrow at being banished from England, calling his sentence a 'speechless death' that will prevent his tongue from 'breathing native breath' (1.3.172–3). Yet Mowbray's eloquent lament fails to influence the monarch who has banished him; as King Richard says, 'It boots thee not to be compassionate. / After our sentence, plaining comes too late' (1.3.174–5). Richard suggests that Mowbray's speech is a deliberate attempt to move him to mercy and compassion, but that the complaint is belated and ineffective.[1] At this point in the play, then, Richard remains unmoved by another character's attempt to express their emotions. Several lines later, however, Richard does show mercy to Bolingbroke after noting the emotional state of Bolingbroke's father, John of Gaunt: 'Uncle, even in the glasses of thine eyes / I see thy grieved heart' (208–9). These apparently transparent signs of Gaunt's inward grief cause Richard to reduce Bolingbroke's ten-year banishment by four years. Of course, there may be political as well as emotional reasons for Richard's decision to show mercy to Bolingbroke and not Mowbray. Nevertheless, Richard's description of Gaunt's 'sad aspect' (209), and his subsequent reduction of Bolingbroke's sentence, opens up larger questions about the play's interest in the representation of grief and the nature of pity. In what circumstances do individuals feel – or fail to feel – pity for one another? What is the most effective means of eliciting sympathy from others? Is it possible to separate the play's politics from its concern with sorrow and compassion?

In the latter stages of *Richard II* it is Richard himself who becomes the subjugated individual pleading for pity. Through his attempts to describe his own 'unseen grief' (4.1.297) Richard attempts to move the play's other characters – and implicitly its audiences and readers – to compassion. Yet the extent to which we ought to sympathise with him has long been a matter of critical discussion and debate. In the nineteenth century, William Hazlitt suggested that we feel 'neither respect nor love' for Richard, but that he is none the less 'human in his distresses … and we sympathize with him accordingly. The suffering of the man makes us forget that he was ever a king.'[2] W. B. Yeats, writing in the early twentieth century, similarly suggested that the play offers a sympathetic portrait of a man 'ill-fitted' to be king: 'I cannot believe that Shakespeare looked on his Richard II with any but sympathetic eyes.'[3] By the latter part of the twentieth century this sympathetic approach was beginning to appear sentimental and even suspect. Andrew Gurr, for example, in his 1984 New Cambridge edition, argued that seeing Richard as a tragic everyman 'projects sympathy for a dead king backwards and puts a gloss on his conduct which is not warranted by the body of the play'.[4] In the same year that Gurr's edition appeared, an article by Scott McMillin discussed the representation of sorrow in the play, suggesting that seeing through tears can be a 'false way of seeing'.[5] In other words, looking at Richard with sympathetic or emotional eyes can blur our vision, and thus impede our judgement. Since the turn of the twenty-first century, however, the play's critics and editors appear to be more at ease again acknowledging the play's capacity to move audiences to sympathy. In his Arden 3 edition, Charles Forker writes that 'sympathy flows naturally towards Richard as tragic victim', while Anthony Dawson and Paul Yachnin suggest that, in Richard's final moments, the 'tragic empathy that Shakespeare has been building towards … gets its fullest expression'.[6]

As this brief overview suggests, it is hard for critics and commentators of *Richard II* to avoid addressing the play's emotionalism, if only to dismiss certain responses as naive or wrong-headed. But we might note that such critics invariably focus on emotional responses *outside* the play: that is, they attempt to identify and describe the sympathetic reactions of audiences and readers. The present chapter, by contrast, examines the various instances of sympathetic engagement and emotional correspondence within the text. It explores the various figured audiences and emotionally engaged onlookers that the play depicts, and the ways in which the play's characters frequently compare their sorrows to other texts and stories. This emphasis upon emotional comparability and intertextuality is intriguingly related to the ways in which *Richard II* is itself embedded in a larger process of literary imitation, allusion and borrowing. In particular, the chapter considers the ways in which Shakespeare borrows certain situations – and emotion words – from Samuel Daniel's *Civil Wars*. As we shall see, Shakespeare's play not only manipulates the audience's sympathies but also plays an important role in refining and modifying terms such as *sympathy* and *sympathise*. In doing so,

Shakespeare highlights the ways in which pity and compassion are complex imaginative processes, rather than simply automatic or humoral phenomena. At the same time, however, *Richard II* reminds us that such processes can be exploited in the hands of a skilful rhetorician, politician, or indeed playwright.

'For whether love in him did sympathize': Samuel Daniel's *Civil Wars*

The primary meaning of *sympathise* in the late sixteenth century was 'to be affected in consequence of the affection of some one or something else; to be similarly or correspondingly affected; to respond sympathetically to some influence' (*OED*, 1a). Under this definition the *OED* cites Burton's *Anatomy of Melancholy* (1621): '*Capiuaccius*, and *Mercurialis* haue copiously discussed this question [the bodily parts most affected by melancholy], and both conclude the subject is the Inner *Braine*, and from thence it is communicated to the *Heart*, and other inferiour parts, which sympathize and are much troubled'.[7] This sense of correspondence and agreement – sometimes with occult connotations – is evident in John Florio's translation of cognate Italian terms in his *A Worlde of Wordes* (1598). *Simpathia* is translated as 'a sympathie or naturall combination of things naturall in the operation of the powers, nature and qualities, as water in coldnes doth participate with the earth, in moisture with the aire, a natruall passion of one to the other'. Meanwhile *simpathizzare* is glossed as 'to sympathize or agree in nature or disposition'.[8] As these examples suggest, the act of sympathising seems to have been regarded as an essentially passive phenomenon, in which a person, object or bodily part is affected by something or someone else.

By the time we reach Randle Cotgrave's *A Dictionarie of the French and English Tongues* (1611), however, we find that the term *sympathise* is used to describe a correspondence of sorrows: the French word *condouloir* is translated as 'To sorrow, or moane with, to sympathize with the griefe, or paine of', while *sympathiser* is translated as 'To sympathize, or have a fellow-feeling of, to jumpe with in passion, consent with in affection, agree with in disposition'.[9] Taken together, all of these examples remind us that the term *sympathise* was in flux in the late sixteenth and early seventeenth centuries, and that while the sense of correspondence and agreement persisted the word was increasingly used to describe grief and fellow-feeling. Literary texts from this period reflect the earlier occult or physiological conception of *sympathise*, yet they also seem to have played a part in facilitating the shift towards a more complex understanding of sympathy, in which 'sympathising' with others was regarded as an active and imaginative process.

One late sixteenth-century text that employs the term *sympathise* in the earlier sense of correspondence and agreement is Samuel Daniel's *The First Four Books of the Civil Wars between the Two Houses of Lancaster and York* (1595), an epic if unfinished retelling of the War of the Roses, which appears to have been a significant influence on Shakespeare's *Richard II*.[10] In Daniel's poem there are several moments that point to a sympathetic reciprocity between human passions and an anthropomorphised natural world. In Book 1, for example, the narrator describes the downfall of Richard II and the unstable political situation, and notes its impact upon the people of England and the landscape. After describing the appearance of various fearful omens, including 'Prodigious monsters' and other 'gastly fearefull sights', the narrator notes the relationship between the natural world and the woeful populace:

> The Earth as if afeard of bloud and woundes
> Trembles in terror of these falling bloes:
> The hollow concaves give out groning sounds
> And sighing, murmurs to lament our woes:
> The Ocean all at discord with his boundes,
> Reiterates his strange untimely floes:
> Nature all out of course to checke our course,
> Neglects her worke to worke in us remorse.[11]

In this stanza the earth is said to be 'afeard' of the calamity that is about to befall the country, while the respective woes of the people and the environment reinforce each other. This passage might thus be seen as evidence that, for early moderns, human passions are not separate from the outside world, but involve an ecology or 'transaction' between the body and the environment.[12] Mary Floyd-Wilson and Garrett A. Sullivan, Jr, have described this conception of the early modern body, which was, they suggest, 'understood as embedded in a larger world with which it transacts'.[13] Daniel's narrator states that Nature 'worke[s]' remorse in human beings; and so this description might confirm the sense that emotions were things that happened *to* people in the Renaissance: people are acted upon by nature. Yet the *Civil Wars* is not only interested in the sympathy between human beings and the environment: it also represents the emotional affinity between individuals.

Book 2 describes Bolingbroke and Richard's entry into London, and includes the perspective of Richard's 'young afflicted Queen' (2.71). Several critics have argued that Daniel's account of her emotional final encounter with Richard was a significant influence on the final act of Shakespeare's play.[14] The historical Isabel was only a child when she married Richard in 1395, and accordingly is only a minor figure in Hall and Holinshed. Daniel greatly amplifies the Queen's role in the story, and focuses on her emotional response to Richard's plight. In Daniel's version she sees a man on a horse surrounded by crowds, and mistakenly thinks it is Richard, when in fact it is Henry Bolingbroke. Isabel then sees a forlorn individual, and it transpires that this is indeed Richard:

> For whether love in him did sympathize
> Or chance so wrought to manifest her doubt,
> Even just before, where she thus secret prize,
> He staies and with cleare face lookes all about:
> When she: tis o too true, I know his eies
> Alas it is my owne deare Lord, cries out:
> And with that crie sinkes downe upon the flore,
> Abundant griefe lackt words to utter more.
>
> (2.84)

Richard seems to intuit that the Queen is looking at him, and this causes him to pause and look about. Daniel employs the term 'sympathize' here to describe this moment of communication – and perhaps also an exchange of emotions – between the Queen and Richard without the use of words or looks. The narrator suggests that the love between Richard and the Queen brings about a metaphysical affinity between them, and again we might note that this is something that happens *to* Richard: love causes him to sympathise. At the same time, however, the passage raises the possibility that this is simply a coincidence: 'Or chance so wrought to manifest her doubt'. Whether or not there is any kind of sympathetic magic at work here, it is striking that the word *sympathise* appears within a stanza that is highly concerned with the transference and correspondence of sorrow. Indeed it recalls Cleopatra's use of the term in Daniel's contemporaneous *The Tragedie of Cleopatra* (1594): 'Our like distresse I feele doth sympathize'.[15] In this way, the model of sympathy depicted in the *Civil Wars* is not confined to the transactional or bodily paradigm described by some critics of early modern culture.

In this episode of the *Civil Wars* Daniel is more concerned to dramatise Richard's and the Queen's personal tragedy than the wider political questions regarding Richard's competence as king. The Queen states explicitly that she does not value Richard for his kingly status: 'I love thee for thy selfe not for thy state / … I married was not to thy crowne but thee, / And thou without a crowne all one to mee' (2.90). Daniel thus encourages his readers to interpret Richard's tragedy from the Queen's perspective, reminding us that, from the Queen's point of view at least, Richard is a husband as well as a king. She asks Richard to join her sorrow, thus making her grief complete:

> Joine then our plaints & make our griefe ful griefe,
> Our state being one, o lets not part our care,
> Sorrow hath only this poore bare reliefe,
> To be bemon'd of such as wofull are:
> O should I rob thy griefe and be the thiefe
> To steale a private part, and severall share,
> Defrauding sorrow of her perfect due?
> No no my Lord I come to helpe thee rue.
>
> (2.92)

The Queen suggests that the only relief for her sorrow is to combine it with Richard's woe. She says that she has come to help Richard 'rue'; that is, 'To feel sorrow or grief, especially because of a personal circumstance or event; to lament' (*OED*, v.1, 1b). Yet the word could also mean 'To have, take, or feel pity or compassion' (*OED*, 4b) and is therefore a precursor of the modern meaning of *sympathise*; both of these meanings are found in Old and Middle English. As these interrelated meanings of *rue* suggest, sharing the expression of another's grief could be an important part of sharing the grief itself.[16] As we shall see below, Shakespeare explores the meanings of *rue* and related emotion terms in more detail in his own depiction of the Queen in *Richard II*. What is most striking for our purposes, however, is that Daniel employs the term *sympathise* as part of his description of Richard and the Queen's lamentations. While the *Civil Wars* and *Cleopatra* works reflect the earlier meaning of *sympathise* as correspondence and affinity – and perhaps retain some of the word's occult connotations – these texts also point towards the word's later meanings and associations.

Sad stories

Shakespeare's *Richard II* borrows and complicates Daniel's treatment of these ideas, and uses several emotion words that appear in the *Civil Wars*. One of these words is *sympathise*, which appears in a particularly suggestive context in the play's final act. Before that point, however, Richard alludes to the concept of occult sympathy, and the ability of inanimate objects to feel and respond to human passions. In 3.2, after stating that he 'weep[s] for joy / To stand upon [his] kingdom once again' (3.2.4–5), Richard addresses the earth directly and commands it to resist his military foes with a succession of terrifying inconveniences including spiders, toads, stinging nettles and adders. He suggests that the stones beneath his feet will act as sympathetic allies:

> Mock not my senseless conjuration, lords.
> This earth shall have a feeling, and these stones
> Prove armed soldiers, ere her native king
> Shall falter under foul rebellion's arms.
>
> (3.2.23–6)

This speech points to Richard's apparent faith in sympathetic magic: his magical invocation will not only cause the earth to feel but also prompt the stones to fight on his behalf. Forker suggests various possible literary sources of and analogues for this idea, including the fable of Cadmus, Luke's gospel, the myth of Deucalion in Ovid's *Metamorphoses* and *Edward III*.[17] We might also suggest that this passage recalls Daniel's description of the earth 'Trembl[ing] in terror' at the unstable state of England in the *Civil Wars* (1.116). Richard describes his conjuration as 'senseless', which on one level refers to the unfeeling stones that he hopes will respond to his commands; in other words, Richard appears to believe that there are times when senseless objects do experience human feelings.[18] At the same time, however, we should acknowledge that Richard's speech is a political and rhetorical set-piece, in which he attempts to persuade his listeners that rebellion – like the concept of an army of stones – is impossible. Indeed the phrase 'senseless conjuration' may suggest Richard's awareness that the very notion of occult sympathies is fanciful. As we shall see below, this ambivalence towards such concepts is further highlighted in the final act of the play, when the word *senseless* appears in an even more suggestive context.

Richard states that his army of stones will be joined by one of angels, stating that 'heaven still guards the right' (3.2.62). Yet his belief in his divine right to rule begins to look increasingly precarious, and it soon becomes apparent that his metaphorical militia will be no match for Bolingbroke's actual armies. His invocation of sympathetic magic is superseded by an emphasis upon the capacity of narrative and storytelling to elicit sympathy from listeners; yet this model of emotional transference is not without its problems either. Richard breaks off the action of the play to recount narratives that describe others in his predicament:

> For God's sake let us sit upon the ground
> And tell sad stories of the death of kings –
> How some have been deposed, some slain in war,
> Some haunted by the ghosts they have deposed,

Some poisoned by their wives, some sleeping killed –
All murdered.

(3.2.155–60)

Richard's retreat into storytelling – and invocation of the *de casibus* tradition – is also a retreat from reality: his recollection of other murdered kings offers him an effective (and arguably affective) means of concealing his own political shortcomings. Harry Berger, Jr, has commented that Richard's reference to sad stories 'specifies a loose and ambiguous relation to history, since what are to be recounted are not the events themselves but previous accounts, and these may be parabolic, exemplary, false, or fictive, as well as historical'.[19] As Berger points out, the idea that all kings are murdered is something of an exaggeration. Nevertheless, Richard's strategy has a clear rhetorical purpose: he is keen to recount these stories of dead kings – and implicitly take his place within these tales – because he understands that a narrative account of an event can be more compelling and moving than the thing itself. We might also suggest that there is an implicit parallel here between Richard's 'sad stories' and Shakespeare's own use of his literary and historical sources. As Richard asks to be compared to other kings, so Shakespeare invites his audiences to recall other texts in the *de causibus* tradition, and perhaps other retellings of the life of Richard II, including Daniel's *Civil Wars*. This moment thus reminds us that the representation of emotion can be a complex intertextual process, and that at least part of the play's emotional power derives from its relationship to other texts.[20]

Richard's attempt to align his life with other sad stories raises further questions about the complex nature of literary 'identification'. On the one hand, Richard attempts to elicit the pity of his listeners by likening himself to other historical and mythical kings. On the other hand, however, Richard is keen to divest himself of the trappings of rule in order that he can emphasise his essential humanness, and thus his comparability with his subjects. He seeks to increase our identification with him by gesturing towards a form of emotional universalism, and suggests that the capacity to feel – or rather taste – grief is a fundamental aspect of being human:

Throw away respect,
Tradition, form and ceremonious duty,
For you have but mistook me all this while.
I live with bread like you, feel want,
Taste grief, need friends. Subjected thus,
How can you say to me I am a king?

(3.2.172–7)

Richard's appeal to an essential humanness that links kings and subjects constitutes a powerful appeal for pity.[21] At the same time, however, Richard's speech is concerned with politics as well as pity, as his playful use of the word 'Subjected' suggests: he emphasises both his human afflictions and the fact that his majesty has been downgraded. Indeed Richard's attempts to identify with his subjects, like his desire to align his story with that of other kings, is problematic. Dawson and Yachnin suggest that this is the first occasion in the play when Richard stresses 'what he shares with other people rather than what differentiates him from them'.[22] And yet Richard's description of what he shares with others is kept decidedly general. In his attempts to liken himself to both other kings and his subjects, then, Richard has to withhold the specifics of his situation, not least because these might remind listeners of the reasons for his deposition and his shortcomings as king. In this way, the play offers a decidedly ambivalent reflection on the mechanics of fellow-feeling and identification. The act of recognising one's own plight in that of another, as Richard implies here, is a fundamental aspect of humanity, and can play a key role in eliciting fellow-feeling. At the same time, however, the play suggests that notions of resemblance and comparability – perhaps inevitably – work to efface the differences between individuals, and can be exploited for personal or political ends.

The play's ambivalent treatment of compassion and fellow-feeling is enhanced through its representation of the Queen and her reaction to Richard's tragedy. In 3.4 we find the Queen and two ladies-in-waiting discussing the Queen's grief. One of the ladies suggests possible activities that might distract from the Queen's emotions, including bowls, dancing and the recounting of stories: 'Madame, we'll tell tales' (3.4.10). The Queen asks whether such tales will be 'Of sorrow or of joy?', and when the first lady says they can be either the Queen decides she does not want to hear them:

> Of neither, girl.
> For if of joy, being altogether wanting,
> It doth remember me the more of sorrow.
> Or if of grief, being altogether had,
> It adds more sorrow to my want of joy.
> For what I have I need not to repeat,
> And what I want it boots not to complain.
>
> (3.4.12–18)

For the Queen the consolations of narrative are absent. Her pessimistic view is thus strikingly different from Richard's position: telling sad stories would add more sorrow to the Queen's grief and force her to 'repeat' her grief in narrative form. Her comments thus echo Richard's words in 1.3 when he tells Mowbray that it 'boots [him] not to be compassionate' (1.3.174). Nevertheless, in her exchanges with the Gardener in the latter part of this scene, the Queen recalls an archetypal sad story in order to express her grief at Richard's situation: 'What Eve, what serpent hath suggested thee / To make a second fall of cursed man?' (3.4.75–6). The Queen thus compares Richard's tragedy with that of the Fall, recasting Richard as an innocent Adam, tempted and seduced by Eve and the serpent. Here, as elsewhere, the play emphasises the importance of intertexts in authenticating and conceptualising emotional experience.[23] And yet several of these intertextual comparisons border on the far-fetched, or even duplicitous, and thus point to the problems with likening one's emotional experiences to biblical or classical analogues.

The Gardener is convinced that Richard's rule is inept and that 'Bolingbroke / Hath seized the wasteful king' (3.4.54–5); and yet by the end of the scene he appears to be deeply affected by the Queen's grief. Shakespeare thus depicts not only the Queen's reaction to Richard's plight but also the Gardener's reaction to her emotional state. The Gardener recognises Richard's limitations but none the less finds himself sympathising with the Queen, and he resolves to plant a particular kind of flower where the Queen has wept:

> Here did she fall a tear. Here in this place
> I'll set a bank of rue, sour herb of grace.
> Rue e'en for ruth here shortly shall be seen
> In the remembrance of a weeping queen.
>
> (3.4.104–7).

The Gardener suggests that the plant rue – which, as he suggests, was sometimes associated with grace – will signify and commemorate the Queen's 'ruth', or sorrows.[24] But the phrase 'Rue e'en for ruth' is especially suggestive, not least because the words *rue* and *ruth* could both denote sorrow *and* compassion.[25] In this way, the phrase could be seen to describe the Gardener's emotional state as well as his plants: he feels 'rue' for the Queen's 'ruth'. Rather than being a piece of decorative wordplay, then, the phrase can be seen to epitomise the play's complex exploration of the different responses we might have to the suffering of others. The multiple meanings of the terms *rue* and *ruth* means that it is ambiguous whether the Gardener simply feels sorrow because the Queen is sad, or whether he pities the Queen because of her pity for Richard. The phrase suggests that there is a fine line between sorrow and pity, but that both can involve a degree of repetition or imitation. Indeed the chain reaction that the Gardener describes may shape, or at least comment upon, the audience's emotional responses. Like the Gardener, audiences and readers may feel ambivalent about Richard but may nevertheless find themselves feeling 'rue' for the Queen. This passage thus reminds us that early modern texts often attempt to elicit sympathy by figuring instances of sympathy within the text. Here Shakespeare exploits the phonic resemblance between the terms *rue* and *ruth* in order to emphasise their semantic affinity; and, by extension, he encourages us to reflect upon the emotional affinities between the Queen, the Gardener and ourselves. It is intriguing, then, that this sorrowful scene ends with a character toying with different terms that could denote sorrow and compassion, and finding aural – and indeed floral – equivalents, suggesting that Shakespeare was exploring the nexus of words that could describe this complex emotional state.

Senseless suffering

Given the fact that 3.4 ends with a cluster of phonically similar words that could refer to pity and compassion, it is striking that the word *sympathy* appears at the start of the next scene – the so-called 'deposition scene' – almost as if it grows out of the Gardener's fertile wordplay. Fitzwater suggests that his valour is equal to that of Aumerle: 'If that thy valour stand on sympathy, / There is my gage, Aumerle, in gage to thine' (4.1.34–5). This usage resembles other early Shakespearean examples of the word, such as King Henry's 'If sympathy of love unite our thoughts' in *1 Henry VI* (1.1.23), and Lysander's 'sympathy of choice' in *A Midsummer Night's Dream* (1.1.141). In his Arden 3 edition, Forker asserts that 'Shakespeare never uses "sympathy" to mean "compassion, fellow-feeling"'.[26] But the situation is more complex than Forker suggests, not least because – as we have already seen – the meaning of *sympathy* and its cognate terms was in flux during this period.[27] Even if Fitzwater is using *sympathy* in its earlier sense of agreement at the start of 4.1, comparing his rank or condition to that of Aumerle, the scene as a whole is concerned to explore various forms of correspondence and analogy, as Richard employs various rhetorical strategies to elicit the compassion of his onstage (and offstage) audience. As we shall see below, this concern with rhetoric, compassion and correspondence arguably leads to the word *sympathise* being used in Act 5 to describe emotional comparability.

We have already seen how Richard implicitly compares his predicament to that of other historical kings. In 4.1 he also suggests that his life resembles that of Christ, and hints audaciously that his suffering might actually be worse: 'Did they not sometimes cry "All hail" to me? / So Judas did to Christ, but He in twelve / Found truth in all but one; I, in twelve thousand, none' (4.1.170–2). Northumberland asks Richard to read out some 'accusations and grievous crimes / Committed by your person and your followers' (4.1.222–3). Richard responds by extending his Christ-analogy, comparing Northumberland and all those complicit in his deposition to Pilate:

> Nay, all of you that stand and look upon me,
> Whilst that my wretchedness doth bait myself,
> Though some of you, with Pilate, wash your hands,
> Showing an outward pity, yet you Pilates
> Have here delivered me to my sour cross,
> And water cannot wash away your sin.
>
> (4.1.237–42)

By addressing 'all' of the people who 'stand and look upon [him]', Richard collapses the distinction between onstage and offstage audience, and thereby emphasises the intense theatricality of this moment. He describes the piteous reaction of these onlookers, only to raise the possibility that their response to his tragedy may be a performance of pity rather than the thing itself. Richard thus encourages the audience to see themselves as participants within a larger narrative, and interweaves the story of Christ's passion with the still unfolding events of his life.[28] Yet he goes further than this, and suggests that he, too, is complicit in his own downfall: 'Nay, if I turn mine eyes upon myself, / I find myself a traitor with the rest' (4.1.247–8). Richard thus makes himself both a spectator of and participant in his own deposition, and suggests that he has allowed his 'pompous body of a king' (250) to be undecked, thus further encouraging a sense of equivalence between himself and his subjects. Richard's attempts to present himself as a tragic everyman can certainly be seen as 'another confessional misdirection'.[29] Yet we might also suggest that Richard's act of making himself into a spectator of his own tragedy is an effective strategy for eliciting the audience's compassion. Even if we do not pity the self-indulgent King, we might nevertheless find ourselves feeling rue for the ruth that Richard feels for himself. Either way, it becomes hard to disentangle our emotional responses from the various piteous reactions that Richard describes and constructs throughout the scene.

Richard's attempts to describe his subjects' reactions to his plight is another device that Shakespeare borrows from Daniel. In Book 3 of the *Civil Wars* we find Richard imprisoned at Pomfret, where he observes a 'happie' man from his window grazing his cattle: 'O if he knew his good, how blessed hee / That feeles not what affliction greatnes yeeldes' (3.64). This anonymous man's contentment offers Daniel's Richard a means of expressing the 'affliction' that he feels. Richard goes on to imagine a scene of comfort by the fire in which the man hears of others' misfortunes, although interestingly the man does not feel their pain:

> Thou sit'st at home safe by thy quiet fire
> And hear'st of others harmes, but feelest none;
> And there thou telst of kinges and who aspire,
> Who fall, who rise, who triumphs, who doe mone:
> Perhappes thou talkst of mee, and dost inquire
> Of my restraint, why here I live alone,
> O know tis others sin not my desart,
> And I could wish I were but as thou art.
>
> (3.65)

Daniel's Richard imagines that his subjects will recount tales of the rise and fall of kings, but that these stories will not provoke an emotional reaction: they will hear of others' harms but 'feelest none'. Nevertheless Richard hopes that his subjects are curious about his 'restraint', and wants to shape their accounts of him, stressing that his predicament is the result of others' sins. He goes on to suggest that narrative offers a way for his subjects to understand his suffering:

> But looke on mee, and note my troubled raigne,
> Examine all the course of my vext life;
> Compare my little joyes with my long paine,
> And note my pleasures rare, my sorrowes rife,
> My childhood spent in others pride, and gaine,
> My youth in daunger, farther yeares in strife,
> My courses crost, my deedes wrest to the worst,
> My honour spoild, my life in daunger forst.
>
> (3.67)

Here Richard invites his subjects to examine the entire course of his 'vext life', from his childhood through to adulthood. He lists the features of such an account, but does not tell them how to react. Richard goes on to make the unarguable point that, if he had 'beene a heardsman rather then a king' (3.68), his life would have been far more straightforward. Here, then, Richard reflects upon his own life from the perspective of others, although he does not examine, or attempt to describe, their emotions.

These passages from the *Civil Wars* are developed and reconfigured in 5.1 of Shakespeare's *Richard II*.[30] And here the differences between Daniel's Richard and Shakespeare's are as revealing as the similarities. Shakespeare borrows certain elements of Richard's plight from Daniel, including Richard imagining how his tale will be told in the future, but makes the emphasis upon the emotional impact of narration far more explicit. As the scene opens the Queen sees Richard, in what could be read as a reworking of their encounter in Book 2 of Daniel's poem.[31] At this point, however, the Queen's words focus more on an imaginary audience than her own emotional state: 'Yet look up, behold, / That you in pity may dissolve to dew / And wash him fresh again with true-love tears' (5.1.8–10). On one level the Queen is addressing her attendants, but she is also implicitly addressing audiences and readers of the scene, and describing their sympathetic reactions. She goes on to describe Richard as 'the model where old Troy did stand' (11), and as 'King Richard's tomb, / And not King Richard!' (12–13), suggesting that on some level Richard has already become his own ghost. But, even as she does this, the Queen links Richard's tragedy to other stories and legends, suggesting that he is a miniature representation of Troy, another grand narrative of fallen greatness.[32]

It is in this context of narration and emotional response that we find Shakespeare's use of the term *sympathise*. Richard commands the Queen to spend the rest of her days in a nunnery, but also enjoins her to tell his story in the context of other old, tragic tales. In a highly self-reflexive passage, Richard offers a piece of narrative that is simultaneously about the power of narrative:

> Think I am dead, and that even here thou tak'st,
> As from my death-bed, thy last living leave.
> In winter's tedious nights sit by the fire
> With good old folks, and let them tell thee tales
> Of woeful ages long ago betid.
> And ere thou bid good night, to quite their griefs,
> Tell thou the lamentable tale of me
> And send the hearers weeping to their beds.
> For why the senseless brands will sympathize
> The heavy accent of thy moving tongue
> And in compassion weep the fire out;
> And some will mourn in ashes, some coal-black,
> For the deposing of a rightful king.
>
> (5.1.38–50)

The tale that Richard imagines will be so pitiful that the listeners will be sent 'weeping' to their beds; moreover the unfeeling embers of the winter fire will 'weep the fire out', and thus cry themselves out of existence.[33] The fireside is both the physical site of storytelling and a secondary figured audience for the tragic tales that are to be recounted. But what is particularly suggestive is Richard's use of the word *sympathise* to describe the emotional reaction of the 'senseless brands'. The play's editors do not quite agree on the word's meaning here, in particular whether it carries the earlier sense of correspondence or the more 'modern' sense of emotional affinity. Forker glosses the word as 'respond to, or match', while Gurr suggests that it means 'share the feelings of'.[34] And indeed the *OED* includes this passage as an example of meaning 3a, 'To agree with, answer or correspond to, match. *Obs.*' (*OED*, 'sympathize', 3a). Yet the correspondence that Richard describes here is specifically concerned with the power of narrative to elicit an emotional chain reaction.

This speech thus represents a key moment in the history of the term, and can be seen as an early example of the emotional form of *sympathise*, 'To feel sympathy; to have a fellow-feeling; to share the feelings of another or others' (*OED*, 4a; first cited usage 1607). At the same time, however, it is ironic that this innovative usage of *sympathise* refers to the emotional reaction of the 'senseless' brands. This moment could thus be read as an extension of Richard's interest in the capacity of inanimate objects to feel human emotions, like the senseless stones that he refers to in 3.2.[35] Yet the fact that this passage is concerned with an imaginary act of storytelling suggests that the function of the sympathetic brands is a poetic one: they offer Richard a powerful metaphorical means of expressing his faith in the ability of language to move others. In his evocative description of this new form of sympathy, even inanimate objects will be moved: not due to an occult or physical process, but by the sad stories recounted by Richard's figured narrator.

In this description of the senseless brands, then, Shakespeare borrows the dramatic situation and the term *sympathise* from two separate passages in Daniel's *Civil Wars* and combines the two, inserting the word into this new context. Indeed later writers seem to have recognised the power of Richard's speech and to have picked up on and appropriated Shakespeare's use of the word *sympathise* to describe the exchange of grief and compassion. In Richard Niccols's poem *Sir Thomas Overburies Vision* (1616), for example, Overbury's ghost appears and starts to tell his sorrowful tale:

> When in my chamber walls, the very stones
> Sweat droppes for teares to heare my greiuous grones;
> As sencelesse, they would simpathize my woes,
> Though my sad cries were musicke to my foes.[36]

Here Overbury describes both the sympathetic reaction of the senseless stones, and the unsympathetic reaction of his foes, to whose ears his cries are 'musicke'. Yet the combination of the specific terms *senseless* and *sympathise* suggests that Niccols is drawing upon and echoing Richard II's speech.[37] We have seen how Richard II tries to associate his tale with other tragic narratives; perhaps here, in an analogous way, Niccols attempts to link his complaint poem with other tragic tales, including Shakespeare's play. *Richard II* thus seems to have played an important part in reshaping and refining the meanings of the term *sympathise*, as Shakespeare drew upon, and in turn influenced, other writers. In other words, this process – whereby the word is associated with ideas of emotional borrowing and imitation – seems to have been made possible by a process of literary borrowing and imitation.

Yet it is worth emphasising that there is something duplicitous about the Shakespearian image that Niccols is drawing upon. In Richard's speech we are invited to imitate the emotional response of the senseless brands, who 'sympathize' with the Queen's tale; yet we do not get to hear the tale that they have heard. Stanley Wells has written that this is a moment when 'the audience is made aware of the play as a mimetic representation, in which they are conscious of the play as play, the actor as actor; for the performers they are watching are in fact enacting the "lamentable tale", and the audience are the hearers who, if the actors succeed, will go "weeping to their beds"'.[38] This analysis perhaps underestimates the extent to which Richard's description of storytelling may distract audiences from the ways in which their emotions are being manipulated. Indeed we might legitimately ask whether the 'lamentable tale' (5.1.44) that Richard imagines constitutes a fitting summary of the events of *Richard II*. His keenness to convert the action of the play into a tragic narrative might thus be seen as politically – as well as aesthetically – motivated: the story that Richard wants to be told about him is not necessarily the same story that the play has told us. Niccols's poem borrows this striking image of insensible objects weeping after hearing the story of a fallen individual – but we need to remember that Shakespeare's Richard has his own particular political agenda, and wants to exonerate himself through the art of rhetoric.

For pity's sake

We have seen, then, that much of *Richard II* is self-consciously concerned with the question of whether we should feel pity for Richard; or, to put it another way, whether subjects – or audience members – should feel sympathy for the monarch. But the play is also interested in the question of whether the monarch himself should feel pity for his subjects; this applies to Richard in the first act of the play, and his successor, Bolingbroke, in the final act. Recognising this aspect of *Richard II* might help to illuminate one of the most controversial parts of the play: the so-called Aumerle conspiracy in 5.2 and 5.3. These scenes, which involve the discovery of Aumerle's plot against the new King and Bolingbroke's subsequent forgiveness, are often dismissed by critics precisely because of their emotional inappropriateness – that is, as a comic interlude in an otherwise serious play. Leonard Barkan describes this episode as 'a piece of slapstick about a wayward son', while Forker suggests that 'Shakespeare complicates our response to the fresh crisis … by allowing the parental disagreement to degenerate into farce'.[39] But this approach seems to underestimate the interest and complexity of these scenes: and I want to conclude by suggesting that this episode reflects the play's larger concern with the imitative and rhetorical aspects of compassion.

In 5.2, York discovers Aumerle's plot against Bolingbroke and resolves to inform the King of his son's treason. The Duchess then attempts to move York to pity by reminding him of their similarity: 'Is he not like thee? Is he not thine own?' (5.2.94). She suggests that her experience of giving birth gives her an even more sympathetic outlook: 'Hadst thou groaned for him / As I have done, thou wouldest be more pitiful' (5.2.102–3). This emphasis upon the Duchess's perspective recalls the play's focus on the relationship between Richard and the Queen. Indeed it is worth noting that the Duchess's role in this scene is a Shakespearian invention, suggesting that Shakespeare was especially interested in exploring the effects of female pity upon his audience. York is certainly capable of pity, as we see at the start of this scene in his vivid description of Bolingbroke's triumphant procession into London and Richard's ignoble entry behind him. Like the Gardener in 3.4, York acknowledges Bolingbroke's claim to the throne, but none the less appears to feel pity for Richard, and weeping makes him 'break the story off' (5.2.2). However, York fails to feel pity for his own son, and he remains entirely unmoved by the Duchess's complaints, preferring to paint her as a subversive and uncontrollable female: 'Make way, unruly woman' (5.2.110).

When the Duke and Duchess confront Bolingbroke in 5.3, York specifically tries to persuade Bolingbroke against feelings of pity: 'Fear, and not love, begets his penitence. / Forget to pity him, lest pity prove / A serpent that will sting thee to the heart' (5.3.55–7). Clearly York is warning

Bolingbroke about the political problems that will beset him if he allows a conspirator to go free; he also offers a more generalised warning that pity can be dangerous and play with our reason. When the Duchess arrives on the scene she tries to convince Bolingbroke that her arguments are, as it were, from the heart, in contrast with her husband's pleas:

Pleads he in earnest? Look upon his face.
His eyes do drop no tears; his prayers are in jest;
His words come from his mouth, ours from our breast.
He prays but faintly and would be denied;
We pray with heart and soul and all beside.

(5.3.99–103)

For Phyllis Rackin, 'the stiff, rhymed verse and degraded language, together with the frantic and indecorous stage business, are not so much "ceremonial" as they are ridiculous'.[40] Rackin does go on to concede that the scene may have a symbolic or thematic function: 'An obvious function of the scenes with Aumerle and his parents is to illustrate in the microcosm of a single family the dissolution of sacred bonds in the macrocosm of the usurped state. But this symbolic point could have been made with genuinely pathetic scenes, so the problem of comic tone remains' (p. 275). However, it is hard to say what a 'genuinely pathetic' scene might look like, while the extent to which this episode has a 'comic tone' depends to a large extent on how it is performed.[41] York again tries to dismiss his wife's sympathetic efforts, calling her a 'frantic woman' (5.3.88). And yet, if we dismiss the Duchess's language as stiff and degraded, and the accompanying stage business as 'frantic', as Rackin does, then this implicitly aligns us with York's misogynistic views.[42] Moreover, the play as a whole is intensely preoccupied with the problems of expression and formality that Rackin casts aside, and the tension between human emotion and linguistic form: as the Queen puts it in 2.2, 'Conceit is still derived / From some forefather grief' (2.2.34–5).

The Duchess hopes that, just as her words come directly from her breast, they will gain direct access to Bolingbroke's heart: 'in thy piteous heart plant thou thine ear, / That, hearing how our plaints and prayers do pierce, / Pity may move thee "Pardon" to rehearse' (5.3.125–7). Like Richard, the Duchess constructs an idealised audience, and describes their emotional response to her plight. The passage is, as the Oxford editors suggest, 'anatomically bizarre', yet it is nevertheless rhetorically persuasive.[43] Despite York's warnings, the Duchess's appeals to Bolingbroke's 'piteous heart' are effective, and Aumerle is pardoned. This scene thus represents a rare instance in Shakespeare's works – contra Lucrece, Isabella and Paulina – of a woman's pleas for pity being heeded by a powerful man. It would appear that Aumerle is pardoned because of his mother's effectiveness at persuading Bolingbroke of the authenticity of her emotions. This scene thus recalls the moment in 1.3 with which we began, when Richard reduces Bolingbroke's sentence because of Gaunt's pain for his son. And yet, Bolingbroke's pardon of Aumerle – like the mercy that Richard showed to Bolingbroke in 1.3 – is bound up with larger political agendas. As Bolingbroke puts it, 'I pardon him, as God shall pardon me' (5.3.130). Thus, while Bolingbroke pardons Aumerle, imitating the Duchess's 'ruth' for her son, it would seem that Bolingbroke wants God, in turn, to imitate his act of compassion, and to pardon him for usurping the crown.

This intriguing scene, then, not only extends the play's ambivalent concern with pity and compassion, but also reminds us that its rhetorical, emotional and political concerns cannot be easily separated. The interpretative dilemma that the play poses with regard to Richard's character – and whether or not we should sympathise with his plight – is part of its larger preoccupation with the ethics and aesthetics of pity. The critics cited at the start of this chapter, who offer varying accounts of the appropriate way of responding to the play and its protagonist, are not necessarily right or wrong in their assessments; yet the play highlights the extent to which such responses to Richard are bound up with larger political and ethical concerns, and cannot be disentangled from the various figured acts of pity and compassion depicted within the text. By depicting pity as a form of chain reaction, in which individuals react to other individuals' pity, Shakespeare demonstrates the extent to which sympathy is frequently imitative, mediated and relational. This complex theorising of pity in *Richard II* and other works of this period seems to have required a new word, as Shakespeare and his contemporaries associated the terms *sympathy* and *sympathise* with emotion and fellow-feeling. The play's representations of figured compassion are integral to the ways in which the audience's emotional reactions are shaped and influenced; but they also point to the complex, varying and unpredictable nature of such responses. In this way, *Richard II* confronts us with one of the fundamental paradoxes of being a subject, or indeed a human being: to feel compassion for others is a key aspect of humanity, and yet the play simultaneously warns us of the dangers of such feelings, and reminds us that our capacity for feeling pity for pity's sake – 'Rue e'en for ruth' – can leave us open to manipulation.

Notes

1 Richard's use of the term *compassionate* here is somewhat obscure, and it appears to mean something akin to piteous, rather than inclined to pity. This is the *OED*'s only cited example of this usage, and even here the *OED* is uncertain of its meaning: 'Displaying sorrowful emotion; sorrowfully lamenting; or ? moving pity, piteous' (*OED*, 1c). Quotations from *Richard II* are taken from Charles Forker's Arden 3 edn (London: Methuen, 2002). Other quotations from Shakespeare are taken from Gary Taylor and Stanley Wells (eds), *The Oxford Shakespeare: The Complete Works*, 2nd edn (Oxford: Oxford University Press, 2005).

2 William Hazlitt, *The Complete Works of William Hazlitt*, ed. P. P. Howe, 21 vols (London: J. M. Dent, 1930-4), vol. 4, pp. 272–3.

3 W. B. Yeats, quoted in Nicholas Brooke (ed.), *Shakespeare: 'Richard II', A Casebook* (Basingstoke: Macmillan, 1973), p. 105.

4 Andrew Gurr (ed.), *Richard II* (Cambridge: Cambridge University Press, 1984), p. 22.

5 Scott McMillin, 'Shakespeare's *Richard II*: Eyes of Sorrow, Eyes of Desire', *Shakespeare Quarterly*, 35 (1984), 40–52 (p. 41). In *Imaginary Audition: Shakespeare on Stage and Page* (Berkeley: University of California Press, 1989), Harry Berger, Jr, similarly argued against the idea of Richard as a weak king who is none the less 'effective in theatrical terms'. He writes: 'Such a distinction between political and theatrical effectiveness is in my opinion a chimera' (p. 74). Berger proposes that we should regard Richard as a character who deliberately performs and displays his emotions for political ends: 'The emotions he stages are those that perpetuate – and are privileged by – the royal, religious, and chivalric rituals of a sacramental world' (p. 135).

6 Forker, 'Introduction', p. 43; Anthony B. Dawson and Paul Yachnin, 'Introduction' to their Oxford edn of *Richard II* (Oxford: Oxford University Press, 2011), p. 71.

7 Robert Burton, *The Anatomy of Melancholy* (Oxford, 1621), p. 48.

8 John Florio, *A Worlde of Wordes, or Most Copious, and Exact Dictionarie in Italian and English, Collected by John Florio* (London, 1598), p. 372.

9 Randle Cotgrave, *A Dictionarie of the French and English Tongues* (London, 1611), s.v. *condouloir* and *sympathiser*.

10 On the links between the *Civil Wars* and *Richard II* see, for example, George M. Logan, 'Lucan–Daniel–Shakespeare: New Light on the Relation between *The Civil Wars* and *Richard II*', *Shakespeare Studies*, 9 (1976), 121–40; Gurr, 'Introduction', pp. 10-14; and Forker, 'Introduction', esp. pp. 140–4.

11 Samuel Daniel, *The First Fowre Bookes of the Civile Wars between the Two Houses of Lancaster and York* (London, 1595), 1.115–16.

12 See Gail Kern Paster, Katherine Rowe and Mary Floyd-Wilson, 'Introduction: Reading the Early Modern Passions', in Paster, Rowe and Floyd-Wilson

(eds), *Reading the Early Modern Passions: Essays in the Cultural History of Emotion* (Philadelphia: University of Pennsylvania Press, 2004), p. 18.

13 Mary Floyd-Wilson and Garrett A. Sullivan, Jr, 'Introduction: Inhabiting the Body, Inhabiting the World', in Floyd-Wilson and Sullivan (eds), *Environment and Embodiment in Early Modern England* (Basingstoke: Palgrave, 2007), p. 2. See also Mary Floyd-Wilson, *Occult Knowledge, Science, and Gender on the Shakespearean Stage* (Cambridge: Cambridge University Press, 2013).

14 See Forker, 'Introduction', p. 143, and Dawson and Yachnin, 'Introduction', pp. 54–6.

15 Samuel Daniel, *Delia and Rosamond Augmented. Cleopatra* (London, 1594), sig. I4v.

16 The idea that it was beneficial to have a companion in misery was proverbial. See R. W. Dent, *Shakespeare's Proverbial Language: An Index* (Berkeley: University of California Press, 1981), C571: 'It is good to have company in misery'. This proverb also informs several Shakespearean tragedies, and is alluded to in *The Rape of Lucrece*, when Lucrece expresses her desire for 'co-partners' in her pain: 'And fellowship in woe doth woe assuage' (790).

17 See Forker's longer note to 3.2.24–5 (p. 493).

18 The term *senseless* anticipates Plutarch's definition of *sympathie* in Holland's 1603 translation of the *Morals*: 'A fellow feeling, as is betweene the head and stomacke in our bodies: also the agreement and naturall amitie in divers senslesse things, as between iron and the load-stone' (Plutarch, *The Philosophie, Commonlie Called the Morals*, trans. Philemon Holland (London, 1603), sig. 6a1v). The passage also recalls Titus's description of the stones that appear to weep in 3.1 of *Titus Andronicus*: 'though they cannot answer my distress, / Yet in some sort they are better than the Tribunes / For that they will not intercept my tale. / When I do weep they humbly at my feet / Receive my tears and seem to weep with me' (3.1.37–41).

19 Berger, *Imaginary Audition*, p. 120.

20 Forker points out that this passage was itself imitated by later writers, including Robert Baron's *Mirza* (1655): 'Come my good lord … you and I / Will sit, and tell sad stories' (*Mirza: A Tragedie, Really Acted in Persia, in the Last Age. Illustrated with Historicall Annotation* (London, 1655), p. 95). See Forker's longer note to 3.2.156 (p. 494).

21 Bridget Escolme offers a brief discussion of this passage, and comments that '[g]rief here is such a palpably physical passion and such an ordinary part of the human condition that it seems logical to describe it as being apprehended in the mouth, like daily bread' (*Emotional Excess on the Shakespearean Stage: Passion's Slaves* (London: Bloomsbury, 2014), p. 169).

22 See Dawson and Yachnin's note to 3.2.174–7.

23 See Cora Fox, *Ovid and the Politics of Emotion in Elizabethan England* (Basingstoke: Palgrave, 2009).

24 Ophelia alludes to this idea when she lists rue as part of her collection of flowers and herbs in Act 4 of *Hamlet*: 'We may call it herb-grace o' Sundays' (*Hamlet*, 4.5.180–1).

25 *Rue* could mean both 'Sorrow, distress; penitence, repentance; regret' (*OED*, n.1) and 'Pity, compassion' (*OED*, n.2), while *ruth* could mean 'The quality of being compassionate; the feeling of sorrow for another; compassion, pity' (*OED*, 1) and 'Sorrow, grief' (*OED*, 3).

26 See Forker's note to 4.1.34.

27 See my discussion of the usage in *Titus* in '"O, what a sympathy of woe is this": Passionate Sympathy in *Titus Andronicus*', *Shakespeare Survey*, 66 (2013), 287–97.

28 See Gary Kuchar, *The Poetry of Religious Sorrow in Early Modern England* (Cambridge: Cambridge University Press, 2008), pp. 48–61, on this aspect of the play. On 5.1 he writes that 'Isabel wants desperately to see Richard as Christ and herself as Magdalene but the scriptural narrative fails to map onto her lived experience' (p. 52). See also Forker, who comments that 'Shakespeare raises the concept of Richard as alter-Christus only to undermine it by wry equivocations and strategies of scepticism' ('Introduction', p. 78). For a discussion of early modern religious debates concerning the possibility of indentifying with Christ see Jan Frans van Dijkhuizen, *Pain and Compassion in Early Modern Literature and Culture* (Cambridge: D. S. Brewer, 2012), ch. 2.

29 Berger, *Imaginary Audition*, p. 63.

30 See Forker's note to 5.1.40–50.

31 The episode in Shakespeare's play is slightly different from the corresponding section in Daniel's poem, where it comes before the deposition. Dawson and Yachnin note that 'the touching devotion of the lovers and their mutual compassion are similar in both texts' (see their note to 5.1).

32 Heather Dubrow describes the stories of Troy and Eden as 'paradigmatic narratives for the interpretation of loss in early modern England' in *Shakespeare and Domestic Loss* (Cambridge: Cambridge University Press, 1999), p. 10.

33 Richard's image anticipates Miranda's comment about the sympathetic logs carried by Ferdinand in *The Tempest*: 'When this burns / 'Twill weep for having wearied you' (3.1.18–19). The concept is also alluded to in *King John* when Arthur states that 'the fire is dead with grief' (4.1.105).

34 See Forker's note to 5.1.46–7, and Gurr's note to 5.1.46.

35 John Joughin has discussed this speech in '*Richard II* and the Performance of Grief', in Dermot Cavanagh, Stuart Hampton-Reeves and Stephen Longstaffe (eds), *Shakespeare's Histories and Counter-Histories* (Manchester: Manchester University Press, 2006), pp. 15–31. Yet while Joughin has some suggestive remarks concerning Richard's 'evaluation of the poetic experience of language' (p. 20), he does not comment on Richard's use of the term *sympathise* or its significance.

36 Richard Niccols, *Sir Thomas Overburies Vision. With the Ghoasts of Weston, Mrs. Turner, the Late Lieftenant of the Tower, and Franklin* (London, 1616), p. 11.

37 Niccols wrote several complaints and elegies, which, as Andrew Hadfield has noted, show 'a considerable debt to Edmund Spenser and, to a lesser extent, to Michael Drayton' (*ODNB*, s.v. 'Richard Niccols'). But in this particular complaint we can also detect an allusion to Shakespeare.

38 Stanley Wells, 'The Lamentable Tale of *Richard II*', *Shakespeare Studies* (Tokyo), 17 (1978–79), 1–23 (p. 1).

39 Leonard Barkan, 'The Theatrical Consistency of *Richard II*', *Shakespeare Quarterly*, 29 (1978), 5–19 (p. 14); Forker, 'Introduction', p. 41.

40 Phyllis Rackin, 'The Role of the Audience in *Richard II*', *Shakespeare Quarterly*, 36 (1985), 262–81 (p. 274).

41 The recent BBC production of *Richard II*, which was part of its adaptation of the second tetralogy *The Hollow Crown* (directed by Rupert Goold, Richard Eyre and Thea Sharrock, BBC Two, 30 June–21 July 2012), powerfully showed that this episode of *Richard II* need not be played for laughs; on the contrary, the Duchess of York's entreaties for her son's life were powerful and moving, notwithstanding Bolingbroke's comments about the scene being changed to 'The Beggar and the King' (5.3.79).

42 My argument here resonates with Bridget Escolme's contention that the early modern theatre 'was a place for pushing at the boundaries of what society regarded as the legitimate expression of emotion, for interrogating and debating those boundaries' (*Emotional Excess*, p. xviii). The Duchess might thus be regarded as an early modern character whose emotional expression, as Escolme puts it, 'disrupts and exceeds authority, convention, and the acceptable boundaries of sanity and subjectivity' (p. xxviii).

43 See Dawson and Yachnin's note to 5.3.125–7.

7

What's happiness in *Hamlet*?

Richard Chamberlain

THE EMOTIONS ARE NOT simply a matter for literature: critics have them too. Or, more interestingly, perhaps, they play an important role in the critical process which goes far beyond any naively expressive response to the emotional content of literary works. The reading of *Hamlet* presented here raises this as a problem in the theory and history of emotions, in that it foregrounds the questions of what happiness and unhappiness are, and of how they might best be deployed in acts of criticism. Happiness, one might think, must be scarce enough in this play, and indeed it is, at least as this emotion is conventionally conceived. However, the play's very negativity is what allows it to speak of happiness as something not actual but potential, as something perceived fleetingly, in the debased world of the play, through imagined moments of fortunate coincidence. Underlying this reading is the principle that happiness, potential or utopian as it is, is fundamentally collective, to be experienced by individuals through and because of the state of social relations in a historical moment, and that only in such a state can happiness, conceived as a spontaneous and uncoerced event, occur.[1] Against this background, the ideological character of individual critics' understanding of what happiness means becomes clearer, reflecting light upon the question of whether happiness, in a particular situation, is to be considered a good thing or a bad.

What's happiness?

In his recent study *The Unrepentant Renaissance* Richard Strier has wittily highlighted the role of the emotions in critical analysis, asking 'Whence the gloom?' of all those operating in the shadow, as he sees it, of new historicism.[2] There is a refreshing élan in his taking to task of such critics for their unremitting social pessimism, the sense they give that human possibilities are constrained not only by the baleful effects of power, but also by what can be demonstrated within the narrow terms of a particular academic discourse:

> The picture of the Renaissance and Reformations that I have sketched is deeply at odds with the picture that has characterized a great deal of literary study of the period, certainly with regard to England, for the past few decades, and indeed for decades before that. One doesn't hear much, in this scholarship and criticism, of man being 'born to be happy' in this world. Being 'civilized' is equated with being repressed rather than being 'jocund', 'affable' or 'liberal'. (p. 6)

Such criticism, Strier here makes one feel, simply plays into the hands of those forces seeking to restrict the full expression of human powers and capacities for the sake of their own material interests. Indeed, despite interpreters' assiduous erasure of the tracks to maintain an image of due professional seriousness, emotions of delight and enjoyment must surely, on occasion, motivate individual acts of criticism; it seems a reasonable assumption, too, that whole scholarly careers devoted to certain authors, periods or genres must have had obscure beginnings in feelings akin to pleasure. In this attack, Strier follows in the rational-humanist traditional of William Empson, who in the mid-twentieth century was regarded as a maverick for expressing so openly his emotional response (one of 'loathing') to the affective repressiveness of the academic institution of English at that time, particularly with regard to its Christian-conservative consensus on John Donne.[3] Yet Strier's liberating attempt to criticise what Empson calls 'the habitual mean-mindedness of modern academic criticism, its moral emptiness combined with incessant moral nagging, its scrubbed prison-like isolation' (p. 159) leaves itself open to the objection that, in celebrating (in the words he quotes from C. S. Lewis) 'the beautiful, cheerful integration' of Renaissance culture (p. 14), he settles for the world as it is, and as it then was, with all its human misery. In the same way that, as Strier points out, Greenblatt's self-styled 'dialectical' approach is ultimately undialectical in consistently underlining the restrictive operations of power, Strier's own 'bumptious' Renaissance can appear complacent in its overestimation of the possibilities for happiness, and its attendant freedom, in an untransformed world.[4]

Nevertheless, these quietist aspects of Strier's – in part – socially critical approach are to be distinguished from those bland exhortations to look on the bright side of life heard in some quarters of emotions research. Such appeals, or even demands, are conceived as redressing a balance, correcting a 'bias', as if the adoption of an allegedly inoffensive middle way is the best response to the world's problems; they are thus decidedly ideological. Darrin M. McMahon represents such a view when he asks,

> Are historians of emotion a negative lot? Do they give greater weight to angst and animosity, sadness and fear than they do to the positive human emotions? Indeed, might the field of the history of emotions as a whole suffer from something of a 'negative bias', a tendency to accord greater prominence to the role played by negative emotions in constituting the human past?[5]

This line of questioning leads him to wonder 'How … might it be possible to put a little more joy in the history of emotions?' (p. 104), as if this would, self-evidently, be beneficial. It is clear from McMahon's essay that he means not just to promote the *study* of emotions such as happiness and joy but to encourage specialists in the social sciences and humanities to adopt a more cheerful outlook themselves, and to convince them to push such forced happiness on the world at large through the perceived authority of their research. In his view those who study the emotions do 'suffer' from a negative bias and are in need of 'remedies' (p. 104). But the analogy of mathematical or electrical negativity and positivity in this instance is inappropriate. What are these 'negative' emotions with which critics, sociologists, psychologists and humans at large are afflicted? What makes sadness at the death of a friend or anger at widespread injustice 'negative'? What makes cheerful connivance at the suffering of others 'positive'? The essential error is to think of happiness and unhappiness as opposites; in fact, they do not possess the convenient symmetry which such talk of 'positive' and 'negative' emotions takes for granted. The 'negative' psychology and economics which McMahon triumphantly declares moribund (p. 106) are (or were) right in so far as they identified misery as the present condition of humanity; they are thus, in that at least, to be mourned. Curiously, he refers to things the continuing existence of which might be thought to render this manufacture of happiness less than honest or desirable – 'class conflict and exploitation, social injustice and poverty' (p. 106) – but is able to place these calmly to one side as if, rather than systemic evils, they are merely passing misfortunes to be counterweighted by good news stories. The assumption that real, feigned or self-convinced feelings of happiness or joy are automatically preferable to ones of unhappiness is evident here, and informs the affirmative, anaesthetised, depoliticised chorus of contemporary culture.

The cheerful approach to the emotions thus misses the point that, at least in present historical conditions, all emotions are mixed. For example, any feeling of happiness we might think we experience is inevitably tainted from the outset by awareness of suffering, whilst the promotion of happiness by the culture industry (and now, it seems, academia) is complicit with violence and exploitation. In the good society, by contrast, happiness – which, at present, is at best a fleeting glimpse of something other or elsewhere, and at worst constitutes self-delusion amounting to psychiatric illness (a persuasive idea which McMahon appears to find laughable (p. 106)) – would be the condition of a general wellbeing in which all can flourish. That good society, however, cannot be produced by minor adjustments to living conditions, and certainly not by advocating a positive mental attitude, but only through a revolutionary transformation of the material basis of society. Socially radical objections to the kind of pessimistic misery identified by Strier in Greenblatt and the new historicists are available. For Alexander Ezekiel Chang, a reading of the emotions grounded in the aesthetic dimension of Marx's early thought offers a way beyond the affirmative relationship of much contemporary theory to the oppressive structures of society. In contrast to what he sees as the acceptance of the existing social order enshrined in 'affirmative' theories of affect influenced by Gilles Deleuze and others, the aesthetic dimension offers a negativity able to critique the conditions currently productive of so much human unhappiness:

> The multiple and ungeneralisable iterations of affect and affect theory performatively refuse the negative as an attempt to escape being subordinated to identity. However, it is precisely this negativity that is maintained and mobilised through the aesthetic, and which can be used to make the distinction between more recent affect theory and Marxist approaches to sensuous experience.[6]

For such approaches, grounded in Theodor Adorno's critical theory, a text like *Hamlet* has a powerfully utopian effect *because* it is negative: shrouding the potentiality of its hopefulness in the blackness of reality, problematising the relation between the object and its concept (p. 238). In Adorno's words, quoted by Chang in his epigraph, 'Aesthetic experience is … promised by its impossibility. Art is the ever broken promise of happiness' (p. 235). Reading Shakespeare can thus show us that what we say about the emotions has profound consequences for what we think about justice, ethics and society. The discourse of the emotions, which can lead towards liberation or away from it, is ultimately central to the sphere of politics.

What happens

According to John Dover Wilson, '[b]efore attempting to interpret a scene in Shakespeare there is one question which it is well to deal with first: in what mood are the principal characters when it begins?' His account of emotion in the play forms part of a lifelong project of 'elucidating' *Hamlet*, to which the study quoted here, *What Happens in 'Hamlet'* (1935), is central.[7] Furthermore, any Shakespearian scene, it seems from his account, depends upon this matter of affect. The observation is characteristic of his criticism in its confident assertiveness: it shares with the book's title a vaunted comprehensiveness of grasp, an exhaustive understanding of everything that *happens* in the play, and why it happens, a definitive solution to its mysteries. Its emphasis on the emotions is equally typical of its author, who also wrote *Shakespeare's Happy Comedies* (1962), and it informs his reading of the play with an almost obsessive persistence. For instance, Ophelia, 'of ladies most deject and wretched', as he notes, is decidedly unhappy as she attends the performance Hamlet has devised (p. 175). In the same scene, most of the other characters, by contrast, are feeling quite pleased. Gertrude, he tells us, 'comes to the play with a glad heart, for she sees hopes of Hamlet's recovery in his interest in such amusements' (p. 174). Similarly, we learn that 'Claudius is as delighted as the Queen when in the preceding scene he hears from Rosencrantz and Guildenstern that Hamlet proposes to entertain them all, for it pleases him to learn that his nephew's mind is occupied with anything so healthy and innocent' (p. 174). Hamlet, in turn, is said to look forward to his 'mousetrap': 'His mood seems calm and self-controlled' (p. 175). The conversation with Horatio which precedes the performance is called 'his one perfectly serene and untroubled moment in the whole play' (p. 176).

It is as if the emotions have a significance for Dover Wilson which undermines his capacity to control them. They appear to be central to his whole worldview and critical project, yet the dangerously uncontrollable element which threatens to derail his whole project. He not only places them at the centre of his account of a morally and ideologically consistent play but is powerfully subject to them himself. *What Happens in 'Hamlet'* shares this emotionally charged register with the play it discusses. Its genesis is explained in 'The Road to Elsinore: Being an Epistle Dedicatory to Walter Wilson Greg', where Dover Wilson presents his earlier self, in November 1917, as 'one of those few fortunate but *unhappy* [my emphasis] men of military age whom a government department even in the fourth year of hostilities had not yet "released" for war service' (p. 2). Working both for the Board of Education and the Ministry of Munitions, ground down by hard but uninspiring war work, by the pressure of the conflict itself, and, as seems inevitable (although this goes unmentioned), perturbed by news of the revolution in Russia, he confides that 'my spiritual condition was critical, not to say dangerous, a condition in which a man becomes converted, falls in love, or gives way to a mania for wild speculation' (p. 3). The article by W. W. Greg, 'Hamlet's Hallucination', which explodes into this fragile spiritual and emotional situation, is the starting point of a critical relationship which Dover Wilson describes in terms of a troubled and disturbing love affair: 'You may have guessed something of this, but you cannot know it all; and as the story of how you forced yourself into my life will explain to others the origin and purpose of this book, you must bear with the telling of it' (p. 2).

As Terence Hawkes has shown, Dover Wilson's dismay at the proposition put forward by Greg (that the implication of the play-scene, in which Claudius remains unmoved by the dumb-show's imitation of his own supposed actions, is that the Ghost's version of events is unreliable) is an index of the ideological investment in a certain 'inherited' reading of *Hamlet* by a certain kind of conservative English culture, and one symbolised by his own name:

> Greg's attack, after all, is on the smooth surface of the play, seen as the product of Shakespeare the 'rational playwright', but effectively, of course, created by an 'orthodox' interpretation which seeks for unity, progression, coherence and, if possible, sequential ordering in all art, as part of a ruthless and rigorous process of domestication. There is no obvious way of placating Greg's objections to that sort of *Hamlet* for they constitute a frontal assault on what he terms the 'inherited beliefs' – that brand of literary Tsarism – which reinforce and sustain it. And the assault is certainly not Fabian in character. It is directly, violently Bolshevik.[8]

The element of the unpredictable, the disorderly, introduced into Dover Wilson's *Hamlet*-world, and his perception of the historical world, by Greg's ingenious speculative reading thus has palpably political implications. The shoring-up of an existing order is felt to depend upon the 'rationality' – the predictability, regularity and unambiguous causality – displayed by both play and playwright. In the face of the problems Greg raises, with a mischievous rigorousness reminiscent of Hamlet himself, with the possibility of randomness, coincidence and error, the sanguine social and political order defended by Dover Wilson begins to totter. What may have been even more upsetting for him, however, is the idea that such indeterminacy might in some way lead to more happiness rather than less.

Nevertheless, the emotional tenor of his autobiographical reflections is not wholly unhappy. In acknowledging the contribution made by Stanley and Joan Bennett, and that of George Rylands, at gatherings in Cambridge, he says that 'I got much discipline and encouragement out of those hours, which rounded off the happy enterprise of seventeen years in the gayest possible manner' (p. 22). Indeed, enjoyment and excitement characterise the tone of this preface, at least as much as anxiety and confusion do:

> I hope, as I have said, that the fun of the thing has not altogether evaporated. And if the reader would catch something of the initial – and final – excitement, let him plunge straight into Chapter v and begin asking himself the question with which you first sent me mad. Did Claudius see the dumb-show? and if not, why not? It is just because I think the posing of that problem a turning-point in the history of Shakespearian criticism that I have written this book. (p. 23)

The ideological project of *What Happens in 'Hamlet'* is grounded in the emotional register of Dover Wilson's writing, which dwells upon happiness and unhappiness in many forms. The 'mad' or 'crazy' search for a rational but all-encompassing solution to the problems raised in Greg's 'Hamlet's Hallucination' links this to the question of what happens, of happening, and the nature of the event. He presents the coming-into-being of the book as a series of happenings, coincidences, fortunate and unfortunate conjunctions, and serendipitous relationships, yet the element of the unpredictable, uncertain or free as perceived by Greg threatens the social system which it is Dover Wilson's self-appointed mission to preserve.

Hap

The role of language is essential to Shakespearean artworks in their negative-dialectical dislocation of actual happiness from its concept. Moreover, in this connection, a particular coincidence or conjunction of like-sounding words in the English of his time, much used in the plays, seems especially important. These words include 'hap', 'haply', 'perhaps', 'hapless', 'mishap', which are all to do with fortune, luck, chance, accident or event, and also 'happiness', 'happy', 'happily', which are used both of fortunate happenings and of an early modern emotion which some people suppose they still experience today. In short, Shakespeare's texts play across the strong family ties between these words deliberately and creatively, and this linkage is key to understanding the reflection upon happiness, and its opposite, in *Hamlet*.

Thus, when Hamlet says, of the Ghost's anticipated reappearance in 1.2,

> I pray you all,
> If you have hitherto concealed this sight
> Let it be tenable in your silence still
> And whatsomever else shall hap tonight
> Give it an understanding but no tongue …
>
> (1.2.244–8)[9]

the word signifies an event: whatever *happens* tonight. But, in their fearful state, there is also a shade of 'whatever shall *chance* to happen, or, consequently, whatever *fortune* befalls us', invoking the sense of *hap* as luck or fortune. This feeling of the unpredictability of events, and the intervention of fortune in affairs, informs the scene, with Hamlet saying just before:

> I will watch tonight.
> Perchance 'twill walk again.
>
> (1.2.240–1)

Thus 'hap' can signify event, or an event shaped by the randomness and unreliability of fortune or misfortune. When Claudius observes of his plan to send Hamlet to England,

> Haply the seas and countries different
> With variable objects shall expel
> This something-settled matter in his heart
> Whereon his brains still beating puts him thus
> From fashion of himself.
>
> (3.1.170–4)

this adverbial form introduces the element of happiness: this is what may happen if we (and he) have good fortune, and this would be a happy outcome for everyone, about which we should feel glad. When the Queen says,

> And for your part, Ophelia, I do wish
> That your good beauties be the happy cause
> Of Hamlet's wildness.
>
> (3.1.37–9)

she means that it would be a good or happy thing if it 'happened' to be Ophelia's charms which had driven the prince out of his wits (which is, of course, also Polonius's hope). Earlier, there is play on this theme, when

Rosencrantz replies to Hamlet's description of Polonius as a 'great baby' still in his 'swaddling clouts' (2.2.381–2),

> Happily he is the second time come to
> them, for they say an old man is twice a child.
>
> (2.2.321–2)

His chancing upon the swaddling clouts a second time is good luck for him and will increase his happiness in his simple enjoyment of life, as he has also come to his second childhood. Happy events occur happily, that is, as a matter of chance, or perhaps at the behest of the fickle Goddess Fortuna. This, however, is not a merely personal occurrence. It is also necessary to trace the social implications of this conjunction of hap and happiness.

How does happiness happen?

A common idea concerning happiness is that of its elusiveness. It is a notion to be found in the play at moments such as this:

> HAMLET … Good lads, how do you both?
> ROSENCRANZ As the indifferent children of the earth.
> GUILDENSTERN Happy, in that we are not ever happy. [ouer-happy F]
> On Fortune's cap we are not the very button.
> HAMLET Nor the soles of her shoe.
> ROSENCRANZ Neither, my lord.
> HAMLET Then you live about her waist, or in the middle of her favours.
> GUILDENSTERN Faith, her privates we.
> HAMLET In the secret parts of Fortune? O, most true –
> she is a strumpet. What news?
>
> (2.2.220–31)

Happiness, conceived as good fortune, is fickle: glimpsed one minute and gone the next. What is here the witty turning of a commonplace can, however, become, in liberal reflections upon happiness, a point of principle. Happiness is something we seek after, but will never find. M. Andrew Holowchak usefully summarises this 'elusiveness' thesis concerning happiness:

> On philosophical analysis, happiness proves as elusive as it is alluring. First, though most recognize its importance, philosophers disagree greatly about just what makes people happy. Among the early Greeks, Socrates, Plato tells us, believes that happiness is virtue, which he equates with knowledge. Aristotle defines it as virtuous activity, which has both a social and an asocial dimension. Plato in *Republic* sees it as a form of justice. The Epicurean and Cyrenaic

> philosophers identify it with pleasure, but each school disagrees on what pleasure is. In more recent times, Sigmund Freud states that happiness is immediate erotic satisfaction. Immanuel Kant says happiness is a moral exercise of duty. John Stuart Mill links it to the freedom for self-determination.
>
> There is also a second philosophical issue: Happiness for whom? Ought I to regard my own happiness above the happiness of others? If so, to what extent? If not, how does the happiness of others factor into how I ought to act?[10]

Happiness in many of these formulations is individualistic; certainly, in the final dilemma, 'others' are a problem for it, not central to achieving it for the self. The other and the self are conceived as separate and antagonistic in this survey. It does not ask whether happiness of the self is possible at all without the happiness of the other, or how it is possible to be 'happy' in a world where others are miserable. Ultimately, though, such questions are felt not to matter, because it is all an enigma:

> Finally, if happiness is an end of human activity, is it the sole end? If it is not an end, what role does it play in a good life?
>
> In short, happiness is puzzling: all of us desire it, but there is widespread disagreement over what it is and how it is to be had. Happiness truly is as elusive as it is alluring. (p. x)

Whilst some of these ancient accounts of happiness, such as Plato's, do acknowledge a public dimension to the emotion, the elusiveness of happiness can act as a convenient excuse for complacency about never doing anything to achieve it. In contrast to the positions Holowchak lists here, for Marxists, happiness (as a collective state in which the individual can flourish) is necessarily the end of all human activity: both the state of society towards which revolutionary efforts are directed and the autotelic, self-sustaining purpose of human life itself, even if at present frustrated and perverted by exploitative social relations.

The elusiveness of happiness is thus by turns ideological, objectively true and utopian: utopian, in that there cannot be a prescriptive formula for happiness – there has to be something extempore, surprising, unaccountable about it (which might be possible in a world not dictated by the treadmill of capitalist competition); objectively true, because it is exasperatingly difficult to find, or rather to achieve, in presently existing society; ideological, because for bourgeois thinkers, who consider happiness a merely personal, and all-too-fleeting, state, that difficulty is ultimately a regrettable, but acceptable, fact of life. Such bourgeois happiness cannot nowadays be represented in serious literature, unless as already, or about to be, lost: to depict it would be intolerable sentimentalism, as in the cosiness of the Victorian hearth. The disparity between the represented state and the real world of its own creation is too huge for bourgeois ideology to ignore, so instead it insists that images of true happiness must be bad art. Serious art, for the bourgeois critic, must thus register discontent, the almost pleasurable, unscratchable longing called up by human unhappiness in class society, for those who can afford to entertain it. The Renaissance, in those moments at which it seems most embarrassingly alien to modern sensibilities, thinks it is acceptable to represent happiness directly. But for us, happiness must be a 'puzzle' (Holowchak's Preface is titled 'The Puzzle of Happiness'), and elusive both as a concept and as a reality. It is 'alluring' too, like a fetishised commodity, and this is really the point: that happiness itself is an ephemeral signified which skitters over the horizon as soon as its latest consumer signifier is purchased.

For Marx, on the other hand, happiness is not really elusive or ambiguous: it is a state in which each individual lives in and for every other individual. This understanding of happiness as human freedom is plain enough: 'In place of the old bourgeois society, with its classes and class antagonisms, we shall have an association, in which the free development of each is the condition for the free development of all'.[11] It is the reality of this state of affairs that is 'elusive' because of the obstacles which the capitalist order, understandably enough, seeks to put in its way. In fact, it is not unattainable so much as proscribed. Consequently, whilst happiness is an emotion, and so psychological, physiological and individual, it is also deeply *political*. This is an understanding of happiness as a state which cannot occur in a society based upon mutual antagonism and economic competition, with all the forms of violence and repression which go along with them. A good (fair, equitable, just, free, nurturing, creative) society is one in which one can be happy, and is at the same time a necessary precondition for happiness. For communists, the end and purpose of all human activity is to create the conditions for all human beings to flourish. It is therefore nonsensical to suppose that human beings, the *social* species, can be authentically happy in a society where others are miserable, or where, in fact, their own happiness is directly or indirectly the result of someone else's despair. Whilst 'happiness' is felt to be experienced commonly enough, this emotion must be regarded as a travesty of the rich and humanly fundamental meaning of the concept.

Thus, happiness isn't (cannot be) just personal: it is collective, shared and social. Whilst contemporary approaches to early modern emotions have stressed their *cultural* nature, their cultural construction, cultural conditioning and cultural impact,[12] this culturalist emphasis is liable to miss the vital importance of the *social* nature of happiness: that it is a social fact to be desired and defended, and that that the individual's happiness is dependent upon the state of that social order within which they live their lives. Authentic individual happiness can only occur in the 'good society', which is a condition of possibility for collective happiness.

One consequence of this is that happiness is in the future (or at least that it isn't in the present or the past); that is to say, happiness is, for us, only potential, not realised. As something (hopefully) possible, but (unfortunately) not actual, happiness is also something desired. Happiness is a utopian emotion: it has its being in no actual place or time, yet it is all around us as a desired collective and individual state. We are surrounded by glimpses of happiness, or rather of its possibility, by fleeting epiphanies of what such a feeling would, or could, be like, mixed with continual disappointment at the difficulty of realising the 'good society' which would make it possible. One of the advantages (but also of course disadvantages) of this utopian or non-existent dimension of happiness is that it cannot be easily controlled – owned, defined, compartmentalised, administered, administrated, coerced – except in the sphere of ideology, where many interests claim to possess it, to control access to it, to have the secret of it, to have achieved it on our behalf and in our interests. But that other, utopian happiness, is always hanging around, like Hamlet around the lobby, to give the lie to all these claims to have realised it, or be able, or about, to produce it.

What's unhappiness?

Hamlet is a play about unhappiness: we have the prince's melancholy, Claudius's guilt, Gertrude's fear, the Ghost's anger, Ophelia's despair. It is also a play about happiness, in a sense: a false sense, in that Claudius asserts repeatedly that everyone is happy when they are not, or are merely misrecognising their emotions as such. Our impression is that this is a miserable place, and a miserable society. In the final scene, as he lies dying, Hamlet implores Horatio to

> Absent thee from felicity awhile
> And in this harsh world draw thy breath in pain
> To tell my story.
>
> (5.2.331–3)

Here he reconfirms the impression, once again, in addition to conventional contempt for the world, that 'Denmark's a prison' (F, 2.2.242). We recall how, in the first lines of the play, the sentinels are mainly concerned to establish their identities in a world obscured by darkness and the possibility of deceit: 'Stand and unfold yourself' (1.1.2). Francisco is the first to unfold himself in another sense; that is, to tell us how he feels:

For this relief much thanks. 'Tis bitter cold
And I am sick at heart.

(1.1.6–7)

This state is a common one in the world of the play, pervading it as does the anxieties about identity. The scene is full of foreboding – everyone knows that a ghost is about to appear, and that the spectre will reveal to Hamlet that a royal murder has been committed and is going unpunished. Beyond that, the sombre opening contributes to the tragic sweep of the play as a whole: something is 'rotten in the state of Denmark' (1.4.190), and so we are presented with a society which, some might argue, needs to be purged by the tragic sacrifice of the Prince.

Whilst Francisco's immediate meaning is that he is 'sick at heart' because of the cold he has endured on his long watch, it is important that he is *unhappy*. The next expression of such angst is Horatio's:

BARNARDO Say, what, is Horatio there?
HORATIO A piece of him.

(1.1.18)

It would be possible to act this as indicating that darkness conceals everything but his offered hand (as a note in Harold Jenkins's edition suggests),[13] but it might otherwise be read to suggest his own fractured or damaged self – that he is 'not all there' or, like Francisco, 'sick at heart'. Perhaps Jenkins is right to suggest that he is, as a sceptic, seeking to 'reserve full participation' from their ghost-watch, but that scepticism runs beyond the bounds of this encounter, and contributes to a critical strain within the play which suggests that nothing in Denmark can offer a whole or coherent existence. A question thrust at us from the start is thus, who can be happy in the *Hamlet*-world, and who cannot?

Hamlet's unhappiness is the concern from the first time we see him; only after his encounter with the Ghost is it, for some, a question of madness. But this un*hap*piness is prophetic of what has happened, and is about to happen:

O cursed spite
That ever I was born to set it right!
Nay, come, let's go together.

(1.5.186–8)

Hamlet, at least in the earlier part of the play, rejects his destiny, not only in being reluctant to carry out the revenge which fate or the heavens has decreed for him but also in continually thwarting the role, identity and duty he has been assigned within the symbolic order of Denmark by Claudius and the version of reality that king is trying to establish there. Whilst one might see Claudius's strategy as being to separate Hamlet from his fellows, from Horatio, and his loyal friends among the soldiers and gentlemen, as well as the common democratic rabble, who first support Hamlet and then Laertes, Hamlet here redefines his task of setting the time right as a collective one: at first he alone is born to it, but then this is changed so that they 'go together' to embark upon the task.

So is the *Hamlet*-world one of totalitarian control, or of effective challenges to such control? There is an interesting tension in the play between an atmosphere of casualness and informality and a more deeply 'administered' reality of which we are given suggestive glimpses. Hamlet lounges disconsolately in the throne room and indulges freely in asides to the adjacent theatre audience, greets wandering players and conducts impromptu rehearsals, swans about in the lobby and perhaps, at the end of the play, wonders whether to have the fencing there or in some more formal chamber; the King and his chief minister are able to conceal themselves freely behind sundry wall hangings without drawing attention to themselves, the dialogue banters about fairly informally and even racily, all things considered, between monarchs and surly princes, and between members of the royal family and courtiers, ministers, ladies, actors, students and gravediggers. Despite being the centre of power in a military nation powerful enough to defeat Norway and subdue England to its will, Elsinore seems to be garrisoned by no more than a handful of nervy and maladroit guards. Yet, at the same time as we are partly aware of this strange economy in representing the machinery of state, we are sensitised to that machinery in subtler and ghostly form, feeling that the spying behind arrases signifies a developed system of surveillance, that the sentinels *do* stand for an army massing just out of sight, and that Claudius is protected by those 'Switzers' (4.5.97) he asks for upon Laertes's furious return. It is a curiously dysfunctional totalitarian state, in which the means of tyranny are supposedly there, but somehow never manage to manifest themselves fully at the level of direct representation.

Claudius's Elsinore is, then, quite a good reminder of our own historical situation. Whilst we, as the audience, are aware that this is a world characterised by unnecessary misery, and that the bloated so-called happiness of some is dependent upon the impoverishment and repression of others, the forces of ideology insist that everything is fine, and that in fact everyone is happy and should be uncritically carousing in celebration of the fact. All this is underpinned by increased paranoia, surveillance, degradation of civil liberties, the distraction of foreign wars and even (every so often) hopeful but unconvincing rhetoric about royal nuptials constituting a new start for the nation as a whole.

However, even more sinister than such overt symptoms, in Theodor Adorno's view, is the deeper tendency in late capitalist society to seek a seamless identification between the realm of representation and the world, and between the world of ideas and the world of things. This punctual correspondence, inherently false and stifling, but incredibly convenient for aiding the progress of a certain kind of reductive instrumental rationality, makes possible a totalising organisation – an informing *administration* – which he sees as taking hold of the world and its representation, cementing the social conditions which create unhappiness rather than its opposite. In short, the growing congruity between culture (in all senses) and an administrative rationality threatens to end not only the critical function of art, but also to extinguish the capacity for the critical or new from society altogether:

> the equalization of the tensions felt today between culture and its objective conditions threatens culture with spiritual death by freezing. In its relation to reality there is a dialectic of non-simultaneity … When reality, however, dwells upon the current standard, a tendentious levelling of consciousness takes place. The more easily consciousness adjusts to integral reality, the more it is discouraged from going beyond that which is there once and for all.[14]

Indeed, this administered or administrated society might be taken as defining the *unhappy* society in its modern form, one in which the singularity and creativity of what has come to be known as 'culture' is negated, and culture itself is compartmentalised within the, itself thoroughly administrative, dichotomy between 'culture' and 'administration'.[15]

Adorno takes as his example of this administrative reason invading the sphere of culture a brochure he has seen advertising cultural festivals around Europe:

> The reason for such a scheme is obvious: it permits the cultural traveller to divide his time and to seek out that which he thinks will be of interest to him – in short, he can plan his trip according to the same principle which lies behind the organization of these festivals: they are all embraced and controlled by a single comprehensive organization. Inherent in the idea of the festival, however, and of the artistic festival as well, no matter how secularized and

> weakened it might be, is the claim to something unique, to the emphatic event which is not fungible. Festivals are to be celebrated as they come; they are not to be organized only from the perspective of avoiding overlapping. Administrative reason which takes control of them and rationalizes them banishes festivity from them. This results in an intensification into the grotesque which cannot escape the notice of the more sensitive nerves present at these so-called cultural offerings. (p. 118)

Rather as at Elsinore, the genuinely moving, socially life-giving and politically critical force of happiness and festivity has been silently and logically 'rationalized' into something highly irrational but nevertheless effective in achieving its instrumental ends. Adorno is keen to emphasise that this process is not to be blamed on any individual social caste. Stage-managers of the political and cultural scene, like Polonius, are not to be singled out for harsh treatment. 'In the administrated world managers are used as scapegoats almost as frequently as the bureaucrats', he writes,

> the assignment of objective guilt relationships to people is itself a product of prevailing ideology. The total social and economic tendency consumes the material basis of traditional culture, either liberal or individualistic in style. (pp. 118–19)

Nevertheless, it is tempting to take Polonius as an image of 'administrated society', as an index of how far (or how little) Denmark still possesses any capacity for authentic festivity, presented, this time, by means of a comic turn. This is suggested by his reaction to the players, treating them like Adorno's cultural festival: his 'administrative' detailing of literary genres, his eventual appropriation of the actors as a means to cheer the lord Hamlet, his focus on organising their accommodation rather than wondering at their skill, and his determination to use them 'according to their desert' (2.2.465) rather than after his 'own honour and dignity' (2.2.469), as Hamlet insists he does. Similarly, there is his pigeonholing approach to rhetorical figures and his fusty manner of addressing the King and Queen. Polonius tries and comically fails to bring about the all-encompassing victory of what is over what could be, of the existent rather over the utopian, and to make the new political reality of Denmark invulnerable to events, to the buffets of fortune, in a word, to *hap*.

Redoubled happiness

To return to that word, or fragment of a word, *hap*, its bringing together of event, chance and good fortune situate it as a key motif relating to happiness in the personal and social senses. Shakespeare's plays appear to play quite deliberately upon the related senses of hap as fortunes, and as 'joys', or emotion:

> KING Do it, England!
> For like the hectic in my blood he rages
> And thou must cure me. Till I know 'tis done,
> Howe'er my haps my joys will ne'r begin. [were ne'r begun F]
> (4.3.63–6)

Surprisingly, perhaps, Polonius, whom I have just cited as representative of the decidedly 'unhappy' tendency in antagonistic society, shows himself to be quite an enthusiast for this playful, festive species of 'hap':

> POLONIUS [*aside*] Indeed, that's out of the air. How pregnant sometimes his replies are – a happiness that often madness hits on, which reason and sanity could not so prosperously be delivered of. I will leave him and my daughter. (2.2.205–9)

T. J. B. Spencer glosses this happiness as 'felicity of expression'.[16] The expression is felicitous because it is good: it is a good phrase, well expressing the thought. But there is also the sense, hanging around in the form of the word *hap* for luck, chance or fortune, that he has 'happily' found this expression, by a fortunate coincidence of word and thought, that good has come out of accident, and that, moreover, the accidental nature of this good makes it all the more good. It is especially lucky to have found this good phrase, which must be good in itself, and, in being unpremeditated, it is good either in, first, being inspired by forces of goodness – gods or a superior kind of poetic fury,[17] or, second, being an instance of courtly *sprezzatura*. In other words, there is an extra value attached here to *hap*, to fortune, coincidence, spontaneity, the singularity or uniqueness of an event. Things falling out happily are good, by chance, and even better *because* they are by chance. In Adornian terms, then, it is the 'cultural' non-simultaneity of hap or happiness in this complexly mixed sense which makes it powerfully contradict the enshrinement of a timeless, frozen actuality. The possibility of an unpredictable, singular event, of a fortunate, or unfortunate *hap*pening, is what leaves a door open from a completely reified and totalitarian order to social freedom. We might see this, historically, as the expression of a courtly, feudal or quasi-feudal sensibility in the appeal to an aesthetic of graceful spontaneity. But it is also the shadow of a radically democratic one, within which particulars, or individuals, are free to be what they are, rather than being subsumed under the totalising categories of a diseased, 'administrative', rationality.

Indeed, Polonius himself seems to savour the paradox that madness – the opposite of orderly, disciplined, prescriptive, administrative government – can sometimes bring good, or lead to truth.

This is not a new idea to him. Rather, he earlier claims to his man Reynaldo that it is the basis of his policy, and even, it seems, of a whole underlying epistemology:

> See you now
> Your bait of a falsehood take this carp of truth,
> And thus do we of wisdom and of reach,
> With windlasses and with assays of bias,
> By indirections find directions out.
>
> (2.1.59–63)

Despite being later commemorated by Hamlet as 'a foolish prating knave' (3.4.213), who only in death can be 'still, most secret and most grave' (3.4.212), we might have to concede that 'Though this be madness yet there is method in't' (2.2.201–3). The foolish counsellor's would-be Machiavellian practices turn out to be close kin to the kind of dialectical, playful rationality, open to critique and the becoming of new possibilities envisaged by Adorno in his *Negative Dialectics* and *Aesthetic Theory*.

The opposite of Hamlet's 'happy' mad-talk is, of course, Ophelia's, a discourse which is both un*happ*y in unfortunately not coinciding with its intended meaning, and in failing to find anyone at court who can interpret it. As the Gentleman describes it,

> Her speech is nothing,
> Yet the unshaped use of it doth move
> The hearers to collection. They yawn [ayme F] at it
> And botch the words up fit to their own thoughts
> Which, as her winks and nods and gestures yield them,
> Indeed would make one think there might be thought,
> Though nothing sure, yet much unhappily.
>
> (4.5.7–13)

Hap can be unfortunate as well, it seems; her story registers the unhappy state of Denmark and the sharp end of the administrative logic that is trying to set, or to force, it right. Yet her disastrous situation is perhaps the inverse, the negative image of the positive sway of hap, of a social order which would be characterised by spontaneous flourishing: 'They say the owl was a baker's daughter. Lord, we know what we are but know not what we may be' (4.5.42–4). Hamlet's rashness, with which he has dispatched Polonius, for one thing, is perhaps the damaged and dangerous remainder of true happiness, the subverting of deep plots, plans and intentions, as it persists within the diseased wit of Denmark:

Rashly –
And praised be rashness for it – let us know
Our indiscretion sometime serves us well
When our deep plots do fall – and that should learn us
There's a divinity that shapes our ends,
Rough-hew them how we will.

(5.2.6–11)

Hamlet and negative utopia

So, as against Dover Wilson, what *happens* in *Hamlet* isn't something behind or beyond the surface of the play, something exterior to the dialogue, intended by the author, which explains the enigma of the Ghost's message. Rather, what happens is *hap*: the (often) negative manifestation of that principle of liberty, the freedom to be spontaneous, to accept and work with the accidental, or that which is generated by the logic of a thing's development, rather than an externally imposed and prescriptive principle. The formal order of society which underpins the capitalist-imperialist system of production, threatened by the revolutionary events of his time, struggles to find legitimation in the elusive text of *Hamlet*, as Hawkes's essay of 1986 showed:

> As a member of the Newbolt Committee, as we have seen, he insists on the proper, controlled study of literature as essential to a society wishing to avoid the alien barbarities of Bolshevism and to preserve the 'national mind and character', i.e. the integral and coherent structures of a British way of life. (p. 115)

However, it is not just a 'recursive', or 'revolutionary' quality to the text which highlights the inadequacy of the bourgeois reading, but also the crucial role of the emotions, and in particular of happiness, conceived not as a state, nor as a humour, but as an event.

Unhappily (for the purposes of this chapter, at least), *Hamlet* is not the play richest in *hap*-words. *King Lear* has more 'happiness', or at least variants upon and fragments of the word *happy*. The history plays dwell on this group of words at length, exploring their important ideological functions. But it is *Hamlet*'s suffusion with and implication in *time* which makes it speak, silently but unmistakably, of *hap*: of what happens, of unhappiness as the negative image of happiness, of what *could* happen or *should* happen if one is to be turned into the other, both in its imagined Denmark and in really-existing social reality.[18]

This timely and untimely dimension of the play is invested above all in Horatio, *Hor-ratio*, whose name could mean the logic or proportion of the times. Unfortunately, Horatio's world has lots of hap, but not much happiness: much happens, and seems to do so according to 'hap', or chance, but all to bad – unhappy – effect. He insists on the clear display of the bodies and the truthful recital of events because he is so keenly aware of this tendency to hap (or rather mishap):

> But let this same be presently performed
> Even while men's minds are wild, lest more mischance
> On plots and errors happen.
>
> (5.2.377–9)

In the bad society represented by Denmark and its neighbours, the serendipitous principle of *hap* is always turned awry. What would, in a better world, be creative and spontaneous, can here only be harmful. As he indicates, the court at Elsinore has been extremely accident-prone – but subject to mishaps rather than to lucky coincidences. Nevertheless, the intertwined linguistic tendrils of *hap* suggest that somewhere in the English language is a dim, unformed understanding that the good society – utopia or paradise – emerges from event, happening and *becoming*.[19]

Hamlet's intriguingly unsaid final words, perhaps pertaining to the plots and murders that have occurred, could also possibly have referred to something richer:

> I am dead, Horatio. Wretched Queen, adieu.
> You that look pale and tremble at this chance,
> That are but mutes or audience to this act,
> Had I but time (as this fell sergeant Death
> Is strict in his arrest) – O, I could tell you –
> But let it be. Horatio, I am dead.
> Thou livest: report me and my cause aright
> To the unsatisfied.
>
> (5.2.317–24)

The chance events of the play have all been *mischance*. The personified Death, on the other hand, ever-attendant upon the bad society, is *strict* – accurate, insistent, prescriptive. This administrative efficacy on the part of Death is indeed deathly – the deathliness of Adorno's totalised, 'administered society'. One wonders what direct and unambiguous truth it is that Hamlet could tell *us*, truly the great mass of 'the unsatisfied', seeing what he has seen, if only Death were not so efficient at his duties.

Notes

1 See Richard Meek's discussion in Chapter 6, above, for a similar point regarding the word/concept *sympathise*: whilst sympathising might seem to be an unproblematic good, under conditions of tyranny it can become a means of ideological manipulation.

2 Richard Strier, *The Unrepentant Renaissance: From Petrarch to Shakespeare to Milton* (Chicago: University of Chicago Press, 2011), p. 6. Further references will be included in the text.

3 William Empson, *Essays on Renaissance Literature, vol. 1: Donne and the New Philosophy*, ed. John Haffenden (Cambridge: Cambridge University Press, 1993), p. 159. Further references will be included in the text.

4 Strier, *The Unrepentant Renaissance*, pp. 9, 2.

5 Darrin McMahon, 'Finding Joy in the History of Emotions', in Susan J. Matt and Peter N. Stearns (eds), *Doing Emotions History* (Urbana: University of Illinois Press, 2013), pp. 103–19 (p. 103). Further references are included in the text.

6 Alexander Ezekiel Chang, 'Art and Negativity: Marxist Aesthetics after the Affective Turn', *Culture, Theory and Critique*, 53 (2012), 235–47 (pp. 236–7).

7 John Dover Wilson, *What Happens in 'Hamlet'*, 3rd edn (Cambridge: Cambridge University Press, 1951), pp. 174, 9. Further references are included in the text.

8 Terence Hawkes, *That Shakespeherian Rag: Essays on a Critical Process* (London: Methuen, 1986), p. 110.

9 Quotations from *Hamlet* are taken from the Arden 3 edn, ed. Ann Thompson and Neil Taylor (London: Thomson Learning, 2006), unless otherwise stated. Where lines and variants are from the Folio-only passages presented in that edition, this is indicated by 'F'.

10 M. Andrew Holowchak, *Happiness and Greek Ethical Thought* (London: Continuum, 2004), pp. ix–x. Further references are included in the text.

11 Karl Marx and Friedrich Engels, *The Communist Manifesto*, trans. Samuel Moore (Harmondsworth: Penguin, 1967), p. 105.

12 See, for example, Gail Kern Paster, Katherine Rowe and Mary Floyd-Wilson (eds), *Reading the Early Modern Passions: Essays in the Cultural History of Emotion* (Philadelphia: University of Pennsylvania Press, 2004).

13 *Hamlet*, ed. Harold Jenkins (London: Methuen, 1982), note to 1.1.22.

14 Theodor W. Adorno, 'Culture and Administration', in *The Culture Industry: Selected Essays on Mass Culture*, ed. J. M. Bernstein (London: Routledge, 1991), pp. 107–31 (p. 121). Further references are included in the text.

15 Ibid., pp. 117–18: 'Nothing escapes the attention of radically socialized society, which further effects the culture of which it seizes control'.

16 *Hamlet*, ed. T. J. B. Spencer (Harmondsworth: Penguin, 1980), note to 2.2.209.

17 See Spencer's note to 2.2.209–10.

18 See also Mary Ann Lund's discussion in Chapter 4, above, of Robert Burton's Renaissance version of Augustine's happy vision of God, which might be compared with notions of redemptive time in Benjamin and Adorno.

19 See Nigel Wood's exploration in Chapter 5, above, of the similarly complex and unsettling word/notion of *spleen* in the same period.

Part III

The politics and performance of emotion

8

'They that tread in a maze': movement as emotion in John Lyly

Andy Kesson

On Shrove Tuesday 1584, Elizabeth and her courtiers sat down to watch John Lyly's *Sapho and Phao*.[1] They saw a play about the mutual infatuation of the Queen Sapho and the ferry boy Phao, an infatuation engineered by Venus in order to 'conquer' the Queen's virginity (1.1.40). This play therefore asked exacting questions, about royal sexuality and social status, of an audience arranged around a female monarch and her court. As Susan Doran and John Guy have shown, neither virginity nor court patronage was a neutral term in the 1580s, and despite Lyly's modern reputation as a reassuringly conservative courtly playwright, the epilogue to *Sapho and Phao* projects an audience response founded on kinetic, emotive confusion:

> They that tread in a maze walk oftentimes in one path, and at the last come out where they entered in. We fear we have led you all this while in a labyrinth of conceits, diverse times hearing one device, and have now brought you to an end where we first began ... There is nothing causeth such giddiness as going in a wheel, neither can there anything breed such tediousness as hearing many words uttered in a small compass. But if you accept this dance of a fairy in a circle, we will hereafter at your wills frame our fingers to all forms. And so we wish every one of you a thread to lead you out of the doubts wherewith we leave you intangled, that nothing be mistaken by our rash oversights nor misconstrued by your deep insights. (Epilogue, 1–14)

This epilogue presumes bewilderment, giddiness and doubt on the part of its audience, a series of intellectual and emotive confusions explored in the highly locomotive terms of a maze, a labyrinth and a circular, supernatural dance. The very structure of the prose itself is labyrinthine, the first sentence's exemplary 'they' related to the audience only by the second sentence's 'you', so that its rhetorical shape performs the journey it describes. The epilogue expresses the wish (though, significantly, it makes no promises) that each audience member will find 'a thread to lead you out of the doubts' caused by these disorientating movements.

Despite the play's engagement with controversial issues and its epilogue's expectation of audience confusion, Lyly scholars have tended to read Lyly's work as politically and aesthetically straightforward. Leah Scragg aptly describes R. Warwick Bond as '[l]ocked into an equation between the action of the play and the courtship of Elizabeth by the Duc d'Alençon': for Bond, writing in 1902, the play can be explained by 'the author's main purpose of flattering the Queen'.[2] It is useful to think of almost all critical engagements with Lyly's work as locked into this idea, which reached its most authoritative expression in the arguments and title of G. K. Hunter's *John Lyly: The Humanist as Courtier* (1962), in which Lyly's humanist learning is sacrificed in favour of his courtly ambition. This play is instead the very opposite of simple propaganda; despite scholarly assumptions that the play has a 'main purpose' or represents an allegorical 'equation', it ends in a passionate impasse created by narrative indeterminacy and spatial irresolution. Lyly's theatre strives to instil confusion and uncertainty in its audience, challenging them, to use Lyly's spatial metaphor, to lead themselves out of doubt.

This chapter considers the emotional and motive implications of Lyly's writing.[3] It moves from the spatial metaphors of *Sapho and Phao* to the representation of authorship as something uniquely painful in Lyly's prose fiction. It concludes with the onstage creation of a character in Lyly's verse play, *The Woman in the Moon*, which allows us to see painfully emotive subjectivity created on stage in both fictional and literal terms, as a small boy represents an empty body slowly becoming a person. Lyly's spatial metaphors and his exploration of authorship, prose style and character subjectivity make emotive experience physical and unstable. In performance, of course, all emotive representation is active, as the word 'actor' ought to remind us, but in Lyly, as with the epilogue above, audience response is repeatedly cast as an active as well as a reactive process. Lyly's discussion of his own work seems to poise somewhere between the intellect and the passions, as with the metaphor here of the 'labyrinth of conceits'. As a principal dramatist of ambiguity and uncertainty, he is especially helpful in relation to current debates about the history of emotion. Amélie Rorty warns that emotions cannot

> be shepherded together under one set of classifications as active or passive; thought-generated and thought-defined or physiologically determined; voluntary or nonvoluntary; functional or malfunctional; corrigible or not corrigible by a change of beliefs.[4]

Lyly's work endorses Rorty's statement by mixing and thus collapsing these opposites. Lyly's audience members, for example, are neither fully active nor passive in the 'labyrinth of conceits', since they must search for a thread which will then lead them out of their imagined predicament. In Lyly's work, metaphor, prose structure and the notion of indeterminacy all come together in their representation and enactment of emotional change and exchange. Rather than using literary or dramatic or rhetorical texts to shepherd, determine or fix emotion, this chapter emphasises that Rorty's questions are themselves in play in early modern texts, as with Lyly's exploration of divergent and discrepant forms of emotional duress through disorientating physical, kinetic, literally moving experiences.

Space in *Sapho and Phao*

Given this chapter's focus on kinetic space, it is important to acknowledge that this is a controversial idea in Lyly studies, which tends to characterise his plays in terms of their stillness. We have seen that scholars have tended to limit the political scope of his work; the epilogue quoted above has also been used to limit the physical movement and narrative impetus enacted by his plays. G. K. Hunter claimed that '[t]he unusual critical agreement on this point is, fortunately for all concerned, shared by Lyly himself', quoting this epilogue's reference to the play's conclusion as 'an end where we first began'. Hunter is right to note that scholarly consensus here is unusually strong. But that consensus is less in tune with Lyly's writing than Hunter supposes. Even the spatial metaphor that Hunter quotes implies movement, not stasis. As Bilbo Baggins knew when he named his adventures *There and Back Again*, to arrive where you first began entails departure, journey and return.[5] Lyly asks his audience to accept the play as a dance, and accepting a dance is an act of kinetic collusion, of choreographed participation, not an act of removed, distanced spectatorship. Similarly, a labyrinth requires, as Lyly puts it, treading in a maze, and the auricular slip between 'a maze' and 'amaze' engineers a conceptual slip between motion and emotion that routinely informs Lyly's work.

Lyly repeatedly encourages readers and audiences to treat his texts with suspicion, and the epilogue to *Sapho and Phao* merits such suspicion: the play does not end as it first began.[6] The Queen Sapho may still 'sway her sceptre in her brave court' by the end of the play, as Phao describes her at the beginning, but the two boys who encounter her, Cupid and Phao, are changed irrevocably (1.1.9). Cupid switches allegiances from Venus to Sapho, his movement across the stage signalled in both linguistic and gestural terms by his mother's repeated orders to 'Come, Cupid' at the start of his scenes (1.1.55; 4.4.1; 5.1.1). Indeed, Lyly's plays repeatedly stage their narrative tensions in terms of crossing from one highly localised onstage space to another, whether that be Diogenes's refusal to come to Alexander's court in *Campaspe* or Cynthia's eventual agreement to visit the lunary bank in *Endymion*. These lateral movements on the early indoor commercial stage are unlike those associated with the outdoor thrust stage, and scholars more familiar with the latter have tended to misread Lyly's different spatial practice as a non-spatial practice. Cupid's movements in *Sapho and Phao*, connected as they are to his fear of mistreatment and his pleasure in treats, provide one example of the relationship between spatial and emotive change in the play.

The play's male protagonist, however, undergoes the biggest shift in place and passion. Phao opens the play by celebrating with the audience his role as 'a ferryman' and therefore 'a free man', by which he means someone free from courtly worry (1.1.1). But Phao then moves from ferry boy to courtier to exile, role-changes that scholars have tended to treat as purely conceptual, but which imply changes in dress, gesture, props and stage location, and therefore in kinds of stage movement. The play goes out of its way to point out changes in Phao's position: the boy begins and ends the play, and this structure underlines the fact that this is not 'an end where we first began'. He tells the audience at the start of the play of his 'content', 'quiet' and lack of ambition, and he tells them at its close of his intent to abandon his home in order to 'Range rather over the world' and 'entreat for death' (1.1.1–2; 5.3.16–17). That these transitions in location, status and emotion have been understood as forms of stasis is a measure of how poorly Lyly's work is currently understood.

Despite Lyly's reputation as an apolitical or safely royalist writer, these emotional shifts within characters had implications for the audience's experience of the play. In court performance, as we have seen, status at court was represented by proximity to or distance from the Queen. As Janette Dillon puts it, '[r]evels were essentially doing the same job as more overtly functional ceremonies and protocols: seeking to put visitors, participants and spectators literally in their proper places (with all the respect as well as constraint that might suggest)'.[7] Far from being put in his proper place, the play's conclusion demonstrates that Phao, the would-be courtier, has no place at all, and sends him off as an exile. These narrative transitions are therefore political as well as emotive, and such changes within a character's interiority imply an exchange with the audience's own empathetic perceptions.

Certainly for Phao, Lyly's 'labyrinth of conceits' entails emotive movement, not intellectual stasis. When Dillon tells us that '[r]evels might thus invade spaces, adopt positions, shape the body or utter suggestions in ways which would be unacceptable without the framing of play', she reminds us that the epilogue's promise of 'an end where we first began' is accompanied by the anticipation that the audience will feel giddy, physically disorientated. Phao's spatial movement in and out of the court is, for the most part, involuntary, marked by the royal and divine coercion of Sapho and Venus; it is also unhappy and self-destructive. Its representation in front of a court audience articulates and therefore disseminates worries about courtly ambition and its implication for self-volition.

David Bevington's description of the final scene as a 'signification of a concluding harmony' seems therefore to privilege Lyly's statements in the epilogue over the actual content of the final scene, or the wellbeing of the high-status monarch over the suffering of the working-class ferryboy and would-be courtier.[8] The epilogue not only tells the audience they have been moved (in both senses of the word) but informs them that they are now lost in unfamiliar surroundings and will need to rescue themselves from the conclusion of the story: 'And so we wish every one of you a thread to lead you out of the doubts wherewith we leave you entangled' (11–13). Though Lyly's plays have been viewed as static, and have been misleadingly described as comedies, Phao's story stages the traumatic experience of being an outsider at court, and the play's epilogue makes clear how confrontational and disturbing that story might feel to Lyly's court audience. Lyly's work therefore offers a useful site from which to rethink representations of emotion on stage and in prose.

Style, opposition and inconstancy

Given Rorty's warning about a tendency to divide emotions into opposites (active or passive; mental or physical; intended or imposed; treatable or intractable), it is useful to remember that Lyly was himself an early modern opponent to the idea of opposites. His prose style is organised around the idea that apparent opposites will always collapse in on each other. In both the style and content of his work, Lyly brings together and rethinks supposed oppositions and insists on the mutability of supposed constants. As he tells his male readers in a preface to his first work,

> I was driven into a quandary, gentlemen, whether I might send this my pamphlet to the printer or to the pedlar. I thought it too bad for the press and too

> good for the pack. But seeing my folly in writing to be as great as others', I was willing my fortune should be as ill as any's. We commonly see the book that at Midsummer lieth bound on the stationer's stall at Christmas to be broken in the haberdasher's shop, which, sith it is the order of proceeding, I am content this summer to have my doings read for a toy that in winter they may be ready for trash.[9]

Lyly's style uses alliteration and syntactical position to isolate certain nouns and identify them as alternatives: printer or pedlar, press or pack, stationer's stall or haberdasher's shop, toy or trash. But in each case, alternatives turn out to be substitutes, and opposites become affiliated. The supposed status attached to the printer over the pedlar, reinforced by the author's previous belief that 'I thought it too bad for the press and too good for the pack', is soon quashed by the discovery that some, perhaps all printed writing is foolish and destined to be used for wrapping paper. Reinforced by alliteration and syntax, Lyly's central insight here seems to be the transformative implications of time: toys will become trash. But in all his oppositions, it is usually the similitude or similarities between concepts that is emphasised, the proximity of printer and pedlar, press and pack.

In his first work, the prose fiction *Euphues: The Anatomy of Wit*, Lyly's narrator warns that 'neither is there anything but that have his contraries' (p. 43), and spends much of the story showing how 'anything' might approximate its antithesis. In his third play, *Gallathea*, Fortune is described as 'constant in nothing but inconstancy', and this play between inconstant constancy becomes a repeated theme across his work.[10] In *Endymion*, for example, when the title figure wishes to express his love for the moon, he does so by defining, defending and celebrating inconstancy:

> There is nothing thought more admirable or commendable in the sea than the ebbing and flowing; and shall the moon, from whom the sea taketh this virtue, be accounted fickle for increasing and decreasing? … Then why be not twigs that become trees, children that become men, and mornings that grow to evenings termed wavering, for that they continue not at one stay?[11]

Capturing the inconstancy of human life across his prose fiction and his prose drama, Lyly mapped out a celebration of unpredictable and uncontrollable change, but he also depicted the emotive consequences of inconstant Fortune and the tendency of supposedly constant human beings to 'continue not at one stay'.

Lyly was, indeed, celebrated by contemporaries for the unpredictable, protean fluidity of his own writing style. John Hoskyns (1566–1638), for example, specifically commended the 'varieties' of his prose, especially for establishing an authorial voice in his early work which he then abandoned: 'But Lyly himself hath outlived this [earlier] style and breaks well from it'.[12] For Thomas Lodge (1558–1625), Lyly was '*the* famous in facility in discourse', the word 'the' reminding readers that this writer is the superlative and unrivalled proponent of prose 'facility', a word which, like Hoskyns's 'varieties', emphasises stylistic surprise as well as range.[13] Lyly was the best-selling literary figure of the period and was famous for his prose ingenuity. He was also the first major writer to work for the commercial theatre, and indeed he was one of the few early modern writers to begin a dramatic career as an already famous writer, rather than beginning his career in the theatre as Shakespeare and Jonson seem to have done. His writing was therefore highly visible to contemporaries and influenced many of the writers who are now at the forefront of the period's canon: Nigel Wood's identification of Shakespeare's interest in 'shaping fantasies' in Chapter 5, above, for example, can easily be read back to Lyly's formative exploration of such ideas.[14] Lyly's exploration of the emotional life of his characters, as well as his representations of the emotive experience of writing, reading and watching, therefore, have implications for all early modern drama. Lyly's style, like his characters, stories and stage worlds, is protean, and this chapter explores the way metaphors and cues for movement chart out forms of emotive and intellectual flux.

Authorship and bodily pain

Lyly supplies a rich site from which to explore the representation of emotions and rhetoric because his work repeatedly offers reflections on the practice of authorship which are, or purport to be, authorially sanctioned. His prose fiction and plays are full of epistles to various kinds of reader or addresses to various kinds of audience member. The *Sapho and Phao* epilogue is a case in point. It was written and perhaps delivered by a playwright who was, in any case, already famous and associated with the play, its rhetorical style and theatre company, and it reviews and interprets the action presented by the play, fulfilling the same function for the reader of the printed play. But, as we have seen, the epilogue has itself been diversely interpreted, not least because it seems to gloss over the more radical implications of the story. Such audience addresses provide useful but problematic reflections on the emotive life of theatrical storytelling.

The subtitle of Lyly's first work, *The Anatomy of Wit*, together with its paratextual material, explicitly casts the author as an anatomist, defining authorship and the act of exploring the concept of wit as something physical, bodily and invasive. The history of emotion has in part been defined by a struggle over the relationship between body and mind, as when Rorty warns against a bifurcation that distinguishes, on the one hand, 'thought-generated and thought-defined' and, on the other, 'physiologically determined' emotion, or when Gail Kern Paster tells us that, in the early modern period, 'the psychological had not yet become divorced from the physiological'. Lyly's title, Richard Sugg suggests, shows 'an interest in piercing, isolating, defining, and knowing what was otherwise tantalizingly abstract'.[15] Sugg's language is itself emotive here ('interest', 'tantalizingly'), and Lyly's title took a hold on contemporaries. The title was influential, being the first time the word had been used outside of a specifically medical context, and its influence can be seen in Stubbes's *Anatomy of Abuses* (1583), Greene's *Arbasto: The Anatomie of Abuses* (1584), Nashe's *Anatomy of Absurdity* (1589) and Robert Burton's *Anatomy of Melancholy* (1621), the latter book connecting the word firmly to the history of emotions.[16]

But Lyly's prefaces to the *Anatomy* complicate any easy relationship or opposition between body and mind by insisting on the importance of authorship, rhetoric and reading to emotive experience. We might, then, think about the way the title *Anatomy of Wit* makes interiority physical or embodies mentality whilst also tying that process to concepts of authorship, style and reception. Given the controversy over the relationship between body and mind explored by this book, particularly in relation to the current critical orthodoxy that early modern individuals were subject to their bodily humours, it seems important that the title of the period's best-selling literary work ambiguously explores these ideas: it could mean 'the body belonging to wit', 'an attempt to embody wit or capture it in bodily terms', or 'the dismemberment of wit'.

As the first prefatory epistle puts it, '[t]he surgeon that maketh the anatomy showeth as well the muscles in the heel as the veins of the heart', and if he gets that process wrong he is liable to mockery or abuse from his spectators: 'It may be that fine wits will descant upon him that, having no wit, goeth about to make the Anatomy of Wit' (p. 28). Attempts to depict emotional interiority in rhetorical form, then, have emotional implications for both author and audience. Lyly tells his readers that 'the tender youth of a child is like the tempering of new wax, apt to receive any form' (p. 35), and his description of his own writing and reception process makes clear that rhetoric is similarly apt to receive any form, and to be vulnerable to descanting.

As we have seen, Lyly's rhetorical style is itself a form of anatomisation, of making and then unmaking physical connections between language. Alliteration, rhyme, wordplay, syntax and contextual allusions are all used in Lyly's writing to build parallels and discrepancies between words and concepts. Patricia Parker reminds us of the importance of rhetorical choices and wordplay in early modern texts, suggesting that we 'adapt the title of Judith Butler's recent *Bodies That Matter* into a sense of words (as well as bodies) that matter, and of language itself not just as mattering but as providing a crucial aspect of what a materialist criticism (or editing the "material Shakespeare") might attend to'. For Parker, language is reduced to 'the minor or merely verbal' by a critical tradition that still looks for 'novelistic forms of psychologizing associated with Bradleian character criticism, or the continuing influence of largely eighteenth-century assumptions about character, chronology, or logical consistency as well as singularity and authenticity'.[17] Lyly's status as a rhetorical exemplar in the period and his stylistic experimentation and compositional emphasis on wordplay make him a particularly fruitful site for rethinking such assumptions. As the idea of the anatomy makes clear, for Lyly, writing was a physical and emotive process.

Despite his misgivings, Lyly's first work was not only popular among readers but unprecedentedly so. Published in December 1578, the *Anatomy*'s reception appears to have encouraged a revised version of the first work as well as a sequel, *Euphues and His England*. Four years later, Lyly's two *Euphues* books had already been printed at least twelve times, and would continue to be reprinted until 1636. This means that representations of emotive life in Lyly need to be taken seriously by historians of emotion because they were so visible to his culture at large. Because Lyly comments on the process of being read, as well as the process of writing, these representations are also important for anyone interested in the histories of authorship, reading or reception.

What did it feel like to be the most famous and best-selling writer of your generation? Painful:

> [I]t falleth out with me as with the young wrestler that came to the games of Olympia, who, having taken a foil, thought scorn to leave till he had received a fall; or him that being pricked in the finger with a bramble, thrusteth his whole arm among the thorns for anger. For I, seeing myself not able to stand on the ice, did nevertheless adventure to run; and being with my first book stricken into disgrace, could not cease until I was brought into contempt by the second

> – wherein I resemble those that having once wet their feet care not how deep they wade. In the which my wading, Right Honourable, if the envious shall clap lead to my heels to make me sink, yet if your Lordship with your little finger do but hold me up by the chin I shall swim, and be so far from being drowned that I shall scarce be ducked. (p. 158)

One advantage of working with Lyly and passion is his generous reflection on the emotive process of writing. Though we should be cautious about treating such passages autobiographically, they have much to tell us about representations of the experience of authorship. Lyly is writing here to the Earl of Oxford, his new literary (and, later, theatrical) patron, and he is writing in the wake of an extraordinary response among book buyers to his literary output. By the time he wrote this preface, Lyly had not only written the first version of *The Anatomy of Wit* but revised it into a longer work which celebrated and took advantage of the success it had achieved. Lyly was now writing a preface to a sequel to that work, a practice which in itself suggests the decision to exploit the prestige of the earlier book – and thus an awareness of his own incipient and immediate popularity. And yet, in this epistle, Lyly conjures authorship as something dangerous and sad: a wrestler defeated in public, a man who sadistically forces himself to suffer ever greater sensations of pain, and, in the most disturbing image of all, someone captured by 'the envious' and forced to undergo simulated drowning. And yet, despite these dangers, this passage is also an oblique meditation on stubborn agency: if held up by Oxford's little finger, Lyly says, 'I shall swim'.

These painful metaphors for writing and reception have much to tell us about a writer who introduces himself to his readers as an anatomist and went on to dramatise the pain of courtly life. These are, once again, highly kinetic images, depicting writing as dangerous, torturous and emotionally painful. In *Endymion*, Lyly used the figure of Sir Tophas to push his stylistic games to an extreme and thus to parody the notion of rhetoric as peril. Sir Tophas proposes to kill 'two lads' because, '[l]arks or wrens, I will kill them' (1.3.20–1). The verbal proximity between lads and larks is enough to bring the boys into danger, as Tophas confirms when he says, 'Birds or boys, they are both but a pittance for my breakfast' (23–4). He later asks, 'Let me see, do you not bleed?' because 'Commonly my words wound' (58–61). His later intention to 'slaughter' these same boys is pacified by their (apparent) humanist erudition, which turns on their ability to argue over the different meanings of the homophones *Mars*, *mass* and *mas* and

Ars, *ass* and *as*: 'The Latin hath saved your lives', Tophas tells them (107). These comic overstatements are nevertheless further iterations of the idea that Lyly sketched out in the title of his first work, the prefaces to his prose fiction and the audience addresses of his plays: that language is a vehicle and rhetoric a space for the exploration of emotive pain as both physical and kinetic. As in the *Sapho and Phao* epilogue, these images of wrestling, pricking and drowning imply a miscegenation of agency and subjection; as with the *Anatomy of Wit* metaphor, these very bodily images fuse with concepts that might otherwise seem non-somatic: scorn, anger, disgrace, contempt and envy.

These physical images of authorship reverberate throughout Lyly's second work. When Euphues tries to counsel his friend, Philautus replies, 'Without doubt, Euphues, thou dost me great wrong in seeking a scar in a smooth skin, thinking to stop a vein where none opened, and to cast love in my teeth which I have already spit out of my mouth' (p. 183). The title of the earlier work seems to make Euphues the object of anatomisation, but here he is very much cast as someone who observes and meddles with others' bodies. Once again, the metaphorical import of these comparisons is bodily, emotive and kinetic: love is something to cast in and spit out of your mouth. Since Philautus is trying to discourage his friend's curiosity in his own mental state, these metaphors serve the further purpose of refusing access to Philautus's thoughts, using physicality as a barrier to interiority.

'See we cannot, guess we may': imagining reception

Although Lyly only wrote two books about Euphues and Philautus, their fictional lives would continue to be narrated by a range of new writers, including Robert Greene, Anthony Munday, Thomas Lodge and Barnabe Riche.[18] These continuations of the characters' fictional biographies are another indication of Lyly's sudden and unprecedented impact on the literary culture around him, and demonstrate writers and publishers attempting to capitalise financially on this success. But they also demonstrate the emotive consequences of Lyly's work for his readers, some of whom were also writers who continued and rewrote his characters' biographies. Reading Lyly's prose fiction in light of their immediate impact on readers, writers and publishers helps to emphasise the way in which his writing invited responsive readership and thus writerly response. The second and final of Lyly's *Euphues* stories leaves the two men separated in space and differentiated in their emotional states, but it also hands over the characters to the reader:

> Gentlemen, Euphues is musing in the bottom of the mountain Silixsedra, Philautus married in the isle of England. Two friends parted; the one living in the delights of his new wife, the other in contemplation of his old griefs. What Philautus doth they can imagine that are newly married; how Euphues liveth they may guess that are cruelly martyred. I commit them both to stand to their own bargains. For if I should meddle any further with the marriage of Philautus it might haply make him jealous, if with the melancholy of Euphues it might cause him to be choleric; so the one would take occasion to rub his head, sit his hat never so close, and the other offence to gall his heart, be his case never so quiet. I, gentlewomen, am indifferent, for it may be that Philautus would not have his life known which he leadeth in marriage, nor Euphues his love descried which he beginneth in solitariness; lest either the one being too kind might be thought to dote, or the other too constant might be judged to be mad. (p. 354)

'I … am indifferent': it seems a curious place to leave two characters whose adventures you have just narrated, and an equally curious place to leave your readers. Lyly seems to suggest that the affective fictional world might at any point leak into the real one, or, perhaps more alarmingly, that the real world might shade into the fiction. Katharine Craik has proposed that 'immersion in a *literary* environment might have shaped, and sometimes imperilled, masculine subjectivity', but whereas Craik emphasises 'the ways that literature affected the material body', Lyly enables us to examine how each affected the other.[19] For despite the apparent certainty of the men's opposite mental states, the one delighted, the other grieving, Lyly's narrator worries that further narration will provoke jealousy or choler, cuckoldry or offence. This dilemma is avoided by the narrator's indifference, his determined neutrality, which is represented as preventing the reader from thinking one character a dotard or judging the other to be mad. Even Lyly's readership seems subject to transformation: this text constructs them as 'gentlemen' one moment, 'gentlewomen' the next. In Lyly's work, enquiry, writing and reading can all incite pain, and even fictional characters are in danger of being psychologically changed by the decisions made by their narrator or readers. Perhaps most importantly of all, in the hands of Munday, Riche, Greene and Lodge, Lyly's characters became serialised, allowing us to see the opposite process described by Craik, as readers became writers and reading matter became material for rewriting.

As we can see, all readers are implicated in these decisions, since they share the narrator's investment in the story. This is, perhaps, the element in Lyly's narrative craft that best explains the hold that his stories took on his readers, for Lyly repeatedly states that his fictional worlds require imaginative intervention from their readers in the real world. This *Euphues* story, for example, begins with a preface to female readers which opens with an emphasis on reading as an act of active imagination:

> Arachne having woven in cloth of Arras a rainbow of sundry silks, it was objected unto her by a lady, more captious than cunning, that in her work there wanted some colours; for that in a rainbow there should be all. Unto whom she replied, 'If the colours lack thou lookest for, thou must imagine that they are on the other side of the cloth; for in the sky we can discern but one side of the rainbow, and what colours are in the other, see we cannot, guess we may'. (p. 161)

Lyly invites his readers to be not only active but supplementary, casting the limits of representation as an impetus for the onlooker to 'imagine'. A modern idiom talks of readers becoming 'emotionally invested' or 'involved' in their reading. Lyly seems to project reading as a passionate act of creation, particularly when a text refuses total representation and thus requires readerly participation: 'See we cannot, guess we may'. As with the other Lylian images we have seen – his audience caught in a labyrinth and seeking to find their way out, some of his readers seeking to execute him, or the notion that the act of narration and reception had consequences for a character's sexual status – the writing here calls for collaborative and creative readership. The reader is expected to 'imagine' as well as 'guess' the fictive worlds they encounter.

These calls for imaginative reception continue into Lylian drama: his first play, *Campaspe*, for example, opened at court with the following prologue:

> Whatsoever we present we wish it may be thought the dancing of Agrippa his shadows, who in the moment they were seen were of any shape one would conceive, or lynxes, who, having a quick sight to discern, have a short memory to forget. (Court prologue, 13–16)

This is a difficult sentence, and the most important thing to grasp is that its syntactical logic includes a sleight of hand, as its subject switches without warning from the performers ('the dancing of Agrippa his shadows': the necromancer's demons) to the audience ('lynxes' with 'a quick sight to discern'). This transition from the play to the audience means that the reference to Agrippa's shadows is a reference to the audience members as well as the actors. The play is thus asserted to be the responsibility of those who 'conceive' it, the audience. Agrippa's shadows, like Arachne's rainbow, are indefinable, supernatural things. They might seem to represent interpretative impasses, but nevertheless serve to prompt, rather than impede, active cognitive responses. As with his readers, Lyly asks audience members to be actively creative and collaborative in both the fictional story and its affective context. These dancing shadows are not quite the responsibility of the actors or the audience, but a complex fusion of the two. In short, the syntax has tacitly fused actor and audience together, once again troubling common oppositions between performer and onlooker. Lyly asked his audience, in the *Sapho and Phao* epilogue, to 'accept this dance of a fairy in a circle'. Accepting a dance implies the decision to take part in what Barbara Ravelhofer calls 'the sartorial, kinetic, iconic and verbal languages of the event', rather than to spectate.[20] Judith Bryce defines dance as a simultaneously 'coercive and enabling' process, and the *Campaspe* prologue repeats this notion of performance as an active, supernatural dance between audience and actors.[21]

This emotively conceptual dancing between performer and audience is endemic to early modern rhetoric and theatre. Parker reminds us that dramatic rhetoric challenges our distinction between a character and its writer: 'Wordplay itself, of course, already complicates the certainties of characterological integrity or the assigning of a particular speaker's intent, operating as it does in ways often independent of any given character's control.'[22] Likewise, a defining feature of early modern drama is the characters' ability to inhabit the fictional and the real worlds at once, what Robert Weimann calls a blending of representational and presentational modes.[23] In his prologues, epilogues and other paratextual material, Lyly insists on the audience's and readers' collusion in the world of wordplay and performance.

In an epilogue to *Campaspe*, Lyly tells his audience that '[o]ur exercise [the performance] must be as your judgment is, resembling water, which is always of the same colour into what it runneth' (Blackfriars epilogue, 4–6). Characteristically for Lyly, the phrasing leaves it unclear whether it is the performance or the audience's judgement which resembles water, a syntactical conundrum which once again muddles distinctions between actor and onlooker and reinforces the central statement that performance 'must be as your judgment'. Katharine Eisaman Maus has described all early modern drama as 'radically synecdochic' in that it urges or forces its audiences into using 'partial and limited presentation as a basis for conjecture about what is undisplayed or undisplayable'.[24] Lyly's work anticipates these ideas but also maps out something bolder and more bizarre, at least to anybody used to thinking of performance as the product of authors, actors or directors, when he claims it to be the imaginative responsibility of the audience only. In both his prose fiction and his drama, Lyly demands that readers and audiences supplement synecdochic representation, making rhetorical and performative representations only the initial stages in cognitive and affective imagination. Indeed, in the *Campaspe* prologue, Lyly seems to suggest that dramatic representation is entirely the result of audience response. 'Whatsoever we present we wish it may be thought … lynxes … [with] a quick sight to discern': this syntactical slip from play to audience locates the former within the remit of the latter, and relocates the affective qualities of performance entirely within the audience's 'quick sight to discern'.

The Woman in the Moon and emotive creativity

As we have seen, Lyly has a well-established but misleading reputation for elite, cerebral and static writing. On the contrary, he repeatedly stages the experience of telling, hearing or being part of a story as something emotionally and physically moving. In the play *Sapho and Phao*, the boy Phao is captivated by a story ('I pray, tell on'), is inquisitive ('Was not the god angry to see you unkind?') and is 'driven … into divers conceits' (2.1.64, 59). The storyteller announces her intention to 'place [Phao] in the plain path of love', but at the story's end Phao reaffirms that 'to yield to love is the only thing I hate' (39–41, 131–2). This is a story told to transform an emotional state; instead, it prompts an emotional response but defies its fictional author's intent, further entrenching the listener in his or her emotional resolve. In *Gallathea*, the title figure feels 'terror' and 'horror' upon hearing a story (1.1.155–7), whilst in *Endymion* Eumenides leaves the stage announcing that his curiosity to hear an old man's autobiographical story 'hath so melted my mind that I wish to hang at your mouth's end' (3.4.2). Here Lyly stages a kind of rhetorical urgency, a passionate need to experience narrative process on the part of a character speaking as they hurry to leave the stage. As Lynn Enterline reminds us, classical rhetoric aimed to move the listener 'in ways that are not purely cognitive', and the relationship between language and dramaturgy here fuses together emotive and kinetic movement.[25] These stories are told on stage and so, for all their apparently static implications, their effect on their listeners is visual as well as oral, and, from Phao's plea for the speaker to continue to Eumenides's promise to 'hang at your mouth's end' as he leaves the stage, the script is alive with invitations to the actor to display emotive affect.

The rest of this chapter explores these ideas of stage choreography, character and affect by looking at Lyly's one verse drama, *The Woman in the Moon*, in which a character is created on stage, requiring the actor to use body and voice to represent nascent interiority and affect. Cora Fox has explored how 'Ovidianism … reveals the way the self can outlive the body': here Lyly's highly Ovidian drama explores a body that predates the self.[26] If Lyly set about exploring *The Anatomy of Wit*, he now required a boy to represent an anatomy without wit, passion or soul. This play begins with the world's sovereign god, Nature, and her two female sidekicks, Concord and Discord. A female ultimate deity is, at least in European theology, rather unusual, even before Christianity came to dominate the Continent's worldview. According to the Bible, usually considered an authority on such matters, God created man in *his* image. 'Furthermore God said, Let us make man in our image according to our lickenes'; 'Thus God created the man in his image: in the image of God created he him'; 'The Lord God also made the man of the dust of the grounde, and breathed in his face breath of life, and the man was a living soule'. There are two accounts of creation in the Bible, but in both woman is an afterthought: 'And the rybbe which the Lord God had taken from the man, made he a woman, and broght her to the man'.[27] The secondary by-product of a spare rib, woman is framed between her two male authority figures in the ultimate love triangle.

In the later 1580s, however, *Woman in the Moon* staged an entirely different creation scene. In this play the ultimate god, Nature, is female. The prologue calls her the 'only Queen' of the play and she is treated by other gods and the humans in the play as almighty creator: 'Thou sovereign Queen, and author of the world, / Of all that was or is, or shall be framed'.[28] Even in pre-Christian European literature, this view of nature is unusual: in Ovid's *Metamorphoses*, 'there was one face of nature in the whole world, which was called chaos', and Ovid is unable to say what transformed Nature's face ('deus et melior … natura', 'god and a better nature').[29] In Lyly's play, Nature is the ordering principle, the author of the world. At the start of the play she has already created men, who are all shepherds, so that their social status is, in early modern terms, comparatively low. They plead with her to create a woman, and she promises them '[a] female … Like to yourselves, but of a purer mould' (1.1.51–2). She tells her handmaidens, 'Now, virgins, put your hands to holy work, / That we may frame new wonders to the world' (55–6). Though it is ambiguous, the word 'Now' is allowed to suggest that this new work is 'holy' in a way that the creation of men was not, and certainly Nature makes it clear to her on- and offstage audience that this woman is the most perfect of her works: 'Herein hath Nature gone beyond herself, / And heaven will grudge at beauty of the earth / When it espies a second sun below' (78–80).

This (so far unnamed) woman is Nature's masterpiece, but she also challenges Nature's own identity, forcing her to go 'beyond herself'. At her first appearance in the play, the 1597 quarto is unsure how to describe this new human: early modern spelling means that this 'second sonne' could be a new heavenly body or a new kind of man.[30] Stage directions are similarly uncertain: the quarto describes the human as '*Image*' until she is given the power of speech, when the stage direction, '*Image speaks*' (85.1) is immediately followed by a speech prefix combined with a stage direction: '*Pandora kneeling*'.[31] The quarto therefore grants her agency, identity and a name only once she speaks: before then, 'Pandora' is an image and 'she' is an 'it'.[32] Lyly here anticipates the journey Marjorie Garber traces in many Shakespearian characters, in which 'the basic rhythm of movement, from personal name to lost name to new name or name regained, can be felt as animating the life – and sometimes the death – of the hero'.[33] Though she is granted motion earlier in the scene, it is Pandora's ability to express herself verbally which leads the quarto to grant her human identity.

The image's first, mute moments on stage are captured in terms of costume, choreography and emotion. When curtains are drawn from Nature's workshop, the audience sees '*an Image clad*' amongst '*some vnclad*' (1.1.56.2). The clothed image is brought forward and Concord is told to 'join the spirit with the flesh in league', at which point a stage direction tells us that '*Concord fast embraceth the image*', and then '*The image walks about fearfully*' (74-74.1; 77.1). Finally, Nature orders Discord to 'unloose her tongue' (83). This is, then, an anatomy without wit slowly gaining interiority and emotional life, a process scripted by a series of stage directions unprecedented in Lyly's or any other early modern plays.[34] The image's silence is an important part of its performance: as we shall see, much of Pandora's struggle over agency will concern control of her own tongue and body.

In the rest of the play the jealous planets decide to take over Pandora's mind, to 'signorize awhile', to 'tyrannize' (135, 140), as they variously put it. This continues until the end of the play, when '*She awakes and is sober*' (5.1.258.1). Every utterance Pandora makes from her first speech and until the final scene is made under the influence of one of the god-planets. Her first speech in praise of Nature, then, is the only one she gives in her own person until her final three speeches of the play. Since the quarto only awards her her name as she delivers this speech, and combines the speech heading with a direction, '*Pandora kneeling*', this seems at best an ambiguous stage image of agency. On the printed page, it looks even more problematic. The quarto cannot quite capture who this thing or what this person is: an image who, speaking, suddenly becomes a person. Lyly rewrites creation using rhetorical and dramatic means that cannot be fully captured in the space of the quarto.

With its image of a new person coming into being, *The Woman in the Moon* represents a very different exploration of the emotive life of agency. The affective stage direction, '*The image walks about fearfully*', is only the first time in the play that Pandora undergoes distress as the result of an intervention by a god who not only observes but takes pleasure in observation: in this case, it is Pandora's fearful walk that prompts Nature to boast that this is her perfect creation. Later, Saturn is the first god to overtake her mind:

> I shall instil such melancholy mood
> As, by corrupting of her purest blood,
> Shall first with sullen sorrows cloud her brain,
> And then surround her heart with froward care;
> She shall be sick with passions of the heart,
> Self-willed and tongue-tied, but full fraught with tears.
>
> (1.1.144–9)

The audience then sees Pandora undergo a succession of changes in mood, and the quarto makes clear that these changes are kinetic in action, giving an unusually full and idiomatic range of stage directions to describe her behaviour: '*She plays the vixen with everything about her*', '*She hits him on the lips*', '*She strikes his hand*', '*She thrusts her hands in her pocket*' and '*She winks and frowns*' (1.1.176.1–206.1). These directions represent a choreography of emotional distress, most of them entailing actions which denote the refusal to speak, or to allow others to speak. Alan Dessen and Leslie Thomson, for example, observe that frowning is 'a rarely signaled silent action', and winking may be still rarer, since they do not include an entry for it.[35] If it was proverbial 'to play the vixen', then that usage does not appear to have been attested before Lyly. In *Have with You to Saffron-Walden* (1596), a text which makes reference to Lyly's *Mother Bombie*, Thomas Nashe (1567–*c.*1601) describes a woman, '*who, howsoeuer shee scolds and playes the vixen neuer so, wilbe borne with*', suggesting that a vixenish woman may be something like a shrew.[36] Lynda Boose reminds us that in early modern culture shrewishness, at least, was located in women at the point of their tongue, and related to linguistic rather than physical language, and Nashe's use of 'vixen' seems to have the same implications.[37] But Pandora's stage directions, on the other hand, either offer opportunities for non-linguistic or unscripted noise, as is the case with '*She plays the vixen*', or pertain to the refusal to speak. They are therefore associated with wordless, perhaps silent, actions.

Pandora's playing, too, seems unusual. Alan Dessen and Leslie Thomson assert that 'play' or 'playing' most often appear in stage directions to describe music, offering only the playing of chess or similar games, together with sword play, as other uses of non-musical 'play' or 'playing' in stage directions.[38] The *Woman in the Moon* direction therefore seems a uniquely theatrical use of the word, and Dessen and Thomson similarly describe the quarto's continued use of the word 'image' to describe Pandora before she achieves full subjectivity as 'atypical', and offer no comparable example.[39] Pandora's playing the vixen therefore captures her unique position as a character that has been created by one character and is now controlled by another: her passionate state is both theatrical and meta-theatrical, feigned and felt.

Pandora's vixen-playing has a limited choreography built into it, since the shepherds enter directly after this stage direction: 'See where she sits ...! Beware, she sleeps!' (1.1.177–8). The boy therefore needed to interpret and fulfil the direction, which seems to require a series of actions of some duration, and then settle down into sleep. These moments are observed (and, in the case of her violence, felt) by the shepherds around her, but Saturn too watches her actions from above. He celebrates with the audience his ability 'to build the ruin of this dame, / And spot her innocence with vicious thoughts' (1.1.230–3). Throughout the play Pandora is a puppet whom the god-planets psychologically invade. *The Woman in the Moon* was written in the same years as *The Spanish Tragedy* and *Dr Faustus* (late 1580s to early 1590s), and, whilst it is not possible to determine which plays came first, they show that the early commercial theatres saw a succession of plays that staged mortals watched and controlled by supernatural beings. In all three plays, however, the extent of supernatural power over the mortals is in question, and, by staging that relationship in dramatic, spatial terms, all three ask questions about agency, plotting, genre and emotion. Brian Cummings has explored 'the discursive pressures exerted in theology and belief throughout English culture in its extended reformations', looking in particular at Donne and Milton, but these pressures had dramaturgical effects too.[40] This is an era pervasively concerned with popular ideas of predestination, and these successive onstage representations of a world in which gods can predict, anticipate and direct human beings ask questions about the hidden agencies that dictate and control affective life.

Lyly's exploration of the relationship between anatomy and wit was therefore an examination of agency, mental experience and the pain of creativity. Carol Thomas Neely tells us that '[i]n the early modern period only a handful of plays and playwrights represent madness and then only sporadically; just three models beget variations'. These are 'prestigious, elevated' tragic madness, 'nominally mad' comic figures who 'catalyze plot chaos', and 'play-within-play performance by Bedlamites for the sane'. Elsewhere Neely describes onstage madness 'as a state of dislocation – separated in part from the self who performs and the spectators who watch – but not as a supernatural invasion'.[41] *The Woman in the Moon* appears to represent madness differently. Critics often describe Shakespeare as breaking from 'traditional' or 'conventional' modes of rhetoric, theatre, storytelling or genre. But generic categories, and particularly those of the plays we now label comedies, were far less well defined in the early period of the playhouses than we now assume, and endings less fortunate or inexorable than we think.[42]

It is therefore important to record how peculiar and unexpected, in a word, how eccentric Shakespeare's contemporaries could be in the early years of London commercial theatre. Enterline traces the way 'Shakespeare creates the convincing effects of character and emotion for which he is so often singled out as a precursor of "modern" subjectivity'.[43] Such effects were already being worked out before Shakespeare started writing. In another of Lyly's plays, *Mother Bombie*, the character Silena, repeatedly described as a fool, tells the audience that '[m]y name is Silena, I care not who know it, so I do not'.[44] From its earliest years, London commercial theatre subjected subjectivity to rhetorical and dramaturgical exploration. Because Shakespeare took part in that process, and later became an important part of the history of psychoanalysis, we are still haunted by that exploration.

Lyly therefore offers the opportunity for rethinking the emotive politics of a play like *Sapho and Phao*, and for understanding that such politics are not only part of the play's text but part of its performance. Lyly's writing is famous for its use of rhetorical exempla, using narratives drawn from classical precedent to make new statements about Elizabethan England, and *Sapho and Phao* is one play-length exemplum, not only reflecting but challenging a court organised around male courtiers and a virgin Queen. Lyly reminds us, too, that rhetoric, writing and performance are peculiarly combative and kinetic processes. His images of wrestling and dancing both allude to activities that are competitive as well as collaborative. Bryce describes dancing as 'coercive and enabling', and dancing and wrestling blend agency and passivity in their mix of intended and imposed physical exertion. Above all, when Lyly creates a character onstage her first action is to walk about fearfully. Treading in a maze, drowning in envy and dancing with demons: throughout his work, Lyly defines authorship, spectatorship and rhetoric as something moving, painful and emotive, and reminds us that the history of emotion is connected to the political and performative life of rhetoric.

Notes

1 For 'highly probable' arguments about the play's dating, see Leah Scragg, 'Introduction', in Lyly, *Sapho and Phao* (Oxford: Malone Society, 2002), pp. xvii–xviii. Quotations from the play appear in text and are taken from Lyly, *'Campaspe' and 'Sappho and Phao'*, ed. G. K. Hunter and David Bevington (Manchester: Manchester University Press, 1999 (1991)).

2 Scragg, *Sapho and Phao*, p. xvii; R. Warwick Bond (ed.), *The Complete Works of John Lyly*, 3 vols (Oxford: Clarendon Press, 1902), vol. 2, p. 366.

3 For more on the semantic slippage between motion and emotion see the Introduction to the present volume.

4 Amélie Oksenberg Rorty (ed.), *Explaining Emotions* (London: University of California Press, 1980), p. 1.

5 J. R. R. Tolkien, *The Hobbit, or, There and Back Again* (London: Allen and Unwin, 1937).

6 For another challenge to 'static' Lyly see Kent Cartwright, 'The Confusions of *Gallathea*: John Lyly as Popular Dramatist', *Comparative Drama*, 32 (1998), 207–39.

7 Janette Dillon, *The Language of Space in Court Performance, 1400–1625* (Cambridge: Cambridge University Press, 2010), p. 104.

8 John Lyly, *'Galatea' and 'Midas'*, ed. G. K. Hunter and David Bevington (Manchester: Manchester University Press, 2000), p. 142.

9 John Lyly, *'Euphues: The Anatomy of Wit' and 'Euphues and His England'*, ed. Leah Scragg (Manchester: Manchester University Press, 2003), p. 30. All subsequent quotations are taken from this edition.

10 Lyly, *'Galatea' and 'Midas'*, 1.1.22–3.

11 John Lyly, *Endymion*, ed. David Bevington (Manchester: Manchester University Press, 1996), 1.1.42–52.

12 John Hoskyns, *Directions for Speech and Style*, ed. H. H. Hudson (Princeton: Princeton University Press, 1935), p. 16.

13 Thomas Lodge, *Wits Miserie, and the Worlds Madness* (London, 1596), p. 57 (my emphasis).

14 For more on Lyly's importance to early modern literary culture see Andy Kesson, *John Lyly and Early Modern Authorship* (Manchester: Manchester University Press, 2014).

15 Richard Sugg, *Murder after Death: Literature and Anatomy in Early Modern England* (Ithaca: Cornell University Press, 2007), p. 206.

16 On Burton, see Mary Ann Lund, Chapter 4, above.

17 Patricia Parker, *Shakespeare from the Margins: Language, Culture, Context* (Chicago: University of Chicago Press, 1996), pp. 2–3, 16.

18 For further details on this process and its implications, see Kesson, *John Lyly*, pp. 85–96.

19 Katharine A. Craik, *Reading Sensations in Early Modern England* (Basingstoke: Palgrave Macmillan, 2007), pp. 3–4 (emphasis in original).

20 Barbara Ravelhofer, *The Early Stuart Masque: Dance, Costume and Music* (Oxford: Oxford University Press, 2006), p. 6.

21 Judith Bryce, 'Performing for Strangers: Women, Dance and Music in Quattrocento Florence', *Renaissance Quarterly*, 54 (2001), 1074–107 (p. 1102).

22 Parker, *Shakespeare from the Margins*, pp. 16–17.

23 Robert Weimann, *Shakespeare and the Popular Tradition in the Theater: Studies in the Social Dimension of Dramatic Form and Tradition*, ed. Robert Schwartz (Baltimore: Johns Hopkins University Press, 1978), pp. 80–1.

24 Katharine Eisaman Maus, *Inwardness and Theater in the English Renaissance* (Chicago: University of Chicago Press, 1995), p. 32.

25 Lynn Enterline, *Shakespeare's Schoolroom: Rhetoric, Discipline, Emotion* (Philadelphia: University of Pennsylvania Press, 2012), p. 19.

26 Cora Fox, *Ovid and the Politics of Emotion in Elizabethan England* (Basingstoke: Palgrave Macmillan, 2009), p. 3.

27 *The Geneva Bible: A Facsimile of the 1560 Edition*, introduced by Lloyd E. Berry (Peabody: Hendrickson, 1969), sig. 1v.

28 John Lyly, *The Woman in the Moon*, ed. Leah Scragg (Manchester: Manchester University Press, 2006), Prologue, 6, 1.1.31. Unless otherwise stated, references from the play are taken from this edition.

29 Ovid, *Metamorphoses: Books I–VIII*, trans. Frank Justus Miller and rev. G. P. Goold (Cambridge, MA, and London: Harvard University Press, 1977), p. 2 (my translation).

30 John Lyly, *The Woman in the Moone* (London: William Jones, 1597), sig. A3.

31 The final quotation is taken from the quarto, sig. A3. Scragg prints '*Pandora.* (*Kneeling*)', 1.1.87.

32 On interpellation, naming and the psyche, see the introduction to Judith Butler, *The Psychic Life of Power* (Stanford: Stanford University Press, 1997).

33 Marjorie Garber, *Coming of Age in Shakespeare* (London: Methuen, 1981), p. 78.

34 There is nothing comparable in any of the examples in Alan C. Dessen and Leslie Thomson, *A Dictionary of Stage Directions in English Drama, 1580–1642* (Cambridge: Cambridge University Press, 1999).

35 Dessen and Thomson, *Dictionary of Stage Directions*, p. 97.

36 *The Works of Thomas Nashe*, ed. Ronald B. McKerrow, 5 vols (Oxford: Blackwell, 1958), vol. 3, p. 111.

37 Lynda E. Boose, 'Scolding Brides and Bridling Scolds: Taming the Woman's Unruly Member', *Shakespeare Quarterly*, 42 (1991), 179–213.

38 Dessen and Thomson, *Dictionary of Stage Directions*, pp. 165–6.

39 Ibid., p. 119.

40 Brian Cummings, *The Literary Culture of the Reformation: Grammar and Grace* (Oxford: Oxford University Press, 2002), p. 281.

41 Carol Thomas Neely, '"Distracted measures": Madness and Theatricality in Middleton', in Suzanne Gossett (ed.), *Thomas Middleton in Context* (Cambridge: Cambridge University Press, 2011), pp. 306–14 (p. 306), and *Distracted Subjects: Madness and Gender in Shakespeare and Early Modern Culture* (Ithaca: Cornell University Press, 2004), p. 49.

42 The classic study in relation to comedy is M. C. Bradbrook, *The Growth and Structure of Elizabethan Comedy*, new edn (London: Chatto and Windus, 1973), see esp. p. 75; for a more recent assumption that there was such a thing as traditional comedy in the 1580s see Suzanne Gossett, 'Middleton and Dramatic Genre', in Suzanne Gossett (ed.), *Thomas Middleton in Context* (Cambridge: Cambridge University Press, 2011), pp. 235–42.

43 Enterline, *Shakespeare's Schoolroom*, p. 1.

44 John Lyly, *Mother Bombie*, ed. Leah Scragg (Manchester: Manchester University Press, 2010), 2.3.18.

9

(S)wept from power: two versions of tyrannicide in *Richard III*

Ann Kaegi

'Be it lawful that I invocate thy ghost / To hear the lamentations of poor Anne': as Lady Anne addresses these words to a corpse, we might suppose her question to be rhetorical, but Anne has already questioned whether 'honour may be shrouded in a hearse', and despite the vehemence of her ensuing declamation she betrays niggling doubts about the effectiveness of her lamentation, describing her tears oxymoronically as a 'helpless balm'.[1] However heightened her emotions, the grammatical mood of her utterance is the optative subjunctive: Anne does not assume so much as *wish* that her obsequies will be judged lawful by the church.[2] Why the uncertainty? Although the events depicted in *Richard III* occurred at a time when intercessory prayers and public displays of weeping and wailing for the dead were orthodox features of late medieval funerary ritual, the doctrine of purgatory to which such mourning rites were closely allied was repudiated by Protestant reformers. Consequently, by the time Shakespeare wrote his play (*c.*1592–93), only scattered vestiges of these practices survived and strict reformers were pressing to have them expunged from Elizabethan burial ritual.[3] While Anne's misgivings about the lawfulness and efficacy of her obsequies are anachronistic within the play's historical frame, they address and are symptomatic of the post-Reformation context in which *Richard III* was first performed (*c.*1593–94). The colloquial directness of Richard's commencing 'Now' (1.1.1) collapses time into the momentariness of performance; by contrast, Anne's hesitancy dissevers 'past' from 'present' by summoning up remembrance of the rupture which the intervening Reformation had caused in the late medieval culture of mourning.

This chapter focuses on one of the consequences of the Protestant Reformation highlighted in the first part of this volume: its transformation of the relationship between the living and the dead, a transformation which shapes the expression of grief, the representation of mourning and the purpose of remembrance in Shakespeare's *Richard III*. At a time, late in Elizabeth's reign, when public displays of vociferous mourning were increasingly regarded as faithless and excessive and denounced by reformed clergy as superstitious, 'heathenish' and 'popish',[4] Shakespeare populates his play with grieving women who repeatedly interject into the masculine soundscape of chronicle history the sharp plaints and bitter curses of feminine lament.[5] Far from stifling the sound and suppressing the spectacle of immoderate mourning, Shakespeare exploits the 'affective and emotional license' often accorded maternal lamentation in male-authored early modern texts to broach the dangerous subject of tyrannicide.[6] That he does so in a play depicting the rise to power and brief reign of the king on whose violent overthrow the Tudor regime was founded makes the conjunction of political matter and affective speech in *Richard III* of particular interest in the history of emotion. The insistence of the play's women on remembering the dead and publicly wailing their loss, despite attempts to suppress their cries, becomes a means of denouncing and eventually of actively resisting tyranny. In Act 4, the mounting toll of suffering finally prompts three of the four grief-stricken women featured to lament rather than relish a former rival's misery: instead of envy and enmity Elizabeth feels 'pity' for Anne, Anne 'mourn[s]' for Elizabeth and the Duchess of York movingly reveals that she has 'wept' for Margaret (4.1.83–4; 4.4.55). By transforming their anguish into compassion rather than bitter reproach, these three lamenting women belatedly prepare the ground for an end to civil war and supply an ethical and affective warrant for tyrannicide that leaves Margaret isolated in her unassuaged hunger for revenge (4.4.56), her alienation from the emerging affective and political compact signalled by her self-exile to France (4.4.109). The treasonous speech which issues from their sympathetic alliance is ultimately sanctioned by the dead who appear as ghostly revenants before the decisive battle at Bosworth. At a time in Elizabethan England when mourners were supposed to regard the dead as the departed, 'spoken not to, but about, as one no longer here', in *Richard III* the dead speak to the living not only within the frame of the play but also beyond it through the medium of performance which transforms actors into 'walking shadow[s]' (*Macbeth*, 5.5.23) of persons long deceased.[7] *Richard III* thus resumes and renovates the dialogue between the living and the dead which the Protestant Reformation had threatened to end.

Plaintive speech: complaint, lament and malediction

Although women are most associated with plaintive speech in *Richard III*, the first person reported to have exploited complaint to sway the sympathies of a listener is a man. Approaching Clarence as he is escorted under guard to the Tower of London, Richard casts suspicion on the Queen for securing his brother's imprisonment. According to Richard, Elizabeth has a history of exploiting her sexual hold over the King to confine her opponents to the Tower:

> Was it not she and that goodman of worship
> Anthony Woodville, her brother there,
> That made him send Lord Hastings to the Tower,
> From whence this present day he is delivered?
>
> (1.1.66–9)

Clarence shares Richard's scornful estimation of Edward's pliancy. In his jaded view Edward's habit of subordinating affairs of state to sexual affairs is such that 'there is no man is secured / But the Queen's kindred, and night-walking heralds / That trudge betwixt the King and Mistress Shore' (1.1.71–3) – the heralds' trudging indicating the frequency of Edward's nocturnal amatory liaisons. Although they profess their hostility to the effeminising power of complaint, Edward's brothers recognise that power has shifted in 'this weak-piping time of peace' (1.1.24). While scornful of Lord Hastings's adoption of the abject posture of a 'humble suppliant' to the King's mistress, they concede that his strategy succeeded: 'Humbly complaining to her deity / Got my lord Chamberlain his liberty' (1.1.76–7). They nevertheless regard his resort to this demeaning stratagem as symptomatic of an alarming inversion of social and gender hierarchy at court: the Lord Chamberlain has been displaced from the King's bedchamber by a royal mistress, a prominent courtier obliged to sue to an adulterous city wife. Edward's elevation to the throne of Elizabeth Grey (née Woodville), a widow of modest rank formerly allied to the Lancastrians, has debased the royal blood and demeaned the King's brothers, who must now 'be her men and wear her livery' (1.1.80). Accustomed to power and high office, they are now 'the Queen's abjects, and must obey' (1.1.106) – 'Why, this it is when men are ruled by women' (1.1.62). It is perhaps surprising that a discourse thus tainted by its association with sexual impropriety and branded as demeaning and effeminising by Clarence and Richard in the opening scene should none the less prove critical to the legitimation of tyrannicide in *Richard III*. However, it is not sex but death, in particular the shared experience of close bereavement by the play's women and their mutual need to mourn the dead, which transforms complaint into a potent political idiom in the drama.

Pathos is a form of power, particularly in the theatre, and it is Anne Neville who provokes, then swiftly quells, the first stirrings of pathos in *Richard III* and initiates, through her ritual lamentation, the process of memorialisation on which the play's mourning women insist in staunch defiance of Richard's attempts to silence their complaints. Her first entrance is jarring, however: for all its solemnity, the thinly attended funeral cortège she accompanies would have struck Elizabethan playgoers as incongruous and disordered. Aptly described by Michael Neill as 'exercises in secular ostentation', regal and aristocratic heraldic funerals were meticulously arranged and closely regulated exercises in social symbolism.[8] Elaborate heraldic funerary pageants reinforced the status quo by staging the prevailing social hierarchy in processional form. Their inclusion of a ceremony of succession known as the offering, in which the titles, rights, powers and obligations of the defunct were passed on symbolically to the heir, projected the ordered and legitimate transfer of status and authority, further emphasising the continuity and solidarity of the ruling elite.[9] The meagre funeral procession of Henry VI imparts precisely the opposite and provides a potent visual reminder at the outset of the play that the legitimacy of the royal title is disputed and the succession remains insecure, the former King's body not yet having been interred even as his deposer, Edward IV, sickens (1.1.136-7). Anne's assumption of the role of chief mourner is also unorthodox and doubly transgressive.[10] The stipulation by the College of Arms that principal mourners be of the same sex as and proximate in social rank to the decedent was reinforced in an Elizabethan ordinance, which likewise declared that 'a man being deade hee to have only men [principal] mourners at his Buriall, and at a woman's buriall to have only women mourners'.[11] A violation of heraldic custom and Elizabethan ordinance, Anne's presence at Henry VI's funeral is also unhistorical. Shakespeare notably departs from his chronicle sources in having Anne not only preside over King Henry's burial procession but also claim to be the wife of Henry's son Prince Edward, whereas they record that she was not in attendance (or in London) and was betrothed to the Prince but as yet unwed when he was stabbed by Richard in his 'angry mood at Tewkesbury' (1.2.226). Anne is thus accorded by Shakespeare, and herself firmly claims, the heightened status of a grieving widow.

If Anne's occupancy of the role of principal mourner would have struck Elizabethan playgoers as anomalous, so too would the manner in which she mourns over the corpse of Henry VI. The social and political functions of the heraldic funeral took precedence over the emotional needs of the bereaved, yet Anne halts the cortège to exclaim her sorrow and implore vengeance, violating heraldic custom to assert the primacy of her grief.[12] But there is more to it than that: her actions, verbal and gestural, evoke Catholic funeral rites which Protestant reformers had been striving to uproot since the reign of Edward VI.[13] As Patricia Phillippy observes, Anne's command that the pallbearers 'Set down … [their] honourable load' (1.2.1–2) to enable her loudly to lament her loss in a London street 'carries the trace of the Catholic practice in which the cortège made frequent stops at public crosses, shrines, and taverns' to summon the community to join in intercessory prayer for the deceased.[14] Although vestigial prayers for the dead remained in the Elizabethan *Book of Common Prayer* (much to the alarm of zealous reformers), the church's repudiation of the doctrine of purgatory and the cult of saints removed the purpose of intercessory supplication and with it a source of consolation for the living.[15] A pre-Reformation historical personage, Anne appears unhistorically mindful of Protestant objections to late medieval funerary observance. As noted above, this anachronistic mindfulness is expressed as hesitancy and results in a hybridised display of public grief whose emotional currents repeatedly turn mourning ritual awry. Although she characterises Henry VI as a 'holy king' (1.2.5, see also 27) and appears to be on the point of venerating him as a saint,[16] she stops short of seeking saintly intercession when she summons the ghost of the dead King 'To hear the lamentations of poor Anne' (1.2.9). Addressing the corpse directly, she vents her misery and weeps unreservedly, her anguished cries openly proclaiming her woes while Henry's wounds become receptacles for her abundant tears (1.2.12–13). This sorrowful spectacle is richly evocative of the Virgin Mary's tearful contemplation of Christ's wounds. Described by Katharine Goodland as 'the most prevalent and resonant cultural symbol of mourning prior to the Reformation', Mary's lamentation over the crucified Christ had featured as a plaintive interlude in the medieval cycles of Corpus Christi plays and been portrayed in icons of the pietà (familiarly known as 'Our Lady of Sorrows') displayed in churches throughout England.[17] Representations of the Sorrows of Mary were meant to provoke 'sympathetic suffering' in onlookers, thereby enabling them to experience the Passion for themselves.[18] Anne's exclamatory 'Lo!' (12) similarly directs observers to 'Behold!' the King's wounds, but while her sorrowful tears may stir compassion she doubts whether they provide a spiritual salve for the departed.[19]

Anne craves intimate and, above all, *effective* communion with the dead but such communion proves elusive. Instead of feeling that she is aiding and communing with the dead, she feels isolated and disempowered at the height of her grief. Denied the consoling ritual of collective mourning and suspecting that her tears and prayers are ineffectual, she abruptly abandons lamentation for malediction. Anne's formal lament lasts for a mere nine lines (1.2.5–13) – hardly sufficient for the pallbearers to catch their breath and rest their limbs. By contrast, her initial curses extend across the next thirteen lines (14–26); after Richard enters, her maledictions and calls for vengeance occupy a further dozen lines (1.2.60–5, 100–1, 110, 129, 143, 148). The suddenness of the shift from lamentation and veneration to imprecation and vituperation, and the striking imbalance between the two forms of woeful utterance, are symptomatic of the sundering of grief from agency in the late Elizabethan burial rite.

In turning from tearful plaints to bitter curses Anne substitutes one method of using the voice as an instrument of power for another. However, by resorting to an even more deviant form of speech associated in Elizabethan England with female insubordination and witchcraft, she displays the lack of moderation and fortitude which reformers attributed to uninhibited displays of grief, denounced as 'wommanish' and condemned as 'popish' (Catholic) or 'heathen'.[20] The pronouncement by the Protestant theologian Andreas Gerhard Hyperius (1511–64) that 'it is very uncomly and wommanish to lament without measure', and his admonishment of those who indulge in a 'womannish kinde of wayling and shricking', are typical criticisms of unrestrained mourning.[21] In the words of Shakespeare's Lafeu, 'Moderate lamentation is the right of the dead, excessive grief the enemy to the living' (*All's Well*, 1.1.48–9).[22] Much as Anne's loud plaints and copious tears violate prevailing Elizabethan norms of moderate mourning, so do her maledictions, as they too denote a failure to be reconciled to death. Like prayers for the dead, maledictions (from the Latin, *male* = badly, *dicere* = to speak) are intended to shape the future, but where the former are benevolent the latter are malevolent. Both aim to transform passion into effect, grief into consequence. As forms of invocation, both make the voice 'an instrument of bodily agency' and presuppose that speech can be highly effectual.[23] Both are also potentially consoling: faith in intercessory prayer offers the bereaved the comfort of believing that they can continue to speak to and assist the deceased, while malediction offers the marginalised and disempowered the tantalising prospect of exacting retribution merely by speaking. As Kate Brown and Howard Kushner observe, 'the fantasy of malediction' is that the body of someone so abject 'can generate a voice so powerful as to translate outrage into vengeance, disrupting the narrative of its own exclusion'.[24]

Made wretched by events which she was powerless to control and doubtful whether she can help the dead, Anne seeks to exercise power over the living by using malediction to translate emotion into utterance and utterance into vengeful consequence. Christina Larner comments that early modern women employed curses as weapons: 'the cursing and bewitching women were the female equivalent of violent males. They were the disturbers of the social order'.[25] Gazing at the fatal 'holes' (1.2.14) in Henry's mutilated body, Anne wants her words to wound if they cannot heal. While she hopes that her curses will inflict retaliatory injuries on Richard to prevent him from escaping punishment for the misery he has caused, they pose an additional threat: the supposed power of malediction to shape the future imperils Richard's ambition to manipulate the present (1.1.120) and so plot his way to the crown, moment by moment. Anne seeks retributive justice but at the cost of perpetuating the cycle of violence, as is evident when she curses Richard's future wife and implores that their firstborn be 'Prodigious, and untimely brought to light' and of a countenance so 'ugly and unnatural' that its mother takes 'fright' (1.2.21–3). Her chilling words echo Richard's description of how he was born

> Deformed, unfinished, sent before … [his] time
> Into this breathing world scarce half made up,
> And that so lamely and unfashionable
> That dogs bark at … [him].
>
> (1.1.20–3)

If fulfilled, Anne's curse would impose another Richard on the world and so prolong the cycle of trauma and retribution. Unnervingly, Richard's sudden arrival and duplication of her command to set down Henry's corpse generates the impression that her maledictions have inadvertently 'conjure[d] up this fiend' (1.2.32) and may already be going horribly awry.

To effect his planned seduction of Anne (1.1.152–8) over the freshly bleeding corpse of the King he murdered, Richard deftly appropriates the affective power of feminine complaint to wrong-foot Anne and turn her imprecations back on herself.[26] Moments earlier he had disparaged the topsy-turvydom which Edward's cupidity had allegedly bred at court, forcing even those of royal blood to imitate the servility of a Petrarchan lover and flatter the Queen to 'keep in favour with the King' (1.1.79). Yet Richard now adopts the fawning posture which he formerly derided and sets about wooing Anne in a textbook exercise of Petrarchan love-making. Richard's capacity to both weep and refrain from weeping plays a major part in Anne's seduction in the Folio version of the scene. In the Folio text Richard convinces a sceptical Anne of her emotional hold over him by telling her of his singular restraint in stoically refusing to weep on hearing 'the piteous moan that Rutland made / When black-faced Clifford shook his sword at him' (F, 1.2.162–3), and later when he was 'Told the sad story of ... [his] father's death' (F, 1.2.165) – occasions when the other men present 'had wet their cheeks / Like trees bedashed with rain' (F, 1.2.161, 167–8). 'In that sad time', he remarks, 'My manly eyes did scorn an humble tear' (F, 1.2.168–9).

Richard's characterisation of his refusal to cry as 'manly' aligns him with neo-Stoic 'rigorists' but, for an Elizabethan audience, it sets him at odds with other prominent Protestant theologians who viewed askance the absence of grief.[27] His fondness for swearing by St Paul is notable in this context: John Calvin accused those who cited Paul's 1 Thessalonians 4:13 in support of suppressing the passions of 'misus[ing] this testimony ... to establish Stoic *apatheia*, that is, an iron insensibility, among Christians' when there is 'nothing of the kind in Paul's words'.[28] Bishop John Jewel (1522–71) contended that '[t]he father if he feele not the death of his sonne: or, the sonne if he feele not the death of his Father, and haue not a deepe feeling of it, he is vnnaturall', because such feelings were implanted by God.[29] But how and to what degree ought the passion of grief be manifested in signs of mourning? Performativity makes this question especially vexed, for as Hamlet notes, 'all forms, moods, shows of grief ... are actions that a man might play' (*Hamlet*, 1.2.82–4). Richard boasts in *3 Henry VI* of his ability to 'wet ... [his] cheeks with artificial tears' (3.2.184), and dupes both Anne and Clarence (1.4.224–6) with timely weeping in *Richard III*. Although Anne's tears are not false, the fact that they 'pour' from her eyes (1.2.13) is another feature of her conduct which violates the model of mourning sanctioned toward the close of Elizabeth's reign. The title of Thomas Playfere's popular sermon 'The Meane in Mourning' summarises the reformed ideal. Taking Luke 23.28 as his text ('Weepe not for mee, but weepe for your selues'), Playfere (*c.*1562–1609) counsels '[t]hat we must not weepe too much', citing Niobe (who 'by ouermuch weeping was turnde into a stone') as evidence '[t]hat too much of a thing is nought'. While 'immoderate weeping is condemned, *in nature, ... in reason, ...* [and] *in religion*', not weeping shows a lack of love: 'So that if we weepe so little as that we weepe not at all, we weepe too little'. Above all, he cautions, 'we must not bee like the Stoikes which were neuer at all moued'.[30] The faithful mourner must thus chart a course between the Scylla of 'ouermuch weeping' and the Charybdis of remaining dry-eyed.

Consumed by a mix of anguish and outrage, Anne is wholly unprepared for the spectacle of a weeping Richard. Though she suspects that he is a 'dissembler' (1.2.170), her pained familiarity with Richard's remorselessness persuades her that her eyes alone 'have drawn salt tears' (1.2.151) from his and that his tears attest his love.[31] Troubled that her woe may be unavailing, the thought that she nevertheless wields passionate sway over her one-time enemy proves seductive. When Richard surrenders his sword (1.2.160), Anne succumbs to the temptation of believing that her beauty has transformed a powerful adversary into a 'poor devoted suppliant', a pitiless murderer into a pious penitent (1.2.192, 201). Her indulgence of this fantasy has the opposing affect of the Marian model it travesties, as it quells audience sympathy for her and is duly ridiculed by Richard on her departure (1.2.213–39). By the end of their encounter Richard has supplanted Anne as chief mourner, restoring a semblance of customary order to the cortège while subverting its function by substituting the regicide for one whom he bereaved. Immediately after Anne's departure he jettisons the role, terminates all mourning ritual and, in a mockery of the pared-down Elizabethan burial rite, proposes to 'turn yon fellow in his grave, / And then return lamenting to … [his] love' (1.2.245–6).

Anne's pliancy to Richard's flattery is calamitous and weakens the residual affectiveness of her plaints. As Richard is quick to remark, Anne's moral failure stems from her memorial failure:

> Hath she forgot already that brave prince,
> Edward, her lord, whom I some three months since
> Stabbed in my angry mood at Tewkesbury?
>
> (1.2.224–6)

Disarmed by Richard's professed adoration of her 'heavenly face' (1.2.168), Anne succumbs to self-idolatry and, within months of his murder at the hands of her would-be seducer, she permits herself to forget her husband's manifold virtues – virtues to which Richard liberally attests (1.2.224–30). Anne has publically wailed the dead but she has conspicuously failed to persist in her remembrance of them. Although she addresses her laments to Henry VI and denounces the 'hand' and 'heart' that murdered him, her own misery is her refrain (1.2.16–26). Anne laments the demise of the former King and her princely consort but we may suspect that it is the loss of her own hopes for which she chiefly grieves.

Although Richard mocks Anne's forgetfulness, she is not unique in this failing. When Elizabeth protests of having 'too long borne' his 'bitter scoffs' and threatens to inform the king of his 'gross taunts' (1.3.103–6), Richard denounces her 'lewd complaints' to Edward (1.3.61) and reminds this self-styled 'great queen' (1.3.108) that, in the recent wars over the succession, she and her then husband Sir John Grey 'Were factious for the house of Lancaster', as was her brother Lord Rivers (1.3.127–9). Richard does not hesitate to repudiate or refashion the past: pressed by Anne, he repeatedly denies then tersely 'grant[s]' that he was the 'executioner' of Henry and her husband but shifts responsibility for their demise on to her (1.2.99, 115–22). Later, when he tries to convince Elizabeth to persuade her daughter to marry him, he urges her to 'Plead what I will be, not what I have been' after she reminds him that there is nothing he can swear by that he has not wronged (4.4.334). Richard is an avid student of history, albeit of a particular sort: keen to summon up remembrance of the past when it serves his present purposes, he shows the aptitude more of the politician than the historiographer. But his self-appointed role as chronicler proves short-lived, as Margaret loses patience, steps from the margins of the court (where, ghost-like, she has lingered unseen and unheard by others onstage) and commands audience (1.3.157–9).

Margaret's refusal to be silently consigned to 'woeful banishment' (1.3.190) and so be rendered dead to English historical remembrance highlights a central feature of the play's formal and thematic engagement with the past. The outer frame of *Richard III* is formed by a pair of speeches (1.1.1–40 and 5.7.15–41) in which two would-be kings, Richard and Richmond respectively, seek to bury the past for opposing ends. Its inner frame is constructed of speeches to, in memory of and by the dead. The outcome and perceived legitimacy of Richard and Richmond's respective ambitions is crucially dependent on the affect – and consequent political effects – of this inner frame of woeful remembrance. An embodiment of 'sorrow's rage' (1.3.278), Margaret is both revenant and remembrancer. Her unhistorical presence at court is a pointed reminder that Elizabeth's current 'honour, state, and seat' were hers (1.3.112), yet her efforts to trouble the consciences of her onstage auditors and make them 'bow like subjects' and 'quake like rebels' (1.3.161–2) fail, not least because her remembrance of the past is as partial (in both senses of the word) as theirs.[32] Unremitting in tabulating the wrongs she has endured, the deposed Queen expresses no remorse for the suffering she has inflicted. She remembers 'too well' (1.3.118) that Richard is 'A murd'rous villain' (1.3.134), yet must be reminded of her cruel mockery of the Duke of York 'When … [she] didst crown his warlike brows with paper' and then proffered a cloth with which to wipe away his tears that was 'Steeped in the faultless blood' of his slaughtered child, Rutland (1.3.171–5). Richard attributes Margaret's misery to the fulfilment of the curse which his father laid on her for her 'bloody deed' (1.3.176–8), and succeeds in uniting the formerly divided court in hatred of her by reminding them of her cruelty – as Margaret wryly observes (1.3.185–7). Though she agrees with her detractors that her continued existence is her 'shame', that is only because she has lived to see her hopes 'butchered', not from a sense of guilt (1.3.276–8). Far from admitting blame or expressing remorse, she refers to Rutland dismissively as 'that peevish brat' (1.3.191).

Anne denounces Richard as demonic because he knows no 'touch of pity' (1.2.69–70), but pitilessness is the quality which most typifies the preponderance of characters in *Richard III* until Act 4. When Clarence urges his executioners to 'Relent, and save … [their] souls', First Executioner dismisses his counsel as 'cowardly and womanish' (1.4.236–7). Though Clarence detects 'some pity' in the face of Second Executioner, First Executioner responds to his entreaty, 'A begging prince what beggar pities not?' by stabbing the Duke 'thus, and thus' (1.4.239–43). When Catesby informs Hastings 'That this same very day your enemies … must die at Pomfret', Hastings is unmoved: 'I am no mourner for that news, / Because they have been still my enemies' (3.2.47–50). Far from mourning their demise he anticipates that he 'shall laugh' in a year's time to think that he 'live[d] to look upon their tragedy' (3.2.55–7). Not even Catesby's reminder that ''Tis a vile thing to die … / When men are unprepared' can temper Hastings's delight in the sudden downfall of his adversaries and his ghoulish anticipation that 'some men else that think themselves as safe' will soon be dead (3.2.62–6). And when Hastings discovers that his own head shall shortly grace the executioner's block, he is urged to 'Make a short shrift' by Catesby: 'the Duke would be at dinner', Catesby explains coolly, 'he longs to see your head' (3.4.99–100).

For much of the play misery does not elicit sympathy; instead a combination of pain and resentment fuels a ruthless longing to see others suffer. If 'York's dread curse prevail so much with heaven', Margaret reasons, 'Why then, give way, dull clouds, to my quick curses' (1.3.188, 193). Because she too stands accursed for her cruelty, Margaret's maledictions do not prompt others to mend their ways. Thus although her curses provoke a powerful bodily response in Buckingham and Rivers (who note how their 'hair doth stand on end to hear her curses' (1.3.304–5)), her onstage listeners are otherwise unmoved by her vituperative outbursts during the first court scene. Far from demurring when Richard dismisses Margaret as a 'Foul wrinkled witch' (1.3.164) and 'withered hag' (1.3.212), they supplement his sexist and ageist efforts to marginalise her as 'lunatic' (1.3.254) and dismiss her menaces as 'False-boding' and 'frantic' (1.3.247). Not one to miss an opportunity to display mock-piety, Richard alone admits the validity of Margaret's denunciations: 'I cannot blame her, by God's holy mother; / She hath had too much wrong' (1.3.306–7). Those, like Elizabeth, who seek to absolve themselves of culpability none the less 'have all the vantage of this wrong' (1.3.310) and show no sign of relinquishing it. Margaret's dire imprecations leave her hearers momentarily unnerved but morally unaffected until it is too late for them to make amends (see 3.4.97–8; 4.4.74–6; 5.1.25). Like one of the Furies the former Queen feeds on 'sorrow's rage' but offers no hope of an end to butchery; her rancorous curses, like Anne's, merely perpetuate an internecine war of words. The translation of grief into malediction offers the consoling hope of retribution; however, it withholds any prospect of an end to suffering and leaves unquenched the desire for pre-eminence that impels the repeated resort to violence and resultant longing for vengeance. As Margaret acknowledges, retributory curses can only bring about 'repetition' of past harms (1.3.165). In so doing they would make the future nothing more than another iteration of England's woeful past.

'Woe's scene'

Patricia Phillippy observes that 'the scene of early modern death – that theatrical exit to the tiring house of the grave – is one in which gender is performed and constructed': mourning is the duty of women while consolation is the preserve of men.[33] The representation of Edward's impending and actual demise in *Richard III* adheres to this pattern. Males predominate as Edward belatedly attempts to persuade his 'wrong-incensèd peers' to make 'fair love of hate' (2.1.50–1), with Elizabeth the only female present. This gender imbalance is perhaps unsurprising in a scene in which the King is striving to create a 'united league' (2.1.2) among his factious peers, though Edward makes a point of instructing Elizabeth that she is 'not exempt in this' (2.1.18). 'Wife,' he commands imperiously, 'love Lord Hastings, let him kiss your hand, / And what you do, do it unfeignedly!' (2.1.21–2). The gender distinction is not just a matter of numbers, however; it extends to the roles performed by those who attend the dying and mourn the dead. Despite having been the 'tardy cripple' (2.1.88) who ensured that Clarence's reprieve was delayed, Richard smoothly assumes the guise of moralist, pronouncing 'This is the fruit of rashness' (2.1.133) after Edward lashes out at himself and his court on learning of Clarence's death. Richard then adopts the role of consoler, suggesting to the lords 'let's in / To comfort Edward with our company' (2.1.137–8). Elizabeth neither moralises nor attempts to console; when she re-enters moments later it is 'to wail and weep' (2.2.33) in a paroxysm of feminine grief. The Folio version directs that she enters '*with her hair about her ears*', her physical (and stereotypically feminine) disarray supplementing her verbal expression of 'black despair' (2.2.35) to create a 'scene of rude impatience' (2.2.37), for which she is reproved by the Duchess of York. By contrast on his entrance Richard counsels restraint in mourning. His blunt assertion that 'none can cure their harms by wailing them' (2.2.90) was orthodoxy in Elizabethan England, as discussed above. Buckingham similarly urges the 'cloudy princes and heart-sorrowing peers' to temper their grief and 'cheer each other in each other's love' (2.2.99–101). They should consider the living not the dead and take comfort in the thought that, having 'spent our harvest of this king, / We are to reap the harvest of his son' (2.2.102–3).

How the Duchess of York responds to Elizabeth's display of extreme grief is revealing. Rather than attempting to console Elizabeth, the Duchess claims a right to a share of her sorrow and does so in eerily commercial terms – 'So much interest have I in thy sorrow / As I had title in thy noble husband' (2.2.46–7). Her focus is on establishing that her grief is greater because she has 'bewept a worthy husband's death' (2.2.48) and suffered the deaths of two of her sons, 'two mirrors of his princely semblance' (2.2.50). 'Thou art a widow', she notes, tallying up their respective losses, 'yet thou art a mother' (2.2.54). Although Elizabeth has been twice widowed, Elizabeth's princely sons are still alive. The Duchess affirms her right to exceed Elizabeth's plaints and 'drown' her cries, the distress of the newly widowed Queen 'being but a moiety' of the Duchess's amassed sorrows (2.2.58–60). The shared experience of intimate bereavement does not trigger sympathy even in the presence of manifest anguish; instead, it prompts renewed rivalry for pre-eminence as if totting up their dead was their sole remaining means of accruing status. Disturbingly, Clarence's children remind their aunt that she 'wept not for … [their] father's death'; they cannot now be expected to shed 'kindred tears' when their 'fatherless distress was left unmoaned' (2.2.61–3) by her. The universal lack of compassion is exemplified by the antiphonal claims by Elizabeth, Clarence's children and the Duchess to have suffered the 'dearer' loss:

QUEEN: Was never widow had so dear a loss.
BOTH CHILDREN: Was never orphans had a dearer loss.
DUCHESS OF YORK: Was never mother had a dearer loss.

(2.2.76–8)

They sound less like mourners than rival merchants reckoning up their accounts at the end of a bad day's trading, such is the damagingly 'parcelled' (2.2.80) and competitive rather than communal and sympathetic culture of mourning to which they have become habituated. Despite resorting increasingly to complaint and having growing cause to lament, the failure of the grieving women in *Richard III* to pity anyone's distress but their own for much of the play makes them complicit in the antipathy that enables Richard's rise to the throne. Only when they are filled with foreboding after having been prevented from visiting the young Princes in the Tower does their desire for an end to the slaughter finally surpass their yearning for ascendancy and vengeance.

'A woman's war'

The affective potential of plaintive speech and its inherent unruliness are illumined and exploited in the play's early stages by a plethora of speakers, but its effectiveness as a mode of persuasion (and dissuasion) is uncertain, with notable successes offset by equally notable failures, and its usefulness as a means of resisting tyranny is far from apparent after Anne grows 'captive to … [Richard's] honey words' (4.1.75). Yet as the threat posed by Richard's 'Insulting tyranny' (2.4.54) becomes more apparent, so the latent capacity of feminine lament to voice, impel and sanction resistance gathers strength. Richard and his co-conspirator Buckingham are clearly apprehensive of how London's citizens will respond to Hastings's sudden execution, Buckingham expressing concern to the mayor that they 'may / Misconster us in him, and wail his death' (3.5.59–60). Buckingham worries that the citizens' loud show of collective grief may issue in civil unrest – a scenario which Shakespeare develops in *Julius Caesar*. As it is, Buckingham's attempt to 'play the orator' (3.5.93) and sway the citizens to endorse Richard's coronation fails: to Richard's anxious question, 'How now, my lord, what say the citizens?' (3.7.1), he replies abashedly, 'The citizens are mum, and speak not a word' (3.7.3). Their fear that the emotional volatility of communal mourning will spill over into violent resistance to Richard's enthronement as king is unrealised; however, the stony refusal of London's citizens to sanction tyranny marks an important turning point in the play.[34]

The nadir and the zenith of the affective power of complaint occur in close proximity. In the Folio version, Elizabeth invites Anne and the Duchess of York to 'look back' and join with her in imploring the Tower's 'ancient stones' to 'Pity … those tender babes / Whom envy hath immured within … [its] walls' (4.1.98–100). Whether Elizabeth is right to dismiss her plaints as 'foolish sorrows' (4.1.104) depends partly on whether she directs her plea upstage or out to the audience as playgoers may well be moved to pity, and the capacity to feel pity is politically charged in *Richard III*. Easily overlooked amidst the expressions of foreboding by this grieving trio are several key developments in the drama's emotional trajectory. Perhaps the most important of these occurs when Elizabeth disavows envy of Anne's glory, wishes her successor 'no harm' and pities her complaints (4.1.59–60, 83), expressions of sympathy which Anne soulfully reciprocates by mourning for Elizabeth (4.1.84). Moments earlier Elizabeth augmented the forces of resistance by urging Dorset to 'cross the seas / And live with Richmond, from the reach of hell' (4.1.37–8). In the play's purgatorial politics, her timely (and altogether human) intercession saves Dorset 'from this slaughterhouse' (4.1.39) and sends the Earl a symbolically important adherent, as Dorset is allied, through his mother's two marriages, to both the Lancastrian and Yorkist branches of the Plantagent family. Elizabeth then plays a decisive role in securing the marriage on which the new Tudor dynasty would be founded by outmanoeuvring Richard rhetorically when he attempts to lure her into persuading her daughter Elizabeth to be his next bride. Although Richard is outwitted by her clever use of interrogatives (4.4.338–46), Stanley's disclosure that Elizabeth 'hath heartily consented' that her daughter shall instead marry Richmond (4.5.17–18) clarifies her intentions. By protecting two of her children from Richard's grasp Elizabeth uniquely avoids dying 'the thrall of Margaret's curse' (4.1.41).

Elizabeth's success in duping Richard consolidates the shift in the balance of rhetorical power first signalled by the stonily silent citizens. The significance of Elizabeth's conduct in the so-called 'wooing-by-proxy' scene lies not merely in her withstanding Richard's enticements to 'drown the sad remembrance of … [his] wrongs' (4.4.227), but in her determination to remember not only her own suffering but also that of all those whose loved ones Richard has butchered and who, like her, will 'wail it with their age' (4.4.309–14). The moral, marital and affective sanction which the grieving Elizabeth gives the alliance with Richmond lends a vital measure of legitimacy to the Earl's revolt. Before Elizabeth and Anne depart, the Yorkist matriarch too endorses Dorset joining in league with Richmond. Reflecting on the 'Eighty odd years of sorrow' that snatching at glory has brought her and her family, she benevolently wishes Dorset 'good fortune' to guide him, Anne 'good angels' to guard her and Elizabeth 'good thoughts' amidst her distress (4.1.87–92). The onset of sympathy sees these three lamenting women mourn communally for the first time in the play, and having formed a pitiable alliance they help to consolidate the political and military compact against Richard while Elizabeth promotes the marital union that will enable peace. In so doing their affective alliance makes possible a future different from the past.

'Why should calamity be full of words?' (4.4.120). In *Richard II*, Thomas Mowbray distinguishes the manly arbitrament of arms from 'a woman's war, / The bitter clamour of … eager tongues' (1.1.48–9). Before Margaret leaves for France, Elizabeth presses her predecessor to 'teach me how to curse mine enemies' (4.4.111). Instructed that her woes will ensure her words are 'sharp and pierce' (4.4.119), Elizabeth persists in questioning the value of loud lamentation, dismissing her plaints as 'Poor breathing orators of miseries' (4.4.123). Ultimately she resolves that even if they 'Help not at all, yet do they ease the heart' (4.4.125), allowing that the act of expressing woe may expel pent-up pain from the body. But the vehement articulation of grief does more in *Richard III* than 'ease the heart'; with tragic belatedness, it eventually awakens compassion from its long slumber. And once they begin to pity each other's suffering, Elizabeth, Anne and the Duchess of York cease to direct their clamorous complaints at one another in mutual recrimination and direct their rhetorical weaponry jointly on the tyrant Richard. Intercepted as he leads his army from London, Richard threatens to prevent the heavens from hearing the accusatory clamour of his mother and Elizabeth by drowning the exclamations of 'these tell-tale women … with the clamorous report of war' (4.4.143–6). However, the Duchess will not be dissuaded from interrupting his expedition and utters her 'most heavy curse', which she claims will 'in the day of battle tire … [him] more / Than all the complete armour that … [he] wear'st (4.4.177–9). Her malediction burdens Richard with the knowledge that, in the approaching battle, his mother's 'prayers on the adverse party fight' (4.4.180). Although the Duchess is not proposing to take up arms against her son, as Richard is now king her avowal of support for the forces of rebellion constitutes an act of discursive treason under Elizabethan statute. So too does Margaret's urgent plea for God to 'Cancel … [Richard's] bond of life' (4.4.72), and Elizabeth's repeated claim that Richard's crown is 'usurped' (4.4.134–6, 288, 292, 302–7). The definition of treason had first been expanded to include 'words or writing' in the 1534 Treason Act, which had been framed by Thomas Cromwell in the aftermath of Henry VIII's break with Rome. The statute defined a traitor as

> any person or persons … [who] do maliciously wish, will or desire by words or writing, or by craft imagine, invent, practice or attempt any bodily harm to be done or committed to the King's most royal person, the Queen's or their heirs apparent, or to deprive them or any of them of the dignity, title or name of their royal estates, or slanderously and maliciously publish and pronounce, by express writing or words, that the King our sovereign lord should be heretic, schismatic, tyrant, infidel or usurper of the crown …[35]

The inclusion of 'treason by words' in the Henrician statute was innovative; previously treason had been more narrowly defined as an attempt to kill a king, his queen, the heir apparent or high-ranking officers of the Crown.[36] For an Elizabethan audience, however, the utterances of all three women constitute acts of 'treason by words'.

The language of feminine complaint is thus not only very affecting in *Richard III* but also deeply political. The moral and affective warrant which Elizabeth and the Duchess of York grant Richmond's rebellion is critical in transforming an act of invasion and usurpation into a sanctioned act of tyrannicide. It is not Richmond's battle oration but the female chorus of communal woe which precedes it that affectively legitimates armed resistance to tyranny in Shakespeare's play. Before the Reformation in England the living had spoken to and on behalf of the dead in mourning ritual; on the night before the battle at Bosworth in *Richard III* that temporal trajectory is reversed and its spiritual valency altered to a political one when the dead appear as revenants and speak to the living 'for fair England's sake' (5.4.137). Addressing Richard and Richmond as the rival generals dream, they urge the tyrant to 'Despair and die' and his would-be deposer to have a 'Quiet untroubled soul' (5.3.154–5). But long before the battle against Richard was won at Bosworth, three grieving women took steps to make 'smooth-faced peace' (5.7.33) possible, and they did so by feeling sympathy for one another's grief and mourning each other's losses. Perhaps the most profound emotional reformation articulated in *Richard III* is that undergone by the Duchess of York who urges her dead husband's tormentor to 'triumph not in my woes' for, she reveals to the embittered Margaret, 'I have wept for thine' (4.4.54–5). As 'orators of miseries' the play's lamenting women tell a different version of English history to the one recorded in the great Tudor chronicles, for they memorialise a woeful history of loss centred on the suffering of bereaved women and on female remembrance of the dead. Theirs is a traumatic history of grief, its poignancy and its ambivalent potency, both violent and restorative. This is a different history of England, and a different version of Shakespeare's enlivening dialogue with England's dead from the one to which we have long been critically attuned.

Notes

1 *Richard III*, 1.2.8–9, 2, 13. Quotations are taken from John Jowett's Oxford edition, based on the First Quarto of 1597 (Oxford: Oxford University Press, 2000).

2 See Janis Lull (ed.), *King Richard III*, updated edn (Cambridge: Cambridge University Press, 2009), note to 1.2.8. References to the First Folio (F) version are to this edition.

3 In a compromise characteristic of the Elizabethan Settlement, the Elizabethan *Primer* retained traces of intercessory prayer as did the Elizabethan *Book of Common Prayer* (1559), to the alarm of ardent reformists who denounced the 1559 Prayer Book as 'an unperfected book, culled & picked out of that popish dunghill, the Mass book full of abominations' ('An Admonition to the Parliament' of 1572, cited in Daniel Swift, *Shakespeare's Common Prayers: The Book of Common Prayer and the Elizabethan Age* (Oxford: Oxford University Press, 2013), p. 148). See also Eamon Duffy, *The Stripping of the Altars: Traditional Religion in England, 1400–1580*, 2nd edn (New Haven: Yale University Press, 2005), pp. 565–93; and Clare Gittings, *Death, Burial and the Individual in Early Modern England* (London: Croom Helm, 1984), pp. 42–59.

4 See Ralph Houlbrooke, 'Civility and Civil Observances in the Early Modern English Funeral', in Peter Burke, Brian Harrison and Paul Slack (eds), *Civil Histories: Essays Presented to Sir Keith Thomas* (Oxford: Oxford University Press, 2000), pp. 71–3. See also Gittings, *Death, Burial and the Individual*, pp. 43–4; Ralph Houlbrooke, 'Death, Church, and Family in England Between the Late Fifteenth and the Early Eighteenth Centuries', in Houlbrooke (ed.), *Death, Ritual, and Bereavement* (London: Routledge, 1989), p. 34; and David Cressy, *Birth, Marriage, and Death: Ritual, Religion, and the Life-Cycle in Tudor and Stuart England* (Oxford: Oxford University Press, 1997), pp. 398–403.

5 See 'Patriarchal History and Female Subversion', in Phyllis Rackin's *Stages of History: Shakespeare's English Chronicles* (Ithaca: Cornell University Press, 1990), pp. 146–200; Phyllis Rackin and Jean E. Howard, *Engendering a Nation: A Feminist Account of Shakespeare's English Histories* (London and New York: Routledge, 1997); Nina S. Levine, *Women's Matters: Politics, Gender, and Nation in Shakespeare's Early History Plays* (Newark: University of Delaware Press, 1998).

6 Patricia Phillippy, *Women, Death and Literature in Post-Reformation England* (Cambridge: Cambridge University Press, 2002), p. 110.

7 Duffy, *Stripping of the Altars*, p. 475. Duffy refers here to the 1552 burial rite. Funeral ritual remained 'one of the most recalcitrant areas of continuing Catholic practice' in Elizabeth's reign (Duffy, *Stripping of the Altars*, pp. 577–8), partly because the burial rite in the Elizabethan Book of Common Prayer was itself 'a palimpsest of rival ideologies' (Swift, *Shakespeare's Common Prayers*, p. 154).

8 Michael Neill, *Issues of Death: Mortality and Identity in English Renaissance Tragedy* (Oxford: Clarendon Press, 1997), p. 270. See also Jennifer Woodward, *The Theatre of Death: The Ritual Management of Royal Funerals in Renaissance England, 1570–1625* (Woodbridge: The Boydell Press, 1997), pp. 17, 23.

9 Gittings, *Death, Burial and the Individual*, pp. 176–9; see also her 'Urban Funerals in Late Medieval and Reformation England', in Steven Bassett (ed.), *Death in Towns: Urban Responses to the Dying and the Dead, 100–1600* (Leicester: Leicester University Press, 1992), pp. 170–83 (pp. 177–8); Woodward, *The Theatre of Death*, pp. 28, 30–5; Ralph Houlbrooke, *Death, Religion, and the Family in England, 1480–1750* (Oxford: Oxford University Press, 1998), p. 261; and Katharine Goodland, *Female Mourning in Medieval and Renaissance English Drama* (Aldershot: Ashgate, 2005), p. 141. According to Gittings, the first recorded attendance at a funeral by members of the College of Arms took place in 1463, less than a decade before Henry VI's death in 1471, but it was in the sixteenth century that the heraldic funeral reached its zenith ('Urban Funerals', p. 176).

10 The First Folio (1623) stage direction specifies Lady Anne's role as '*being the mourner*' (1.2 SD). All references to the First Folio text (F) are to Lull's New Cambridge edition. Further references will be given in the main text.

11 Egerton MS 2642, fol. 168, cited in Woodward, *The Theatre of Death*, p. 17; Phillippy, *Women, Death and Literature*, p. 133; Goodland, *Female Mourning*, p. 143.

12 Gittings, *Death, Burial and the Individual*, p. 179, and 'Urban Funerals', p. 178.

13 See Gittings, *Death, Burial and the Individual*, esp. pp. 39–59, 102-23, 131–50; on the heraldic funeral see pp. 166–87. See also Gittings, 'Urban Funerals'; Duffy, *Stripping of the Altars*, pp. 448-503, 565–93; Houlbrooke, 'Death, Church, and Family', pp. 25–42; Houlbrooke, *Death, Religion, and the Family*, pp. 220–95; Ronald Hutton, *The Rise and Fall of Merry England: The Ritual Year, 1400–1700* (Oxford: Oxford University Press, 1994), pp. 73–110; Cressy, *Birth, Marriage, and Death*, esp. pp. 379–455; and Swift, *Shakespeare's Common Prayers*, pp. 127–50.

14 Phillippy, *Women, Death and Literature*, p. 131.

15 As Ralph Houlbrooke observes, '[t]he reformers' repudiation of intercession for the dead took away what had hitherto been the most important religious purpose of funeral rites' (*Death, Ritual, and Bereavement*, p. 40).

16 Anne will later describe Henry VI as a 'dead saint' (4.1.65; 'dear saint' in F).

17 *Female Mourning*, p. 2; see also Duffy, *Stripping of the Altars,* p. 260.

18 Duffy, *Stripping of the Altars*, p. 259. See also Susan C. Karant-Nunn, *The Reformation of Feeling: Shaping the Religious Emotions in Early Modern Germany* (Oxford: Oxford University Press, 2010), pp. 161–5. On the continued presence of 'Marian moments' in plays of that period, see Regina Buccola and Lisa Hopkins (eds), *Marian Moments in Early Modern British Drama* (Aldershot: Ashgate, 2007).

19 See Goodland on female weeping 'as a form of resistance to male control' in the N-Town cycle's *Raising of Lazarus* and in medieval English Lazarus plays more generally (*Female Mourning*, pp. 37ff).

20 Richard responds to Margaret's vituperation by denouncing her as a 'Foul wrinkled witch' (1.3.164) and a 'hateful, withered hag' (1.3.212), and accuses two other women he deems social upstarts, 'that monstrous witch' Elizabeth, and 'that harlot strumpet Shore', of having 'withered up' his arm through witchcraft (3.4.73–7). A witchcraft sceptic, Reginald Scot, observes in *The Discovery of Witchcraft* (London, 1584) that 'one sort' accused of witchcraft are women who are 'sullen, superstitious, and papists; or such as know no religion'; another are vulnerable women ('miserable wretches') who have fallen out with their neighbours and 'wished evil luck unto them all; perhaps with curses and imprecations made in form'. When some whom she cursed subsequently die or fall ill, they ignorantly suppose their diseases 'to be the vengeance of witches' (Book 1, ch. 3, pp. 7–8).

21 Andreas Gerhard Hyperius, *The Practice of Preaching, Otherwise Called the Pathway to the Pulpit* (London, 1577), pp. 171–2, 174, cited in Jennifer C. Vaught, *Masculinity and Emotion in Early Modern English Literature* (Aldershot: Ashgate, 2008), p. 1 n. 1.

22 For a trenchant critique of the ideal of moderation as a profoundly coercive instrument used to justify the restrictive exercise of social, religious and political authority in early modern England see Ethan H. Shagan, *The Rule of Moderation: Violence, Religion and the Politics of Restraint in Early Modern England* (Cambridge: Cambridge University Press, 2011).

23 Kate E. Brown and Howard I. Kushner, 'Eruptive Voices: Coprolalia, Malediction, and the Poetics of Cursing', *New Literary History*, 32 (2001), 537–62 (p. 545). They are describing malediction, but the claim also applies to intercessory prayer.

24 Ibid., pp. 545–6.

25 Christina Larner, *Witchcraft and Religion: The Politics of Popular Belief* (Oxford: Oxford University Press, 1984), pp. 86–7.

26 See Phillippy, *Women, Death and Literature*, p. 133.

27 Ralph Houlbrooke defines 'rigorists' as admirers of the Stoics who 'insisted that grief and intercessory prayer were equally futile' (*Death, Religion, and the*

Family, pp. 222–5). Alec Ryrie argues that the prevailing consensus among post-Reformation English and Scottish Protestants was anti-Stoic (*Being Protestant in Reformation Britain* (Oxford: Oxford University Press, 2013), pp. 18–21. Erin Sullivan observes that Thomas Wright's rejection of a Stoic approach to the passions 'was not unusual' but that his emphasis on their 'vertuous' function in encouraging people to fulfil their Christian duties '*was* atypical' (see Chapter 1, above). Wright's Catholicism is key: writing of the German context, Susan Karant-Nunn notes that the tendency to praise restraint and to regard Mary's outpouring of grief at the Passion as excessive broadly distinguishes Lutheran and Calvinist theologians from their Catholic counterparts for whom 'Mary stands … as an incentive and a model to feel strongly. Christians should aspire to weep and to love as she did' (*Reformation of Feeling*, p. 169).

28 Cited in Houlbrooke, *Death, Religion, and the Family*, p. 223.

29 John Jewel, *An Expositio[n] vpon the Two Epistles of the Apostle S. Paul to the Thessalonians* (London, 1584), p. 300.

30 Thomas Playfere, 'The Meane in Mourning' (London, 1596), pp. 1, 7–10, 20. Playfere dedicated the printed version of his sermon, originally preached during Easter week in 1595, to Lady Elizabeth Carey.

31 In the First Folio Richard confesses that he has never 'shed remorseful tear' (F, 1.2.160).

32 Margaret's presence is unhistorical, as she was imprisoned after the defeat at Tewkesbury in 1471 and after Louis XI ransomed her in 1475 she was exiled to France, where she died in 1482, the year before Richard Gloucester was crowned.

33 Phillippy, *Women, Death and Literature*, p. 211.

34 See Ann Kaegi, '"What say the citizens" in Shakespeare's *Richard III*?', *Journal of Early Modern Studies*, 2 (2013), 91–116 (pp. 104–9).

35 Cited in Rebecca Lemon, *Treason by Words: Literature, Law, and Rebellion in Shakespeare's England* (Ithaca: Cornell University Press, 2006), p. 8. Elizabeth's Treason Act of 1571 was modelled on the 1534 statute but it extended the definition of 'treason by words' to include 'writing, printing, preaching, speech, express words or sayings' (cited in Lemon, *Treason*, p. 9).

36 Ibid., p. 5.

10

The affective scripts of early modern execution and murder

Frederika Bain

A BRIEF ANECDOTE APPEARS in the *Mémoires* of the valet of Louis XVI: on being informed of his coming execution, the monarch requested the account of the death of Charles I in Hume's *History of England* (1754–61), which he read over for days leading up to the event. 'Louis would appear to be using Hume's narrative', the historian Donald Siebert suggests in recounting the story, 'as a script for his own imminent tragic performance.'[1] Apparently the effort was successful, as his affect and mien at the guillotine were praised for their grace and regal quality. Louis's study of Hume's account may be an especially overt use of a description of an execution as a guide to behaviour and emotion at being put to death, but it is one in accordance with the tacit aims of the genre. The emotions, or lack thereof, of all participants in the spectacle of state-ordered death appear shaped by convention in numerous accounts, found in both drama and cheap print.[2] The ruler who orders the execution, the executioner, the condemned, the spectators who bear witness to the event: all have their parts to play and their emotions to convey. This chapter demonstrates the ways representations of affect – conventional and departing from convention – are used in early modern depictions of execution and murder for political arguments and to point to larger questions of rightful rule and tyranny. The usual relative lack of emotion, and the stylised nature of those emotions shown, demonstrate the appropriateness of the execution and thus by extension the legitimacy of the ruler who has commanded it. Conversely, in a killing – a murder, not an execution – ordered by one characterised as a tyrant or usurper, strong or inappropriate emotion is often expressed by those who order, witness and undergo it.[3]

Complicating the question of affective scripts is the possibility, and advisability, of emotional control. Gail Kern Paster's groundbreaking *Humoring the Body* and many of the chapters in the contemporaneous collection *Reading the Early Modern Passions* argue for a humoral understanding of early modern psychological and emotional states, a necessary insight but one that must be joined with other bases for appreciating early modern affect.[4] Humoral theory, Paster shows, might lead to a perceived inability to completely school the passions: the greater their physiological basis, the less under conscious control they could be.[5] At the same time it is clear that there was an implicit understanding in the early modern period of the possibility of control, as in *ars moriendi* texts and *specula principis*. This chapter reads these devotionals and conduct books for indications of how actors in scenes of state-ordered death should play their roles and examines descriptions in drama and cheap print of the degree of fulfilment of these prescribed affective functions. It draws upon a group of broadside and pamphlet execution narratives from the late sixteenth to the mid-seventeenth century, including accounts of the regicide of Charles I, and upon Thomas Preston's (1537–98) *Cambyses, King of Persia* (1569) and Shakespeare's *Richard III* (*c.*1592–93).[6] These plays illustrate the differing ways dramatic works may treat displays of emotion in reference to the question of tyranny and execution, the former providing a straightforward illustration of the elements of the argument and the latter complicating them. The discussion begins with an overview of the formal elements of typical execution narratives and then addresses each of the participants in the scene: king, executioner, condemned and spectator.

Execution narratives

Little passion commonly attends the execution narrative. English broadside depictions may use such words as 'tragical' to describe a death, but these are stylised rather than affective phrasings: the participants do not evince, or evoke, a feeling of tragedy.[7] Lawful executions in dramatic works are likewise productive of little emotion in the characters, and what exists is often conventionalised. Margaret Owens, tracing the often-marked similarities between execution spectacles and theatrical performances, shows that participants in the former resembled actors in that they 'were expected to perform designated roles and to reproduce prescribed behavioural and rhetorical formulas in front of a crowd of spectators'.[8] However, the salient elements in accounts of executions are not emotional displays but recountings of the crimes of which the condemned are convicted, transcripts of their speeches and prayers on the scaffold and physical descriptions. A relatively frequent emphasis on clothing enhances the theatricality of the execution scene, complete with its costumed actors.[9] Convicted during a sensational trial in 1615 of being an accomplice to the poisoners of Sir Thomas Overbury, Sir Gervase Hewlys wore to his execution

> a black Suit and Jerkin with hanging sleeves, having on his head a crimson satten Cap, from the top downwards, and round about laced, under that a white linnen Cap, with a border, and over that a black Hat with a broad Ribbond, and a ruffe Band thick couched with a lace, and a pair of skie-coloured silk stockings, and a pair of three soaled shooes.[10]

Several lines of Francis Bacon's (1561–1626) account depict Hewlys's garb, but no mention is made of his emotional state – though in the transcript of his speech Hewlys announces that 'it rejoyceth' him to see his friends in the audience.[11] Regina Janes, in her monograph on beheading, offers a similar list of what she terms 'rules for representing scaffold dramas', including an exhaustive description of the physical surroundings.[12] This latter element also creates a sense of verisimilitude desirable in what were often touted as eyewitness reports.

In most cheap print accounts, exchanges between the victim and the headsman, if present at all, are short and conventional. They primarily cluster around three acts: the headsman asking for and receiving pardon, the condemned paying him for his careful work, and then the condemned either telling the headsman to strike when ready or warning him to wait until given the sign, often a movement of the arm or a set phrase – 'Lord Jesus receive my soul' – indicating that prayers are done and he or she is spiritually ready to die. Comparatively little is said of the moment of killing, which is most often encompassed in a single clause: the headsman 'severed his neck with one blow' or 'did his office' or, more poetically, gave 'his heavy blessing'.[13] Janes likewise notes the elision of the moment of death, pointing out that accounts '[s]top with the axe or leap to the head held up: [they] never mess with Mr. In-Between. This is the place the sympathetic imagination does not want to go; this is where morbid curiosity lodges.'[14] The very paucity of emotional display, however, begs imaginative recreation on the part of the reader, while that emotion which is shown illustrates the widely varying spaces occupied by the passions in the early modern imaginary.

King

That emotion felt but unexpressed is an ideal of kingship throughout the medieval and early modern period is shown in the many mirrors of princes written in these centuries. Desiderius Erasmus (1466–1536), in his *Education of a Christian Prince* (1516), deems as 'lowest and most wretched … slavery to vice and degrading passions. What more abject and disgraceful condition can there be', he asks, 'than that in which the prince, who holds imperial authority over free men, is himself a slave to lust, irascibility, avarice, ambition, and all the rest of that malicious category?'[15] A century later, James VI and I's charge in *Basilikon Doron* (1616) to his son echoes these strictures: 'Embrace trew magnanimitie, not in beeing vindictiue … but by the contrarie, in thinking your offendour not worthie of your wrath, empyring ouer your owne passion, and triumphing in the commaunding your selfe to forgiue.' He amends his advice, however, to warn, 'But on the other part, let not this trew humilitie stay your high indignation to appeare, when any great oppressours shall presume to come in your presence; then frowne as ye ought.'[16] It was more important for a king to triumph over his own baser self than over his opponents, yet overmuch control should not hinder his employment, or enactment, of that anger for its correct purpose, rebuking his enemies. Thomas Elyot (1490–1546) warns as well in *The Boke Named the Gouvernour* (1531) that a ruler ought to display affability rather than wrath and coldness, though Elyot focuses more on the possibility that a haughty or ireful affect may cause the people to rise up against their king; his emphasis is on the practical, tactical benefits of dispassion more than on an ideal.[17]

The exemplary monarch's control of his emotions, particularly anger, has been widely discussed. Geneviève Bührer-Thierry sums up the consensus: 'If anger was reprehensible for all mankind, it was still more so for kings, who were supposed to know how to control the movements of their flesh and how not to allow themselves to get carried away.'[18] Gerd Althoff argues that kingly anger from the twelfth to the fourteenth centuries was conceptualised less as a personal sense of rage and more as a tool of justice: numerous laws warn that the penalty for particular wrongdoings is both a fine and incurring the wrath of the king.[19] Thus *ira regis* could indeed be rightfully expressed, but its occasions and modes of expression were to be carefully modulated, and it was to be given rein only when appropriate, as a punishment itself or as the impetus for an act of punition or war. Althoff explains that therefore kings who are to be coded negatively are shown as uncontrollably giving in to rage: 'Anger as a determinant of royal action appears at exactly that moment when the king is to be revealed as unjust.'[20] Ann Marie Rasmussen likewise traces the battle fury of Tristan in the romance of *Tristan and Isolde* as an appropriate spur to heroic action rather than a personal lack of control.[21] Conversely, Althoff points out that anger's established opposites, justice and charity, are the hallmarks of a Christian king and are thus appropriate emotions to feel and convey. Nor should the expression of non-violent emotions be inordinate: Jennifer Vaught also shows that the strong emotion shown by Shakespeare's Richard II and Marlowe's Edward II signals their weakness as kings, though she points out that the usurpers of their thrones, stoic men of restrained passions, are not coded as wholly positive either.[22]

A king who could not control his emotions, then, could not control his conduct, including the appropriate wielding of the prerogative of execution, and showed himself to be a tyrant or weakling or in some other way inherently undeserving of his position. The question of tyranny versus legitimate rule is one of particular importance in the early modern period.[23] The subject is not only discussed in *specula principis*, pamphlets and political treatises; it also repeatedly motivates dramatic works. One of the most transparent is Preston's *Cambyses*, which reads like an exemplum on the nature of the tyrant turned into a drama.[24] The play's extended title, not included in the edition cited, includes a preview highlighting the important role state-ordered execution could play in the representation of a good versus a bad king: the action shows King Cambyses's 'one good deed of execution, after that many wicked deeds and tirannous murders, committed by and through him'.[25] The prologue further clarifies that he is a lawful king by blood and upbringing but falls into tyranny through lack of self-control: 'He in his youth was trained up, by trace of virtue's lore; / Yet (being king) did clean forget his perfect race before' (19–20).

A large component of Cambyses's fall involves his giving in to anger rather than controlling it. The first execution he orders, of the corrupt judge Sisamnes, is represented as a legitimate exercise of royal power, correctly rebuking grievous wrongdoing, whereas his later killings are neither lawful nor appropriately motivated. The King heeds the Commons' Complaint against Sisamnes's cruelty and corruption, pronounces the sentence without betraying undue anger, and correctly orchestrates the execution without taking too personal a role in it. Immediately afterwards, though, Cambyses begins his descent, first by getting drunk. Calling for wine before his next, illegitimate killing, he exclaims, 'I must drink to make my brain somewhat intoxicate' (527). His decision illustrates the view, perhaps most famously expressed in Descartes's *Passions of the Soul* (1649) but available in pre-Cartesian thought as well, that, while it is impossible to control the passions themselves, the will may partially restrain the body's response to them.[26] Here Cambyses is represented as *choosing* not to exercise control. Subsequently his temper becomes quick and his pride tender, possible indications in themselves of his unfitness for rule that also lead to devastating consequences. His excessive anger at his counsellor's mild suggestion that he might be inebriated drives him to order the counsellor, Praxaspes, to bring out his own son for him to kill. Cambyses shoots an arrow through the boy's heart and cuts out the heart to show it pierced through the centre, to prove to the anguished father that he is not too drunk to shoot straight. Nor does he allow the machinery of justice to orchestrate the appropriate ritual of the death; there is no trial, and he himself murders rather than employing the headsman. Afterwards Cambyses continues to show fury in further killings, of his brother and his wife. None is a legitimate exercise of monarchical power; he has become a tyrant.

Displays of emotion and their implications for fitness for rule are more complicated in Shakespeare's *Richard III* than the argument based on expression or suppression illustrated in *Cambyses*. Richard is a master at manipulating others' emotions, primarily by counterfeiting his own, showing sympathy and outrage to Clarence and admiration and tenderness to Anne. Clarence attempts to convince himself and others that Richard must love him because Richard acts as though he does: told by the murderers who sent them, Clarence protests, 'It cannot be, for he bewept my fortune, / And hugged me in his arms, and swore with sobs / That he would labour my delivery'.[27] Previously, though, Richard has told these men that 'fools' eyes fall tears' (1.3.352); only fools express uncontrolled and truly felt emotion.

At the same time that the play leads the audience to distrust Richard's excessive affective control for the manipulative power it conveys, it questions those swayed too easily by their own or others' passions. Richard is contemptuous of those whom he can manipulate with his feigned affect and of what he sees as their lack of emotional restraint, and at times we are encouraged to share in his scorn. After winning Anne over the corpse of her dead father-in-law through his rhetorical virtuosity, he roundly condemns her for her emotional capitulation: 'And will she yet abase her eyes on me, / That cropped the golden prime of this sweet prince, / And made her widow to a woeful bed?' (1.2.249–51) he asks, before his bitterly mocking speech praising his previously unsuspected physical attractiveness. Ironically, however, it is Richard's *lack* of complete emotional control, betrayed in his soliloquies and conversations with his hired killers, that proves the most significant to his final representation. In these speeches he shows anger, impatience and contempt rather than the justice, compassion and charity that kings ought rightfully to display, and his exposure of the lack of authenticity of the latter is a powerful indication to the audience of his status not as 'fool' but as unworthy king.

Executioner

In early modern English accounts of legitimate executions, the headsman says little or nothing; he is primarily a function rather than a character.[28] The representation of emotion, therefore, when it does exist, is especially telling in descriptions of the hangman, signalling a specific intent on the author's part. Hannele Klemetillä has written extensively on medieval hangmen, primarily as depicted in French miracle and mystery plays; these plays often give executioners a much more prominent role than English texts, portraying them with violent scorn, hatred and disgust.[29] Though her focus is not on affect, Klemetillä argues for the didactic purposes of these hangmen's representations; while they are overwhelmingly portrayed as callously indifferent to the suffering of their victims, she discusses one instance in *La Passion d'Auvergne* (1477) in which John the Baptist's executioner Maliferas is represented as deeply distressed by and guilty about the act he is about to perform. She argues that his emotion is shown as heightened to point to the lesson that the saint should not have been killed.[30]

Executioners are very rarely represented in medieval mystery plays as remorseful, though the great majority of those they kill – saints, monks, nuns and, most emphatically, Jesus – are coded as dying unjustly. They are either supposed to be so personally irredeemable that they lack any sense of compassion, as Klemetillä contends, or so abject as to be unable to participate in communally accepted norms of emotional behaviour. That is, their (lack of) emotion may be either personal or based on collective norms of appropriate expression. In early modern English sources the phenomenon of the executioner who hesitates to kill or regrets doing so appears with more frequency, again coding the killing as murder rather than legitimate execution. Elyot recounts how an executioner's emotional response keeps him from killing a condemned man in whom he recognises the indicators of kingship: 'beholding [his] honourable porte and maiestie … he therfore all tremlyng, as constrayned by feare, dyd lette fall out of his hande the swerde wherewith he shulde haue slayne Marius, and leuyng him untouched, fledde out of the place'.[31]

Only a rightful ruler could order a legitimate execution, and only when undertaking a legitimate execution was the headsman afforded institutional protection against familial vengeance, penalty of law and mortal sin. An event that brought into sharp focus the question of an acceptable warrant for an executioner was the beheading of Charles I. Charles was not, of course, the first monarch to have been executed, but a significant issue in Royalist responses is that it was not another monarch, as in other cases, who demanded his head; it was Parliament, a headless body. One of his epitaphs refers to the 'ASSASINES; whose weale HEE sought, / Even then when they His MURDER wrought / With horrid Plots, that HEADLESS He / (And in HIM Church and State) might be'.[32] This passage prosodically captures the affective aims of its author, the hissing and panting 'S' and 'H' sounds and the capital letters of the crucial words transmitting horror at the act, while the capitalised 'He', 'His' and 'Him' show an almost religious reverence. Charles's speech transcripts and many Royalist accounts of the regicides' trials argue Parliament had no authority to order a death, especially the death of a king; repeatedly referring to the act as 'murther', they maintain that even to contemplate killing a king was treason. This left the executioner's own position gravely unprotected; one William Hulet was convicted in 1660 under Charles II of high treason and executed for having struck the blow that killed Charles I, though it was never proved he had done so.[33] The executioner, who was dressed in a mask, including false beard and hair, has never been conclusively identified.

A common element in narratives of legitimate execution is the headsman's receiving pardon before killing. This shrives his soul of the sin of murder, in so far as he is only acting as the instrument of the monarch, and makes it clear that he executes not on the basis of any animus of his own and that his dutiful performance is understood by the condemned. In a characteristic cheap print description, M. Tyler of Bristol says to his executioner, 'I pray thee do thy work in mercy, for I forgive thee with all my Heart, and I also pray to God for to forgive thee.'[34] The hangman responsible for the execution of Charles I may not have received pardon, however, and several who might have done the killing are represented as feeling deep emotion relating to it: reluctance to do the deed, trepidation while doing it, and remorse and fear afterward. For instance, several reports of the regicide trials note that it had been difficult to find someone willing to undertake the execution; the official headsman, Richard Brandon, had refused, as had all thirty-eight soldiers selected as possible candidates.[35] And while some accounts, including *The Black Tribunall* (1660), describe the condemned monarch as offering a general pardon to all, at least one other text, the *Confession of Richard Brandon the Hangman* (1649), argues that the executioner was not forgiven.[36] The speaker of the latter admits that he did behead King Charles and adds affective details: 'His Majesties denying to forgive him, when he fell down upon his knees unto him, hath very much troubled his conscience', such that 'euen at the very point of time when he was to give the blow, a great pain & ache took him round the neck' and has continued ever after – causing him to feel on his own body the hurt he had done to his king's. The speaker adds that he has become afraid of the dark and has had to have a candle burning while he sleeps.[37] Whether or not this account is accurate is less important than that it conveys the guilt the author believed the hangman *should* have felt.

Cheap print works may also use expressions of hangmen's feelings beyond remorse to demonstrate their disapproval of Cromwell and Parliament. In *The Rump* (1662), a Royalist compilation of satirical verses on the Rump Parliament, 'The Hangman's Last Will and Testament' repeats the refrain 'I and my gallows groan'.[38] They groan because they have not been able to hang anyone recently, the implication being that they would have liked to have hanged some members of Parliament, identified by name and disagreeable characteristics in the song. The speaker of 'The Hangman's Joy and the Traytor's Sorrow' (1660), a 'merry dialogue' also written during the Interregnum, similarly expresses the desire that the business of execution will pick up soon.[39]

Dramatic works likewise follow the convention that assumed hangmen's emotions primarily in the face of a warrant from an unworthy king. In the one scene in *Cambyses* of a legitimate execution, the headsman, appropriately called 'Execution', asks Sisamnes's pardon for preparing to kill him, and the condemned man readily gives it, freeing the executioner from guilt. Conversely, the King afterward forces his counsellor Praxaspes into a conflicted role akin to executioner by ordering him to bring forth his own son to be killed, for which Praxaspes is unambiguously blamed by others. Bound by his position to obey, he is nevertheless shown as culpable in his complicity, and he expresses horror at what he is forced to do. In later killings Cambyses employs two agents to strike the blows, but instead of 'Execution' they are identified as 'Cruelty' and 'Murder', the change in their designations underscoring the different status of these deaths. And even these characters, embodiments of vices, cannot perform their required offices unmoved: 'With heavy hearts we will do all your Grace doth say', they respond when ordered to kill the Queen (1111).

The stage directions and speech prefixes in *Richard III* also question the legitimacy of the ruler in the names given to his chosen agents of execution. Those Richard hires to kill Clarence are called 'Executioners' the first time they enter in the stage directions of the six quartos, while in the Folio they are 'Murtherers'. In the quartos their speech prefixes are 'Execu.' and 'Exec', but in the Folio they are 'Vil.', presumably 'Villain'. In all cases, Richard first greets them as 'my Executioners'.[40] Is what Richard has sent these men to do a just execution or an unlawful murder? Among the indications it is a murder is the fact that emotions are expressed by the killers as well as by Richard and Clarence over the course of the scene. The agents act in some respects as professional hangmen; preparing to kill Clarence, the Second Murderer says to the First, 'Come, shall we fall to work?' (1.4.151). This is a job; they do not feel murderous towards their intended victim. They clearly express that they are working for the King: when, meeting them, Clarence says, 'Thy voice is thunder, but thy looks are humble' (1.4.166), the First Murderer answers, 'My voice is now the King's, my looks mine own' (167). Being asked by Clarence how he has offended them, one answers, 'Offended us you have not, but the King' (1.4.177). By the King they mean Edward; however, their only dealings have been with Richard, who has usurped his place by sending them to perform an execution by an official warrant that Edward has since countermanded. They are not official hangmen, because Richard is not yet King – and never will, in the play's view, be a legitimate king. They fall into, and understand themselves to be in, a grey area between true instruments of the state and murderers-for-hire, as the shifting speech prefixes and stage directions suggest.

Another demonstration of this confusion is that they ultimately express more emotion than official executioners conventionally do. They originally seem to lack passion – and compassion – entirely. Their eyes, says Richard, 'drop millstones' rather than tears (1.3.352), aligning them with the stereotypically emotionless hangman as well as with Richard himself, of whom the killers later jibe that he can only weep 'millstones, as he lessoned us to weep' (1.4.239). Richard expresses concern that they will be seduced into pity by Clarence, and though they initially scoff at the possibility, they do feel qualms of conscience as they approach the murder. This occurs before they encounter Clarence; they are shown as hesitating not because of his eloquence but because of their dawning realisation that the killing is wrong. When the First Murderer says they need not fear because they have a warrant from the King, the Second protests that they lack a warrant from God, a concern official executioners under a legitimate king do not evince. The Second Murderer ultimately refuses to join in the killing; if this acknowledgement of his ability to choose demonstrates that he is not a professional hangman, it is demonstrated still more clearly in his emotion surrounding that choice.

Condemned

The case of the condemned is more complicated than that of the executioner or the monarch; no simple equation exists in which emotion shown equals an illegitimate execution, emotion contained a legitimate one. Though anguish on the part of the condemned may be designed to be read as a sign that their deaths are wrongful, other wrongly condemned prisoners adopt a saintly calm that demonstrates they are better Christians than their accusers and killers. This is the attitude of the great majority of the Protestant martyrs in John Foxe's *Acts and Monuments* (first published in 1563), as exemplified by John Rogers (*c.*1500–55), the 'protomartyr', who 'constantly & cherefully tooke hys death wyth wonderfull pacience'.[41] Margaret Owens discusses 'three distinct paradigms of exemplary deaths' at execution, 'the innocent martyr, the penitent culprit and the resistant transgressor'; though her focus is not on their emotions, each type is characterised by certain affective details. She also notes that when Sir Walter Ralegh was preparing to be executed, his spiritual adviser was '[t]aken aback at Ralegh's apparent "confidence and cheerefulnesse"', these presumably not being emotions within the usual range.[42]

In general, less rather than more emotion on the part of the dying is valued. As in *specula principis*, the view of the passions as an unwilled force at least partially liable to manipulation by the conscious will is implicit in *ars moriendi* guides. Both are concerned to a greater extent with appropriate conduct than with appropriate feeling, though there is a tradition in later examples of the genre towards convincing the mind before, or as a means to, schooling the affect. Guides to the art of dying well became popular after the publication of the first *De arte moriendi* texts in the early and mid-fifteenth century and continued to be written through the early modern period. Though they vary in some particulars, what constitutes 'a good death' remains essentially the same, including a Stoic acceptance of one's fate and the ability to master one's emotions rather than giving way to fear, anger or misery. Henry Suso warns his readers in his *Horologium sapientiae* (*c.*1339), which contains early *ars moriendi* elements, that they are 'by youre desires inordinate / And eeke of othir mo our self han we / Brought in-to this plyt and wrecchid estat'.[43] The focus here is on the problem of *feeling* inordinate desire, not necessarily on how one responds to those feelings.[44] *De arte moriendi* itself counsels that a good Christian 'should not be sorry nor troubled, neither dread death of his body … but gladly and wilfully, with reason of his mind that ruleth his sensuality, he should take his death and suffer it patiently'.[45] Three centuries later Jeremy Taylor (*c.*1613–67) counsels that those dying should refrain from rebellion against God's decrees, impatience, peevishness and other inappropriate emotions; here, however, he offers logical arguments by which the dying person can persuade herself or himself away from these untoward passions: 'That sorrow is hugely tolerable which gives its smart but by instants and smallest proportions of time. No man at once feels the sickness of a week or of a whole day, but the smart of an instant ... And what minute can that be which can pretend to be intolerable?'[46] Performing a sort of calculus of the emotions, Taylor attempts to divide pain or other inducements to untoward behaviour into units small enough to be borne with patience and calm.

Even condemned criminals were able to experience, or enact, a good death. In execution narratives, shows of emotion on the part of the condemned may be glossed by the writer to ensure that they are read appropriately. We are told that when Arnold Cosbie 'burst foorth into bitter teares' when sentenced to die for murder in 1591, it was in repentance for sinning, not despair at being executed: he 'grieuously lamented both his follie and his fall, wishing that he had neuer beene borne to performe an act so detestable, whereby he had lost the fauour of his prince, and good will of hir people'.[47] By his own affect he affirms the rightness of his death sentence. Conversely, the fear that Robert Drewrie, a Benedictine friar, displays at being killed in 1607 is shown to be a manifestation of his wrong-headed religion. The author of his execution narrative earlier has made it clear he is not in sympathy with Drewrie's 'very dangerous and Traitorous' faith and depicts the condemned man's demeanour in the moments before he is to be hanged so as to imply that he has finally come to understand the error of his beliefs. Drewrie is described as

> often looking about him, as hopinge there was some mercy for him, for feare appeared very plainely in him[;] when he felt ... his expectation to be deceiued, he caught fast holde with his left hande on the [h]alter aboue hys head, and very hardly was inforced to let it goe, but held so for a pretty while. If this were not an aparant hope of life, I refer it to better Iudgements then mine owne.[48]

Drewrie fears death, the author implies, since he cannot die secure in the hope of heaven; again the account affirms his rightful punishment.

At times the execution is put in an overtly positive light, as in the pamphlet titled 'The happy conuersion, contrition, and Christian preparation of Francis Robinson, gentleman. Who for counterfetting the great seale of England, was drawen, hang'd, and quartered at Charing-Crosse' (1618).[49] The author Henry Goodcole (*c.*1586–1641), a 'preacher of the Word of God', implies that if it has taken drawing and quartering – the mechanics of which are described briefly and unemotionally – to effect Robinson's conversion and contrition, they have been well worth the doing, and the execution can indeed be termed a 'happy' one.[50] Many Royalist descriptions of Charles I's sentencing and execution also praise his mildness, generosity of spirit and kingly demeanour, such as Henry Leslie's 'Martyrdome of King Charles I' (1649), which emphasises that he 'endured his crosse with such cheerfull patience' as resembled that of Jesus.[51]

Cambyses's wife is another who bears her coming death with Christian grace and fortitude. Her demeanour is cast into particularly vivid relief in comparison to her husband's uncontrolled (and pagan) fury; while he growls, 'Thou cursed Jill, by all the gods I take an oath and swear, / That flesh of thine these hands of mine in pieces small could tear' (1058–9), she sings, 'with a joyful heart to God a psalm I mean to sing, / Forgiving all' (1123–4). The other victims in the play are represented with varying emotional reactions that likewise work to characterise the King. Sisamnes, rightfully executed before Cambyses becomes a tyrant, pardons the headsman and calmly gives his blessing to his son, Otian, the implication being that those who know they are being punished appropriately can accede to their deaths as falling within the natural order of things. Others, lacking this assurance, are left with a fearful sense of the world turned awry; Cambyses's brother Lord Smerdis, stabbed to death by Cruelty and Murder, does not go gently, but cries out that 'the king is a tyrant tyrannious, / And all his doings be damnable and pernicious' (724–5). Not only has he not had time to prepare spiritually to die, confessing and being shriven; he also is implicitly represented as understanding that as a tyrant Cambyses does not have the proper authority to sentence him to death.

In *Richard III*, as well, the terror of the condemned may point to the illegitimate nature of his or her killing. Clarence's anguished reactions demonstrate that his is not a valid execution, though this reading is complicated by the negative portrayal of Clarence as weak and helpless, prey to night terrors and begging the gaoler not to leave him. Though he has been given no official notice of impending execution, he is warned through a dream and awakens expressing fear and horror at the dream-death. Confronted with the murderers' stated intent to kill him, Clarence appeals to the machinery of justice, saying that he has not been convicted or sentenced, so how can he be executed? No pious resignation, no chastened guilt are expressed for wrongdoing justly punished, as in conventional depictions of official executions. The play later offers the spectacle of Richard's victims, including Clarence, speaking from beyond the grave: during the night before the final battle at Bosworth, eleven ghosts visit the sleeping Richard and Richmond, bidding the former to 'Despair and die' and the latter to be cheerful and comforted. The ghosts' affect as they describe their deaths is no longer overtly anguished and fearful, but they express pain enough to arouse the corresponding pain of guilt and horror in Richard, who is at last moved by others' expressed emotions as he has moved others by the same means throughout the play. He reacts by questioning whether or not his killings were instances of tyrannical murder, equivocating, 'Is there a murderer here? No. Yes, I am' (5.3.184) and then concluding that he has committed '[m]urder, stern murder in the highest degree' (5.3.197). This sense of the illegitimate nature of his actions, brought on by the ghosts' demonstrated affect, vanquishes him to a greater extent than the physical battle; as he tells Ratcliffe, 'shadows tonight / Have struck more terror to the soul of Richard / Than can the substance of ten thousand soldiers' (5.3.216–18).

Spectators

In execution narratives, as Owens points out, '[t]he audience also contributed to the proceedings by enacting a repertoire of responses – derision, silent sympathy, gasps of horror, cheers, applause – at appropriate moments'.[52] Martyrologies of Charles I emphasise the infamy of his murder by representing spectators as so moved by its horror that their emotional control breaks down. Marcus Nevitt quotes a pamphlet portraying even ducks and spirits as mourning Charles's death, but he argues that 'the evils of the execution find their most appropriate imaginative correlate in the extreme emotional responses of women', who at least two pamphlets tell us 'wept bitterly'.[53] One fainting woman is at the foreground of John Weesop's painting *An Eyewitness Representation of the Execution of King Charles I* (1649), and Nevitt points to 'the disproportionate predominance given to … [her] emotional reaction', while the execution itself is 'relegat[ed] … to a tableau played out by curiously indistinguishable men in the background'.[54] The wrongness of his death, in short, may be better expressed by the portrayal of a strong emotional reaction to it rather than by a portrayal of the actual event.[55]

In *Cambyses* spectators' responses correspond clearly to the degree of tyranny associated with each killing. Despite the gruesome nature of the scene in which Sisamnes is executed – he is flayed on stage after his head is cut off – a strong portrayal of the passions is lacking. Sisamnes's son expresses his grief for this just death by situating himself within a generic category and pointing to the correct emotion for this category: 'What child is he of nature's mold could bide the same to see, / His father flayed in this wise? O, how it grieveth me!' (465–6). His affect is conventional rather than heart-sick. He also implies that he has read the execution more as a rhetorical move than as a tragedy, demonstrating he has correctly assimilated the lesson to be learned: 'O king, to me this is a glass: with grief in it I view / Example that unto your grace I do not prove untrue' (469–70).[56] Praxaspes, another spectator, agrees the execution is a noble act. Far more affective language appears at Cambyses's next, illegitimate, killing. The boy's mother screams and cries in the longest speech of the play, bemoaning her 'blubbered eyes' (582), her 'heavy heart' and its 'spiteful pangs' (583, 584), calling Cambyses 'of tiger's brood! / O tiger's whelp' (593–4). The emotion expressed by the court likewise grows with the King's continued killings; they weep and wail. Even the Vice Ambidexter loses to some extent his habitual detachment and cries, at the murder of the Queen, 'Ah, ah, ah, ah! I cannot choose but weep for the queen! … Oh, oh, my heart, my heart! Oh, my bum will break! / Very grief torments me that scarce I can speak. / Who could but weep for the loss of such a lady?' (1126–30). In contrast, when the King is accidentally stabbed to death with his own sword at the play's end, Ambidexter swears, 'The devil take me if for him I make any moan' (1171). In both drama and cheap print the spectators, as external to the scene, bear witness through their emotional responses to justice carried out or miscarried; their office is the external validation that, as reported, mirrors the writer's own estimation of events.

A partial example of a spectator's anguish in *Richard III* is Lady Anne's lamentation over King Henry's corpse; here, however, Shakespeare's mastery at defying and redefining literary convention complicates the argument considerably.[57] Anne's misery at viewing if not a murder then its aftermath is vividly expressed:

> Lo, in those windows that let forth thy life
> I pour the helpless balm of my poor eyes.
> O, cursed be the hand that made these fatal holes;
> Cursed be the heart that had the heart to do it;
> Cursed the blood that let this blood from hence.
>
> (1.2.12–16)

However, elements of the speech and the scene following it complicate the equation of spectator's grief with wrongful murder. Anne's phrasing and figures recall conventional and formulaic aspects of mourning: the coldness of keys and the paleness of ashes, to which she likens Henry's corpse, were both proverbial, and the speech's introduction has echoes of ceremonial mourning. 'Set down, set down your honourable load … Whilst I awhile obsequiously lament / Th'untimely fall of virtuous Lancaster', she directs the bearers, as though preparing the scene for a set piece (1.2.1–4). More striking, and a greater complication, is that this anguish, whether represented as deeply felt or conventional, is obscured by Anne's agreeing to marry Richard at the end of the scene, as his represented skill at emotional manipulation overpowers, without nullifying, her grief and hatred. Throughout the play Richard performs, or attempts to perform, the four roles of king, executioner, victim and mourning spectator, three within this scene: he admits to killing Henry and Edward, promises to mourn and bury the former, and invites Anne to stab him in retribution. Such a multivalent performance calls these roles, and their generic conventions, into question.

As this chapter has argued, expressions of emotions at state-ordered deaths usually follow predictable patterns. Devotionals and other didactic texts implicitly or explicitly call for certain modes of affect, while most execution narratives, read in quantity, reveal a uniformity of emotion that shows their authors working within established generic expectations. Emotions that exceeded the conventional script in extent or diverged from it in kind raised questions about the legitimacy of rulers and the appropriateness of the executions, as *Cambyses* so effectively demonstrates. But even conventionalised depictions of the passions are not represented as corresponding to pre-established formulae. Rather, authors show the participants in these scenes as truly feeling their emotions and truly expressing what they feel. This elision of the gap between appropriately presented and genuinely felt emotion has a naturalising effect not only on these depictions, heightening their apparent realism and therefore their truth value to their intended audience, but also on their argument, strengthening and even fundamentally shaping it. For if events have moved the participants spontaneously to feel and express emotion, the author's interpretation of those events is therefore presented as validated. It is precisely this appearance of authenticity that makes Richard III's feigned displays of emotion so seductive to his auditors within the world of the play, while at the same time audiences continue to find Shakespeare's constructed character, with the far different emotions displayed in his asides, equally persuasive as the portrait of a consummate villain. Perhaps it was this show of authenticity which made the martyrologies of Charles I, with their portrayal of the King's saintly mien, so convincing to their readers, and which likewise led Louis XVI to imitate the English king's performance in an attempt to legitimise himself, as Charles had followed his culture's script in shaping his own affect to reaffirm his legitimacy as a ruler at the very moment his execution called it into question.

Notes

1 Donald Siebert, *The Moral Animus of David Hume* (Newark: University of Delaware Press, 1990), pp. 51–2. Many thanks to Matthew Lauzon for bringing this incident to my attention.

2 Anna Wierzbicka offers a more general view of what she terms 'emotional scripts', larger-scale societal attitudes defining appropriate emotion, in *Emotions across Languages and Cultures: Diversity and Universals* (Cambridge: Cambridge University Press, 1999), p. 240. I am grateful to David Bagchi, in Chapter 2, above, in this volume for introducing me to this source.

3 See Zirka Filipczack, 'Poses and Passions: Mona Lisa's "Closely Folded" Hands', in Gail Kern Paster, Katharine Rowe and Mary Floyd-Wilson (eds), *Reading the Early Modern Passions: Essays in the Cultural History of Emotion* (Philadelphia: University of Pennsylvania Press, 2004), pp. 68–88, for a discussion, in reference to conventional early modern portrait poses, of the structured, conventionalised nature of much of what may now be read as individual, personal expression. This argument can be extended to written as well as pictorial representation.

4 Gail Kern Paster, *Humoring the Body: Emotions and the Shakespearean Stage* (Chicago: Chicago University Press, 2004); Paster, Rowe and Floyd-Wilson (eds), *Reading the Early Modern Passions*.

5 Paster, *Humoring the Body*, p. 241.

6 Some of the non-Caroline cheap print surveyed can be found in the first two volumes of Leigh Yetter, *Public Execution in England 1573 to 1868* (London: Pickering and Chatto, 2009), a remarkable eight-volume compendium of facsimiles of cheap print execution narratives.

7 For broader discussions of execution narratives, see both the introduction to Yetter, *Public Execution*, and Katherine Royer's comprehensive and meticulously researched *English Execution Narratives 1200–1700* (London: Pickering and Chatto, 2013).

8 Margaret Owens, *Stages of Dismemberment: The Fragmented Body in Late Medieval and Early Modern Drama* (Newark: University of Delaware Press, 2005), p. 121.

9 See Royer, *English Execution Narratives*, ch. 4, for an expanded discussion of clothing in execution narratives.

10 Francis Bacon, *A True and Historical Relation of the Poysoning of Sir Thomas Overbury* (London, 1651), p. 68. Bacon presided over the trial along with Sir Edward Cooke, but his account was not published until after his death.

11 Bacon, *True and Historical Relation*, p. 70.

12 Regina Janes, *Losing Our Heads: Beheadings in Literature and Culture* (New York: New York University Press, 2005), p. 45

13 This latter phrase appears in George Whetstone, *The Censure of a Loyall Subiect* (London, [1587]), p. 25.

14 Janes, *Losing Our Heads*, p. 45. 'Mr. In-Between' is Janes's half-ironic term for the body at the moment of death.

15 Desiderius Erasmus, *Education of a Christian Prince*, trans. Neil M. Cheshire and Michael J. Heath (Cambridge: Cambridge University Press, 1997), p. 24.

16 James VI and I, *Basilikon Doron or His Majesties Instrvctions to His Dearest Sonne, Henry the Prince*, in *Political Works of James I*, ed. Charles Howard McIlwain (Cambridge, MA: Harvard University Press, 1918), p. 41.

17 Thomas Elyot, *The Boke Named the Gouvernour*, vol. 2, ed. Henry Croft (New York: Burt Franklin, 1967), ch. 5.

18 Geneviève Bührer-Thierry, '"Just Anger" or "Vengeful Anger"? The Punishment of Blinding in the Early Medieval West', in Barbara Rosenwein (ed.), *Anger's Past: The Social Uses of an Emotion in the Middle Ages* (Ithaca: Cornell University Press, 1998), pp. 75–91 (p. 75).

19 Gerd Althoff, '*Ira Regis*: Prolegomena to a History of Royal Anger', in Barbara Rosenwein (ed.), *Anger's Past: The Social Uses of an Emotion in the Middle Ages* (Ithaca: Cornell University Press, 1998), pp. 59–74.

20 Ibid., p. 67.

21 Ann Marie Rasmussen, 'Emotions, Gender, and Lordship in Medieval Literature: Clovis's Grief, Tristan's Anger, and Kriemhild's Restless Corpse', in C. Stephen Jaeger and Ingrid Kasten (eds), *Codierungen von Emotionen im Mittelalter / Emotions and Sensibilities in the Middle Ages* (New York: De Gruyter, 2003), pp. 174–91.

22 Jennifer Vaught, *Masculinity and Emotion in Early Modern English Literature* (Aldershot: Ashgate, 2008), chs 3–4.

23 W. A. Armstrong, 'The Elizabethan Conception of the Tyrant', *Review of English Studies*, 22 (1946), 161–81; Rebecca Bushnell, *Tragedies of Tyrants: Political Thought and Theater in the English Renaissance* (Ithaca: Cornell University Press, 1990); Mary Ann McGrail, *Tyranny in Shakespeare* (Lanham: Lexington Books, 2001).

24 Thomas Preston, *Cambyses, King of Persia*, in *The Minor Elizabethan Drama, vol. 1: Pre-Shakespearean Tragedies*, ed. Ashley Thorndike (London: Dent, 1958). Subsequent references appear in the text, with line numbers in parentheses.

25 Thomas Preston, *A Lamentable Tragedy Mixed Ful of Pleasant Mirth, Conteyning the Life of Cambises King of Percia* (London, 1570).

26 René Descartes, *The Passions of the Soul*, trans. and ed. Stephen Voss (Indianapolis: Hackett, 1989), pp. 43–4. See Erin Sullivan, Chapter 1, above, in this volume for an illuminating discussion of pre-Cartesian theories of mind–body integration and duality.

27 William Shakespeare, *King Richard III*, ed. James Siemon (London: A. & C. Black, 2009), 1.4.243–5. Subsequent references appear in the text.

28 'Hangman' and 'headsman' need not be terms confined to their specific modes of killing but may both refer to 'more generally, an executioner, a torturer' *OED*, 'hangman'.

29 Hannele Klemetillä, *Epitomes of Evil: Representations of Executioners in Northern France and the Low Countries in the Late Middle Ages* (Turnhout: Brepols, 2006), and *The Executioner in Late Medieval French Culture* (Turku: Turun Yliopisto, 2003).

30 Klemetillä, *Epitomes of Evil*, p. 225.

31 Elyot, *Boke Named the Gouvernour*, pp. 15–16.

32 A. B., *An Epitaph* (London, 1649), ll. 17–20.

33 See Heneage Finch, *An Exact and Most Impartial Accompt of the Indictment, Arraignment, Trial, and Judgment … of Twenty Nine Regicides* (London, 1679).

34 James Bent, *The Bloody Assizes* (London, 1689), p. 44.

35 Finch, *An Exact and Most Impartial Accompt*, p. 268.

36 Anon., *England's Black Tribunall* (London, 1660); Richard Brandon, *The Confession of Richard Brandon the Hangman (upon His Death Bed) Concerning his Beheading His Late Majesty, Charles the First* (London, 1649).

37 Brandon, *The Confession of Richard Brandon*, p. 6.

38 Anon., 'The Hangman's Last Will and Testament', in Alexander Brome (ed.), *Rump, or, An Exact Collection of the Choycest Poems and Songs Relating to the Late Times* (London, 1662), p. 149.

39 Anon., *The Hangmans Joy, or the Traytors Sorrow* (London, 1660).

40 Siemon's note to the speech prefix 'Murderer' at 1.4.84 references the distinction outlined in *3 Henry VI*: 'To Richard's question – "Think'st thou I am an executioner?" – King Henry [VI] replies: "If murdering innocents be executing, / Why then, thou art an executioner" (5.6.30–3).'

41 John Foxe, *The Unabridged Acts and Monuments Online* (1570 edition), www.johnfoxe.org [accessed 1 December 2012].

42 Owens, *Stages of Dismemberment*, p. 130.

43 Quoted in Christina von Nolcken, '"O, why ne had y lerned for to die?": *Lerned for to Dye* and the Author's Death in Thomas Hoccleve's *Series*', *Essays in Medieval Studies*, 10 (1993), 27–51 (p. 23).

44 This question is taken up by later authors as well: Thomas Wright (*c.*1561–1623) warns, 'The flesh molesteth us … with an army of unruly Passions; for the most part withdrawing from goodness and haling to illness, they toss and turmoil our miserable souls' (*The Passions of the Mind in General* (1601), ed. William Webster Newbold (New York: Garland, 1986), p. 327), while Juan Luis Vives (1493–1540) maintains that emotions are bestowed by God so that erring humanity may be guided towards good and away from evil by their desires (Carlos G. Noreña, *Juan Luis Vives and the Emotions* (1538; rpt Carbondale: Southern Illinois University Press, 1989), pp. 147–8).

45 Frances Comper (ed.), *The Book of the Craft of Dying and Other Early English Tracts Concerning Death* (New York: Arno, 1977), p. 7.

46 Jeremy Taylor, *Rule and Exercises of Holy Dying* (Princeton: Longman, Hurst, Rees and Orme, 1808), p. 86.
47 Arnold Cosby, *The Manner of the Death and Execution of Arnold Cosbie* ([London], 1591), p. 3.
48 Anon., *A True Report of the Araignment, Tryall, Conviction, and Condemnation, of a Popish Priest* (London, 1607), p. 15.
49 Henry Goodcole, *A True Declaration of the Happy Conuersion, Contrition, and Christian Preparation of Francis Robinson* (London, 1618).
50 For a discussion of the political implications of early modern 'happiness', see Richard Chamberlain, Chapter 7, above.
51 Henry Leslie, *The Martyrdome of King Charles* (The Hague, 1649), p. 19.
52 Owens, *Stages of Dismemberment*, p. 121.
53 Marcus Nevitt, *Women and the Pamphlet Culture of Revolutionary England, 1640–1660* (Aldershot: Ashgate, 2006), pp. 56–9. See Leslie, *Martyrdome of King Charles*, p. 18; and Anon., *The Life and Death of King Charles the Martyr* (London, 1649), p. 6.
54 Nevitt, *Women and the Pamphlet Culture*, p. 57.
55 Over time, accounts of spectators' reactions to Charles I's execution have a tendency to become more highly coloured, as in Laurence Echard's account in *The History of England* (1720): 'Women miscarry'd, many of both Sexes fell into Palpitations, Swoonings and Melancholy, and some, with sudden Consternations, expired' (quoted in Donald Siebert, 'The Aesthetic Execution of Charles I: Clarendon to Hume', in William Thesing (ed.), *Executions and the British Experience from the 17th to the 20th Century* (Jefferson: McFarland and Co., 1990), p. 7).
56 The didactic role of the early modern execution spectacle is commonly accepted; see Michel Foucault, *Discipline and Punish*, 2nd edn, trans. Alan Sheridan (New York: Vintage Books, 1995); Petrus Spierenburg, *The Spectacle of Suffering: Executions and the Evolution of Repression* (Cambridge: Cambridge University Press, 1984); and Andrea McKenzie, *Tyburn's Martyrs* (London: Continuum, 2007) for a representative sampling of the range of this argument.
57 For a fuller discussion of Anne's mourning speech, see Ann Kaegi, Chapter 9, above.

11

Discrepant emotional awareness in Shakespeare

R. S. White and Ciara Rawnsley

EMOTIONS-BASED COMMENTARY ON early modern literature, and Shakespeare in particular, may suffer from a reductiveness due to reluctance to reflect multiple emotional states present simultaneously, either within an individual as 'mixed emotions', or between different characters often listening 'at cross purposes', or between characters and the audience ('dramatic irony'). This perceived deficiency arguably stems from three basic assumptions that can be challenged. First, there has been recently an emphasis on the physiological approach to emotions, which suggests that early modern theory analysed feelings as primarily stemming from the body.[1] In general terms this approach is clearly justifiable in the light of humoral theory and Galenic medical conceptions. However, if we fail to look beyond it as an explanation for affective states in early modern texts, we risk very simplistic conclusions, as specific circumstances and affective responses become more complex than such an approach can accommodate. Second, there is a critical tendency to compartmentalise clearly defined emotional states for the sake of analysis – anger, pity, melancholy, shame and so on – rather than noticing that many states of feeling are transitional or inseparably multiple.[2] Even the important (if differing) philosophical accounts of 'the Passions' in general by Robert Solomon and Thomas Dixon tend to represent affective states as definably discrete.[3] As Erin Sullivan has shown in Chapter 1, above, precedents are the great early modern theorists Thomas Wright (*c.*1561–1623) and Robert Burton (1577–1640). They follow Aquinas in particular, analysing passions and affections as capable of categorisation into taxonomies. Third, in cases where mixed emotions *are* acknowledged, they tend to be only those presented as binary opposites suggested by oxymorons ('very tragical mirth', 'that I must love a loathed enemy', and so on).

The aim of this chapter is to show that Shakespeare pre-eminently works at a more complex and multiply integrated level when dealing with 'mixed emotions'. This is an important aspect to the cultural transportability and temporal longevity of his plays. To use a musical metaphor, his dialogues are constructed multivocally like madrigals, discriminating each emotional refrain and melody from the others, playing off different emotional registers and patterns, allowing them to change, and finally merging them in harmony. By contrast, 'Marlowe's mighty line' is most often deployed in monologues rather than conversation, more or less like arias or sonatas, mirroring the swell of single emotional states rather than the intermingling of many. As mentioned in the Introduction to this book, even the term *emotion* was in flux when Shakespeare was writing his plays and could signify many things at once, which seems significant when considering the playwright's layered approach to depicting emotions. The broad task undertaken here is to devise a mode of analysis subtle and flexible enough to allow us to understand how Shakespeare makes mixed emotions function on the stage, since this aspect of his drama is so characteristic as to be 'the dyer's hand' in his work.

Although works of early modern literature such as Philip Sidney's *Arcadia* bear witness to the fact that what we call mixed emotions were depicted and experienced, a nomenclature to describe the phenomenon seems to have come later in the seventeenth century. The first record of the phrase 'mixed [mixt] passion' comes in Samuel Purchas's *Purchas His Pilgrimage* (1613), describing the lion's view of man 'with a leering countenance, expressing a mixt passion of dread and disdaine', and again describing the currents in a river, 'as with a mixt passion of feare and disdaine'.[4] The image of the currents in a river is analogous to the strands in a madrigal. Next, Burton in *The Anatomy of Melancholy* (1621) writes in the opening section, 'Democritus to the Reader':

> I did for my recreation now and then walke abroad, and looke into the world, & could not choose but make some little obseruation, not … to scoffe or laugh at all, but with a mixt passion, *Bilem saepè, iocum vestri mouere tumultus*, I did sometime laugh and scoffe with *Lucian*, and Satyrically taxe with *Menippus*, weepe with *Heraclitus*, sometimes againe I was *petulanti splene cachinno*, and then againe *vrerebilis ecur*, I was much mooued to see that abuse which I could not amend.[5]

When Burton writes 'Of the Moouing Faculty' we find the following comprehensive listing:

> The good affections are caused by some obiect of the same nature, and if present they procure ioy, which dilates the Heart, and preserues the body: If absent, they cause Hope, Loue, Desire, Concupiscence. The *Bad* are *Simple*,

> or *mixt*: *Simple* for some bad obiect present, as sorrowe which contracts the Heart, macerates the Soule, subuerts the good estate of the body, hindering all the operations of it, causing Melancholy, and many times death it selfe: or future as Feare. Out of these two arise those mixt affections, and passions of anger, which is a desire of revenge, Hatred which is inveterate anger, Zeale which is offended with him which hurts that he loues, and ... a compound affection of Ioy and Hate, when wee reioyce at other mens mischiefe, and are grieued at their prosperitie, Pride, Selfe-loue, Emulation, Envy, Shame, &c. of which elsewhere. (p. 38)

Although this description seems to regard certain passions and affections as intrinsically complex and 'mixt', both quotations none the less suggest there can be interplay between different feeling states activated by one situation.

In 1633 Thomas Taylor in *Christs Victorie over the Dragon* describes how we should regard the overthrow of enemies of Christ with both joy and compassion: 'With mixt affections; consider them as men, so humanity bids us sorrow in their ruine; consider them as men in whom the will and justice of God is revealed, and now piety steps in, and makes us rejoyce in the righteousnesse of it'.[6] In the same year Richard Capel in *Te[mp]tatio[n]s their Nature, Danger, Cure* has a subheading (Section III) denoting 'Of mixt Tentations wherein Satan joynes with us, and wee with him' where, for example, 'mixt tentations wherein lust and Satan doe tye together'.[7] He describes the apprehensions of a guilty conscience: 'mixt passion working feares in the heart, and complaints in the conscience of a man; for as the sin is bad, so it doth trouble because it threatens the wrath of God, and is accompanied many times with a fore-feeling of the wrath to come'. To fall to temptation might be enjoyable but the pleasure is mixed with apprehension of inevitable punishment to follow. Capel also points to complicated responses to situations in which we must make the best of a bad lot, as when we borrow money from a usurer in order to fulfil some worthy need even though usury is a sin: 'This is a mixt act of willingnesse, which is construed to be naturally, done unwillingly, but willingly accidentally' (p. 44). While these few examples hardly provide enough basis for a theory of emotional *mélanges*, they show that early modern writers could acknowledge affective states consisting of more than one emotion felt at the same time.

One possible, modern approach lies in retrieving and adapting an idea from a neglected critic, Bertrand Evans. In *Shakespeare's Comedies* (1960) and the sequel, *Shakespeare's Tragic Practice* (1979), Evans constructed a tool of analysis of Shakespeare's theatrical craft that he called 'discrepant awareness'. He posited 'exploitable gaps between awarenesses' applied first between characters on stage and the observant audience, and secondly between characters themselves.[8] The theory worked well for the comedies – almost too well, in fact, since it is presented as something of a repetitive formula – not so well for the tragedies, perhaps because the device is intrinsically more relevant to comedy as stimulus to detached laughter. A drawback is that the analysis focuses only on the differences and individual limitations between what each character (and an audience) consciously *knows* in terms of what the other characters know, or are doing. However, our suggestion is to shift the emphasis from *knowing* to *feeling*, and to look at 'discrepant *emotional* awareness' between characters at any one time in the action. In his chapter on movement as emotion in John Lyly, Andy Kesson has shown how important discrepant emotional awareness was both to the creation and the reception of Lyly's work. Similarly, we believe that such an approach can help us to recognise and value not only Shakespeare's craftsmanship in plotting scenes but also the emotional complexity generated in situations involving several characters with differing emotional points of view. A range of feeling states and experiences are aroused in different personages, leading to complexities of 'mixed emotions' not only in individual characters but also the ensemble, and the audience, so that the whole emotional impact is both a sum of, and greater than, each individual's limited but strongly felt, affective perspective. In order to illustrate how this approach might work in practice, we will now look in turn at a single scene from an early play, *The Two Gentlemen of Verona*, and then at a late play, *Cymbeline*, and its lengthy, final 'movement' (in the musical sense) – examples chosen because they are driven by emotions rather than simply untangling narrative complications.

Discrepant emotional awareness in action: *The Two Gentlemen of Verona*, 4.2

Act 4, scene 2 of *The Two Gentlemen of Verona* may well be the first scene Shakespeare wrote in which he presents 'mixed feelings', between characters and also between characters and audience, with any degree of complexity. Evans argues that in the possibly preceding comedy, *The Comedy of Errors*, there is 'only one discrepancy in awareness' (that the audience knows there are two sets of twins whereas the characters do not), but that here Shakespeare 'exploits multiple gaps that involve no fewer than six notable secrets'. When Evans looks at 4.2, he uses the terms that encapsulate his approach: '[Julia] *knows* all. Her *discovery* raises her abruptly to our level of *awareness*' (our emphasis).[9] This may be true in terms of what Julia 'knows' by way of information and 'discovery', but it is not so in terms of her feelings – she does not 'know all' of what other characters are feeling, and she certainly does not share the audience's fuller view of emotional changes in the scene. Evans's interest effectively stops when he has shown Julia's omniscience taking over from Proteus's, and Proteus revealed as 'the trickster tricked'. These are basically matters of plot and dramatic irony, and they do not tell the whole story of emotional expressiveness, the personal avoidance, and mutual engagement between characters. Our interest lies not so much in gaps in knowledge but between feelings, and how the audience is made aware of these and even implicated, and we argue that these emotional mismatchings are crucial to the dramatic effect and affect of the scene. From this point of view, Julia is trapped in her necessarily limited feeling-state caused by betrayal, humiliation and lost love, just as effectively as she is trapped in her disguise. Likewise, Proteus and Silvia speak from their own respective emotional states, as the result of their accumulated roles in the play up to this point. The audience has a further and yet more complex layer of understanding of the conflicting emotions of all three main characters who are not on the same wavelength with each other. This more inclusive view is not shared by Julia despite her being the central, suffering consciousness in the scene, and certainly not by Proteus, nor Silvia. The audience also has access denied to the characters of an overarching, generic knowledge that this play is a comedy. We exercise a tolerance of anxiety in the expectation that 'all will be well'.

In our following commentary on 4.2, we dwell not on the formal poetic qualities like versification or imagery, nor on the adroit theatrical craftsmanship, but on the shifting emotional points of view. These give the scene a broader range of 'passions' than is felt by one character alone. The pivotal scene, set underneath Silvia's chamber window outside the palace of the Duke of Milan, begins with the entrance of Proteus alone. He summarises the situation, which includes not only the narrative twists but his own compromised feelings. Conceding that he has been 'false to Valentine' he now proposes to 'be as unjust to Thurio' by pretending to woo Silvia ostensibly on Thurio's behalf, but in fact for his own selfish ends. He feels penitent in the knowledge that Silvia 'is too fair, too true, too holy' to be 'corrupted' with his 'worthless gifts' based on disingenuous falsehood since he has broken faith with Julia. The more Silvia has berated him for this, the more 'spaniel-like' Proteus feels in his fawning love for her. Having explained the tangled 'mixt passions' caused by his own infidelity, Proteus spots Thurio: 'But here comes Thurio. Now must we to her window, / And give some evening music to her ear.' (4.1.1–17).[10] Proteus's cratylic name announces his reprehensibly changeable behaviour and feelings which have led him into these betrayals that are both emotional and moral, against Julia, Silvia, Valentine (who honourably loves Silvia) and Thurio, whom Proteus is deceiving.

Already we have a situation of some emotional range and intricacy that increases with the respective arrivals on stage of the other characters. Thurio is accompanied by musicians, and Proteus duplicitously assures his 'stooge' that they will be wooing Silvia on his behalf (4.2.18–25). Proteus's emotional situation becomes more entangled, though without his knowledge, when the miserable Julia, disguised as a page boy, arrives in the company of the Host of the tavern. Her feelings are the subject of discussion:

> HOST: Now, my young guest, methinks you're allycholly. I pray you, why is it?
> JULIA: Marry, mine host, because I cannot be merry.
> HOST: Come, we'll have you merry. I'll bring you where you shall hear music and see the gentleman that you asked for.
> JULIA: But shall I hear him speak?
> HOST: Ay, that you shall.
> JULIA: That will be music.
>
> (26–34)

With hindsight we see here the origins of Viola 'like patience on a monument' in *Twelfth Night*, her feelings kept as secret as her disguised identity ('as secret as maidenhead'). Julia skirts around the cause for being 'allycholly' with a despondently muted quip ('because I cannot be merry') though to the knowing audience she reveals that in her emotional state of hopeless love, despondency and wry self-criticism, the 'music' will be the sound of Proteus's voice, no matter how badly he has treated her. Suffering from betrayal and love melancholy, she is as good as invisible to the other characters on stage except the Host, and Proteus later lies that she is dead. However, Julia becomes for the audience the character through whose feelings we interpret events, even though she is a bystander heard only by the audience.

Music is always a calibrator of moods in drama as it is in the cinema, and here the sound as well as sense equally bear diverse and poignant meanings. Julia has ears for only one of the 'musicians', which makes her especially prone to hear her own preoccupation mirrored. When '*Music plays*', the song ('Who is Silvia? what is she / That all our swains commend her?' (37–8)) is in the vein of a Spenserian pastoral lyric praising the beauty of Silvia, 'excelling … each mortal thing' (48–9), but to the Host's surprise the apparently innocuous words simply deepen Julia's mood:

> HOST: How now! are you sadder than you were before? How do you, man? The music likes you not.
> JULIA: You mistake. The musician likes me not.
> HOST: Why, my pretty youth?
> JULIA: He plays false, father.
> HOST: How? out of tune on the strings?
> JULIA: Not so; but yet so false that he grieves my very heart-strings.
> HOST: You have a quick ear.
> JULIA: Ay, I would I were deaf. It makes me have a slow heart.
> HOST: I perceive you delight not in music.
> JULIA: Not a whit, when it jars so.
> HOST: Hark, what fine change is in the music.
> JULIA: Ay, that 'change' is the spite.
> HOST: You would have them always play but one thing?
> JULIA: I would always have one play but one thing …
>
> (53–69)

They are in different emotional worlds, and, no matter how gently the kind-hearted but insouciant Host tries to lift her spirits, Julia is predominantly and punningly aware of the singer as 'false' and inconstant in both emotional and moral senses. She speaks through allegory (again like Viola in *Twelfth Night*) in finding the 'jars' in the music, a deeper link that understandably escapes the notice of the commonsensical and uninvolved Host who plays a significant but unobtrusive part in the scene's emotional design.

Norman Sanders makes the interesting observation that the 'asides' about music between Julia and the Host provide 'one of the earliest occasions in Shakespeare where a specific personal issue is linked allusively to the universal'.[11] Sung by the fickle Proteus, the words ironically harp on the 'holy, fair and wise' constancy of the exemplary Silvia, whose beauty and virtue create a unity of being 'kind as she is true'. The qualities she represents, at least in the song's words, are in stark contrast to the deplorable contradictoriness of Proteus's feelings and actions. To make matters even worse for him, a subtext is Proteus's misogynistic suggestion that it is the woman's very constancy that causes men to love women and desert even their own faithful lovers. All this intensifies Julia's suffering, unable as she is to hear the song in a less self-referential light, while it amplifies the audience's understanding of Proteus's 'cunning drift':

JULIA: But, host, doth this Sir Proteus that we talk on often resort unto this gentlewoman?
HOST: I tell you what Lance, his man, told me, he loved her out of all nick.
JULIA: Where is Lance?
HOST: Gone to seek his dog, which tomorrow, by his master's command, he must carry for a present to his lady.

(70–6)

To the alert audience, this is a particularly galling, semi-comic reminder of Launce's self-sacrificial love for his dog, a parody version of Julia's own constancy to her equally ungrateful love-object. Next, Julia gives an embedded stage direction, 'Peace! stand aside: the company parts', signalling the departure of the now irrelevant Thurio and musicians. This leaves Proteus alone, as he thinks, since Julia is unobserved, while the Host is by now asleep as we hear in another embedded stage direction at the end of the scene.

Silvia enters 'above', in both physical and moral senses, to thank the musicians for serenading her. She recognises Proteus's voice, and introduces into the scene a new, refreshingly candid emotion, anger:

My will is even this,
That presently you hie you home to bed.
Thou subtle, perjured, false, disloyal man,
Think'st thou I am so shallow, so conceitless
To be seduced by thy flattery,
That hast deceived so many with thy vows?
Return, return, and make thy love amends.
For me – by this pale queen of night I swear –
I am so far from granting thy request
That I despise thee for thy wrongful suit,
And by and by intend to chide myself
Even for this time I spend in talking to thee.

(90–101)

As the object of three men's love, Silvia is just as emotionally implicated as Proteus but she has been consistent in her own feelings and actions as Valentine's betrothed, giving her moral authority to be vehemently clear-headed in her contempt for Proteus's behaviour. She delivers her passionate attack in two senses, expressed *with* anger and *against* the man's fickleness. The fluent momentum of her poetic language and her outraged tone carry the feelings to the audience, as if some emotional dam has broken under pressure.

Proteus is now driven into a series of lies, and the audience is made aware again of the suffering presence of Julia, the other emotional touchstone in a triangle of discrepant emotional states:

> PROTEUS: I grant, sweet love, that I did love a lady,
> But she is dead.
> JULIA (*aside*) 'Twere false, if I should speak it,
> For I am sure she is not buried.
> SILVIA: Say that she be, yet Valentine, thy friend,
> Survives, to whom, thyself art witness,
> I am betrothed. And art thou not ashamed
> To wrong him with thy importunacy?
> PROTEUS: I likewise hear that Valentine is dead.
> SILVIA: And so suppose am I, for in his grave,
> Assure thyself, my love is buried.
> PROTEUS: Sweet lady, let me rake it from the earth.
>
> (102–12)

Silvia's indignation and Proteus's self-pitying pleading, falsehoods, and hair splittings are counterpointed by Julia's hurt indignation, adding yet more affective layers to a scene already rich in contrasting feelings:

> SILVIA: Go to thy lady's grave and call hers thence,
> Or, at the least, in hers sepulchre thine.
> JULIA (*aside*): He heard not that.
>
> (113–15)

By this stage Julia's pert 'asides' need not be delivered as private self-communings but as direct addresses to the audience, since our sympathies are most strongly sympathetic to her plight. In the dramatic design she speaks to – and for – us, rather than to herself, providing a framing perspective through which to judge the 'inset' drama between Proteus and Silvia. He continues defiantly to accuse Silvia of being 'obdurate' and asks for her picture so that at least he can admire her 'shadow' even if the 'substance' is unattainable, a distinction tartly commented upon by Julia who is still dwelling on his hypocrisy.

Proteus's exit line, proclaiming he will rest 'As wretches have o'ernight / That wait for execution in the morn' (126–7), is histrionic in the light of Julia's genuine suffering, further emphasising his insensitivity and culpable acts towards everyone. His words prove he is the 'shadow' without moral 'substance', but Julia ruefully realises that she is a 'shadow' in her insignificance to him. Now left alone on stage, Julia and the Host finish the scene:

JULIA: Host, will you go?
HOST: By my halidom, I was fast asleep.
JULIA: Pray you, where lies Sir Proteus?
HOST: Marry, at my house. Trust me, I think 'tis almost day.
JULIA: Not so; but it hath been the longest night
That e'er I watched, and the most heaviest. *Exeunt*

(131–7)

This beautifully muted closure to the emotional complexities of the scene strikes a note of both weary suffering and comedy, leaving unrelieved Julia's distress while also diminishing this consciousness that 'life goes on' for others, in the longer perspective offered by the Host's falling asleep. It is also yet another first for Shakespeare – drawing attention to the gathering darkness that must have been enveloping the audience itself after the afternoon performance in a gentle premonition of the impending climax of the play as a whole, and subliminally linking the moment with the proverbial, emotionally loaded sense, 'the darkest hour is just before the dawn'. The 'insomnia Sonnets' (27–30) seem to indicate it was an emotionally tricky time for him to navigate.

It is tempting to use a culinary metaphor in describing the 'emotional thickening' of this scene, but we could also maintain the musical analogy set up in the scene itself. The initial, single instrument of Proteus's voice is gradually joined, overtaken and subsumed by others in an increasingly madrigal-like or even operatic arrangement of varying passions carried by the different voices – by turns full of pathos, righteous anger, confusion, mendacity and a final, muted and gently comic 'full close'. Considering this was Shakespeare's first attempt at romantic comedy, a genre that he partially inherited from Lyly, partially found in his prose source ('Felix and Felismena' in Montemayor's *Diana*), but also largely invented himself in its dramatised form, the scene is an impressive demonstration of emotional range while maintaining perfect clarity and comic control at the level of plot.[12]

When he found a winning formula, Shakespeare used it again and again. Straight away in this case, since the final *ensemble* scene in *The Two Gentlemen* follows the same pattern in opening with a single character (Valentine in this case) relishing his solitude, and then adding more characters each with different emotional viewpoints, gradually disclosing, complicating, exploiting and finally reconciling discrepant emotional awarenesses. Other scenes similarly constructed along conflicting emotional lines spring to mind: scenes in *Measure for Measure*, *All's Well That Ends Well*, *Troilus and Cressida* and *Othello*, and many others are at least comparable. Such scenes are targeted by Evans for analysis of 'discrepant awareness' but in a somewhat mechanical, plot-based fashion, not as emotional encounters, leaving out the fluctuating and dynamic feelings that primarily drive the action. At the same time, this shows that the two concepts, structural and emotional, go hand in hand, supporting each other in the dramatist's design as a whole. It is tempting to think that unfolding and discrepant *emotional* awareness is the more compelling technique as an explanation for Shakespeare's manifestly effective, emotionally charged scene-building.

Cymbeline and the transformation of suffering into joy

To show that discrepant emotional scene-building is a central Shakespearean dramatic ploy, we jump to the end of his career where he still uses it. In fact he returns to the very same kinds of sources and plots, since *The Two Noble Kinsmen* has more in common with *The Two Gentlemen of Verona* than merely their names. Why Shakespeare went back to dramatising romance at the end of his career we cannot know. The older story that appealed to Victorian sages was that he entered an 'autumnal' period of his psychic life, all passion spent after a tragically inclined mid-life crisis. Hard-headed cultural materialists might these days suggest he was simply exploiting theatrical fashion as audiences turned away from satirical, citizen comedy and towards the kinds of plays popularised by Beaumont and Fletcher (the latter Shakespeare's collaborator on *The Two Noble Kinsmen*). But this in turn ignores the fact that it was Shakespeare himself who, long before, had pioneered and perfected the mode of adapting to the stage 'mouldy tales' found in romances and tales for children.[13] The more likely explanation is that he had never abandoned his taste for such stories and was again concentrating his attention on their inward, emotional rhythms. Central to these sources are the primacy of feelings over intrigue, comedy, plotting, suspense or even characterisation, which is often perfunctory in these plays. These forms of structural linking become secondary in the romances to shifting moods in affectively constructed scenes. As with Viola and Orsino in *Twelfth Night*, Isabella and Angelo in *Measure for Measure* and Helena and Bertram in *All's Well that Ends Well*, we find the dramatist apparently capriciously putting characters into the very kind of situation that their dominant passion makes impossible to deal with, and seeing how they will emotionally react. This ploy recurs insistently in the late romances and the situations become more extreme, bizarre and challenging: Marina in the brothel; Innogen waking to find herself beside a headless figure dressed in her husband's clothes; Antigonus pursued by a bear; a statue coming alive to effect the return of a wife to her husband and a mother to her daughter. It is the feelings, the discrepant emotional reactions, that matter more than the skill in handling elements of plotting and disclosure.

Issues of dramatic craft and also the sheer fictiveness of the presentation have been seen not as strengths but weaknesses in the late plays. Many critics suggest that the improbable scenes so prevalent in *Cymbeline* function to undercut the play's emotional power. Arthur Kirsch repeatedly comments on *Cymbeline*'s 'deliberate self-consciousness', claiming it 'calls attention to itself as a dramatic fiction', and 'its dramatic effect is to keep the audience at least partially disengaged from … the action and characters'.[14] Similarly, R. A. Foakes claims the play's 'deliberate emphasis on chance, accident, and the improbable' functions as a means of 'preventing us from identifying ourselves with a character, or taking the action too seriously'.[15] More recently, Susan Snyder has suggested that 'the conscious fictionality of [the] action, its improbabilities and miraculous turns of event, including manifestations of the divine', serve to create 'a certain distance between audience and stage action'.[16] However, even if such detachment operates for the audience, we shall argue that the primary and more functional aspect of these unrealistic scenes is not 'the action' *per se* but the radically fluctuating emotions stirred by the action.

In particular it is the endings to these plays that exemplify dramatic strategies of discrepant emotional awarenesses, and *Cymbeline* is an obvious and daring example. Here Shakespeare seems to be toying in leisurely fashion with his material and his audience, at his own pace unveiling one set of revelations after another, teasing us to think this is surely closure only to follow up with yet another revelation, deferring the ending once again in order to exploit and resolve emotional fluctuations. Each of these revelations depends not so centrally on a simple recognition but on changing emotional states in each character until equilibrium is reached. The death of the wicked Queen whom the King had dearly loved requires him to rethink retrospectively his whole relationship with her; returns of the long lost Princes and of his daughter whom he had driven off in Lear-like rage again necessitate an affective reorientation in him; the return of Posthumus to Innogen is predicated on emotional reconciliation and forgiveness, after the man had treacherously wagered on his wife's fidelity and chastity. These are not simply matters of clearing up misunderstandings and sorting out plot entanglement but of forging settled feelings of happiness out of negative and conflicted emotional states, weaving joy from suffering through a series of transitional crises that involve changing discrepant emotional awarenesses. They represent not just a series of timely disclosures but the creation of new, more stable, emotional territory for each character, the closing section of the madrigal when competing strains of feelings are steadily resolved into harmony.

In *Cymbeline* the beginning of the end starts long before the final scene, and the various resolutions take up the whole of the fifth act, proceeding with a pageant-like rhythm. In 5.1 Posthumus enters at the beginning of the battle, conveniently drafted into the Roman army. A bloody cloth, morbid token given to him by Pisanio to 'prove' he has murdered Innogen, becomes a symbol of Posthumus's guilt: 'Yea, bloody cloth, I'll keep thee, for I once wished / Thou shouldst be coloured thus' (1–2). As the mistrusting husband, he is now plagued by remorse, but significantly not with penitence. In his confused moral and emotional state, he still believes Innogen was unfaithful but has (misguidedly) forgiven his wife 'For wrying but a little' (2–5). However, he feels so guilty about his actions in ordering the death of Innogen that he is hoping he will be killed in the imminent battle between Britain and Rome. Moments before the battle begins, Posthumus in a surge of patriotism decides to discard his Italian apparel and fight for Britain instead, declaring, ''Tis enough / That, Britain, I have killed thy mistress-piece; / I'll give no wound to thee' (19–21). If nothing else, Posthumus's confused psychology at this time tears him in different directions and establishes his own state as one of extreme, self-induced, mixed emotions. In this aspect of the presentation, Shakespeare has added significantly to the story of such 'chastity wagers' in traditional stories, which invariably forget about the husband who abandons his wife, only to resurrect him at the end of the story exhibiting neither remorse nor a sense of having missed his wife. Feeling no emotional conflict, such an unrepentant return brings only narrative closure.[17] By contrast, Shakespeare dedicates a long section of the narrative (almost all of Act 5) to Posthumus, making him suffer at length and accept full responsibility for his morally reprehensible actions, thus supplying a more emotional human dimension to the marital reconciliation. Also unusually, as Helen Cooper points out, Shakespeare prolongs the process by showing Posthumus forgiving his wife *before* learning she is innocent, which once again underscores his remorse and paves the way for a more satisfying, emotionally touching reunion.[18]

The next step in Posthumus's redemption comes when he defeats the Italian rogue, Giacomo (5.2), visually suggesting a newfound capacity to recognise his own inner conflicts and overcome the feelings of sexual insecurity and jealousy exploited by the Italian's mischief-making. However, it is important that Giacomo is disarmed but not slain, since he must later disclose his villainy in order to effect the happy ending. The next three scenes resolve the larger war between Rome and Britain and re-introduce Belarius, Guiderius and Arviragus as 'war heroes'. Posthumus, despite his heroic part in the battle, is still burdened by a guilty conscience. He decides to externalise his inner state of self-loathing by again donning Roman attire, hoping for literal imprisonment and execution by the British: 'Most welcome, bondage, for thou art a way, / I think, to liberty' (5.5.97–8). Given his partially unredeemed ethical status, evidenced by his continuing suspicion of Innogen, the image is true to the evolving emotional movement towards eventually shedding his guilt fully and reaching atonement worthy of reconciliation with his wife.

While Posthumus is in prison, he falls asleep, and in this critically much-maligned scene he is visited by the ghosts of his parents and brothers. They circle him while he dreams, followed by the god Jupiter who descends on the back of an eagle accompanied by lightning and thunder. For years, scholars rejected Posthumus's vision as not being Shakespeare's work, deeming it crude and gratuitous: 'the apparitions and their rubbish … are not only, one swears, not Shakespeare's, but could hardly have been perpetrated even by the perpetrator of the worst of the rest of the play', fulminates Granville-Barker.[19] Far from being meretriciously supernatural, however, the scene is crucial in the emotional pattern towards resolution, and it explicitly raises the issue of discrepant emotions. The family ghosts do not berate Posthumus but instead complain about his circumstances, reproaching Jupiter, god of orphans, for not protecting him from 'this earth-vexing smart' (5.5.136). Why did Jupiter allow Giacomo to 'taint [Posthumus's] noble heart and brain / With needless jealousy' (159–60), they ask, and why was Posthumus put through the ordeal of war only to have his successes 'all to dolours turned' (174)? They rail against what they see as the injustice of his suffering: 'Since, Jupiter, our son is good / Take off his miseries' (179–80). Jupiter in turn does not apologise for Posthumus's miseries or admit any flaw in his design, but asserts that the man's sufferings will be alleviated, subtly reminding the audience that Posthumus is still not ready for dramatic forgiveness that must come as a 'gift' on repentance: 'Whom I love best, I cross, to make my gift, / The more delayed delighted' (195–6). Posthumus will be 'happier much by his affliction made' (202), an enigmatic phrase that describes Shakespeare's overall approach in *Cymbeline*. That the flawed protagonist must experience hardship to compensate for his failings will deepen the pleasure of his final happiness, not only as part of the moral purpose but also the emotional pattern. Unfortunately the innocent victim or even dramatic plaything is Innogen, who endures more than others and without cause, reminiscent of the respective fates of Lavinia, Ophelia and Cordelia. Jupiter leaves a tablet with a gnomic prophecy on the chest of Posthumus, who is unable to comprehend: ''Tis still a dream, or else such stuff as madmen / Tongue, and brain not; either both, or nothing' (238–9). 'Be what it is', he wryly concludes, 'The action of my life is like it' (241–2). Elijah Moshinsky, director of the BBC's televised version of *Cymbeline*, uses the same paradoxical distinction to mirror the audience's limited understanding of the dramatist's larger scheme: 'the confusion of the play is like life: it's bizarre and emotionally penetrating, and psychologically intense. And very lifelike.'[20]

Instead of being taken to the gallows, Posthumus is summoned by the King, setting up the final, ensemble scene of the play that unravels the tangled strands of the plot in a series of revelations and reconciliations. Each is 'a mark of wonder' (5.6.366), leading steadily towards a miraculous, happy ending. Bernard Shaw deemed the scene 'a tedious string of unsurprising denouements sugared with insincere sentimentality'; Robert Adams found it 'cramped', claiming 'so many complications accumulate that by the end of the play only strenuous efforts by a contortion artist can get us out of them'. Meanwhile, Richard Meek describes it as a 'remarkable' and 'radical experiment', yet ultimately an '*un*satisfactory' one.[21] However, the complications and improbabilities are functional, creating for the audience a gathering desire for order, while also heightening the sense of wonder. More importantly, the emphasis, indeed the whole point of the scene, lies not in the ingenuity exercised in untangling the knots in the plot but in its extraordinary range of constantly shifting emotional states in individuals, stage groups and audience alike.

George Bernard Shaw, using his dramatic instincts in a playful way, proves the point in an almost perverse way. In *Cymbeline Refinished: A Variation on Shakespear's Ending* (1937), Shaw, by reducing the 1000 lines in Act 5 of *Cymbeline* down to about 400, first shows that if Shakespeare had been primarily interested in the plot then he could have considerably streamlined its resolution. Second, Shaw changes the whole emotional timbre from wonder and mystery to something more comic and down to earth. His Iachimo is less a villain than a plain-speaking trickster, claiming his wager was simply to 'spend a night' in Imogen's bedroom, and that he did so in great physical discomfort. Third, the moral understanding slowly and painfully wrung from Posthumus by Shakespeare, leading to his reconciliation with Innogen, is radically revised by Shaw to reveal the man as a callous believer in 'means justifying ends' while his wife is resolutely unforgiving until the end:

> IMOGEN: I am a woman, and this man my husband,
> He would have slain me.
> POSTHUMUS: Do not harp on that.

Invited to join in with the general merriment, Imogen responds, 'I will not laugh. / I must go home and make the best of it / As other women must', to which Posthumus curtly replies, 'That's all I ask'.[22] Shaw's rewriting reveals more of the distinctiveness of Shakespeare's design in purposefully raising *admiratio* rather than comedy, and using emotion as well as ethics to renew marital harmony in his closure. We now turn to seeing how this operates in detail.

Each character is changed emotionally in response to the stream of revelations. First, the King knights the three 'outlaws' for their valiant service in battle, not yet knowing they are his own sons, and regrets that the fourth 'poor soldier that so richly fought, / Whose rags shamed gilded arms' (5.6.3–4) could not be found and likewise rewarded, again not knowing his identity as his son-in-law. The first revelation turns on affective reevaluation when the doctor Cornelius enters announcing, 'The Queen is dead' (27), reporting that before dying she confessed to hating both Innogen and Cymbeline and had planned to poison them. Since we were informed earlier in the play that she suffered from a 'fever with the absence of her son' (4.3.2), her ending is not surprising as an event though it is in the manner. 'How ended she?' Cymbeline asks, 'With horror,' replies Cornelius, 'madly dying, like her life, / Which being cruel to the world, concluded / Most cruel to herself' (5.6.30–3). The internal and external violence of her passing effects a punitive poetic justice, and the news of her treachery acts as an emotional catalyst for the King who had no idea of his wife's wickedness: 'O most delicate fiend! / Who is't can read a woman?' (47–8). He is genuinely perplexed, hurt and galvanised into revaluation: 'Mine eyes / Were not in fault, for she was beautiful … nor my heart / That thought her like her seeming' (62–5).[23] It is the first in a steady succession of moments of emotional anagonorisis, though the revelation of facts is less significant than the affective changes they cause. Indeed, if the ending is judged purely in structural terms it might well be seen as unsatisfactory because, as Meek has carefully argued, the revelation of facts 'seem[s] to overwhelm the story rather than clarify it'.[24] This may be a sign that Shakespeare was not primarily concerned with narrative neatness but was aiming at some other effect here, focusing not on the plot details *per se* but on the succession of transformative and recuperative emotional states.

Next, the Roman prisoners are ushered on stage, and with them the remaining characters: Lucius, Giacomo, Posthumus and Innogen (Fidele), the last two still disguised and unrecognisable to each other or anyone else. Lucius begs Cymbeline to spare his page, Fidele: 'I have surely seen him' (92), says Cymbeline upon regarding his disguised daughter, a first dawning glimmer of recognition that is apparently not based on external markers (Innogen's disguise is so convincing no one even suspects she is a woman), but rather his intuitions and feelings. Like his sons earlier and Lucius after them, Cymbeline takes an instant liking to Fidele – 'Thou has looked thyself into my grace' (94) – reinforcing the romance notion that inherent goodness cannot be hidden, only camouflaged. Cymbeline's unconscious recognition of his daughter, based on intuition and emotion rather than logic, leads him to offer 'Fidele' any boon in his power to grant, which he assumes will be used to spare his master Lucius from the fate awaiting the rest of the defeated Roman army. In the next surprising twist, however, Innogen turns away from her master: 'No, no. Alack / There's other work at hand' (102–3). She has spotted something 'Bitter to [her] as death' (104) as she stares at Giacomo. 'Wherefore ey'st him so?' (114), inquires Cymbeline. Innogen requests to talk to the King 'in private' (115) and the pair move off to the side. This brief pause helps to heighten the suspense and also provides an opportunity for Belarius and the boys to express amazement that Fidele is alive – 'but we see him dead' (127) – and for Pisanio to recognise his mistress: 'she is living' (128).

On their return, the King orders Giacomo to step forward and Innogen makes her demand: 'My boon', she declares to the startled spectators, 'is that this gentleman may render / Of whom he had this ring' (135–6). In line with the wager tradition, Innogen has fortuitously seen in Giacomo's possession her own ring, but, unlike the traditional tricksters who are reluctant to explain how they came by the token(s), Giacomo breaks down emotionally and declares he is 'glad to be constrained to utter that / Torments me to conceal' (138–9). He explains his part at length, to Cymbeline's mounting frustration: 'I stand on fire' (168); 'Nay, nay, to th'purpose' (179). We too are anxious for the Italian to 'Come to the matter' (169), but the delay serves a purpose, since Giacomo's confession foregrounds in embellished detail his newfound penitence that otherwise might seem perfunctory. Colouring his tale with emotional expressions like 'O, would our viands had been poisoned, or at least / Those which I heaved to head!' (156–7), he confesses he is the villain, the 'wretch' (181), who acted 'Most vilely' (198).

If Shakespeare had been concerned only with economy of action (as he was, for example, in the accelerated denouement of *The Winter's Tale*), then at this stage the heroine would come forward and remove her disguise, her honour restored and her chastity confirmed before all those who wronged her. But instead he delays the climax a little longer, concentrating on untangling and clarifying the remaining array of emotional responses. It is not Innogen who reveals herself after Giacomo's speech but Posthumus, cursing the 'Italian fiend' (210) but then descending into furious self-reproach, culminating pitifully in 'O Innogen! / My queen, my life, my wife, O Innogen, / Innogen, Innogen!' (225–7). His speech further rehabilitates our sympathy, since he at last acknowledges publicly his wife's faithfulness, which is essential for the coming reconciliation: 'The temple / Of virtue was she' (220–1). Only now does Innogen speak: 'Peace, my lord. Hear, hear' (227). She is still disguised, however, so Posthumus does not recognise her, and in his hysterical remorse he strikes the 'scornful page' (228) to the ground, a stark reminder of the violence she has suffered at her husband's hands (recalling too the way Orsino berates Cesario/Viola at the end of *Twelfth Night*). Innogen's fall galvanises Pisanio, until now a spectator, to come forward in dismay and reveal her true identity: 'O my lord Posthumus, / You ne'er killed Innogen till now. Help, Help!' (230–1). Shakespeare emphasises the wonder of the moment through Cymbeline and Posthumus's baffled reactions to the revelation that Innogen is alive:

> CYMBELINE: Does the world go round?
> POSTHUMUS: How come these staggers on me? …
> CYMBELINE: If this be so, the gods do mean to strike me
> To death with mortal joy
>
> (232–5)

Still the dramatist tantalisingly defers the marital reunion. Innogen repulses the servant, accusing him of poisoning her – 'O, get thee from my sight!' (237) – which in turn compels Cornelius to explain the Queen's sleeping potion and clarify Fidele's apparently miraculous return from the dead. Only now does Innogen wrap her arms about her husband's neck in love and forgiveness, and he utters one of the most powerful lines of the play: 'Hang there like fruit, my soul, / Till the tree die' (262–3).[25] After the violent chaos of the last few minutes, the moving simplicity of this sentiment makes it stand out like a beacon, highlighting Posthumus's remorse and devotion. It is a moment signalled by Shakespeare as one in which discrepant emotional states have at long last moved into harmony.

The remaining revelations occur summarily but without haste, still in a rhythm of steady unveiling of emotional truths. Simply listing these events draws attention to the fact that they are, as critics have complained, plentiful to the point of apparent redundancy. However, for an experienced playwright to create his ending in the way he does suggests that we need to retrieve some dramatic, emotional and atmospheric functions beyond narrative thoroughness. Cymbeline tearfully embraces his estranged daughter, 'How now, my flesh, my child?' (264), and finally gives her his blessing (267–8). He informs Innogen of her stepmother's death and Cloten's disappearance, which prompts Guiderius to come forward and admit to killing the bumptious and dubiously legitimate prince. Cymbeline feels reluctantly forced to condemn Guiderius to death, which motivates Belarius to intercede: 'This boy is better than the man he slew' (303). The old soldier explains the kidnapping, confessing that his name is not Morgan but Belarius, and that the two boys Polydore and Cadwal are really the princes Guiderius and Arviragus. Cymbeline is at first incredulous, but remembers that Guiderius had a red, star-shaped mole on his neck, 'a mark of wonder' (366), which Belarius can verify. Guiderius's mole, in another gesture towards romance and folk story sources, recalls the mark used to identify Innogen earlier, though this time it is 'a mark of wonder' in a more tonal sense, betokening not only identification but also the spirit of amazed joy. Cymbeline's astonishment at finding his lost sons quickly gives way to overwhelming joy, 'O, what am I? / A mother to the birth of three? Ne'er mother / Rejoiced deliverance more' (369–71), which in turn opens the way for the reunion between Innogen and her brothers.

All that remains is the uncovering of Posthumus as the 'forlorn soldier that so nobly fought' (406), which finally proves him worthy of Innogen in Cymbeline's eyes. His admission is backed up by Giacomo, who prostrates himself before Posthumus, expecting his life will now be forfeit as punishment for slandering Innogen. Instead, in a move that defies all traditional wager stories, Posthumus decides to pardon Giacomo, bidding him 'Live, / And deal with others better' (420–1). Caught up in the spirit of moralistic forgiveness, Cymbeline decides to free all the Roman prisoners, magnanimously declaring, 'Pardon's the word to all' (423). Yet still a puzzle remains, Jupiter's coded tablet. With some sophistry, a soothsayer manages to coax a reading out of the riddle that fits the events that have just occurred, concluding that Jupiter foretold 'peace and plenty' (458). Shakespeare seems to be gently poking fun at our desire to make sense of life, when life is a senseless riddle best left to the amusement of gods. Regardless, Cymbeline is inspired to continue paying the tribute to Rome as a sign of mutual respect, allowing the play to end not only with joyful unity on an emotional plane, but also in a vision of national reconciliation: 'Never was a war did cease, / Ere bloody hands were washed, with such a peace' (484–5).

It is an ending worthy of the best 'wonder' tale (the word itself occurs ten times in the play), its effect made all the more compelling for the steady, rhythmic pace of the sequence of denouements. On the narrative level, the ending ties up loose threads, resolving twisted expectations, disguises, wild improbabilities and multiple confusions. More significantly, however, it also satisfies on an emotional level since there is a transformation of different states of individual suffering, conflict and turbulence and multiple discrepant emotional awarenesses into collective and cathartic joy. Throughout, the action hovers dangerously close to tragedy, but actual disaster strikes nobody except the villainous Queen and her dispensable son, a mark of Shakespearian tragicomedy. The King blundered in his remarriage and his dealings with Rome, but Britain survives; a father loses his children, but they are restored to him unharmed; Posthumus and Innogen both believe each other dead, but they do not kill themselves as each has contemplated, and are reunited in marriage; Giacomo has caused disharmony by his actions, but his life is spared because of his penitence; and the Romans are conquered, but in the end they are set free. Shakespeare seems to have purposely prolonged his characters' sufferings and courted the potential for disaster so as to inspire in the audience a longing for a happy ending, which, when it finally arrives, 'The more delayed delighted'. The ending is emotionally effective also because it does not attempt to negate all the suffering and turmoil the characters (and audience) have endured in the play: Posthumus's irrational and overwhelming sexual anxiety; the murky violation of Giacomo's voyeurism; Innogen's psychological and physical suffering at the hands of her husband, father and stepmother. These sinister emotions are not entirely forgotten, nor is the existence of sorrow and failure denied, but a miraculous contrast is provided to these dark undercurrents, offering hope that the characters may in the future be 'happier much by [their] affliction made'.

It is a function of the dramatist's concentration throughout on feelings, and especially discrepant emotional awarenesses, that the ending represents a rich fusion of extreme and changing states coming from within the characters as they adapt to circumstances. Critics may have been lukewarm in their estimation of *Cymbeline* and it is admittedly a difficult play for modern readers, filled with moments that defy logical interpretation. But if the lack of rational logic is seen as intended and redefined as portraying the logic of dreams telling a tale of emotional changes,[26] then what emerges are the inner processes taking place in individuals caught in moments of intense transition, and finally reconciled one with another in re-established familial and affectionate bonds reinforced by a spirit of mutual forgiveness. Concealed, conflicted and mixed emotions gradually clear in changing circumstances and acceptance of moral responsibilities, as if the clouds have parted. The presentation suggests that such a process in which characters are given a 'second chance' in life must inevitably take time – as it does in *Pericles*, *The Winter's Tale* (sixteen years) and *The Tempest* – as the discrepant emotional states generated by often outlandish events, sins of commission, errors of faith and judgement committed by characters, and individual, emotional problems, so the implication runs, cannot be solved in an instant or by a single revelation like the existence of twins.

A working lifetime separated *The Two Gentlemen of Verona* from *Cymbeline* but we find more in common between the plays than meets the eye. Perhaps curiously, our examples can be taken to confirm both approaches to emotions that have been mooted. It is possible, for example, to employ a theory of dominant passions, even humours, in each character. Both Julia and Innogen are melancholy and patient to an almost self-martyring degree, Proteus is pathologically fickle while Posthumus is constitutionally jealous, Silvia is proud and choleric, Giacomo is a liar, the King is repeatedly deceived by appearances. However, and at the same time, these self-consistent traits do not seem as interesting as the 'emotions' in the early modern sense of 'moving things' that mutate in response to circumstances and to human interactions, the 'agitation of mind … deriving esp. from one's circumstances, mood, or relationship with others' (*OED*, 'emotion', 3a; first cited usage 1602). This is where 'discrepant emotional awareness' operates, at the point where the fixed passion bends, adapts or changes in the light of fluctuating situations and in resistance to others. It is arguably what makes Shakespearian affective encounters still plausible as explanations of complex human behaviour.

Notes

1 The most influential of these are Gail Kern Paster, *Humoring the Body: Emotions and the Shakespearean Stage* (Chicago: University of Chicago Press, 2004) and Gail

Kern Paster, Katherine Rowe and Mary Floyd-Wilson (eds), *Reading the Early Modern Passions: Essays in the Cultural History of Emotion* (Philadelphia: University of Pennsylvania Press, 2004).

2 For discussions of these emotional states see Gwynne Kennedy, *Just Anger: Representing Women's Anger in Early Modern England* (Carbondale: Southern Illinois University Press, 2000); David Konstan, *Pity Transformed* (London: Duckworth, 2001); Douglas Trevor, *The Poetics of Melancholy in Early Modern England* (Cambridge: Cambridge University Press, 2004); and Gail Kern Paster, *The Body Embarrassed: Drama and the Disciplines of Shame in Early Modern England* (Ithaca: Cornell University Press, 1993).

3 See Robert C. Solomon, *Not Passion's Slave: Emotions and Choice* (Oxford: Oxford University Press, 2003); and Thomas Dixon, *From Passions to Emotions: The Creation of a Secular Psychological Category* (Cambridge: Cambridge University Press, 2003).

4 Samuel Purchas, *Purchas His Pilgrimage* (London, 1613), pp. 37, 549. Unless otherwise indicated, contemporary early modern texts are dated and quoted from Early English Books Online (EEBO).

5 Robert Burton, *The Anatomy of Melancholy* (London, 1621), p. 1.

6 Thomas Taylor, *Christs Victorie over the Dragon* (London, 1633), p. 479.

7 Richard Capel, *Tentations: Their Nature, Danger, Cure* (London, 1633), ch. 4, sect. 3, p. 43.

8 Bertrand Evans, *Shakespeare's Comedies* (Oxford: Clarendon Press, 1960), p. 1. See also *Shakespeare's Tragic Practice* (Oxford: Clarendon Press, 1979).

9 Evans, *Shakespeare's Comedies*, pp. 9, 17.

10 Quotations from Shakespeare are taken from *The Complete Works*, ed. Stanley Wells and Gary Taylor, 2nd edn (Oxford: Oxford University Press, 2005).

11 Norman Sanders (ed.), *The Two Gentlemen of Verona* (Harmondsworth: Penguin, 1968), p. 36.

12 For further discussion of Lyly see Andy Kesson, Chapter 8, above.

13 The phrase 'mouldy tale' was used by Ben Jonson in reference to Shakespeare's *Pericles*, another late romance. See 'Ode (to himself)', in *The Oxford Book of Seventeenth Century Verse*, ed. H. J. C. Grierson and G. Bullough (Oxford: Clarendon Press, 1934), pp. 179–80.

14 Arthur Kirsch, '*Cymbeline* and Coterie Dramaturgy', *English Literary History*, 34 (1967), 285–306.

15 R. A. Foakes, *Shakespeare: The Dark Comedies and the Last Plays: from Satire to Celebration* (London: Routledge, 1971), p. 103.

16 Susan Snyder, 'The Genres of Shakespeare's Plays', in Margreta de Grazia and Stanley Wells (eds), *The Cambridge Companion to Shakespeare* (Cambridge: Cambridge University Press, 2001), pp. 83–97 (p. 95).

17 See for instance 'The Wager on the Wife's Chastity', in *Folktales of Chile*, ed. Yolando Pino-Saavedra (Chicago: University of Chicago Press, 1967), no. 37,

pp. 189–94; and 'The Chest', in *Popular Tales of the West Highlands*, ed. J. F. Campbell (Edinburgh: Edmonston and Douglas, 1860–62), vol. 2, no. XVIII, pp. 9–16.

18 Helen Cooper, *The English Romance in Time* (Oxford: Oxford University Press, 2004), p. 290.

19 Harley Granville-Barker, *Prefaces to Shakespeare* (London: Sidgwick and Jackson, 1927–47), vol. 2, p. 236. For a more modern discussion see Roger Warren (ed.), *Cymbeline* (Oxford: Oxford University Press, 1998), pp. 54–5.

20 Quoted in Warren (ed.), *Cymbeline*, p. 56.

21 George Bernard Shaw, 'Cymbeline,' in *Shaw on Shakespeare: An Anthology of Bernard Shaw's Writings on the Plays and Production of Shakespeare*, ed. Edwin Wilson (London: Cassell, 1961), p. 63; Adams, *Shakespeare: The Four Romances* (New York: Norton, 1989), p. 62; Richard Meek, *Narrating the Visual in Shakespeare* (Farnham: Ashgate, 2009), p. 192.

22 George Bernard Shaw, *Geneva, Cymbeline Refinished, & Good King Charles* (London: Constable and Company, 1946), pp. 131–50 (pp. 148–9). The female protagonist of Shaw's play is called 'Imogen' following the Folio text rather than the Oxford text's 'Innogen'.

23 The phrase 'Who is't can read a woman?' ironically applies to Posthumus too, blinded as he is by his sexual anxiety.

24 Meek, *Narrating the Visual*, pp. 192–6.

25 See Caroline Spurgeon, *Shakespeare's Imagery and What It Tells Us* (Cambridge: Cambridge University Press, 1952), p. 293, who claims this moment as the culmination of a train of organic imagery in the play.

26 See Ruth Nevo, '*Cymbeline*: The Rescue of the King', in Alison Thorne (ed.), *Shakespeare's Romances* (Basingstoke: Palgrave Macmillan, 2002), pp. 91–116.

Afterword

Peter Holbrook

Samuel Johnson said that reading Shakespeare would help 'a confessor predict the progress of the passions'.[1] Shakespeare's works have always been a prime location of powerful and intense feeling, telling us that passion is not just an unavoidable but a positive aspect of human experience. 'O, you are men of stones!' cries Lear at the end of his play to those around him: there is something morally wrong with restraint of feeling at this dreadful moment.[2] Cold-heartedness, lack of feeling, a cool, detached perspective on life: all that is declared by Lear to be less-than-human. As Johnson's remark indicates, Shakespeare's centrality in Western culture has to do with the intense feeling his works depict and generate. Leonard Digges's commendatory verses for the First Folio assert that Shakespeare will 'never die' until (what is unlikely) some new poet can 'out-do' the '[p]assions of Juliet, and her Romeo'; and, because what Shakespeare depicts will never 'with more fire' or 'more feeling be expressed' than what we find in his 'volumes', he will 'live eternally'.[3] In the 1640 edition of Shakespeare's poems, Digges claimed audiences were 'ravish'd' by the quarrel between Brutus and Cassius in *Julius Caesar* (*OED*'s first instance of 'ravish' in the sense of 'To transport (a person, the mind, etc.) with the strength of some emotion' is dated to 1390). And in the 1660s, Margaret Cavendish, the Duchess of Newcastle, said Shakespeare could 'express the diverse, and different humours, or natures, or several passions in mankind': 'in his tragic vein, he presents passions so naturally … as he pierces the souls of his readers with such a true sense and feeling thereof, that it forces tears through their eyes'.[4]

My own guess is that while the endorsement and celebration of passion we find in Shakespeare's texts was not exactly unprecedented (Chaucer and Marlowe come to mind), Shakespeare, more than any other writer of his day, made the emotional life of human beings the essence of art. Of course, and as this collection demonstrates, numerous authors of the period, John Lyly,

Thomas Wright, Robert Burton among them, were concerned to explore, stimulate and even honour the passions.[5] And we must not overlook the vehement emotion of much religious culture, both Catholic and Protestant, at this time (something sermons and liturgy were designed simultaneously to promote and control, as David Bagchi shows in Chapter 2).[6] Yet for the most part, it seems to me, there remains something exterior, scripted, rhetorical, denotative about the expression of passion in writers before Shakespeare.[7] In Shakespeare himself, however, as the quotations from Johnson, Cavendish and Digges imply, it is as if feeling itself speaks rather than is spoken about. And as I've suggested, Shakespeare seems to ascribe an especially high *value* to the emotional life: feelings have cognitive power, enable some things to be seen in their true light; lack of feeling, callousness, comes across as a form of psychological or moral blindness, an inability to see naturally and clearly what is there (Goneril, Regan, Edmund, Cornwall are blinded in this sense, no matter how clever they at times appear).[8] One can go further: Shakespeare often presents not just highly emotive human experiences but a world with all the qualities of mind and feeling – a mindful, ensouled world that *feels with* humanity.[9]

There is a political point to be made about Shakespeare and strong feeling: he thinks about feeling in relation to freedom. In some ways this is to be expected. The ancient world bequeathed to the Renaissance an understanding of freedom (personal and political) that saw it as bound up with the ability to keep feeling in check, to place the passions under the control of reason. For Cicero the natural order was that '[r]eason … commands, and impulse obeys'.[10] Horatio is a good, free, character because, like any self-respecting Renaissance Stoic, he is one who, 'in suffering all, … suffers nothing', is not 'passion's slave' (3.2.65, 71). As a result he cannot be cowed by a tyrant like Claudius: there is nothing the latter can do to force Horatio to act wrongly. When you neither fear a tyrant nor want what he can give, you are free no matter what. Reason guarantees freedom.

Shakespeare sometimes seems to hold this view, essentially that of ancient schools of philosophy such as Platonism and Stoicism as well that of a classicising author like Milton, for whom 'rational' or 'true liberty' involves keeping 'upstart passions' under reason's sway.[11] But at other times the opposite is the case, and he endorses the notion that acting unreflectively and passionately in accordance with one's desires is freedom's essence. Impulsiveness, impetuosity, a creative, spontaneous, free-wheeling approach to existence – that, the plays and poems so often declare, is true success in life. Can anyone seriously propose that *Romeo and Juliet* endorses a prudent, lukewarm, milquetoast attitude to love? To be in love in that play is to realise some potential in one's nature that otherwise lies dormant: love here is a mode of freedom, even when uncontrolled.

The present volume is an attempt to think through some ways of conceptualising emotion in early modern texts apart from 'humoralist' physiological models.[12] This is where the question of freedom comes in. For, to the extent that the volume questions humoral psychology as a total explanatory framework for understanding early modern discourse about emotion, it might be seen as of a piece with recent, *anti*-materialist ways of conceiving human experience, by thinkers who are asking whether we are ultimately nothing more than material objects (in the same way that chairs or elementary particles are material) or whether human consciousness makes a fundamental difference, making us ontologically distinct from other natural phenomena. If we aren't distinct, but simply subject to the same laws matter is (matter conceived as *without* mind or soul) it is hard to find a place for agency, freedom.[13] A recent response to this problem, and one rejecting the materialist account of the world, is the philosopher Thomas Nagel's *Mind and Cosmos*. For Nagel, 'emergentist' theories (the belief that mind emerges from matter) are fundamentally implausible, as are attempts to reduce consciousness to physiology.[14] Nagel is unpersuaded that physicalism or materialism offers an all-encompassing account of human experience. Likewise, in the Renaissance, as this collection demonstrates, humoralism was not the only system available for understanding human emotion.[15] Other discourses – religious, aesthetic, philosophic – played a role. As Meek and Sullivan write: 'Understanding emotion in the Renaissance was part of the larger project of understanding the human, and accordingly it required insights from all of its philosophical, spiritual, physiological and creative engagements' (p. 6).

To reiterate: part of what is at stake here is freedom. If we are merely bodies in space, our conduct determined by (for instance) various commixtures of vital or elementary liquids, what remains of agency, free will? *Mutatis mutandis*, this would seem to be as much a problem for physical materialists today as it was for humoralist natural philosophers of the sixteenth century.[16] And of course it is a problem too for a dramatist representing human conduct – are one's characters the playthings of irrational, impersonal mechanisms, or do they transcend determinism?

A danger of current conceptions of the human as so many physical (unconscious) processes bundled together is that they devalue humanity by undermining the idea of human autonomy. It's this understanding of the human that Hamlet rejects in his denunciation of the fleshy materialism of Claudius's court: 'What is a man, / If his chief good and market of his time / Be but to sleep and feed? A beast, no more' (4.4.34–6). What appals Hamlet is a view of 'man' as *mindless*, as nothing more than a *body*, the helpless slave of his appetites and hence the easy tool of a tyrant. It is no accident that similar physico-reductionist views of humanity are propounded today, in manically capitalist societies that demand that everything be subordinated to commodity production and consumption, that people should therefore not waste their time studying useless subjects such as the humanities, the real and only point of human life being, in fact, getting and gaining and the satisfaction of physical needs (drink, sex, food) – in short, that what is necessary is that people live an *animalistic* life untethered to any higher, richer account of what it might be to be human. But Hamlet insists that such a life is unworthy (it is servile as well as stupid) of a rational creature.

Shakespeare's *Coriolanus* presents a picture of freedom that can remind us of Hamlet's complex understanding of this notion. Up until the pivotal scene with his mother Volumnia, when Coriolanus backs down from his mission to destroy Rome, he has, arguably, been at the mercy of the humour of choler (Shakespeare's source, North's translation of Plutarch, points up the dominance of this humour in a marginal note drawing attention to 'The force of anger').[17] But it is in response to Volumnia's long speech that Coriolanus experiences what can only be described as an emotional breakdown, signified in the wonderfully expressive stage direction, '[he] holds her by the hand, silent' (4.3.182). To put the point simply: it is words, an appeal to mind, imagination *and* feeling, not a random physiological event, that causes Coriolanus finally to do what he feared he might when, in the Volscian camp, he set eyes on his family – that is, to 'melt' (5.3.28) and abandon his (inhuman) aspiration to live up to the Second Watch's description of him as 'the rock, the oak not to be wind-shaken' (5.2.112). In doing so, of course, he shows himself to be human in Hamlet's sense: that is, a rational creature, not 'a beast … want[ing] discourse of reason' (*Hamlet*, 1.2.150).

This tremendous theatrical moment is worth dwelling on. Hitherto Coriolanus has refused to acknowledge his connection to others – famously, he has sought to live 'As if a man were author of himself / And knew no other kin' (5.3.36–7). In taking Volumnia's hand he acknowledges that, as Donne put it, '[n]o man is an island, entire of itself; every man is a piece of the continent, a part of the main'.[18] He has sought to banish 'affection' (5.3.24), or emotion, but now he is brought low, reminded how vulnerable he is, how helplessly attached to others. He thought to show himself not to be 'such a gosling to obey instinct' (5.3.35), but all that is now forgotten. The key thing, however, is that Shakespeare sees this breakdown and back-down as a gain. As Coriolanus himself anticipates, this (rediscovered) connectedness will be fatal, the Volscians will never forgive such an egregiously insulting betrayal of their cause. Nevertheless Shakespeare presents this moment of 'melting' as a moment of salvation. It is not only Rome that is saved by Coriolanus's decision to abandon his quest for revenge, it is he himself, since it is better to be a 'boy of tears' (5.6.106), brought to his knees by emotion, than to remain 'the oak not to be wind-shaken'.

Paradoxically this humiliation makes Coriolanus freer. From a common-sensical viewpoint this is surely wrong: freedom means not being interfered with, being left alone, doing one's own thing. But what if freedom in this sense involved the inability to connect – that is, a disability, an *inhibition* of one's free power to act? Isn't being trapped inside one's self, inside fantasies about oneself as a natural force for example, a diminishment or obstruction? What if one's wishes prevent one from fulfilling a normal human need to connect with others? Then 'freedom' would be a prison, an impoverishment and disability. Whereas Romeo and Juliet's passion leads to an expansion of experience, Coriolanus's equally powerful drive would constitute a narrowing, a disability.

It would take too long to develop this line of thinking here, but arguably it is the case that there is something anxious, miserable and reactive about Coriolanus prior to the moment in which he extends his hand to his mother. He is driven by something (let's call it a humour) that controls him, irrationally and arbitrarily. But in that moment of silence with his mother he acquires a blessed clarity about himself and his needs, a new self-control. And, paradoxically, this moment of self-mastery presents itself as one of self-dissolution, a fatal 'melting' of the self, a flowing into and with others.

This notion of a self affectively linked to others, and to the world itself, is expressed in a motif of Shakespeare's writing we find in a famous passage in *A Midsummer Night's Dream*: Oberon describes to Puck how once he

> sat upon a promontory,
> And heard a mermaid on a dolphin's back
> Uttering such dulcet and harmonious breath
> That the rude sea grew civil at her song,
> And certain stars shot madly from their spheres
> To hear the sea-maid's music.
>
> (2.1.149–54)

What comes through is how alive and dynamic the world is: the barbarous or wild sea is rendered civil by the mermaid's song; the stars shoot 'madly' from their spheres, overcome by a swooning, uncontrollable desire for the sea-maid's music. We see a world quickened with life and desire – reality is not a series of stable, separable entities but, rather, a whole, or continuum, of mobile and plastic moments of togetherness or interaction. Likewise, in the speech portraying Ophelia's drowning, a 'sliver' or slender branch of the willow tree is 'envious' – full of spite and ill will. It is the sliver's breaking off that precipitates Ophelia's death, as, clambering to hang her 'weedy trophies' on the tree, she falls into the stream, which is itself 'weeping' (4.7.174, 176). It is a rich, mysterious, startling vision, both tree and brook participating fully in the tragedy: far from being mere elements of the scene, inert background for the high drama of Ophelia's death, they are themselves agents within it. This is a way of representing reality that isn't well captured by recourse to Renaissance theories of 'correspondence' or 'chains of being' (what I am talking about is somehow less systematic and orderly than such doctrines suggest) or by treating the malice of the tree, or the brook's grief, as mere 'metaphors': they seem not merely illustrative but, rather, constitutive of the essential strangeness, the mystery, of what is going on. Once again, it is the dynamism of Shakespeare's perception that is noteworthy: neither tree nor brook is a mere static, unfeeling substance, securely situated at the bottom of a hierarchy of human, animal, thing, etc.: instead they are passionate participants within the drama, and understanding Ophelia's death requires understanding her relatedness to them.

In this vision everything reaches out to and involves everything else. Nothing is absolutely alone, including we humans: everything is folded within a complex whole. Of course Shakespeare is capable of taking the opposite position, that flowers and rivers for example are completely without affect or mindedness. But it is remarkable how frequently the contrary view turns up: the drops of dew on the flowers Titania places on Bottom's brow look like tears, as if aware of 'their own disgrace' (*A Midsummer Night's Dream*, 4.1.55, and 50–5). This is to apprehend the world as instinct with feeling and value – not as a mere blank, a meaningless material space of cause and effect – and to look forward to ways of apprehending the world that we are perhaps beginning to recover today. We might compare here the stress on relatedness in the modern philosopher Alfred North Whitehead (1861–1947), a keen admirer of Shakespeare who was also significantly influenced by English Romantic poetry: what was required, thought Whitehead, was 'the abandonment of the notion that simple location is the primary way in which things are involved in space-time. In a certain sense, everything is everywhere at all times. For every location involves an aspect of itself in every other location.' Whitehead sought to overthrow the scientific-mechanistic view of the world that regarded the fundamental basis of reality as mindless, unfeeling, valueless matter, a view that, he supposed, undermined human freedom and creativity. As he summarised this perspective: 'Each molecule blindly runs. The human body is a collection of molecules. Therefore, the human body blindly runs. And therefore there can be no individual responsibility for the actions of the body'.[19] In the vision I am attributing here to Shakespeare we might say that nature is socialist not capitalist: rather than each item in the material world existing in absolute, competitive isolation from every other, each is instead part of a complete whole forever and profoundly communing with each and every part of itself.[20]

To conclude: the present collection seeks to show the ways in which Renaissance writers and thinkers, not least Shakespeare, imagined human life as capable of emotional *freedom*. Humoral psychology, which bears a rough analogy to physical-reductionist pictures of the human today, downplays the role of agency in human life, since one no more chooses one's basic 'humour' than one does one's neurophysiology. No one can doubt the formidable influence and explanatory power of such physical accounts of humanity. But we must hope to find other ways of talking about ourselves – perhaps in religion, art, philosophy, perhaps in writers like Shakespeare? These would be ways of talking that enabled us to believe in and act upon our own collective and individual sense of agency.

Notes

1 Samuel Johnson, 'Preface to the Edition of Shakespeare's Plays' (1765), in *Samuel Johnson on Shakespeare*, ed. H. R. Woudhuysen (London: Penguin, 1989), p. 125.

2 On this point, and Shakespeare's anti-Stoicism generally, see Richard Strier, *The Unrepentant Renaissance: From Petrarch to Shakespeare to Milton* (Chicago: Chicago University Press, 2011), esp. p. 53. The quotation from *Lear* is found at 5.3.262 in *The Complete Works of Shakespeare*, 6th edn, ed. David Bevington (New York: Pearson, 2009). All quotations from Shakespeare are from this edition.

3 See the facsimile in *The Riverside Shakespeare*, gen. ed. G. Blakemore Evans (Boston: Houghton Mifflin, 1974), p. 71; spelling modernised.

4 *The Riverside Shakespeare*, ed. Evans, pp. 1846–7; spelling modernised.

5 Thus Erin Sullivan notes of Wright his readiness to acknowledge 'the productive

work passionate sensitivity might accomplish in the devotional life' (p. 30); and Mary Ann Lund sees Burton as 'stress[ing] a principally affective route towards union with God' (p. 88).

6 Bagchi argues that *The Book of Common Prayer* may have functioned as 'a mechanism of control' for the congregation's emotional life, warming and cooling the feelings as appropriate (p. 58).

7 A more positive view of the relation between rhetoric and emotion, emphasising the way in which 'the history of emotion is connected to the political and performative life of rhetoric', is to be found in Andy Kesson, Chapter 8, above, p. 197.

8 Nigel Wood, in Chapter 5, above, writes that 'Theseus and Lysander [in *A Midsummer Night's Dream*] realise … that the excessive and extreme can be revelatory' (p. 114). Proper feeling helps us see better.

9 A point made by Richard Meek, Chapter 6, above. He notes that Samuel Daniel's *Civil Wars* epic sometimes 'point[s] to a sympathetic reciprocity between human passions and an anthropomorphised natural world' (p. 133); Shakespeare's Richard II 'appears to believe that there are times when senseless objects do experience human feelings' – though Meek also observes that Richard's faith that England's 'earth' will 'have a feeling' and loyally spurn the rebels (*Richard II*, 3.2.24–6) is perhaps meant to be understood as a mere 'political and rhetorical set-piece'.

10 See Cicero's *On Duties*, ed. M. T. Griffin and E. M. Atkins (Cambridge: Cambridge University Press, 1991), pp. 39–40.

11 John Milton, *Paradise Lost*, ed. John Leonard (London: Penguin, 2000), XII, ll. 82, 83, 88.

12 See the Introduction to this book, in which the editors call for 'greater scholarly attention to the marked pluralism of early modern emotions theory' (p. 13) and for approaches that show how 'intellectual traditions beyond Galenic humoralism shaped Renaissance thinking about emotion'.

13 See for instance Meek and Sullivan's observation that what Richard Strier has termed 'the new humoralism' of recent early modern literary scholarship resembles 'new historicism in its questioning of individual agency' (Introduction, p. 5).

14 Thomas Nagel, *Mind and Cosmos: Why the Materialist Neo-Darwinian Conception of Nature Is Almost Certainly False* (New York: Oxford University Press, 2012).

15 Thus, for example, Meek observes that Shakespeare's *Richard II* 'highlights the ways in which pity and compassion are complex imaginative processes, rather than simply automatic or humoral phenomena' (Chapter 6). See also the editors' comment that we need to attend 'to the other systems of knowledge' that early modern 'people used to conceptualise … emotional experience' (Introduction, p. 6).

16 The editors notice a certain affinity between Renaissance humoralism and contemporary neuroscience (see p. 4 of their Introduction and also their note 9).

17 See North's Plutarch in Philip Brockbank's edition of *Coriolanus* (London: Methuen, 1976), p. 342.

18 *John Donne: The Major Works*, ed. John Carey (Oxford: Oxford University Press, 2000), p. 344.

19 See Whitehead's *Science and the Modern World* (1926; repr. London: Free Association, 1985), pp. 113–14, 96. Thomas Nagel, alluded to earlier, sympathises with Whitehead's resistance to mechanistic materialism.

20 See Whitehead's critique of the nineteenth-century social-Darwinist 'struggle for existence': 'in nature the normal way in which trees flourish is by their association in a forest. Each tree may lose something of its individual perfection of growth, but they mutually assist each other in preserving the conditions for survival. The soil is preserved and shaded; and the microbes necessary for its survival are neither scorched, nor frozen, nor washed away. A forest is the triumph of the organization of mutually dependent species' (pp. 256–7).

Index